The Nagle Journal

The Nagle

Journal

A DIARY
OF THE LIFE
OF JACOB NAGLE,
SAILOR, FROM
THE YEAR 1775
TO 1841

Edited by
John C. Dann

Weidenfeld & Nicolson
New York

Published by Weidenfeld & Nicolson, New York
A Division of Wheatland Corporation
841 Broadway
New York, New York 10003-4793

Published in Canada by General Publishing Company, Ltd.

Library of Congress Cataloging-in-Publication Data

Nagle, Jacob, 1762–1841.
  The Nagle journal : a diary of the life of Jacob Nagle, sailor, from the year 1775 to 1841
edited by John C. Dann.—1st ed.
      p.   cm.
  Original ms. in the collections of the Clements Library, University of Michigan.
  Includes index.
  ISBN 1-555-84223-2
  1. Nagle, Jacob, 1762–1841—Diaries.   2. United States—History—Revolution, 1775–
1783—Personal narratives.   3. United States—History—Revolution, 1775–1783—Naval
operations.   4. Impressment.   5. Voyages and travels.   6. Seamen—United States—
Diaries.   7. Seamen—Great Britain—Diaries.   8. United States.   Navy—
Biography.   9. Great Britain. Royal Navy—Biography.   I. Dann, John C.   II. William
L. Clements Library.   III. Title.
E271.N34   1988
973.3'5—dc 19
                                                                          88–9623
                                                                             CIP

Manufactured in the United States of America

Designed by Irving Perkins Associates

First Edition

10   9   8   7   6   5   4   3   2   1

Contents

Acknowledgments

T H E transcribing and editing of the Jacob Nagle Journal has been a lengthy but enjoyable project, brought to completion only with the assistance and support of many persons.

The book could never have materialized were it not for the fact that I have the privilege of directing the Clements Library, and thereby am given the delightful responsibility of following the auction catalogs and visiting the bookshops, searching for treasures such as the Nagle Journal and adding them to the collections. My superiors at the University of Michigan, President Harold Shapiro and Associate Vice President Mary Ann Swain, and the library's Committee of Management have been enthusiastic and supportive at every turn. My staff at the Clements, particularly Arlene Shy, assisted by John Harriman and Noreen Rice, has been gracious in taking over many of my normal responsibilities during frequent absences while bringing the manuscript to completion.

Without Dave Kirschenbaum's cheerful willingness to interrupt his vacation to examine and successfully bid on it, the Clements Library would never have gotten the Jacob Nagle Journal. He is not only a friend and close adviser but the unrivaled master of the auction room. Particular thanks also go to John and Emily Wheeler of Bay City, Michigan, who generously purchased the journal for the library in honor of Emily's parents, Guy Robert (University of Michigan, Class of 1922) and Mary Alice Moulthrop. It was at their beautiful cottage on Lake Huron that we first began to read and appreciate that this was a most extraordinary manuscript.

Soon after its purchase, I shared a photocopy of the journal with Jim Schoff of New York, retired president of Bloomingdale's, longtime board member of the library, adviser, brilliant collector, and a friend such as few have the privilege to know. It was one of the joys of the last two years of his life. He made a transcription of the entire journal, and his enthusiasm and insight, shared in many long telephone conversations and occasional visits, heightened my own excitement during the tedious process of copy editing. I invited him to be my co-editor. He declined, saying the spirit was willing, but at his age, he dare not commit himself to an undertaking he might not be able to complete. His foresight in this, as in all things, was somewhat beyond most of us, but his spirit has remained an inspiration throughout the project.

Many institutions and individuals provided invaluable assistance in the research phase of editing: Bob Warner and the staff of the National Archives in Washington; Roger Knight and all personnel of the National Maritime Museum at Greenwich; Jim Cruse and Carol McKendry of the University of Michigan Library; Tony Farrington of the India Office Library; David Vaisey of the Bodleian Library, Oxford; the staffs of the Historical Society of Pennsylvania, The New-York Historical Society, the Public Record Office at Kew, and of course the Clements Library. Dave Syrett, from the very beginning, shared his vast knowledge of British naval history and sources. Many people helped to document the last period of Nagle's life in Ohio: John Shy and Galen Wilson of the University of Michigan; Claude Latham of Norwalk, Ohio; Kathy Cyr of the Milan Historical Society; Paul Yon of Bowling Green State University; John Miller of the University of Akron; John Grabowski of the Western Reserve Historical Society; Alec J. Holland of Buckler's Hard Maritime Museum; Alan Frost of La Trobe University; Victor Crittenden of Camberra College; Gary Tipping of Beecroft, Australia; Ken Lockridge of the University of Michigan; and Mollie Gillen of Toronto and London. Marian Carson of Philadelphia provided many thoughts and suggestions that have been invaluable. Clarence Wolf of Mac-Manus & Co. of Philadelphia helped me track down and acquire published narratives of some of Nagle's fellow First Fleeters. Dennis East of the Ohio Historical Society found the wonderful obituary notice of 20 February 1841 in the *Stark County Democrat*.

The editor served as his own picture editor and in the process was helped by many people: Marilyn Hunt of the Yale Center for British Art; Shirley Mays of Independence Hall; James Cheevers of the United States Naval Academy Museum; Mrs. Sally Donze of the Stark County Historical Society; Rosemary Block of the Mitchell Library in Sydney; Lindsay McFarlaine of the National Maritime Museum; Stacy Smith of Bay City, Michigan; the picture curators of the Peabody Museum in Salem, Massachusetts, the Pennsylvania Historical Society, the New York Public Library, the Berks County Historical Society, and the Map, Print, and Book divisions of the British Library and the British Museum. Paul Jaronski of the University of Michigan Photographic Services and Dale Austin of Technical Illustration employed their highest skills in taking pictures on short notice in Ann Arbor.

Tom and Pat Cross of Ann Arbor, ardent sailors, kindly read the manuscript and provided me much help with nautical terms. Marshall and Catharine Dann, my parents, read my introductions and made invaluable editorial suggestions. William Strachan, of Weidenfeld & Nicolson, has been all that one could wish for from an editor—critical, supportive, and understanding. Jack Rummel, a most skillful copy editor, demonstrated unusual sensitivity to the peculiarities of Nagle's writing style and a sharp eye in correcting those of the editor. Orelia Dann deciphered several "Nagleisms" that eluded the editor as to their meaning.

Not the least debts of gratitude are due those who have made life pleasanter while the strenuous process of research and book production continued and who listened graciously, without wincing, as an enthusiast related his every latest discovery. In addition to many of the persons recognized elsewhere in my acknowledgments, I include the various members of my family, Nabil Osman and Hugh Bett of London, and Dudley Barnes of Paris. Peter Heydon gave me timely advice and encouragement. The Clearlake Hotel was the ideal home away from home for an author in London. The employees of Knights Restaurant, Ann Arbor's preeminent family-operated "pub," often provided a meal and good company after a long night of scholarship.

There are six individuals whose assistance went far beyond any ability on my part to adequately express my appreciation. Mrs. Marion Rhoads, descendant of Jacob Nagle's uncle, provided invaluable information on the family, took me to the sites in Reading associated with the Nagles and Lincolns, tracked down and commissioned the photographer to take pictures of views of the town in Nagle's era, and has supported the project in every possible way. She is a person of intelligence, energy, and generosity—bearing witness to the exceptional qualities of the Nagle family, which produced her very remarkable cousin Jacob.

Roger Morriss, Keeper of Manuscripts at the National Maritime Museum at Greenwich, has been enthusiastic about the project and has willingly and critically read a draft of the manuscript. Offering many helpful suggestions, sharing his expertise without reserve, he is the epitome of the generous and helpful scholar.

John Harriman, from the time he joined the staff of the Clements Library in 1984, worked closely with me on every aspect of the research and preparation of the manuscript for publication. His meticulous scholarship, his complete willingness to do anything to further the work, and his constant good humor and comradeship have made it a pleasure from beginning to end.

David Bosse, my Curator of Maps at the Clements, is not only a map scholar but a mapmaker as well. He produced the cartographic illustrations for the publisher on very short notice.

Last of all, I want to express my almost incalculable indebtedness to Elizabeth and Walter Hayes, without whose collaboration and unsparing hospitality the volume could never have materialized in its present form. Walter, formerly editor of the London *Sunday Dispatch*, and now vice chairman of Ford of Europe, served for several years in this country as vice president of the Ford Motor Company in charge of public relations. The Hayeses lived in Ann Arbor, and being ardent bibliophiles, they became enamored of the Clements Library, bringing the outsider's appreciation of what a remarkable place it is, easily taken for granted by those closer to home. Elizabeth volunteered as a cataloger at the library and became interested in the Nagle project in its infancy. Since their return to Britain, she has pursued innumerable research leads and she and I worked together to find and select the many pertinent illustrations that grace the pages of the volume. Both Elizabeth and Walter read and reread the transcript of the journal at every stage, gaining a familiarity with it in the smallest detail and making for numerous "seminars" on the fine points while I enjoyed the hospitality of Battlecrease Hall, their delightful seventeenth-century home in Shepperton. Walter read my introductions with the eye of a true editor, and he introduced me to his friend Lord George Weidenfeld, who immediately appreciated the special qualities of the Nagle narrative and committed his firm to its publication. The faults that remain with the volume are my own, but the manuscript benefited throughout from Walter's and Elizabeth's suggestions and support. My indebtedness to them, and to all who have made this project possible, will never be forgotten.

John C. Dann
Ann Arbor, Michigan

A Sketch or Journal of Jacob Nagle from the Year 1775.

My Father was of the German decent & my Mother of the Quaker decent from England my Grand mother of my Mothers Side having two husbands, our Family have Sprung from the Nagles, Lincolns, Rogers, & Booms, &c: A Short time after my Father being high Sherriff in Reading Berks County Pennsylvania State, where I was born. The War broke out, in Boston, about the 28 of April 1775, Massachusetts applyed to the State for assistance, against the Brittish, my Father Received a Capt Commission and Listed a hundred & 25 Riflemen in one Week, and joining with Meriland and Virginia Companies, which amounted to five Companies & marched for Boston in the month of June 1775, during the time he remained there against the Enemy he received a Slight wound, by a Shell, from the Enemy a Cross the bridge of his Nose, after being a Considerable time there, Came home to see his family, Likewise was prefered as Major in the 5th Pennsylvania Rigment which he joined, as the were then, Laying in Phelledelphia Berraks, and took me with him Some time after they joined the army and I went home to Reading In 1776 the Brittish Leaving Boston Landing at Long Island & took New York
In 1777 Lord How Landed at the head of Elk, which washington perceived he went for Philadelphia, therefore he Came to meet him, at this time my Father Sent for me, at this time there was a Number of Officers in Reading upon Liberty, but was demanded to join the army, amongst the Rest was Jacll Bittle, Commesary genral, which my Mother gave him Charge of me, to be delivered to my Father, we went on to join the army, but on the Road he pretended he had Lost some dispatches which was for Washington, the Officers all Returned with him for Seven or eight Miles, when he gave up the Search and we Returned, & Joined the army, the next day, Marching through Wilmington Mr Bittle took me to my Father who was then Leutenant Cornel of the Ninth Rigiment, & Shortly after full Cornel of the Tenth Pensylvania Rigiment, I was then not quite Sixteen, when the army Encamped my Father took me to Cornl Prockter who Commanded the grand park of Artillery, I Laid in his Martee that Night, and the next day I mesed with ajudent Hofman who had the Charge of me, being a Yooung Soldier, we then marched and the army Encamped on the Brandewine on the Right of Shads ford on the high ground, our Artilery was Ranged in front of an Orchard, the Night before the Brittish arived the Infantry hove up a brest work, so that the muzzels of the guns would Run over it, a Cross the Road on the left was a Buckwheat field opposit to a wood, & the Brandewine, between them, the provision waggons being Sent a way we ware three day without Provisions, Excepting what the Penmons brought in to Sell, in their waggons, & what the Soldiers Could

Introduction

I. THE JOURNAL COMES TO LIGHT

*I*N JULY 1982 a New York autograph dealer's auction catalog
arrived on my desk at the Clements Library. The Clements, housed
in a Palladian limestone building on the central campus of the
University of Michigan, is one of America's great caretakers of the
nation's historical past, and as the library director, I most enjoy the
responsibility of adding to its collections of manuscript and printed
source materials. The library is well known in scholarly circles throughout the world for its holdings on the American Revolutionary War, and
actively collects letters, diaries, and maps relating to this eighteenth-
century conflict, where research content is great and price not outra-
geously inflated. Lot number 6 in the Charles Hamilton Galleries sale of
August 12 immediately caught my eye.

Described as "a book-length journal" of 161 folio, handwritten
pages, "A Sketch or Journal of Jacob Nagle from the Year 1775"
purportedly covered the adventuresome lifetime of a Revolutionary
War soldier and sailor who was captured by the British and later
became a sailor in the British navy and merchant service, traveling to
China, Malaya, and Europe. He supposedly served under Lord Nelson
in the Mediterranean, described "floggings, traffic with whores, fights,
drinking bouts," and was later pensioned as a Revolutionary War
veteran.

There were many American soldiers in the Revolution who served a tour of duty on a naval or privateering vessel and not a few who served in the armed forces of both sides. American seamen between 1776 and 1815 constantly risked being impressed or drafted into the Royal Navy if they happened to be at the wrong place at the wrong time. But very few left written records of their lives. When service under Nelson in the Mediterranean, trips to China and the East Indies, and spicy adventures among tippling houses and bordellos were added to this book-length package and by an unknown author, the manuscript sounded too good to be true. Was it an outright fabrication? Was it possibly the draft of an early, unpublished novel? Or could it be one of those rare treasures that occasionally come to light and prove to be all that is promised and more?

Great collections are not built timidly. I called our New York agent, David Kirschenbaum of Carnegie Book Shop, and asked him to take a look at it and see if it "looked right" in terms of its having been written in the early nineteenth century. Mr. Kirschenbaum, who started in the book and autograph business in 1910, has handled a sizable percentage of the great manuscript finds of the twentieth century, and his judgment could be relied upon. He reported that it had the appearance of authenticity. I placed a bid, and we secured the manuscript at the sale, which attracted very few purchasers. When Dave shipped it to Ann Arbor in the latter part of August, I little realized what an important manuscript the Nagle Journal would turn out to be and to what an extent it would dominate my spare moments in the following five years. One glance corroborated his judgment that it was of early-nineteenth-century authorship. There would be no justification for returning it to the gallery for a refund.

In its physical dimensions, the Nagle Journal is eight inches by twelve, a third of an inch thick, contained in homemade brown paper wrappers (added in the latter nineteenth century, after Nagle's death). Laid into the manuscript are a few smaller sheets with textual additions, keyed to the narrative by the author. While evidence points to the late 1820s and 1830s as the probable period of composition, the writing is decidedly eighteenth century in style—a close neat hand, averaging sixteen words per line and forty-one lines per page. The composition is inherently contradictory—its handwriting suggests someone who had frequently set pen to paper, but the phraseology, orthography, and punctuation are those of a man with little formal education—the sort of person who generally avoids writing for fear of showing his ignorance. But as I would quickly come to realize, where Jacob Nagle is concerned, the improbable becomes the expected!

The Nagle Journal, in its original form, is not easily read. It is so closely written that the eye tends to wander from line to line. The author's vocabulary is extensive but colloquial, while his spelling is often phonetic—easy enough to understand when sounded out, but confusing to read. While the author conveys his narrative in complete, if convoluted sentences, he apparently viewed punctuation as a decorative device, to be scattered liberally in order to convey the appearance of learning and scholarship.

Yet behind this facade of misspellings, meaningless commas and semicolons, questionable capitalization, and never-ending sentences is a text not only of great historical importance but of literary ability, even brilliance, particularly when compared with what passed for superior composition in his era. In this Nagle was blessed, perhaps, by his limited formal education. He had a true gift for narrative composition and dialogue. His style was more oral than written. He spoke directly to his readers without any of the turgid formalities and posturing of learned contemporaries, and with every sentence, the reader can hear him telling the story, often in slang, but in a style absolutely true to the times, places, and events so richly described. His phonetic spelling recorded even his pronunciation. The narrator never becomes repetitious except at the end, when the aches and pains of his remarkable life caught up with him, denying him the active life upon which he could weave tale after tale.

From the first "here and there" readings of the Nagle Journal, and more fully as a typed transcript made possible sustained, careful reading, it was apparent that the manuscript was more amazing in terms of the breadth of the author's experiences than even the auction catalog description had suggested. The catalog had mentioned service in the American army and navy during the Revolution, his privateering and capture by the British, his service in the Royal Navy under Horatio Nelson and career as a merchant seaman. It had not noted that he claimed to have been on the flagship of the First Fleet that settled Australia or the governor's barge crew that discovered and selected the future site of Sydney. It omitted his claim to have sailed to both India and China in the service of the East India Company, to have been stranded in South America for an entire decade, and to have survived a full nineteen-year career in the Royal Navy on a dozen different ships.

If Nagle's Journal could be taken at face value, it was clearly one of the most exciting manuscript finds of recent times—a book-length diary by the sort of person who simply does not write memoirs—the story of a man who had personally met "the founder" of his own country (George Washington); shaken hands with Britain's greatest naval hero (Lord Nelson) and been complimented by the first governor of modern Australia (Arthur Phillip); sailed the four corners of the globe; missed death by inches a half-dozen times in hand-to-hand combat, shipwrecks, and barroom brawls; and yet died of natural causes in rural Ohio at the age of 80! Could the story possibly be true?

II. The Journal
Authenticated

HISTORICAL detective work is one of the most exhilarating and at times exasperating activities known to man. The Nagle Journal provided a formidable challenge indeed. Nagle claimed to have served in the American Revolution and he described, at some length, his eventually successful efforts to secure a government pension; the National Archives in Washington was an obvious place to start checking his story. Among the vast collection of applications, there was one forwarded by Jacob Nagle from Canton, Ohio, in 1833, which agreed in substance with the portions of the diary covering the Revolutionary War service and was signed in the same distinctive hand that had written the journal. The War Department had considered his narrative sufficiently credible to have granted him a small allowance, and various muster rolls published by the Pennsylvania State Archives in the nineteenth century included a "Jacob Nagle" in the military unit and time period indicated. He was at least a real person, a Revolutionary soldier, and the writer of the journal.

But at that point, the trail became disturbingly cold. While the journal suggested that its author had completed his days in Ohio, he nowhere appears in a fairly exhaustive list of Revolutionary veterans buried in that state. He was not listed in a volume purportedly containing all persons making up the First Fleet to Australia, and although Governor Phillip, Captain Hunter, Lieutenant Bradley, and Dr. White of the First Fleet—men with whom Nagle claimed rather close contact—all left detailed diaries, none of them contain the slightest reference to him by name. In the vast printed record of source materials on Australian settlement, and in the voluminous, published primary and secondary sources on the Royal Navy between 1781 and 1802, the name of Jacob Nagle never appears.

While Jacob Nagle's name was found to be suspiciously absent from the printed historical record, his father, George Nagle, began appearing with some regularity. The Nagles, German immigrants of substance, were prominent in the early history of Berks County, Pennsylvania, and it seemed logical that another route to information on

Jacob would be through genealogical research. No full-scale Nagle genealogy has ever gotten into print, but through fortunate coincidence, made possible by an alert librarian at the Berks County Historical Society, I had the good luck to make contact with a most remarkable lady, Mrs. Marion Rhoads, the last of this branch of the Nagle family residing in Reading. She not only had compiled a careful, critical history of the family, but welcomed my inquiries about "Cousin Jacob," almost as if she had known him personally. She provided me an obituary notice (published in the Appendix) and a wealth of information on the family. The limited comments in the journal about his family were entirely confirmed, and from the obituary notice I now had his place and time of death, less than a year after the final entry in his journal.

Mrs. Rhoads was able to document the beginning and end of Jacob Nagle's life, but the problem of credibility of the journal remained. The substantive records I had at this point—the journal itself, the pension application, and now the obituary—all contained facts generated by Nagle himself, and while the three sources largely agreed with one another, they left unanswered whether one could believe the remarkable adventures of his active career. Until I could delve into the records of the Royal Navy, the East India Company, and scattered sources on commercial shipping that have survived, the questions would remain. That path of inquiry led to London.

In the present age of computerized records, income taxes, census questionnaires, confidential security files, and credit reports, we tend to assume that citizens of the modern world are documented as never before. In fact, bureaucratic record keeping was as prevalent in the era of the quill pen—perhaps nowhere to a greater extent than in the Royal Navy.

Between the Public Record Office and the National Maritime Museum at Greenwich the activities of the Royal Navy in Jacob Nagle's days are recorded to a degree almost surpassing belief. For any commissioned vessel in service, throughout the world, handwritten logs were kept by the captain, two or more lieutenants, and the master, which contain minute details of location, weather, activities of the crew, ships sighted, foodstuffs ordered and inspected, ship repairs, rigging, and punishments. Crew lists and pay registers document names, places of birth, age, rank, and pay of every man on board. Captains' and admirals' correspondence with naval officials in London tell not only what a vessel is doing but why, fitting it into the larger scheme of overall fleet movement and naval strategy and occasionally providing confidential information unknown to either officers or men at deck level. For any career sailor of the eighteenth-century British navy, we know what he did, what he ate, what he saw, and even the way the wind was blowing, day and night. The India Office Library, now associated with the British Library, contains a similar level of documentation on sailors in company service.

I made four trips to London between 1984 and 1987, and not only did Jacob Nagle's name appear in muster books, pay registers, and log books, but it showed up on every ship in the exact sequence narrated in the journal. When Nagle describes a storm, a change in officers, sighting another ship, or the capture of an enemy vessel, his narrative is confirmed in the log books. While serving on one vessel, HMS *Netley*, he was prize master, often detailed to take captured ships into port. The logs and the captain's correspondence record the captures; the pay registers record and date his absences. The navy instituted a system in the 1780s whereby sailors could make out wills, leaving unpaid wages to their families. A check of the ''N's'' produced such a document, signed by Jacob Nagle and Captain John Hunter of HMS *Sirius*, filled out at Sydney Bay in May of 1788! Nagle not only existed and was a man who told the truth, but he seems to have had exceptional powers of recall.

For a common sailor, who was not privy to command decisions, Jacob Nagle took an unusual interest in what was going on around him. He had a genius for picking up small but important details. And some way or other, he retained the fresh immediacy of the events of decades earlier when setting them on paper. He was a reporter of prize-winning talent.

III. JACOB NAGLE

WHAT, then, do we know about Jacob Nagle? About his physical appearance we know only what is derived from occasional remarks in the journal itself. He noted that in his early twenties, he was ''slim, but very active.'' He was strong and agile, capable of besting larger men in physical combat, and able, until the end of his career, to climb the highest rigging in the middle of a severe gale. He had a ''cast'' to his left eye, presumably meaning that it wandered out of the direct line of focus, at least by the time he was in his late forties. He wore his hair long, tied behind his head. Nagle took considerable pride in his appearance, wearing on shore a carefully tailored roundabout of the finest cloth, a silk handkerchief at his neck, and jewelry—shoe buckles, a gold brooch, rings, and a gold watch. For a sailor of his era, a good ring or pocket watch served not only as a mark of prosperity but as a walking bank account that could be drawn upon in times of emergency.

To understand Jacob Nagle's personality, and perhaps his motivation, it is worth exploring his background. The Nagle family had emigrated from Kefenrod, Germany, in the early 1750s, Jacob's father apparently coming over to Pennsylvania first, followed by Jacob's grandfather, grandmother, and their children. Protestants—members of the Reformed church—they were people of some degree of financial substance and education. The grandfather, Joachim, purchased land in Berks County, built a grist mill, and died at age ninety in 1795 in a state of modest affluence.

George (1735–1789), the oldest son, and the father of Jacob, served in the Pennsylvania militia in the French and Indian War, was a blacksmith by trade, and was appointed sheriff of Berks County in 1770. He held this office of considerable importance in colonial Pennsylvania for five years. At the outbreak of the American Revolution, he raised a company of frontier riflemen, which was one of the first distant groups of soldiers to arrive in Boston. As the seriousness and long-term nature of the conflict became obvious, the states and Continental Congress replaced voluntary militia companies with formally organized regiments. George Nagle was appointed major of the 5th Pennsylvania Regiment in January 1776, lieutenant colonel of the 9th Pennsylvania Regiment in October of that year, and colonel of the 10th Pennsylvania Regiment in February 1777. Drawing upon his wide connections as sheriff in the years before the war, he seems to have been especially capable at recruiting soldiers. He was slightly wounded at the time of the siege of Boston and served continuously with Washington's army through the 1777–78 winter at Valley Forge, when, apparently for a combination of health reasons and conflicts among officers in his regiment, he resigned. In 1776 he had taken son Jacob along with him to the army barracks in Philadelphia, and between September 1777 and the spring of 1778, they were both serving in Washington's army, the father in the infantry, the son in the artillery.

George Nagle operated a tavern in Philadelphia for a brief period after he left the service and then moved back to Reading and opened a store. In 1759 he had married Rebecca Rogers, whose mother had been married twice, first to Mordecai Lincoln, great-great-grandfather of President Abraham Lincoln, and then to Roger Rogers, Nagle's grandfather on his mother's side.

Jacob was one of four children of George and Rebecca Nagle. One of his three sisters, Polly, is known only by Jacob Nagle's diary entry as living somewhere near Philadelphia in 1802. Sister Rebecca married

Thomas McCartle (or McCardle) and lived in the vicinity of Hagerstown, Maryland. Sister Sara married John Webb, a hatmaker in Pennsylvania, New York, and finally at Canton, Stark County, Ohio. Jacob visited and lived at various times with all of them in the last years of his life. Jacob Nagle's father died in 1789, his mother in 1793. His immediate family had all left Reading by the end of the eighteenth century, but brothers and sisters of his father remained there and in nearby towns, many of them occupying prominent positions in their communities and holding local and state offices.

Names, dates, records of landholdings, and wills do not tell us a great deal about the personalities of Jacob Nagle's family, but there are enough clues and facts to speculate on ways in which his background influenced his own character. For the years in which George Nagle held the office of sheriff of Berks County, several letters survive at the Historical Society of Pennsylvania. It would appear that he enjoyed strong connections, politically or through personal friendship, with various members of the prominent Biddle family, and their influence had much to do with his officer's commissions during the Revolution.

In colonial Pennsylvania, the position of county sheriff could be the stepping-stone to considerable personal gain. Political connections in Philadelphia and access to information about land foreclosure made it possible for an astute officeholder to amass considerable personal wealth. George Nagle seems not to have taken advantage of the situation, like his son after him setting a higher store on action than on worldly goods. At the outbreak of the Revolution, when it might have been particularly profitable to have remained in Reading, joined the local militia, and capitalized on the confiscation of Tory landholdings, he opted, although in his forties, for the more adventuresome life of a soldier in the field. Fathers are often role models for sons, and it is not hard to imagine that for Jacob Nagle, who left home at age fifteen in 1777, the rough-and-tumble life of a sailor was a logical continuation of his father's career in the years while he, Jacob, was growing up in the Berks County jail and the military camps of the Revolutionary army.

On the other hand, his solid family background helped to instill the remarkable degree of self-confidence and pride that characterizes Nagle's actions throughout his career. Unlike most of his contemporaries, who tended to judge others on the basis of their rank, their income, and what their family or political connections were, Jacob Nagle judged another man on how well he did his job. He took immense pride in being the best sailor on any ship on which he served and expected similar "on duty" competence on the part of a fellow crewman, whether captain, midshipman, or common sailor. He could drink, carouse, throw a punch, pick up a girl, and tell off an officer with the best of his shipmates, but he chose his moments for each of these activities carefully. There was a shrewd intelligence, a solid self-assurance always present in his actions and an instinct for self-protection that explains his longevity.

Although Nagle in his old age proudly considered himself to be a full-fledged veteran of the Revolution, his army service between the ages of fifteen and seventeen had never taken him beyond the watchful and protective eye of his father. He notes that well into his sailing career, in 1782, at age twenty, he "made a practice of walking the deck till 2 or 3 in the morning, crying and fretting for the loss of my parents, never being so long from home before." Age and the shipboard discipline of the Royal Navy quickly hardened him, but he always retained a degree of childlike naïveté, honesty, and generosity—qualities often associated with sailors of the age of sail, and probably owing to the fact that most of them had gone to sea before they had grown up.

It is hard to understand why Jacob Nagle had so little ambition, and in fact went out of his way to avoid becoming an officer or a captain in the course of his career. If we knew all of the facts associated with his father's resignation from the army, the particulars of which Jacob would have personally witnessed, we might understand it from a psychological point of view. On three occasions within a one-week period near the end of the army's stay at Valley Forge, the father was involved in court-martial proceedings. On June 2, Captain Stake of the 10th Regiment, which Nagle commanded, was brought up on charges of "propagating a report that Colo. George Nagle was seen on the 15th. of May drinking either Tea or Coffee in Serjeant Howcraft's tent with his Whore, her Mother, the said Howcraft and his Family to the Prejudice of good Order and military discipline." The court acquitted Stake, "unanimously of opinion that Captn. Stake's Justification is sifficient." On June 5, Nagle brought charges against his immediate subordinate, Lieutenant Colonel Hubley, for lying about the absence of a Captain Long, causing Nagle to sign a false return for the regiment, "contrary to good order and military discipline." Hubley was acquitted, which, as in the case above, was a slap in the face for Nagle.

Three days later, on June 8, Colonel Nagle himself was brought up on charges relating to the earlier incident of "associating with a Serjeant [Howcraft] in Company with Women of bad reputation in the Serjeants hutt." Nagle was exonerated, but it was shortly thereafter that he and son Jacob left the army.

The historical record is too fragmentary for us to draw any conclusions as to whether George Nagle had committed an impropriety or had been maligned by disgruntled subordinates. In either case, he apparently left the service abruptly and presumably in anger. To a sensitive boy, just turned seventeen, who had clearly enjoyed a degree of privilege because of his father's high rank, the experience must have been traumatic. One cannot help but speculate that the incident left a permanent scar, causing him to avoid the pressures and potential disappointments of command throughout his later career.

Having gone to sea as a boy, he never grew up in terms of fully accepting adult responsibilities. He apparently never bothered to contact his parents after his capture by the British in 1781 and made no serious efforts to get back to the United States. Although he married "a lively hansome girl" in London in 1795, she rated but a few brief mentions in his journal, and we do not know her first name, or the names or even number of his "children," all of whom died of yellow fever in Lisbon in 1802.

Although he obviously had an irresponsible streak in his personal life, when it came to his job, he was always professional. After the American Revolution and a few unsuccessful efforts to get passage home from England to Philadelphia, Nagle enlisted in the British navy that he had formerly served by forced necessity. He remained four years on HMS *Ganges,* most of the time in port at Portsmouth and Spithead. In his journal, he primarily remembered the hard treatment of "Lieutenant Rio." In fact, Lieutenant Edward Riou (1762–1801) probably had a formative influence on making Nagle the excellent sailor that he would show himself to be. Riou was a fanatical disciplinarian, but he was fair and he demanded a crew that was intelligent and "all business" when on duty. Whatever the reasons, Nagle projected a sufficient appearance of ability by 1787 to be specially selected from among a large pool of volunteers to be a member of Australia's First Fleet.

One senses that the Australian expedition had a permanent maturing effect on Nagle's attitude toward service. He had been entrusted with the extra responsibilities of assignment to Governor Phillip's barge crew and regularly rubbed shoulders with the commanding officers of the colony. He had experienced hardship and seen more of the world than the typical British sailor, and it showed in his demeanor. After 1792 he was unwilling to put up with unreasonable treatment, whether from officers, fellow sailors, press crews, or shipowners, and he demonstrated absolute confidence and pride in his abilities.

The high point of his life was his service on HMS *Netley* between 1798 and 1801. He loved his ship, thoroughly respected his captain, and was given considerable responsibility, serving as master's mate and as prize master. In retrospect, it seems a shame that he did not become a

merchant vessel captain when he left the navy; he had all the knowledge, experience, and ability to do so, but there is no indication that he
ever aspired to be more than a common sailor.

He left the Royal Navy in 1802, and in many ways, the subsequent
twenty-three years were a gradual and somewhat sad decline in his
career. There is a general belief that service in the Royal Navy in the
eighteenth century was tantamount to slavery. It is a portrayal that
must have originated largely among landsmen in fear of being
impressed, because Nagle's journal clearly documents that, in general,
British naval captains were capable and shipboard duty was comfortable for the experienced sailor while the life of a merchant seaman was
far worse. The majority of his merchant ship captains between 1802
and 1825 were tyrannical alcoholics, dishonest incompetents, or both;
the ships were chronically undermanned and undersupplied. Nagle
was severely injured in 1806 and suffered from overexposure in ice-
cold water in 1809. Thereafter, sickness and apparent arthritis are
increasingly noted in the journal.

He finally returned to the United States in 1822 and retired from
the sea in 1825, at age sixty-four. He spent the last sixteen years of his
life wandering from place to place, trying to get a pension for his and his
father's military service, and taking odd jobs. One senses that he was
very much a fish out of water, a character probably like nothing the
typical inland American of the 1820s and 1830s had ever seen before,
with his old-fashioned speech, his sailor dress, knapsack, walking stick,
and vast stock of stories. He never stayed put in any one place for more
than two or three years, and in the very last years of his life he did not
live with members of his family, but in boardinghouses of some sort. He
probably was not entirely a welcome visitor, perhaps even something of
an embarrassment to the relatives he visited. He died penniless. But
even in these last years, he retained the remarkable willpower that had
made him a most uncommon, common seaman. His triumph was the
journal, the likes of which no other sailor of his era, British or American, is known to have produced.

IV. THE WRITING OF THE JOURNAL

WHEN, why, and how did Nagle write his journal? Other than minor
variations in handwriting, due to using different pens and slightly
different inks, the manuscript, from beginning to end, has the consis-
tency of appearance of a near final draft, set down on paper over no
more than two or three years, perhaps less.

There are a few internal references that suggest that Nagle had always been a diary keeper. At age twenty, when in prison, he had "a kind of journal and had a great many remarks in the taking of the island of St. Christopher and the French and British fleet." His fellow prisoners convinced him he should destroy the journal so as not to be hanged as a spy. He later noted that he lost a diary of the Australian expedition, possibly in the wreck of the *Sirius* on Norfolk Island in 1790. Combining these statements with the documentable accuracy of his memory, one can probably assume that Nagle kept pocket diaries of some sort throughout his life, possibly reconstituting those that had been lost and revising and expanding them in moments of leisure.

While his bodily infirmities forced him into retirement from active sea duty in 1825, his mind and his memory remained sharp until very near the end of his life in 1841. Between 27 August 1824 and 4 May 1826, he apparently lived with his sister, near Hagerstown, Maryland. From 17 June until 10 December 1827, and from 13 October 1834 to 27 October 1837, he lived with nephew John Webb in Perrysburg, Ohio. During the winter of 1828–29, he lived with his cousin, George Nagle, in Harrisburg, Pennsylvania, and for several stretches of months' and years' duration, between 1827 and 1841, he lived a fairly stationary existence in Canton, Ohio.

Particularly suggestive are the periods between 1830 and 1833, when he was employed by Canton attorneys and Stark County recorders of deeds John Myers and William Bryce, "righting in their offices," and between 1834 and 1837, in Perrysburg, where he was "righting in the Clerks Office" with his nephew. His formal responsibilities were undoubtedly to keep ledgers and make copies of deeds and legal papers, but in his spare moments, it is probable that he pulled together whatever written records of his life he had preserved, drew upon his remarkable memory, and began the "finished" journal that now exists. In 1833 he had composed the short narrative of his Revolutionary War service in order to secure a pension (see Appendix), and if he had not already started the "finished" draft of the journal, that experience may have inspired him to do so.

By the 1830s, the United States was a half century old as an independent nation. With each year, the "old Revolutioners," to use Nagle's phrase, were acknowledged with growing respect and emotion at Fourth of July celebrations, while their numbers were rapidly dwindling. The Canton newspaper described a local celebration in 1834, at which Jacob Nagle gave a toast: "May the sons of America be united as the patriots of the revolution were in '76." For a man who, in his last years at sea, had lived a fairly lonely existence, the respect shown for his military career must have pleased him. The anonymous obituary writer in the Cincinnati paper who "knew him well" noted that "many an hour have we listened to him, recounting the privations he underwent in the continental army, and the perils he encountered upon the waves." This writer apparently was unaware that Nagle had also written out his adventures.

Why did he write the journal? He may, indeed, have had some thoughts of getting it published in order to make money. The 1820s and 1830s had witnessed a vast multiplication of printing offices in small-town America, which in addition to issuing posters, legal forms, and weekly newspapers, would occasionally take on the publication of original books and pamphlets—pure Americana in its crudest and most endearing form. Several Revolutionary War soldiers and sailors of no higher station in life than Nagle's had published their reminiscences by the late 1830s, often selling them door-to-door to keep body and soul together. He may have seen some of them, but Nagle's journal was too long and decidedly too crude in style and expression, and whatever his aspirations, a printer would have been unlikely to have touched it in its existing form. He may simply have written it for his own, and his friends' and relatives', amusement.

One of the qualities of the journal that make it such a valuable and unusual source is the degree to which Nagle records not only the events but also the language, the slang, and the entire mentality of the milieu of the late-eighteenth-century world that had already disappeared by the time he penned his "finished" version of his life's story. In a sense, due to most unusual personal circumstances, Nagle was a living time capsule who had outlived his era and been strangely unaffected by thirty or forty years of change. Shipboard isolated men from the cultural transformations of society as a whole, and between 1777 and 1812, he probably spent a total of less than two years on dry land. In the thirteen years thereafter, he was largely in South America.

It is interesting that, although he had spent several years in the proximity of Portugal on the *Netley* and over ten years in Brazil, he says that he learned no Portuguese. The adage that one can't teach an old dog new tricks would seem to have been especially applicable to Nagle, and it helps to explain why, in the 1830s, he remained so much a product of the previous century. When he describes shipboard experiences or naval action of the 1790s in his journal, his every phrase and reference mirrors the logs and letters of that time, not the era in which he was writing. His sister in Canton, with whom he may have lived while writing the memoir, was a pillar of the local Methodist church, but he was totally oblivious to the proprieties and moral inhibitions of evangelical Christianity, which had so thoroughly transformed the Anglo-American world. In his mind and in his journal, he continued to take his "rambles" in Hogarthian dockside London without a hint of prudery or shame.

Jacob Nagle, whether from a combination of unusual circumstances, isolation from the changing world, or simply perfect satisfaction with the eighteenth-century world he had grown up and operated in, never changed at all. The people of the 1830s listened to his stories of Washington at the Battle of the Brandywine, of privateering during the Revolution, of the strange and unusual lands and peoples he had encountered in Australia and the South Seas, but in various ways they probably showed that they either did not believe or did not understand experiences entirely foreign to their own. In his journal, Jacob Nagle was preserving the record of a life of which he was thoroughly proud. It was, in a sense, his last and most memorable voyage.

V. THE JOURNAL'S HISTORICAL IMPORTANCE

IN terms of traditional history, Jacob Nagle did not make the crucial decisions that changed the world. No single historical event he was a part of, or witness to, hinged upon his presence. The American Revolution would have followed its course and the ships of the Royal Navy would have sailed pretty much as they did without him. It is as a witness, rather than an actor, that he earns an important place in history.

The Jacob Nagle Journal is a historical find of major importance and, in its entirety, unique. It provides not the primary record of the major events themselves, but the connectors between them, the "off the record" activities that officers' letters, official reports, and newspapers left out. Nagle brought to his narrative the distinctive perspective of a private and of a common sailor. Unlike the officers, whose accounts make up almost the only record upon which our eighteenth-century history is based, he had no ax to grind, no decisions to justify, no blame to pass off on other shoulders. From Nagle we learn more about the cutthroat rivalry between the Royal Navy and the East India Company in the Napoleonic era than was ever made a matter of public record. We learn of the little schemes and con games in operation in the Royal Navy—stealing from troops being transported to Gibraltar, officers smuggling liquor, captains and admirals pocketing prize money. And Nagle provides some marvelous vignettes, replete with dialogue, of people who are only two-dimensional figures in the standard sources—tyrannical Lieutenant Riou, idealistic Governor Phillip, pathetic Lieutenant Maxwell, timid Captain Buchanan. On shore, there were the dishonest landlords, the bullies, the crimps, the whores. Nagle does not include these details to sensationalize his narrative or to satisfy old grudges—they simply are part of the entire experience. The details Nagle gives us may be small in themselves, but they are vital to our understanding of what the past was like and the most difficult sort of information to find. Nagle puts meat on the bones of history and provides us a rare perspective to balance the traditional and official point of view.

It would be nice to think that our ancestors were always efficient, honest, sensible, and high-minded. We do sometimes tend to picture our eighteenth-century forebears as possessing a more rational outlook and greater wisdom than our generation. Nagle reminds us forcefully that, even in the Age of Reason, the world, on whatever level, did not operate exactly according to plan. Then, as now, human nature tended to get in the way, and when Nagle was around, it did not go unobserved. In spite of his seeming simplicity, he was a wise man, appreciating that it was the very inefficiencies inherent in human nature that made life, and his narration of it, a source of constant amusement and interest. He never took himself or the world too seriously.

In evaluating the Nagle Journal, one has to question the extent to which he is typical of his time, his "class," his profession. Was he representative of the sailors of his age?

Nagle came from a middle- or upper-middle-class home and he was an American serving in the British navy. But these were not quite such unusual characteristics as one might imagine. There is a popular belief, particularly on the part of Americans, that the Royal Navy was manned by the dregs of society, the sweepings of the London slums. In the height of the Napoleonic Wars, when manpower requirements multiplied far above peacetime levels, almost anyone who had maritime experience and who could walk was fair game for press crews, but even then, and certainly in normal times, the average British sailor came from a home not unlike Nagle's. A man-of-war was a remarkable melting pot, containing sailors from throughout the British Isles—slightly weighted toward natives of coastal towns, Scots, and Irishmen—but on any ship, particularly those that had been to sea for long periods of time, there were always foreigners—Europeans, Indians, blacks and whites from the West Indies, Canadians, and natives of the United States. Jacob Nagle was always enrolled in crew lists as a native of Philadelphia, and there was never a ship on which he served that there were not other Americans, often a fair number of them.

It is probable that Nagle's consciousness of being an American gave him a slight feeling of detachment, a sense, at least after his earliest forced tour of duty, that he was in the navy by choice, and that he could leave it by choice as well. On the other hand, he actually grew to manhood, not on United States soil, but within the wooden walls and dockside streets of British territory. While serving on HMS *Netley*, dealing with a Philadelphia captain of a captured merchant vessel, he had no qualms about obeying the dictates of the flag under which he was serving rather than the one under which he was born.

In the United States, where many people were angered by impressment of their sailors by the British, the citizenship of crews became a heated political issue in the era of the Napoleonic Wars. But in truth, the sailors of this period who were involved in more than localized coastal trade were, to a large degree, citizens of the world. Nagle certainly was of such a mind, and his perspective seems to have been shared by his fellow crewmen. Being an American did not, by itself, make him different in outlook from his peers.

What can be learned from the wealth of existing source materials on the Royal Navy, the East India Company, and the merchant service of the late eighteenth and early nineteenth centuries suggests that Jacob Nagle is very representative of his time and place in history. The discovery of this previously unknown source provides us with a window through which we can view a fascinating and long-gone era from the rare perspective of the common man. The Jacob Nagle Journal deserves a place as one of the more important and most readable diaries of its era.

VI. THE JOURNAL AS A HISTORICAL SOURCE

WHILE the Nagle Journal is an invaluable addition to the corpus of original source materials on British naval history in the late eighteenth century, the American Revolution, the First Fleet to Australia, and merchant shipping in the nineteenth-century Atlantic trade, it must always be kept in mind that it was written as an autobiography. Thus the editorial introductions at the beginning of each chapter provide additional information, much of which Nagle himself was unaware of.

In analyzing the manuscript as personal literature, it becomes obvious that while Nagle enjoyed tracking his path through history, describing the places, the ships, the military actions of which he was a witness, his greatest interest was in people. Nagle introduces a cast of hundreds and tells us minute details of how they lived; this is simply part of the narrative for him, but priceless bits of social history for us. To read and enjoy Nagle one needs little more than Nagle himself, with a few dates added, a few exceptional misspellings and errors corrected, and a bit of additional factual data. For those interested in clarifying some of the more minute details, notes are marked and provided in a separate section at the end of the volume, but the text can be read and understood without consulting them.

The literature on life in the British navy in the period in which Nagle flourished is extensive and highly readable. John Masefield's *Sea Life in Nelson's Time* (1905) being the much reprinted classic, supplemented by M. A. Lewis, *The Social History of the Royal Navy* (1960), C. C. Lloyd, *The British Seaman* (1968), P. K. Kemp, *The British Sailor* (1970), G. J. Marcus, *Heart of Oak* (1975), and N. A. M. Rodger, *The Wooden World* (1986). One of the most recent and useful is Dudley Pope's *Life in Nelson's Navy* (1981 and 1987), a superb, beautifully written study of the seamen of Nagle's time. It is highly recommended that anyone whose interest in the subject is more than passing read it along with Nagle.

Without imposing an exhaustive preface on life at sea in the age of sail, I would emphasize a few basic, even obvious, points worth keeping in mind as one reads the journal. First, although Nagle lived to see the introduction of steam power and would take passage on both Chesapeake Bay and Great Lakes steamers in the 1830s, his shipping career from beginning to end was in sailing vessels. In the modern world, we are so accustomed, whether on land or water, to pushing the button and starting the engine, even in our larger sailing vessels, that it is difficult for anyone to conceive of what it meant to be entirely at the mercy of the wind for motive power, both on the high seas and on inland waterways.

The ships of Nagle's day were greatly affected by currents and by tides, when the wind was not sufficient to counteract their force. Both are yet factors in international maritime commerce—currents used effectively to save fuel, high tides to get over coastal obstructions—but in the age of pure sail, they could become the controlling factor, as in the case with the *Sirius* when it went on the reef at Norfolk Island. Today, the captain can start the engine and go against the tide.

A side effect is that anchors have lost much of their eighteenth-century meaning. The majority of Nagle's ships were equipped with six anchors, one of them being a spare, a sheet anchor, two bower anchors (the "best bower" on the larboard side, the "small bower" on the starboard side), a stream anchor, and a kedge. They were used, as today, to hold a ship in place offshore, but when the wind or current was taking a ship toward shore, and where the bottom did not provide a firm grip, or the power of the wind was so intense as to either cut the cable (actually rope) or force the ship's crew to cut it so as not to turn the vessel on its side, one anchor after another would be used, with destruction awaiting the ship when the supply was exhausted. The bower anchors were primary; the sheet anchor, of the same size, was essentially for emergency use. The stream anchor was smaller and more maneuverable and was primarily used for temporary mooring, and the kedge anchor, smaller yet, and therefore easily transported in a small boat, was used for any number of purposes that would not be thought of as anchoring in the modern sense. Transported by a boat in the appropriate direction away from the ship, and dropped overboard, it was used to pull a ship off a sandbar, or to right a ship whose cargo had caused it to turn on "its beam ends." It was also used to pull a ship up a river, or in open water as a drag or a stabilizing force.

In the age of sail, the ships themselves were designed so as to maximize the flexible usefulness of canvas sail, and routes of travel across the oceans were determined in large part by the nature of prevailing winds. Also, the time a voyage might take, or even the moment a voyage could begin or end, depended upon the unpredictable nature of the wind's direction. A fleet at Spithead could be held up from sailing, or one of Nagle's American ships kept out of the Capes of the Delaware, for not just days but weeks by contrary winds. And while these prevailing winds, which of course change from season to season, determined the course of long voyages, unexpected reversals could easily turn a one-month transoceanic trip into a three-month ordeal, for which provisions might not be adequate.

Sailing ships, made of wood, canvas, and rope, had the qualities of being both tough and fragile at the same time, and both were important. In operating a ship, the general purpose was to crowd as much sail as possible without pushing it beyond the breaking point. It was a constant gamble. Without sufficient sail, the ship would not be taking advantage of the wind to hasten the voyage. Too much, and the sails would tear, or in extreme situations, the spars and masts would be carried over the side. Yet their fragility was important too. If masts and sails did not give under extreme weather conditions, ships would have been blown over, and they occasionally were. Ships of the era carried a sizable quantity of spare parts: sails, masts, spars, and rigging. The crew always included men whose responsibility it was to repair the inevitable and constant damage, but on a long voyage or a long tour of duty, a ship could become woefully short of the replacement stores, making the distant ports and naval supply stations so essential to keeping a single vessel or a fleet at sea. Much of the reason behind seemingly harsh and demanding discipline in this era was to stay as far ahead as possible of the destructive forces that were constantly tearing a ship apart, to make sure that a vessel would be in top shape when it encountered the next gale-force wind. Maintenance before the storm, as much as weather conditions, could make the difference between survival and destruction.

A final point worth making is the fact that, in Nagle's age of sail, it was the land, not the sea, that offered the greatest danger. A well-maintained ship, under a knowledgeable captain and a professional crew, could weather almost any storm at sea, but reefs and rocks, in conjunction with the uncontrollable factors of wind, current, and tide, made landfall a life-threatening experience. In home waters, at least the location of rocks and channels and the prevailing tendencies of winds and currents were known. In the distant reaches of the earth, charts were inadequate to the point of being almost useless. Nagle describes many harrowing escapes in the course of his career, and with few exceptions, they relate not to open water, but to coming into shore.

VII. THE EDITORIAL METHOD

As noted previously, the Jacob Nagle Journal, although the product of pen, ink, and paper, is essentially an oral narrative, much like the transcript of a tape-recorded interview. This is the quality that makes it such a marvelously readable source, but it also requires a more flexible editorial approach than would be the case with the writings of a formally educated writer.

In preparing the manuscript for the reader, I have been guided by one overriding principle: to make it possible for Jacob Nagle to speak directly to his audience in his own words, with a minimum of archaic and meaningless impediments. To the likes of Nagle, the written word was merely a vehicle to transmit the substance of his message. Form, so important to men and women of education, was meaningless to him—he would spell a word two or three different ways on the same page. Nagle's punctuation and his capitalization were entirely without rhyme or reason, yet he had a sense of grammar, and he wrote in complete sentences for the most part, even if he seemingly destroyed them by useless commas and semicolons.

Jacob Nagle's spelling has been preserved exactly as written in the original, except for obvious "slips of the pen," and two other situations noted below. Reading the journal is a corrupting process, and it is very difficult to get through the book and retain any memory of how a word is actually spelled! But after a few pages, the reader will find Nagle's orthographic peculiarities one of the great charms of the journal. The two exceptions noted above are the words "the/they" and "of/off," which most of the time he spelled alike. The modern reader would find it impossible to preserve the flow of the story with these transcribed as he wrote (but did not intend) them, and when he means "they" and "off," the extra letter is added without comment. Where his spelling is so far-fetched as to make it questionable what the word is, a correction is provided after the original in brackets. For the sake of readability, capt[ain], b[oar]d, [k]now, and, selectively, a few other words and names are also generally filled out to their full spelling, the additional letters provided in brackets. Nagle's capitalization, to which like most of his contemporaries he was excessively addicted, defies logic. The majority of his capital letters have been reduced to lower case. The only situation where the process has been reversed, changing lower case letters to capitals, is with proper names. Words and phrases set off in parentheses are Nagle's own, to be found in the original manuscript as superscripts; words in brackets are clarifications provided by the editor.

Punctuation has been changed to agree with his true sentence structure, and paragraphs and chapters have been added, to break up the density of the prose. When Nagle gets involved in one of his wonderful stories, he enjoys adding dialogue, and very effectively. The first-person speaking parts have been set off in quotation marks, as have occasional figures of speech. With a little editorial assistance, Jacob Nagle does speak to us, very much as if he were here today.

The Nagle Journal

CHAPTER 1

In Washington's Army

INTRODUCTION

J A C O B Nagle's career of adventure began in 1776, when, at the age of fourteen, he proudly accompanied his father from Reading, Pennsylvania, to the military barracks in Philadelphia. George Nagle, recently promoted, was going to assume his duties as major of the 5th Pennsylvania Regiment, a position of importance and prominence.

Jacob Nagle spent several weeks in Philadelphia. At that time, after the British evacuation of Boston, it was the center of revolutionary fervor and activity. Congress was in session there, attempting to create an army and debating the issue of independence; Thomas Paine was writing *Common Sense*. News was being brought daily from Washington's headquarters, Canada, and the frontier, making it clear that the country had got itself into a war of long duration. Jacob would be sent back to Reading when his father's unit was ordered to the field, but hometown life must have lost much of its charm once he had tasted the pleasures of the metropolis and the excitement of military preparations in the early stages of the war. When his father sent for him in August 1777, this time to join the army as a regular soldier, it must have been a dream come true.

Despite his lack of military heroics, Jacob Nagle's memoir of this period is of historical interest. When he actually wrote this account, presumably in the 1830s, he was drawing on very distant, youthful memories. As he says in summing up his story of the Battle of the Brandywine, "I then wanted 3 day of being sixteen years of age, and the first action I was ever in, therefore it cannot be expected that I can give the purticulars of the whole that accured." His tale has an episodic character, contrasting with the detail and narrative power of his memories of later service at sea. But even at this very young age, Nagle showed a facility for careful observation and accurate reporting. Although he never returned to Chadd's Ford in later life, his description of the terrain, his memory of which troops were stationed where, and his account of the retreat from the battlefield are exceptionally accurate. The very spot where Proctor's artillery, with Nagle among them, was stationed, on the east side of the Brandywine, is easily identifiable today and is confirmed by other contemporary sources.

The one aspect of Nagle's narrative that is inaccurate, or at least confusing, is the time of battle. The Battle of the Brandywine was not an engagement planned well in advance. It was fought over a hilly, heavily forested countryside, where any single observer's vision was limited. The something like two dozen contemporary descriptions of the battle conflict widely as to when the fighting began, but it was certainly later than Nagle indicates.

General William Howe, who had landed at Elkton, Maryland, and was now near Kennett Square, Pennsylvania, had become aware that Washington had established a line of defense on the east side of the Brandywine, with the center at Chadd's Ford, on September 10. He divided his army, sending General Knyphausen directly toward Chadd's Ford to engage the Americans, while he and General Cornwallis headed upstream to attempt a crossing above the Continental army. It would enable them to attack the Americans from the side and rear and render the entrenchments along the river untenable.

Knyphausen's troops, marching east, encountered the first American scouting parties in the early morning, but it was not until 8:00 or 9:00 A.M. that the artillery was brought up to the heights west of the river and shots were exchanged. Nagle's reference to the British "hoisting the red flag" is interesting and undoubtedly accurate, probably part of an effort to convince the Americans that the infantry was being arranged for a frontal assault. Knyphausen's guns played on the American position, and scouting parties maneuvered, as Nagle observed, between the middle of the morning and the early afternoon. Cornwallis's division successfully crossed the two branches of the river several miles above in the early afternoon, and at about 4:00 P.M. both flanks of the British army attacked. Proctor's artillery and the rest of the troops at Chadd's Ford were forced to abandon their line after an hour's close fighting. Several guns were abandoned, as Nagle indicates, and the retreat toward Chester was set in motion.

As fifteen-year-old Jacob Nagle rode on horseback from Reading to join Washington's army at Wilmington, Delaware, early in September 1777, he could never have imagined the extent of the lifetime journey he had embarked upon. Except for three brief visits to his mother in the fall and winter of that year, he was not to return to his hometown again for twenty-five years.

MY FATHER was of the German decent and my mother of the Quaker decent from England, my grandmother of my mothers side having two husbands. Our family have sprung from the Nagles, Lincolns, Rogers, and Boons [Boones], etc.

A short time after, my father being high Sherriff in Reading, Berks County, Pennsylvania State, where I was born, the war broke out in Boston about the 28 of April 1775. Massachusetts applyed to the states for assistance against the Brittish. My father received a capt[ain's] commission and listed [enlisted] a hundred and 25 riflemen in one week, and joining with Merriland [Maryland] and Virginia companies, which amounted to five companies, and marched for Boston in the month of June 1775. During the time he remained there against the enemy he received a slight wound by a shell from the enemy a cross the bridge of his nose. After being a considerable time there, came home to see his family. Likewise, was prefered as major in the 5th Pennsylvania Rigment, which he joined, as they were then laying in Phillidelphia barraks, and took me with him. Sometime after, they joined the army, and I went home to Reading. In 1776, the Brittish leaving Boston, landing at Long Island, and took New York.

Berks County Jail: Jacob Nagle's Boyhood Home

In 1777 Lord How [Howe] landed at the head of Elk, which Washington purceived he ment for Philadelphia. Therefore he came to meet him. At this time my father sent for me. At this time there was a number of officers in Reading upon liberty, but was demanded to join the army. Amongst the rest was Jack Bittle [Biddle], Commesary General, which my mother gave him charge of me, to be delivered to my father. We went on to join the army, but on the road he pretended he had lost some dispatches which was for Washington. The officers all returned with him for seven or eight miles, when he gave up the search and we returned and joined the army the next day.[1]

Marching through Wilmington, Mr. Bittle took me to my father who was then leutenant cornel of the Ninth Pennsylvania Rigment, and shortly after full cornel of the Tenth Pennsylvania Rigmint. I was then not quite sixteen. When the army encamped my father took me to Cor'l Prockter [Proctor] who commanded the grand park of artillery. I laid in his markee that night, and the next day I messed with Adjudent Hosner who had the charge of me, being a young soldier.

We then marched and the army encamped on the Brandewine [Brandywine] on the right of Shads ford [Chadd's Ford] on the hier ground. Our artilery was ranged in front of an orcherd. The night before the Brittish arived the infantry hove up a brest work, so that the muzels of the guns would run over it. A cross the road on the left was a buckwheat field opposit to a wood and the Brandewine between them.[2]

The provision waggons being sent a way, we ware three day without provisions excepting what the farmers brought in to sell in their waggons and what the soldiers could plunder from the farmers. I went to my father, his rigment being on our right, and received a neats tounge from him, and Mr. Hosner bought some potatoes and butter the evening before the Brittish arrived, and we concluded to have a glorious mess for breakfast. Mr. Hosner gave it to one of the soldiers wives that remained with the army to cook for us in the morning. Early in the morning, she had the camp kittle on a small fier about 100 yards in the rear of the Grand Artilery, with all our delicious meal, which we expected to enjoy (on the 11 of September 1777). The Brittish at this time hoisted the red flag on the top of the farm house on the rige of the hill a breast of us, and their artilery advancing towards us down the ploughed field, we then begin a cannonading. The armies at this time had not completely formed. Unfortunately one of the enemies shot dismounted the poor camp kettle with the fier and all its contents away with it. The woman informed Mr. Folkner. He replied, "Never mind, we have no time to eat now." Therefore we made another fast day.

The cannonading continuing as near as I can guess till a bout 8 or 9 o'clock. The Brittish being in the open ploughed field, we could perceive when they saw the flash of our guns they would leave [stand away from] the gun 2 or 3 yards till the shot struck and then close. We then ceased about an hour, excepting a few shot at different times. The artilery were ordered sum liquor and a cask of water; the soldiers hove in some catriges of powder to make them resolute, but I could not drink it.[3]

The adjudent being an old soldier, expecting it would be a warm day, wished to take a little nap and desired me to come and lay down a longside of him under a wagon that had $13\frac{1}{2}$ shels in for the morter that Cap'n Patterson commanded. We lay down under the waggon, when a shot from the enemy struck one of the hind wheels and carried it way. I cried out to Hosner that the waggon would be down upon him, and I jumped from under. He replyed, "Lay still, you young raskel." The waggon remained firm, but I shifted my quarters.

Our army being formed both right and left wings, Morgans rifelmen on our left upon Shads ford, both in the buckwheat field and the wood, which wood was the opposite side of the Brandewin on the road to come over Shads ford, we being on the higher ground, we could see the manovers of some of the rifflemen and the Hessions on the edge of the wood. The Brittish came on. The action begun in general, both right and left wings, about 10 o'clock. Capt. Pattersons $13\frac{1}{2}$ morter split, which was then useless and sent away.

About this time General Washington came riding up to Col[onel] Procter with his Life Guards with him and enquired how we came on. He informed the general that there was two field pieces on our left wing behind the wood which anoyed us very much and could not be seen except by the flash of the guns and he was then ordering four field pieces to play upon them. Accordingly they aimed for the flash of their guns, so direct, though they could not see the guns, that in 15 or 20 minutes we received no more shot from that quarter. Their guns were either dismounted, or otherwise it was two hot to remain there any longer.

The adjudent rode down to the ford to water his horse. A Hession laying in the brush fired at him and missed him but wounded the horse in the right shoulder. The horse stagered, the adjutent jumped off with his pistols in hand and run up to the spot, which was not more than 15 yards from him, and several of the artilery run down to him, but the Hission could not be found. The Hessions and Morgans rifelmen being both in this wood and some of the American rifelmen in the buckwheat field, I took notice of one in a white frock laying on his back to lead his gun. On the edge of the wood next to the road was some trees cut down, and the Hessions got amongst them; this riffelman fired 7 or 8 shots at them as fast as they came there. The buckwheat being in bloom, they could not see him, but we ware on the highth over him. At length finding no more coming, he crawled on his hands and knees to the fence where he fell in with six more. They all rise and crossed the ford and went to the place he had been firing at them, as we supposed to overhall them.

My fathers rigment being on our right, belonging to Gen. Connoways [Conway's] Bregade, the action continued very heavy during the day. The British advenced to the very works, though our artilery made a clear lane through them as they mounted the works, but they filled up the ranks again. One noble officer, mounting the works, cried out, "Come on my Brittons, the day is our own." At that moment, one of Capt. Joneses brass 9 lbr. went off, and he was no more, with a number more. While at a distance, the Brittish shells that they hove from their howetors [howitzers] never busted, which saved a good many men. One shell, while the fuse was burning, a soldier run and nocked out the tube which provented it from bursting.

When we began to retreat, while the infantry covered us, we had a mash [marsh] or swampy ground to cross with the artillery to get into the road, and the horses being shot, the men could not drag the peaces out. Therefore we had to spike two pieces and a howetor. In the retreat I saw a beutiful

George Washington

charger, all white, in a field next the road with an elegant saddle and holsters, and gold lace housing, and his bridle broke off, and his rider gone. I made an attempt to ketch him, but he was skared, and the enemy keeping up a constant fire, I thought it best to leave him. It coming on night, I was famishing with drouth. Coming to a well, but could not get near it for the mob of soldiers, but falling in with one of the artillerymen, he worked his way through them and brought me water in his canteen. Otherwise I should of fell on the road.

    That night I reached a small town, I think it was called Beggers Town, and the army encamped near it.[4] In the heat of the action close to the orchard that I already made mention of I see some men burien an officer who wore the same dress that my father wore, which was green turned up with read fasings [red facings] and gold lace. I was ready to faint. I run up to the officer and enquired what rigment he belonged to. He informed me he was a colo[nel] belonging to the Virginia Line, which gave me comfort but sorrowful. When we ware encamped, my father was searching for me in the town, and I for him. We could hear of each other, but did not meet till the next day.

I do not pretend to give a discription of the action, only where I was myself. I then wanted 3 day of being sixteen years of age, and the first action I was ever in, therefore it cannot be expected that I can give the purticulars of the whole that accured. The next day the dead were buried and great number of the wonded [wounded] sent to Reading, where every family received one or two, and the remaineder was taken care of in the churches as hospatels. My mother desired them to bring one to her house. As soon as she saw him, she had like to fainted. He was about my age and so much like me that she did not [k]now the difference, but he informed her that his parents lived in Virginia; but having three (3) balls through his body, when nearly healed, the wonds broke out again, and he died.

The army marched in a few days and laid wait for the enemy upon Schulkill. Our artilery was ranged along the ridge of the hill on the road side between the bridge and the enemy. Morgans rifelmen ware in a wood on the opposite side of the road next to Sculkill. The rifelmen begun the action with their advance guard and Hessions [16 September 1777]. But the enemy not being nearanuff, the artilery had not fired a shot, when it begin to rain, that we could not engage. At this time we saw a deserter from the enemy come out of the wood with his musket clubed and crossed the field to our army.

The rain continuing, we begin a march and the enemy likewise. It rained for three days suckcessfully. Beginning of the march, Coln. Procter having a spare horse, he gave him to me to ride—the rain continuing so constant that small runs of water ware overflowed by the rain, that the foot soldiers could scarcely get a cross without swiming in several different places. We came to a regular decented hill, the ground being so soft that they had to onhich the horses from one piece of artilery and hitch them to another till they got them all up the hill. The nights was so dark you could not tell the next man to you. I being a horseback, I kept close behind one of the ammunition waggons but driping wet and shivering with cold. All this time Morgans rifflemen ware on the wings, next to the enemy, against the Hissions, as they could use their rifels, having bearskins over their locks, and every now and then you would give a crack at each other. We could always tell when a Hession fired, from our rifels, cracking so much lowder than our rifels. The second night, being behind one of the amunition waggons, some of the officers being in it, they desired me to come in, making the horse fast to the waggon, which made me warm and comfortable. In the morning the army encamped and made fiers to dry their clothes and refresh themselves at

HMS Augusta*'s Magazine Blowing Up*

the Yellow Springs.[5] The Brittish got into Philadelphia. Washingtons army marched and encamped in the swamp.

While we lay there I had a furlow from the col[onel] to go to Reading to see my mother and friends. Two days after, the action of Jermantown [Germantown] took place. I remained in Reading about a week and then joined the army again at White Mash [Whitemarsh]. Being under the command of Capt. Jones, being detached with two field pieces and five hundred chosen man, marched in the night to Chesnut Hill. The artilery was placed in the high road and the troops on both wings. We expected a party of the Brittish to be on the scout here but we missed them. We remain'd in our station, and the commander sent a number of men and kindled about 4 or 5 hundred fiers on the hill, which allarmed the whole Brittish Army, both in Germantown and Philadelphia.[6] Expecting the whole American army was coming upon them, they fired guns, and the drums beat to arms, and we kept them under arm during the night, but they did not attempt to send out a detatchment. The next day we returned to camp. During the time we lay here, the *Augusto* [*Augusta*], 64 gun ship, was bloun up, by Mud Fort, attempting to get up to Philadelphia [23 October 1777], and about this time we received the news of Gen'l Burguine [Burgoyne] being taken (on the 17 October 1777).[7]

In a short time after, my father went with a small party of foot to Jermantown, the Brittish having brought all their troops into the city of Philadelphia. While scouting there with a guard of sarjent, corporal, and six men, they stoped 14 waggons with provisions going into Philadelphia, sent by the Tories. He turned them about and sent them by another road into camp.[8] The Brittish having information, sent out the light horse. Came in sight of my father, gave chase, expecting the waggons ware ahead of him, but he having a good English blood horse, they could not come up with him till they give up their chase and missed their booty.

General Washington finding the winter setting in, he brought the army over to the Valley forge and built log houses for the troops for the winter [19 December 1777]. I then went home to Reading. In a short time after, I went to camp again and remained sume time and returned again to Reading. On the 18th of June 1778, the whole Brittish army evacuated Philadelphia through the Jarses [Jerseys] for New York and Washingtons army in pursuit of them, and defeated them at Prince town or Monmoth, where Sir Henry Clinton lost 500 men, and they retired by forced marches to Sandy Hook.[9] My father, at this time taking the dropsey through the fatege of the chief of the war, had to leave it. He came home and moved to Philadelphia.

CHAPTER 2

The Privateersman

INTRODUCTION

PRIVATEERING is an aspect of the American Revolution that has tended to be neglected by historians of the conflict. The "privateer" was a privately owned but officially sanctioned ship whose sole purpose was to capture vessels flying the enemy flag during wartime. The incentive on the part of owners and crewmen was profit. Vessels and their cargoes were brought into port, "libeled," "condemned" by vice admiralty courts, and sold at auction, the proceeds divided in legally established proportions between investors, agents, ships' officers, and seamen. The justification, from the government's point of view, was that its merchant fleet could, in part, be transformed into an instant navy at no expense to the state, the enemy intimidated and weakened in its commerce and supply lines, seamanship and trade encouraged, and, it was hoped, supplies and munitions diverted from foe to friend. British naval captains, in their correspondence, characterized American privateersmen as mercenary pirates, but in fact this was a time-honored practice and was employed by all nations until prohibited by international treaty in the nineteenth century. The problem, from the British point of view, was that in American waters, the United States was better equipped to pursue this line of attack. For Jacob Nagle, privateers were his schools in seamanship.

At the commencement of the war, the Continental Congress outlined ambitious plans for creating a regular United States Navy that could counteract British supremacy by protecting shipping, breaking up blockades, even taking on British fleets in battle. But the federal government was new, inefficient, and underfinanced. Though Congress commissioned a number of regular navy vessels during the course of the war, among them the *Saratoga, Confederacy,* and *Trumbull,* mentioned by Nagle, there were never enough of them afloat and manned at one time to launch any concerted naval action. Most of the success U.S. Navy vessels had during the war came when they acted very much like privateers—taking on individual merchant ships or packet vessels, capturing them, and bringing them into American ports for condemnation.

Sometime between June 1778 and late 1779, Jacob Nagle's immediate family moved from Reading to Philadelphia. Colonel George Nagle, Jacob's father, now retiring from active duty, seems to have had some further responsibilities as an army recruitment officer, and as of 1780 he was operating a tavern on Water Street, between Chestnut and Walnut streets, that catered largely to seamen. Jacob probably assisted his parents in operating the establishment and listened with interest to ships' captains and seamen tell of their nautical exploits and worldwide travels. As an eighteen-year-old, he would almost inevitably again have to perform some sort of military service, and early in 1780 he enlisted on board the *Saratoga,* a 16-gun sloop of the United States Navy being built in Philadelphia by Wharton & Humphreys, commanded by Captain John Young.

Jacob Nagle's "cruise of six weeks" in the U.S. Navy was even less glorious than his brief army career. He may have received rudimentary training in seamanship, but the *Saratoga,* lacking necessary equipment, would remain in port until mid-August, and Nagle was impatient for action. In April he requested and received permission of Captain Young to ship on board the *Fair American,* a 16-gun privateering vessel owned jointly by Blair McClenachan and Charles Miller & Co. of Philadelphia, commissioned on 20 April 1780 for a four-month cruise. Duty on a privateer did not officially qualify as military service, but it did protect the sailor from being drafted into the army.

Nagle could not have selected a better ship for acquiring a quick education of the most vigorous sort. McClenachan, a wealthy merchant and shipowner before the war, was the "Midas" of Revolutionary War privateering, having a talent for investing in the fastest ships and hiring the most capable captains.

Stephen Decatur, father of the more famous captain of the United States Navy of the next generation, commanded the *Fair American*, and he did so with daring and ability. The ship slipped down the Delaware River at the beginning of May 1780 and before the end of June had brought in to Philadelphia nine prizes. McClenachan also owned the *Holker*, and in late July, under a new captain, Roger Keane of New England, the *Holker* sailed and joined the *Fair American*. In three months, the two vessels captured more than a dozen ships, successfully bringing into Philadelphia enough of them to make the owner a sizable fortune.

Nagle's cruise on the *Fair American* was completed at the end of October 1780, and the following spring, after briefly signing on and then, because of his parents' disapproval, resigning his place on the European-bound *Jay*, he shipped for two cruises, March–April and July–October 1781, on the 20-gun *Rising Sun*, owned jointly by Francis Gurney and Joseph Carson & Co., and commanded by Samuel Cassin. Nagle says that the ship took twenty-one prizes. The somewhat fragmentary newspaper and vice admiralty court records suggest that less than half of this number were actually brought into port and that the cargoes were not quite as rich as those of the *Fair American*, but like the former ship, the *Rising Sun* compiled a decidedly successful and profitable record for its owners and crew. There are no exact figures available, and Nagle does not discuss the matter in the journal, but his share of the profits from his voyages on the *Fair American* and the *Rising Sun* must have been several hundred pounds. It was enough to help support the family and convince any young man of twenty that the sailor's life had much to commend it as a career.

Nagle, undoubtedly with his father's advice, had chosen his ships well to this point. Both the *Fair American* and the *Rising Sun* were fairly large vessels, the first being 150 tons burden and 16 guns, the second 200 tons and 20 guns, and each with a complement of 130 crewmen. His luck at this point changed. In October 1781, Nagle shipped on a small merchant vessel that went aground off the Virginia coast. He escaped with his life, but made an even more ill-fated choice of vessels for the next voyage. The *Trojan*, of only 50 tons burden and 6 guns, commanded by John Fanning, was commissioned on November 8 for a privateering cruise to the West Indies. It was caught by a violent storm off the Carolinas, lost its foremast, and, while making repairs at sea, on 23 November 1781 fell prey to two British men-of-war, HMS *Royal Oak* and HMS *La Nymphe*.

The specific factual detail that Jacob Nagle provides on this phase of his career, between April 1780 and November 1781, must be read and used with some caution. Documentation on American privateering during the Revolution is limited and incomplete, making it impossible to identify all of the ships captured. The situation is complicated by the fact that Nagle was frequently assigned to take prizes into port, thereby being away from his ship when some of the recorded captures were made. It is also possible that Nagle's memory, after almost half a century, was somewhat faulty. He says that his captain on the *Rising Sun* was named Young; contemporary documents indicate that it was Samuel Cassin.

There has been much debate among historians as to the effectiveness of privateering in furthering the American cause during the Revolution. Naval historians, like regular navy men at the time, have tended to minimize its value, or even suggest that it was a detriment to the overall military effort. There is no question that privateers, with their promises of sizable profits, drew off many of the potential sailors and marines of the would-be Continental navy. Many of the same merchants and shipbuilders who were commissioned to build and supply naval vessels were personally involved in these private ventures, creating obvious conflicts of interest. Had Congress prohibited privateering and established generous prize-sharing regulations for naval vessels they might have launched a regular navy worthy of the name. But the American colonies were dominated by merchants of an individualistic temperament, and the war was in part fought against the very sort of governmental bureaucracy necessary to operate an effective navy. It was not a realistic option.

Privateers were never a match for the Royal Navy but they were a factor in the outcome of the war. After France, Holland, and Spain entered the conflict, some American privateers operated out of European ports, taking vessels even along the British coast. Their economic impact on Britain was slight, but their publicity value, bringing the war close to home and raising insurance rates, was significant. In American waters, the British war effort was absolutely dependent upon trade and supply lines from Europe and from Loyalists in the immediate proximity of occupied territories. The shipping lanes were never closed, but a sizable number of the fighting vessels of the Royal Navy were diverted from military to convoy duty. British merchants, risking not only capture by Americans but impressment of their crews by the Royal Navy, were provided few incentives to venture into American waters. The West Indies were forced to encourage illicit trade with the enemy. Supply ships operated short of normal crew complements and were easy captures when isolated from protected fleets. As a result of all these factors, the war's monetary costs to the British population escalated, helping in the end to break the British nation's will to continue what seemed to be a never-ending and financially draining conflict.

On November 23, when Jacob Nagle and his seventeen fellow crewmen on the *Trojan* were transferred to HMS *Royal Oak,* his service on the American side of the Revolution was abruptly ended. But his privateering experience would serve him well and to a considerable degree shape his twenty-year career in the Royal Navy. More than a year of exceptionally active sea duty, dozens of combat situations, prize crew assignments, storms, and a shipwreck had transformed a landlubber into a competent and versatile sailor, accustomed to meeting challenges and facing danger. He was a British prize of war who proved to be of value well after this war was over.

I THEN inclined for the see [sea]. I entered on board the *Saratoga* State Ship of 24 guns newly built and fitting out.[1] After being a long time a board of her and not [k]nowing when she would go to see, Capt. Young, who commanded her, gave me purmission to go in the *Fair American* of 16 guns under the command of Capt. Decator, and Ajudant Hosner leaveing the army, went capt[ain] of marines on board of her.[2]

We sailed from Chester, where I joined the brig at daylight, for Cape May and then put to see [ca. 1 May 1780]. The first vessel we took was loaded with wine and 30 thousand rope of onions from Maderia [Madeira], bound to New York. We sent her up to Philadelphia and put to see again. We steared our course off New York, where we fell in with a large ship about 400 tons loaded with dry goods and different kinds of fruite bound into New York, but we altered her voige and took her into Cape May. Likewise a schooner with china on board. We sent them to Philada., and I was sent in

Captain Stephen Decatur

the schooner. When the two prises were delivered to the merchants, we were all sent down to Cape May in a small schooner to joine the brig again when she came in again.

On the passage, a beautiful moon light night, we purceived a refugee boat pulling for us. There was about 20 odd of us on board but no arms to defend ourselves, except a short brass piece which was intended to be shiped on the capstain on the quarter deck of the privateer in case of boarding at close quarters. As luck would have it ther was catriges sent with the 4 pounder, but no shot, as it was intended for musket balls. We lashed this piece to the bitts as secure as we could with rope, put a good charge into her; having no balls, the capt[ain] of the boat had a bag full of old nails, hooks, and thimbels, and we filled the peace to the muzzell. When they ware rounding two to come a longside, as they ware stem on, we let fly, which raked them fore and aft, not more than 8 or 10 yards distance. It came on them unexpected, like thunder. The shrieks and moaning were terible. She pulled 26 or 28 ores. Laying for a minnute in that sittuation, and the few that remained unhurt saw our deck full of men, expecting we ware well armed, we saw about 4 or 5 got out their oars and pulled away for the Jarsey shore. The gun carried away the lashing and fell over on the opposite side of the deck, however it was not wanted more. The next day we arrived at Cape May. Mrs. Decator lived there when he went to see, and when the *Fair American* came in, we went on board.[3] By those meanes we had a supply of men during the 4 months cruise.

We put to see again in a few days and sailed for the south. Off Charlestown, of a fine moon light night, we espied a large sail to leeward of us. We bore up and run down so close till we could perceive her ports. She proved to be a 44 gun ship. We halled our wind, and she made sail after us, but we ware soon out of sight of her, and shortly after fell in with an English brig laden with merchandise. Took her and sent her in to Philadelphia.

The next day we fell in with two seventy fours, and it falling a dead calm, we crowded all sail from them, but we still got nearer. We ware nearly in gun shot when a light breeze spring up, and we walked off. We then perceived why we neared them so fast; the line of battle ships, [k]nowing there was a strong currant, let go a ketch anchor, and riding by it, we not observing the current, was drifting down upon them, and if a breeze had not spring up, we should have been under their guns in a quarter of an hour more. However we soon left them and run to the northord and cruised off New York.

We fell in with a Kings Packet from Falmouth bound to New York [*Mercury*, Captain Joseph Dillon]. She mounted 16 six pounders and 4 eighteens, cannonades, and we mounted 16 sixes. We run a long side and gave her a broad side, they returning the same, but the second broad side she struck her colours, but hove the mail overboard. We could hear the screaches of wimen on board. When boarding her we found seven ladies on board going to New York to their husbands that were officers in the Brittish army.[4] Capt[ain] Decator permitted them to remain in their own cabbins and took good care they should not be molested, and when brought to Philadelphia, he got purmission from Congress to send them to New York to their husbands. The English capt[ain] said he would not have struck so soon if it had not been for the ladies being on board.

In a few days after [14 October 1780], we fell in with a Scotch brig loaded with wine and took her [*Richard*]. They informed us there was a Scotch ship from Glasko [Glasgow] a head of us bound to Charlestown [*Richmond*, Captain George Jameson]. At this time we fell in with the *Holker*, Capt. Kaine, and sum times crused together. We both made sail, and about 10 o'clock P.M. we came up with her and gave her a broad side, and she returned it as readily. There was some pollicy in the capt[ain] of the brig informing us of the ship, expecting she would take us. She was a two decked ship, mounting 26 guns, 12, 9, 6 pounders and 4 pounders on the quarter deck and 75 men. She being a lofty ship and the see runing high for our low vesel, she had the advantage of us. She kept on her course with steering sales

Fair American

a low and aloft on both sides, having the wind right aft, but we could run round her under our two topsails. After several broad sides, we both halled off till morning. We received bread and cheese and grog and lay at our quarters till daylight.

At the dawn of day the cap[tain] asked the ships company if they were willing to engage her. They gave three chears and said they would never leave her. We spoke the *Holker* and then run alongside, and the *Holker* on the quarter. We engaged till about 10 o'clock, when our foremast was wounded in two different places. Likewise our mainmast wounded in two different places and cut our riging severly. Likewise the *Holker* was in as bad a situation, besides one man killed and we had one wounded. We hall'd off to repair damages and fished our masts and repaired the riging. Our consort done the same, the enemy continuing under full sail. During the action, about 1 o'clock P.M., we run a long side on the starbourd side and the *Holker* on the quarter. Though she was under full sail, low and aloft, we shot ahead under our two topsails, jibb, and mainsail, and bore up across her bows and raked her fore and aft. The enemy shooting a head, we gave her a broad side on the larboard side. The enemy continuing her course, we fell under her stern and raked hur with several broad sides. At length she struck her colours. The capt[ain], chief mate, and second mate ware all killed, and no one to fight the ship but the boatswain. A British officer pasenger remained on the quarter deck with a musket during the action.[5]

We boarded her and brought all the prisoners on board and sent 10 of our best seamen on board to repair her riging. In the mean time we intended to get provisions and water out of her, being very short of both, but before we could get any on board, a gale of wind came on, and we had to lay two, the ship being high out of water. They put her before the wind for the Capes of Philadelphia, having two prizemasters on board, one from each vessel.

The gale continued for several days. The brig being very light, we had to fill our water casks with salt water, and put some of our guns in the hold, and struck our topmasts. At the same time we had no provisions eccepting two or three bags of bread dust and a quart of water, and when that was expended, we received a half pint of flower, but we could not spare the water. The gale ceaceing, we steared for the Capes of Dellawor. Our water getting shorter, there was a gun barrel plased in the fore top. The man mus[t] bring it down to the scuttle butt on the quarter deck and suck the water through the tuch hole, then return it to the same place before another could have it, but that did not last long, for some of them could not suck it at all. Therefore it was served out a pint pr. man.

Off Cape Hatterass we fell in with another gale of wind, which drove us amongst the shoals. We kept the led [lead] going several nights and days in both chains, and if we had not been so light and drew so little water, we must of perished, but thank God the gale ceased, and a light breeze sprung up from the sothord which brought us to Cape Henlopen. Being a breast of the Hen and Chickens [a shoal off Cape Henlopen], not far from the light house, a north west wind took us all a back and laid her down upon hur beam ends. The see begining to run down the main hatchway, we begin to cut the main mast away, but before the mast was cut half through, the sails gave way and flew to pieces. The vessel then righted; we then let go all our anchors, which was four, bedside a kedge, and struck our topmasts, it blowing amost tremendious from N.W. If we had been blown to see, we must of perished. Our little stock of water was expended.

The third day it cleared off, and a fine sotherly wind sprung up. We got under way and made sail up the river. We had at this time seven English

Cape Henlopen Lighthouse

capt[ains] and about 90 men on board that belonging to the vessels that we had captured during the time we had left Cape May.

We had now got into fresh water where we could satisfy our thirst with water. Being abreast of Wilmington, with a light fair wind and lovely moonlight night, our topgallant masts struck, and our ports down, and guns howsed fore and aft, we looked like a distressed merchantman, when we saw a schooner standing for us, till she came within hail. Taking us to be a merchantman, she ordered us to "Strike, you damned Rebels," and fired a swivel over us. All hands being on deck, the cap[tain] answered, "Aya," and ordered too guns to be cast loose. They heared his orders. They begin to shear off towards the shore and we after them. We then got aground, and the schooner striving to get farther from us, likewise got a ground, and we could not get our guns to bare upon her, but a sloop coming down out side of us, we fired a six pound shot at her and brought her a long side. She proved to be a prise to this refugee, from Philadelphia with dry goods. We put 20 men into her and a six pounder, then pulled for the schooner till we got aground. We then was preparing to bring our gun to bare on the schooner. At that moment the brig got two guns to bare on her, when, giving her two or three guns, cried out for quarters. We got a long side in the sloop. Unfortunately the refugees had put the owners son in irons below, and one of the shot killed him and took a refugees leg off. This refugee, when he saw us, was going up to Marcus Hook, to cut out a brig loaded with flower that lay in the stream. With these two we took in the river, made twenty one prizes we had taken in the cruise.

When we got to Markus Hook, we all hands went on shore, and the prisoners carried the brig up to Philadelphia. The *Confederacy* frigate, laying at Chester, and had all her boats out to press us all, and we all walked round by land to Philadelphia.[6] I reached liberty at 10 o'clock at night, weary and my feet sore. I knocked at the dore. Presently a young woman cousin of mine opened the dore. The moment she saw me, she flew like lightening into the front parlour where my mother and a next dore neighbour was sitting and the table laid for supper. I followed her into the room. Finding my mother did not know me, I sit down in a chair close to the dore and enquired for my father. My mother informed me that he was gone to Chester, expecting his son was pressed by the frigate and she expected him and hur son home every minnute. I having a blanket rooled up over my shoulders, she took me to be a soldier from the army having some business with my father, till the lady that was sitting with her eyed me verry close and new me. "My God, Mrs. Nagle, it is your son." My mother ketched up the candel and came near and new me. The table had been laid, as I before mentioned; we got our supper. My father did not arive till past midnight.

The nex day we larnt that the two richest prizes that we had taken was missing. The schooner loaded with silk was retaken by an English cruiser, and the Scotch ship that fought so brave before mentioned [*Richmond*] was ris upon. The chief of the men being Englishmen, they hoisted the jolly boat out, though full of shot holes, and put the two prize masters into her with some water, bread, and salt beef and set them adrift and made sail for Charles Town. Having a fair wind, they got in. The owners that she was consign'd to seized the ship and gave them five guineas each for bringing her into port. She was valued at 175 thousand Pounds sterling when we took her, and a chest of silver plate, and two boxes of gold watches, her whole [hold] full of dry goods, and wine between decks, and all the boats full of wine, the quarter deck stowed with hampers of cheese, and between every gun in the waist, pipes of wine. One of the men [Thomas Wilkinson] returned to Philadelphia to get his prizemoney and was tried and hung on the island abreast Philadelphia.[7]

During our four month cruise we made a practice of coming in with the most of our prizes, and then put to see again. Coming in with a prize brig through the narrow channel, both being abreast each other, and the prize drawing more water than we did, we strove to give her more room, and we got on the reef, and a heavy surf rolling in upon us, hove her on hur side, the guns being well secured, or otherwise if they had given way they would of stove her side out. All hands got on hur weather side and hur sails all set. While laying in that sittuation a heavy swell and surf came and hove hur clean over the reef. As she was light, she received no damage. We filled hur sails and got into the channel and run up to the prize at the anchoring ground.

Likewise, during this cruise, we ware coming in with three prizes, a large ship with dry goods and West India fruit, a brig loaded with rum, and a sloop with rum. In the mean time an English frigate hove in sight and gave chase. When she came up we fired at her. She being eager to take us, she chased us, and when we run out of gunshot, Decator would heave two till she came nearer, then fier again, and make sail. By this manuver the two headmost vessels got over the barr. The frigate finding they would loose the whole if they continued chasing us, therefore she made after the sloop, and being a long way astern of the other two, she was taken. But I have not given the purticulars of every vessel, as it would be two tegious.

Our cruise now being out, I then [January 1781] shiped on board a large ship bound to France call'd the *Jay*, but my father not being agreeable, I returned the advance and left hur. I then shiped in the *Rising Son* of 20 guns, Capt[ain] Young [*sic*, actually Captain Samuel Cassin] commander, and put to see [ca. 16 March 1781] with a fresh breeze standing to the N.E.[8] We had a good many artilerymen on board that had been discharged from the army, but they being see sick, the capt[ain] sent me up to the main top mast head to look out. Shortly after, I saw a vessel at a great distance to windward. I cried out, "Sail ho!"

"Whereabouts?" replyed the capt[ain].

"On the weather beame," I replyed.

The leutenant then came up with his spyglass but could not see her. I being posetive, and the vessel coming before the wind, nearing us, the capt[ain] came up and by my directions he saw hur before the wind stearing for us. We then beat to quarters. I was then stationed in the foretop with a musket, but when she came down to us, we found she had but six guns on board. She proved to be a Philadelphia brig [*Tristram Shandy*] loaded with wine, shell'd ammons, and reasons [raisins]; was taken by the *Orpheous* [HMS *Orpheus*, 32 guns], Brittish frigate, and sent hur to New York, but being out of provisions and only half barril of water, they bore down upon the first vessel they saw.⁹

We maned her, and as I saw hur first, the capt[ain] sent me in her. We made sale for the Capes and convoyed by the ship. We made the land to the sotherd of Cape Henlopen, call'd the Seven Mile Beach. In the morning the *Rising Son* was a good way to the sotherd of us. A large cutter hove in sight, standing for us, mounting eighteen 12 pounders. We made a signal to the ship. She amediately crowded all sail and came up like a shot. In the mean time the cutter gave us a gun. We hove two. The ship came up and fired a shot athought [athwart] her fourfoot [forefoot], and the cutter returned the same. Capt[ain] Young [*sic*, Cassin] runalong side and spoke her. She proved to be a Merican letter of mark from Sta. Stacia [St. Eustatius] bound for Philadelphia. The capt[ains] new each other.

The cutter undertook to convoy us up, as the refugees was numerous in Delewar River. Getting up between Rede [Reedy] Island and New Castle, with a pleasant moderate breeze and the cutter a head of us, with all hur guns howsed, a refugee boat came out of a creek and made for the cutter. Hur ports being down, thought she had no guns. We ware about a quarter of a mile a stern. When they got close, they up ports and gave them two guns with round and grape. Sunk the boat. The cutter never hove two but stood on her course up the river. Those that were not killed were sunk by the time we came up. There was not more than the remnant of the boat on the surface of the water. We stood on likewise. It apeared cruel, but at this very time, not even an oister boat dare leave Philadelphia for the Capes without being run a shore, and men, wimen, and children, as pasengers, would be plundered, striped and robed and ill treated by these hell hounds, and which is wose, was done by our own cuntrymen and neighbours.¹⁰ What lenity could be shoun to those tories?

When we got up to Chester in our prize, the *Confedrecy* frigate sent her boat on board and took 4 men out, and expecting more to be stowed away below, but could not find us. They left three midshipmen on board with a brace of pistols and cutlashes each. By this time we ware brought to an anchor below Mud Fort. The boat being gon[e], I came out of my whole, and two more that had eskaped. One of the midshipmen I new, Mr. Brown, he said he was glad he had got me, I should be a mesmate of his on board the frigate. I said but little. In a short time after he asked me if I could get them some good wine. I informed him I could. I brought them the strongest and best wine out of the cabin, which was the best on board. The wine went down pleasant and delicious with those young intruders, which I was in hopes we would be clear of by morning. I supplyed them with as much as they required till they made a field bed abaft the binneacal, sit down, and enjoyed themselves. I took good care to supply Mr. Brown and his mesmates with as much as they could swallow. They plased the arms on the binneacal at their feet, supposing every thing was right, as the boat was to return early in the morning to bring them and the rest of us on board the frigate. They being so much intocsicated, they soon fell into a sound sleep.

I went forward to the other two men and told them to have the oars ready at the gangway, while I secured the arms. I went aft to the binneacal and took all the arms away to the gangway. I then crept'd along the gunnel to the stern, till I got the painter of the pilots gig and halled her up along side. We put the arms into the skiff and took our departure and left the young gentlemen to reflect of their misconduct over a glass of wine in the morning. We pulled all night and arived at the Bird and Hand Warf early in the morning. We took the arms to the merchants counting house and made the boat fast in the dock and aquainted the merchant of the prize laying below Mud Fort. He sent men down to bring hur up.

In a few days we went to Cape May and joined our ship. Cruising off New York we fell in with one of Gutteriges [Goodrich's] privateers.[11] We being painted all black and our ports down, we apeared like a dull sailing merchantman, but in truth there was nothing could sail with her that we ever came across. We fixed a grating a cross the bows and a heavy buoy draging under her quarter, crowded all sail, and steared our course. The privateer would sail all round us. At length she lay under easy sail a head of us, thinking herself secure by sailing. We cut away the buoy and the grating and was a long side of her before she could have time to make sail. We took her and brought her in. She was a beautiful brig of 16 guns.

Coming off the Capes of Deleware, we fell in with a nother privateer of our force belonging to Philadelphia. The capt[ai]ns agreed to remain in company. In a few days we fell in with a Brittish convoy of about 40 sail under convoy of a small frigate. Capt[ain] Young [*sic*, Cassin] hailed our consort and told them if they would joine him, they would engage the frigate, as we ware superior in force, and by that means we could take the most of the convoy. They agreed to engage them. We being to windward, we bore down upon them. Our ship was entering amongst the convoy and the

Privateer Taking a British Ship

frigate luffing up for us when we purceived our consort hall'd to the wind and maid all sail away from us. Capt[ain] Young [*sic*, Cassin] was in a great rage, and we were compeled to make off, as the frigate was two supperior for us alone. We crused no more with her.

In a few days after we fell in with a Kings store ship of 26 guns. We run up a long side of her and gave her a broad side, and she returned the same. She engaged for several broad sides and than struck. The cap[tain] protested there was scaresly a shot from us but what hulled him. She was very much shatterd in the steel, and a good many woonded, but none killed outright. We had none killed or wounded. We sent her in and stood off to the south east.

Fell in with a mugion schooner from Charles Town loaded with rice and Indian corn. It being a dead calm, we out boat and maned hur well armed and boarded her without resistance. Her cargo not being of much value in America, she was sent to Cape (Long'd. w.c. 4°42′ East, Lat. 19°46′N.) Fransway [Cap François] on the island of Sandemingo [Santo Domingo]. I was one of the number. As soon as a breeze sprung up, we made sail. Nothing particular accured till we made the island of Sandemingo. About 12 at night we fell into the middle of three mugion privateers. They begin to show lights, seeing there was a stranger in company. We showing a light, they could not tell which was the stranger, and by day light we ware close in with the mouth of the harbour, and the punch mugion privateer close after us, but a French manawar brig sliped her cable and gave hur chase. We got in safe, but the mugion got off. We sold the rice and Indian corn for as much as would load the schooner twice with sugar and coffee, but the prize master which was a pilot belonging to Cape Henlopen found seven tearses [tierces] of rice that belonged to a pasenger in the schooner and was not in the bill of laden [lading]. That private property he smugled and put in his own pocket.[12] Being ready, we took in a cargo of sugar and coffee, and the rest in spacia [specie], and put to see.

On the homeward bound passage to Philadelphia, the prize master treated an old seaman very ill, the best seamon on board and acted as his mate. He beat him cruelly at different times. Still he had to put all his trust in him, as the rest of us was but young sailors. On the passage, making the land with a light air of wind at day light, between New York and Eg Harbour [Egg Harbor] we fell in with 40 sail of Brittish under convoy of a 20 gunship, a schooner and cutter. The schooner and cutter made sale after us. We having some sailor passengers besides our crew, we got out our sweeps and pulled away from them. We mounted only four 4 pounders. We got in shore of them with a leading wind from the eastward. Getting near Little Egg Harbour, a refugee row boat came out to cut us off. We see them coming. We got the 4 guns over on the starboard side. When they got about musket shot from us, we gave them a broad side. They put about and pull'd for the shore as fast as posseble. We gained on the schooner and cutter, they giving up chase. We got into Cape May, and coming to an anchor, the prizemaster went on shore and brought some fresh provisions and liquor on board and served it out to us as a plaster for our sore heads.

In the evening we got under way up the river. A heavy black squall from the N.W. took us all aback, and was nearly capsised, but we got the sails down and furled and let go both anchors and rode it out till morning. The weather clearing up, we got under way and reached nearly to New Cassel that night and came to an anchor, the wind and tide being against us, and set the watch, with orders to call the prize master at the turn of tide. The man that had the first watch remained till we ware all asleep, and having no purticular time, he called me up. I remained up till I got very sleepy, and not finding any one willing to releive me, I fell a sleep and did not wake till the tide had made up a good hour. I call'd the master. He coming on deck and seeing a strong tide runing up, got in a grate rage and hove all the blame on me, though the rest had kept no watch. A scheme came into his head to punnish me, as he was afraid to flog me, being aquainted with my father. He made me get a large oar out and keep pulling and said I should remain there till we arived in Philadelphia, but when we got up to Markus Hook the wind died away and we came to an anchor. We out boat and pulled the master to town. The two of us had to return.

By the time we had got half way to Gloster Point, a breeze sprung up from the sotherd. We seing the schooner coming up with a fair wind, we strove to fetch a wood boat that was near us going up. We got a long side. The vessel going fast through the water and the boat shearing off, the man in the bow being a young sailor, not [k]nowing what to do, he jumped out and left me adrift. It being ebb tide, and the wind up the river acasioned the river very ruff, and having no place a stern to scull the boat, and the tide drifting me down the river, I had to shift my our [oar] from one side to the other to get in shore. Then I poled her with an oar along shore till I came to the first warf, which was a board yard. I made the boat fast and hid the oars. About twelve o'clock at night I started for home.

The old sailer had not furgot the treatment he received from the prise master. He informed the merchant and came the next day to my fathers house for me, the rest of the crew being with him, and went before a Squire and ware sworn and examined in the presence of the prize master and found guilty. He was cut off from all priz money during the two cruises. We had taken in the two cruises 21 prises in the *Rising Son,* which she had taken in our absenc in the schooner a number of them, but we ware entitled to prize money as though we ware on board.[13]

Shortly after, I shiped on board a sloop bound to the Havanna on the Island of Cuba. The capt[ain] was a Londoner, a savage and ill tempered man. When getting to Cape May, he told us he had now got us into blew water and he was determined to stretch our hides.

In a few days 45 sail got under way, the *Trumble* [*Trumbull*] frigate being our convoy. Being out four days, we sprung a leak. We got as much of the cargo on deck as we could, expecing to get to the leak, but finding it in vaine, we put the cargo below again, and it was agreed to put back. Standing in for the land, we made Wollops [Wallops] Island.[14] The wind being from the eastward, we came to an anchor. The wind increasing and hur bullwork [bulwark] but slight, her harse [hawse] broke away to the timber heads, and a refugee coming down upon us from the windward, we cut the cable and stood along shore but could see no entrance.

The capt[ain], after beating and abuseing the men, got the boat out, which was all we had, and put his chest into her, thinking to save his own, but the youngman that was in the boat did not know how to manage her. He held on the painter in the middle of the boat, and she took a shear off. He held on till he got into the stern of her and jumped out and left hur adrift with all the capt[ai]ns property. The refugee closing on us, we run a shore on the island, and the refugee halled off. A heavy surf running, we hove over the squaresal boom to see weather it would drift on shore or drift to see. When I found it drifted ashore, I jumped overboard after it. When it came near the shore, I left the boom and swom for the shore, the rest following me. We all got on shore except the capt[ain], and he could not swim.

I then swam out for the vessel again and got on board. We on rove the gib halyards and downhall and some other small ropes and made fast one end round the capt[ain] under the armpits. I jumped overboard and swam ashore with the other end. Then making a signal to the capt[ain], he jumped overboard, and we run him high and dry. He then told us if we would remain there and save as much of the flower as we could, it should be sold, and we should have our shear to bear our expences homewards. The capt[ain] then beged of me to go on board for his pistols, which was in the cabin. I went on board and one more with me. We cut the mast away, and I got the pistols, but I could not go down into the cabin as I wanted for my shoes and a pair of silver buckels I left there. The windows of the cabin being broke, I saw the sherks [sharks] draging the hams and chees about, and my clothes being there, I dare not venture down for them. We got two bottles of liquor out of a case. The surf was rising and the vessel braking to peices with the surf. We left hur and went on shore.

We had one sailor among us that was born at Chester upon Delewar River. The capt[ain] treated him with cruelty during the time he was on board. If the man looked at him, he would thrash him till he was tired, then send him up to the mast head to remain there; if he saw him look down, he would say, "I know what you think, come down here," and would thrash him again as long as he could. In this manner he treated him till we were on shore. Then this sailor would do no more, and now having his pistols, [the captain] swore he would make him work or shoot him. The pistols were loaded but entierly wet. He snaped the pistols at him several times, but in vain. The sailor at length tackled to him and gave him a severe floging, which made him quiet.

We got the sails on shore out of the surf and pitched a tent and remained there a week. There was only two houses on the island. The capt[ain] boarded at one of them. While I went on board for the capt[ain's] pistols, I left a silk hankerchief and a gold broach [brooch] sticking in the hankerchief, but when I returned they ware missing. I enquired of the men, but they new nothing of them. We saved about 300 barrels of flower, and the capt[ain] got sum flats from the main, and we all went over with the flower. I coming to the house where the capt[ain] boarded, I saw a young woman with my black silk hankerchief on hur neck. I asked her where she got that hankerchief. She very politely informed me the capt[ain] of our sloop had made her a present of it. When I informed her that he had stolen it from me, she wished to return it to me. She apeared to be in much trouble about it. I would not except of the handerchief, but desired she would keep it as a present from me, and the flats waiting to cross over to the main with us all, I left her, and we all crossed over to the main.

We had to make application for a pasport, being in the highth of war. We received a passport from the Squire where we landed and ware to be renewed by the Squires as we traveled through the country. At parting, the capt[ain] gave us two dollars to carry us to Philadelphia in lew of allowing us part for saving 300 barrels of flower. I told him of his theft, but he denied having the gold broach. In taking our departure they informed us it was 254 miles to the citty of Philadelphia. I lost all my clothes excepting what I had on: one shirt, one pair of trousers and a light waiscoat and a west indea lime basket for a hat, without shoes. I make mention of this short sketch, particularly to show the generosity of the capt[ain] to me for saving his life, as there was not one of the five would have ventured to save him when on board, if it had not been for my exertion and assistance.

We travel'd till we came to a small town call'd Snow Hill. I fell in with a gentleman that had been in my fathers house in Reading. He new me and ordered the landlord to give us all sufficient to eat and drink, at his cost, five in number. The farmers in general treated us very kindly when they see our passports and understood that we had been castaway. But on the road we applyed to one rich farmer, an Englishman, as we ware informed afterwards that he was a Tore [Tory], but he would not give us any succar [succor], but ordered us to go about our business.

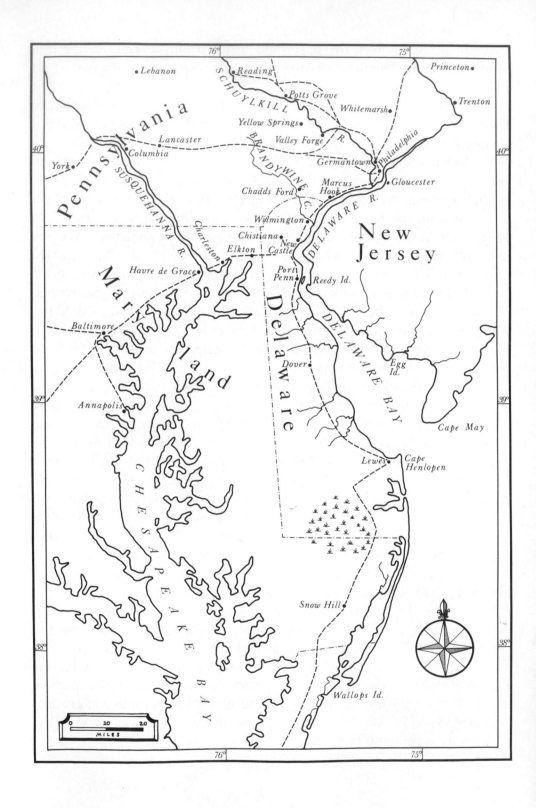

On the road we came to a small boarded house and a young man working at shoemaking, being convenient for travelers. We asked him where we might get lodgings, it being late in the evening, and inform'd him of our situation. He inform'd us that he boarded at a farm house about a mile on the road, but he could not tell weather he would give us entertainment or not, as he new he was a rank Tory, but he told us not to let on that we had seen him, as he would be there by dark, and if we would be Tories for one night, he had no doubt but what we would be well treated. Accordingly we agreed and set out.

Coming abreast the house, we had a long lane to go up to a fine large stone building with a beautiful gress plat and garden befor the dore and apearantly like a small village of Negro huts on the left of the building.[15] The old gentleman was sitting in the porch with a white cap on, taking the air. We approached and enquired if he could be so kind as to give us a nights lodging for the night, as we ware castaway sailors. He told us plainly he could not, as he had entertained a young man a few nights before and in the morning he stole a silver cup and had taken it away with him, therefore he would not entertain any more strangers.

One of the sailors turned round and began to dam the country, and cursed, and wished he was once out of it, and once more in his own country, and there was nothing but rebels here.

"Hush, hush," cried out the Old Tory, "do you know that if some people heard you, they would put you into prison?"

He replyed, "They must then give me some provisions to eat."

"Well, come in lads, and I will give you something to eat."

We thanked him and seated ourselves in a large entry, both cool and pleasant. The old gentleman ordered a large double bowl of milk punch to be brought in and call'd his wife to see that supper was got ready, as he supposed the lads was hungry, and when that bowl was out, he ordered another.

In the mean time we ware asked many questions by the old gentleman conserning the fleet we sailed out with. God forgive us, what we told him we expected was all lies, but after we left the fleet, the *Trumbel* fell in with a Brittish frigate and a twenty gun ship, was taken, and a good part of the fleet, which proved to be tru when we arived in Philadelphia. We informed him the *Trumble* frigate and the most of the convoy ware take by the Brittish, and if we had not been compelled to run on shore, we would of been taken likewise. We could perceive it pleased the old man verry much to hear the news.

Philadelphia

By this time the shoemaker arived and was very inquisitive concerning the news and carried on the joke, though he was a ware of the plot by his directions. We had an elegant supper, and tended by 4 or 5 Negro girls, and the milk punch flew round merrily. After supper being over and sitting a little while, the old man supposed we were tired in traveling, ordered us to be shown to a genteel room in the back part of the house with three good beds. We turned in and slept sound. In the morning we got up early. The shoemaker called us into one of the overseeors houses and had some liquor provided for us, and a harty laugh they had in playing the trick on the old gentleman. In [*sic*, And] thanking them for their kindness, we started, and coming in front of the house, the old gentleman was sitting in the porch. We thanked him for his kindness. Putting his hand in his pocket, drew out a dollar each, and gave to us to bare our expenses on the road.

We traveled on again, and who should overtake us but the capt[ain].

We stoped him and demanded a little more money. He gave us two or three dollars, and then pushed on, and I beleive glad to get rid of us. We arived at Lewis Town, expecting to get up to Philadelphia in some small craft, but we ware informed that the refugees ware so thick in the river that no small vessel could go up or down. We then concluded to travel on. After having a little meriment with some of the Old Tories coine, we went through Dover, and coming near New Castle, we fell in with a wagon master and 12 wagons from the army. He enquiring from whence we came, which I informed him. He being aquainted with my father, he put us all in the wagons. I having no shoes, I could scarecely walk. He rode ahead to New Castel and bought me a pair of shoes and had a dinner provided for us all.

In a few days we arived in Philadelphia, but my feet were so inflamed I could not put them to the flore. The doctors could not cure me, till a young lady next dore came in and saw my feet. She put a large slice of toasted bread, steaped in strong vinnegar, with black ground pepper strewed thick, and applyed it to the soles of my feet, and bound them up. In the morning I walked about the room, and the pain and swelling entierly gone. By being so particular with this ailment, it might be servisable to others. In a short time after, I was taken with the fever and was given up by three doctors that attended me. I was entierly speachless. I motioned to my mother, that was sitting by me weaping, for some water, and as there was no hopes of my recovery, she thought she would satisfy me and gave me some in a tumbler. It turned the feaver, and in fifteen minutes I got better and recovered daily. The doctors expected to see me a corps the next morning and ware amazed to find me recovering. In a short time I was perfectly well.

My father now lived in Water Street, between Shesnut [Chestnut] and Water [Walnut?] Street, kept a public house. Paul Jones arived in a twenty gun ship from France, and a good many of his men boarded at our house.[16] We ware all siting at breckfast when Capt. Fanning came in wanting to ship sum men. He commanded the schooner *Trogan* [*Trojan*], copper bottom (16 guns) [*sic*], bound to the Havanna in the island of Cuba, and I shiped with him at eight half joes for the run and eight dollars in advance.

On the 10th of November 1781, we sailed down the river with loose iice and put to see. On the 20 of said month, we caried a way our main yard, and on the 21st we sprung the mainmast close by the board. We could carry no sail. We begin to fish the mast and get up another main yard. Having no man at mast head to look out, the *Royal Oak* and *Lee Nymph* [*La Nymphe*] Frigate came down upon us before we saw them. They fired a shot. We hoisted our thirteen stripes and hall'd them down again.[17] They sent there boat on board from the *Royal Oak* and took us all on board and took the schooner in tow. They ware bound to the West Indies.

CHAPTER 3

The West Indies

INTRODUCTION

T H E American Revolution is remembered today primarily in its North American context, but the struggle of 1775 to 1783 was very much part of a world war that was more a British–French conflict than simply an American war of independence. The West Indies, particularly the Lesser Antilles, or what were called the Leeward and Windward Islands, stretching in a semicircle east and south of Puerto Rico and the Virgin Islands to near present-day Venezuela in northern South America, were an important theater of military action. Control of the islands was divided among the French, their Dutch ally, and the British. In the eighteenth century the West Indies were economically important as producers of sugar and tropical products, as consumers of European goods, and as centers of trade, much of it illicit, between the North American colonies, South America, and Europe.

The islands also possessed strategic military importance. In the age of wooden sailing ships, naval vessels, after weathering the storms of often lengthy transatlantic crossings from Europe, needed friendly ports for supply and repair. Halifax, Nova Scotia, and New York were the primary stations of the British navy on the North American mainland in the Revolutionary War period, but these harbors were occasionally inaccessible in winter. The French, in ceding Canada to Britain in the peace ending the Seven Years War in 1763, had lost their mainland base altogether and were heavily dependent on an installation at Fort Royal, Martinique, for maintaining a naval presence in American waters.

During the American Revolution, the French tended to dispatch large fleets of battleships, which would cruise in the Leeward and Windward Islands. They occasionally made forays to other parts of the West Indies or to the North American coast if it seemed likely that they might be able advantageously to take on a British fleet or capture one of their island possessions. They would eventually return to French ports for major repairs.

The British maintained a somewhat more permanent naval presence in the Caribbean. They had repair and supply bases at English Harbor, Antigua, at Carlisle Bay, Barbados, at far distant English Harbor, Jamaica, and between 1778 and the end of the war, at Gros Islet Bay, St. Lucia. Hurricanes were potentially disastrous to sailing vessels of this era, and both the French and British attempted, as much as possible, to keep their fleets clear of the Caribbean between July and October.

France entered the war on the American side in 1778. By formal treaty with the United States, she renounced territorial claims on the North American mainland, but reserved the right—and had high aspirations—to seize British islands south of Bermuda. Previous to Jacob Nagle's arrival in the Leeward Islands in early December 1781, there had been a number of major naval battles and a certain amount of island swapping, but neither side had succeeded in delivering the decisive blow. France had seized Dominica, St. Vincent, and Tobago, but this had been countered by British capture of St. Lucia and Dutch St. Eustatius.

However, the pace of events in the West Indies began to quicken in the late fall of 1781. Major portions of both the French fleet, under Count de Grasse, and the British fleet, under Admiral Samuel Hood, had left the West Indies in August, during hurricane season, for the American coast. In September, de Grasse successfully defended the mouth of the Chesapeake Bay against an attack by the combined fleets of Hood from the West Indies and Admiral Graves from New York. This sealed the fate of General Cornwallis's army at Yorktown. Admiral Rodney, senior commander, had earlier returned to England.

A relief expedition for General Cornwallis under Admiral Graves was launched from New York on October 18, but on the 25th, they were joined by HMS *La Nymphe*, bringing dispatches of Cornwallis channeled through New York, which made it clear that they were too late to be of assistance: Cornwallis had surrendered on October 19.

The British fleet returned briefly to New York, and the center of naval action shifted back to the West Indies. Admiral Graves was reassigned to the command at Jamaica. Admiral Hood, with eighteen ships of the line, left New York on November 11 and arrived at Barbados on December 5. De Grasse and the French fleet left the Virginia coast on December 5 and arrived at Fort Royal, Martinique, on the 25th and 26th.

It was a crowded and storm-swept sea into which Nagle's *Trojan* had set sail from Philadelphia in early November. Severe storms not only dismasted the little American privateer but scattered Admiral Hood's fleet. HMS *Royal Oak*, a 74-gun vessel, which had run aground in New York earlier in the spring and been severely damaged by French cannon fire in the engagement off the Chesapeake on September 5, was separated from the rest of the British vessels. The storm reopened old wounds in the aging hull, and Captain William Jenkins was delighted when by chance they encountered, on November 22, the 36-gun frigate HMS *La Nymphe*, returning from its message-carrying assignments between the British fleets. *La Nymphe* already had one prize vessel in company. On the 23rd, Nagle's vessel was captured and on December 14, the *Royal Oak*, accompanied by the prizes, made it into Basseterre Harbor, St. Christopher. Nagle and twenty-eight other prisoners on the ship were sent to the local jail on the morning of December 17. Under normal circumstances, crews of a captured American privateer would probably have been transferred to a prison ship and either encouraged to enlist in the British service or transported to England, where they would have been incarcerated in Old Mill or Forten prisons, but unusual conditions prevailed.

The British fleet at that moment was entirely preoccupied with trying to outguess and outmaneuver the larger French force, made up of the fleet under de Grasse and an army under the Marquis de Bouillé, governor of Martinique, who had surprised and taken St. Eustatius from the British on 25 November 1781. Prevailing trade winds foiled two French attempts to attack Barbados, and on January 11, less than a month after Jacob Nagle arrived on the island, the French fleet appeared at Basseterre, St. Christopher. The island, except for the strongly fortified post on Brimstone Hill, surrendered without a fight, with the agreement that the inhabitants would maintain neutrality during the course of the war. Neighboring Nevis capitulated under the same terms.

Jacob Nagle presents his own story sufficiently well that there is no purpose here in relating all the details of his experiences. But there are a few points that are confusing, particularly the series of events whereby he found himself in the British navy.

When local authorities on St. Christopher surrendered the island to the French in January, Nagle became a free man. Probably because of the neutrality provision of the surrender, it took some time before he obtained a release, but he eventually did, and gained employment, fitting out British merchant vessels that had been captured when the town fell. While he was working there, he was an eyewitness to a notable sea battle between Hood and de Grasse on 25 January 1782. Hood brilliantly outmaneuvered de Grasse but was unable effectively to relieve Brimstone Hill. On 12 February 1782, the post surrendered, leaving the entire island of St. Christopher to the French. Nagle then shipped on board a French coastal vessel in the service of de Bouillé, the governor of Martinique and commander of the military force that had captured Brimstone Hill. He had an understanding with the vessel's captain that when the ship went in to Fort Royal for repairs, he and shipmate William Rigeons would be given a pass to travel to St. Pierre, enabling them to secure passage on the *Holker* or some other American ship back to the United States.

In late February or early March 1782, the French schooner was moored in the harbor at Fort Royal. Nagle and Rigeons were well treated by the French captain and had shore liberty and use of the ship's launch whenever they wished. One day, while on shore, they were approached by a Philadelphia-born sailor named Thomas Moody, who had been captured on an American vessel by the British and impressed into British service. He was serving on board this British ship when it was captured by the French.

Moody had been a British sailor when captured, and as far as the French were concerned, he was therefore liable to imprisonment no matter where he had been born or how he had gotten on the British ship in the first place. Moody had escaped from a French ship in Fort Royal Harbor, and now Nagle and Rigeons befriended him, bought him food and drink, and brought him on board their ship. There undoubtedly was a reward of some sort to be had by anyone who would ''discover'' an escaped prisoner, and one of Moody's ''friends'' spotted them boarding the French ship and turned them in.

That evening, Moody, Rigeons, and Nagle were arrested and taken to a prison for British sailors at Fort Royal, the former as an escaped prisoner, Nagle and Rigeons for abetting an escapee. As the French commissary to whom Nagle later appealed told him, "the man that [you] supported was taken as an English prisoner, if he was an American, and supplying him with provisions and suckering [succoring] him made [you] as good Englishmen as he was a Frenchmen." Nagle wrote to the American consul at St. Pierre, at the other end of the island, but received no response before larger events in the war would intervene and seal his fate.

Nagle incorrectly remembered the duration of his second imprisonment as ten months. This may have been a deliberate misstatement, inspired in the 1830s by his effort to secure as large an American Revolutionary War pension as possible. In reality, he served only two or three months in the Port Royal prison, in company with the crews of the British ships HMS *Iris* and HMS *Richmond*, which had been captured in the Chesapeake on 10 September 1781. On 12 April 1782, Admiral Rodney succeeded, at the Battle of the Saints, in delivering the decisive blow to the French fleet of de Grasse. This victory did not end the war, but it greatly changed the war's complexion, making it clear that the French could not drive the English from the West Indies and enabling the British to save face at the peace table in spite of the loss of the colonies on the North American continent.

Up to this time, the French had maintained a general policy of not exchanging prisoners, using the logic that such trades enabled the enemy to maintain its fleet and prolong the contest. As a result of the debacle at the Battle of the Saints, where more than 10,000 soldiers and sailors were captured, the policy was quickly revised. In May, in preparation for sending the veteran seamen in Fort Royal Prison by ship to France for exchange, the younger and the less able-bodied were transported in a cartel ship to Pigeon Island, off English-held St. Lucia, where they were immediately exchanged. Nagle was among this latter group and was placed on board HMS *Prudent* on 20 May 1782 and transferred to HMS *St. Lucia*. On May 25 he was officially enrolled as a crew member. Like it or not, he was now a regular, "ablebodied seaman" in the Royal Navy!

Before he would embark on the voyage to Australia in the spring of 1787, the grand venture of his long career, Nagle served on the *St. Lucia* and two other vessels of the Royal Navy. The reader of his journal will find it helpful to know a little more about these ships, and about HMS *Royal Oak,* than he tells us himself. The ships provide an interesting cross section of the various types of vessels serving under the British flag in this era. The *Royal Oak* was the sort of ship that gave the navy a bad name. It was a 74-gun vessel with a complement of 624 crewmen. At the time Nagle was brought on board, it was thirteen years old and in very poor condition. It would be decommissioned on its return to England in 1783. The *Royal Oak* had spent the last part of the war in American waters. While typical ships would maintain a high degree of continuity of personnel and build a certain sense of pride in the vessel over the two or three years away from Britain, the *Royal Oak* had been a revolving door in the year previous to Nagle's entry. Large numbers of its original crew had been used to man other vessels, replaced by reassigned men, prisoners, and impressed merchant seamen picked up in Halifax and New York and from captured vessels. There had been a constant and complete turnover among officers as well, and discipline must have been unusually harsh. Nagle was fortunate, himself, to escape impressment on the *Royal Oak*.

HMS *St. Lucia* was a very different sort of ship. The vessel was probably a captured American privateer, the second of that name to fly the British flag during the war. It was commissioned to meet a pressing need for smaller vessels, which could perform coastal surveillance and cartel duties more effectively than the larger ships of the line. The *St. Lucia* was put into British service on 16 May 1782, only nine days before Nagle came on board, and was decommissioned on 23 April 1783, eight days after he left it. Its officers were drawn from HMS *Prudent* and the crew was made up of anyone they could get their hands on. Nagle describes discipline on the vessel as unusually capricious and strict. This was undoubtedly the case, because the officers were young and trying to prove themselves worthy of their rank, the crew, raw and inexperienced, and the duty, monotonous—watching the coast, exchanging prisoners, occasionally chasing down smugglers at a period when the war itself was all but over. Morale on the ship was abysmal.

The end of the war was announced in Gros Islet Bay on 4 April 1783, and plans were made immediately to get the soldiers and sailors home. The sailors of the *St. Lucia* were transferred to HMS *Ardent*, a 64-gun ship that normally had a crew of 500 men. Originally a British naval vessel, it had been captured by the French in 1779 off the English coast, then recaptured at the Battle of the Saints. By this time the British had already commissioned another *Ardent*, so after its return to England, it was renamed *Tiger*. It was decommissioned in 1784. With a crew of sailors, invalids from the hospital on Pigeon Island, and contingents of the 60th, 92nd, and 94th regiments, the ship set sail in company with HMS *Prudent* and HMS *Invincible* from Antigua on June 5 and arrived in Plymouth exactly one month later. Nagle was paid off on August 11. As with other participants in the American Revolution on both sides, Nagle's service was now at an end. He had been taken "home," but as he was a born-again British sailor, the point of discharge was England, not Philadelphia.

Nagle was never one to waste much time feeling sorry for himself, but his journal does imply that circumstances beyond his control now kept him from returning to America, that he had no choice but to reenlist in the British navy, and that in a sense, he therefore would remain a prisoner for years to come. The argument, which fortunately for his own credibility he does not press too hard, deserves to be greeted with skepticism. On his discharge at Plymouth in April 1783, he certainly was paid enough to have bought a passage back to America, had it been his highest priority. The reality is that he was a very normal twenty-two-year-old, and now very much a typical seaman, who was interested in seeing the world and living it up while on shore. For a young American, Philadelphia may have been exciting, but London was the center of the world. His funds lasted for about four months. In September 1783 he volunteered for the navy and was placed on HMS *Scipio*, a recruiting vessel that took him to Spithead. He was assigned to HMS *Ganges* for what would turn out to be a three-and-a-half-year tour of duty.

The *Ganges* was a recently built 74-gun ship with a normal complement of 600 men that had been given to the government by the East India Company while on the stocks in 1779 and launched in 1782. The *Ganges* had seen limited service at the end of the war. Two weeks after Nagle's arrival on board on 28 September 1783, it sailed in company with HMS *Goliath*, HMS *Diadem*, and HMS *Ardent* with supplies and troops for Gibraltar. The *Ganges* transported soldiers of the 18th and 25th regiments, and Nagle's account of the sailors tormenting the raw recruits is the sort of anecdote of shipboard activity that makes the journal such a valuable source for life in the Royal Navy in the eighteenth century.

The *Ganges* returned to Portsmouth with five companies of the 39th Regiment, never to leave port again during Nagle's service on board. Duty was monotonous in the extreme, and when the fleet for Australia came into harbor from the Thames for minor repairs, resupply, and the drafting of enough seamen to bring the crews of the ships up to full complement, Nagle jumped at the opportunity. On 23 March 1787, Nagle and several other acceptable men transferred from the *Ganges* to HMS *Sirius*.

Two of the officers who figure in Nagle's journal in this period deserve particular mention: Lieutenants Isaac Coffin (1759–1839) of the *Royal Oak* and Edward Riou (1762–1801) of the *Ganges,* both remembered by him as particularly stern disciplinarians. Contrary to Nagle's impression that Coffin was an unprincipled Tory who had "runaway" to the British, he came from a prominent New England family and was appointed a midshipman in the navy before the war, in 1774, through the influence of Rear Admiral Montagu. In the eighteenth-century Royal Navy, midshipmen's commissions were highly valued and were the first steps to achieving officer's rank. Boys were generally taken between the ages of ten and fourteen, educated in mathematics and seamanship on shipboard and ashore, and those who showed promise, passed examinations, and gained the favor of their commanding officers were promoted after a few years to lieutenancies. Coffin was rising rapidly in the ranks when Nagle encountered him in November 1781. He had received his lieutenant's commission in January 1778 and had just been promoted to the rank of commander. He joined Hood's flagship, HMS *Barfleur,* when the vessel reached the West Indies, and the admiral thought highly enough of him to have Coffin promoted to the rank of captain and given command of the 74-gun *Shrewsbury* in June 1782. Coffin went on to perform well in his career, charting the St. Lawrence in 1786–88 and serving with great efficiency as commissioner of the navy at Corsica, Lisbon, Minorca, Sheerness, and Halifax, and as superintendent at Portsmouth during the wars with France. He was created a baronet in 1808.

Isaac Coffin's brother John was a noted and much despised Loyalist cavalry leader in the Revolution. What certainly would have surprised Jacob Nagle, had he known it, was that Isaac Coffin was pro-American in his later life. After the war he returned to Boston, where he visited his alma mater, Boston Latin School, and received a Master of Arts degree from Harvard, was painted by Gilbert Stuart, and made close and lasting friendships with several captains of the American navy. He later purchased and paid the expenses for a training ship for New England boys wishing to become seamen, and he left most of his money for the establishment of a nautical academy on Nantucket.

Edward Riou, Nagle's "Lieutenant Rio" on the *Ganges,* was another fascinating character. Riou, in Nagle's memory, was the ultimate disciplinarian. He was, but Nagle did not know what we can know about him, from Riou's papers, which survive at Greenwich. His letters show him to have been a man of unusual intelligence, thoughtfulness, and even kindness, but, without question, an absolute fanatic about cleanliness and shipboard discipline.

In one of his memorandum books, Riou ended a lengthy essay on shipboard cleanliness with the following: "It is no uncommon thing for the most unhealthy and dirty ships—ships never clean, never wholesome,—ships whose crews are neglected by their officers, to be constantly washing and scraping from no other cause than that whilst one half of the ships company are washing and scraping in one place the other half are making dirt in another place. . . . Therefore it is repeated AVOID MAKING DIRT."

Riou had undoubtedly picked up some of his ideas on the importance of discipline from his earlier career, which had included being midshipman on HMS *Discovery* and HMS *Resolution* with Captain Cook on his ill-fated third voyage. To Nagle and his fellow seamen, the lieutenant was an absolute tyrant, but his fanaticism would later save a ship and its crew from almost certain disaster. Two years after Nagle sailed on the *Sirius*, Riou was given command of the *Guardian*, laden with stores for Sydney. The day before Christmas 1789, halfway between the Cape of Good Hope and Australia, it hit a massive iceberg. Most of the crew abandoned ship, but Riou and a skeleton crew kept the vessel afloat for eight weeks, when it was towed back to the Cape by a Dutch whaler. He was promoted to the rank of captain in 1794 and would die gloriously in action under Lord Nelson at the Battle of Copenhagen in 1801.

Nagle's memories of his British service in the early years are primarily of hard duty and harsh treatment. By modern standards, the discipline of the eighteenth-century Royal Navy was often brutal, and these particular ships were in situations that promoted both disobedience and greater than normal resort to the cat-o'-nine-tails—HMS *St. Lucia* because of inexperienced officers and crew, HMS *Ganges* because of the boredom of inactivity. Nagle's complaints had validity for the ship's crews as a whole, but he, on the other hand, demonstrated a lifelong talent for personally making the best berth for himself under even difficult circumstances. On the *St. Lucia*, because he could write, he was assigned the duties of steward, saving him from much of the drudgery of deck duty and giving him access to more and better food. On the *Ganges*, before his term of service was out, he had gotten himself appointed to the crew of the captain's barge, and his experience at that set him up for similar responsibilities on the Australian voyage.

The journal makes it obvious, but so do the ship's logs and the special assignments, that Nagle was not only an unusually capable but also an exceptionally intelligent sailor. With the same ability he had for observing and describing anything important or notable, he knew how to size up a ship and its officers quickly, and then how to make his lot as pleasant as possible. The log books record a few instances in which Nagle received punishment, but they were always at the beginning of his tour of duty. He learned quickly what he could and what he could not get away with. He may have been an unwilling British seaman of limited experience when he first stepped on the deck of HMS *Prudent* in 1782 to begin his Royal Navy career, but by March 1787, when he shipped on board HMS *Sirius,* he was probably as capable as any sailor in the service.

THE *ROYAL OAK* was very leaky, keeping her chain pumps going every quarter of an hour, and hur hand pumps constantly going. Having been in action at Chesspeek with Count Degrass, they kept the frigate with them for fear of sinking. Capt'n Coffin was then first leutenant of the *Royal Oak.*[1]

They ordered us all on the quarter deck, to find out if there were any Englishman amongst us. There ware seven amongs us that had run from the same ship, but the officers at this time were prefer'd on board other ships, and those on board ware strangers to these men, and not known, and the seamen that new them well, even mesmates, would not inform. They over-hall'd one after the other and sent us to the opposite side of the deck. We all passed without mistrust, till the last old Irishman, which was not long from Ierland, and shiped on board for cook, was called. He answered.

The capt[ain] said, ''You will not pretend to say that you are not an Irishman.''

He replyed, ''By Jesus, I never saw the country,'' with a strong Irish brouge on his tongue. The capt[ain], officers, and ships crew burst out in such laughtur, was anough to deafen us. When it was over, the capt'n told him to go along, he was not worth keeping on board his ship.[2]

They had then 90 Americans on board that was compelled to do duty,

Bounty Paid	N°	Entry	Year	Appear-ance	Whence and Whe-ther Prest or not	Place and County where Born	Age at Time of Entry in this Ship	N° and Letter of Tickets	MENS NAMES	Quality	D.D. D.D. or R.	Time of Discharge	Year	Whither or for what Reason	Stragling	Fro[m] in Ledg[er]	Three pence per £	Slop-Cloaths supplied by Navy
									A List of Rebel Prisoners Borne at ⅔ds Allowance									
2330	2.	Nov 1781	Nov 22	Taken in					Edwd Donnelly	2								
				the Rebel					Davd Simison	2								
				Schooner					John Carr	2								
				Trogan Belonging					John Alexander	2								
				to Philadelphia					Jemy Osgood	2								
	5	"		"					James Richason	2								
		"		"					Moses Beard	2								
		"		"					Wm Thomas	2								
		"		"					Thos Brown	2								
		"		"					Jacob Noggle	2	22 Decr 1781			Island of St Christoph				
	40	"		"					Wm Pigeons	2								

Log Entry of HMS Royal Oak *Recording Nagle's Capture*

and Coffin wished to keep us likewise. Two days after we ware taken, they took a Yankee brig which amounted to 30 odd Americans, and the capt[ain] said he would not keep any more Americans for fear they would rise and take the ship.[3] Coffin was American Tory and runaway to the English. While on board, of a moonlight night, we ware sitting in one of the boats out of the way when Coffin, seeing us there, came two us and looking into the boat, he purceived some water in the well. He accused us with making water in the boat ''for a set of dam'd rebels and raskels'' and threatened to flog us all. He made application to the capt'n to flog us all till we went to the pumps, which we refused, but the capt[ain] would not purmit it. The sailors inform'd us if we went to work, as they had comp[e]led the rest of the Americans, they would keep us likewise.

Basseterre, St. Christopher

On the passage, the *Holker* privateer, that we had crused with out of Philadelphia, came down to the frigate and fired a broad side at her and then made sale away from her, but the 74 would not purmit the frigate to chace out of sight, for fear of loozing her. On the passage, one of the Brittish seamen receiv'd two dozen for stealing some of our clothes.

The first island we made was St. Astaci [St. Eustatius]. We luffed up, striving to get in, but the wind being scant, we could not settle [?] in; then they stood on for St. Kits [St. Kitts, or St. Christopher]. The English colours flying in the forts [on St. Eustatius] were then hall'd down, and up went the French colours. The island had been taken [November 26] and was decoying the ships.[4] When they found we stood on, they begin a hot fire upon all the 4 vessels from the forts. They had to bare up to get out of gun shot. We fetched Bassetarr (20 miles in breadth and seven in length, was taken by the French 1782) Roads in the island of Sen't Kitts. Came to an anchor and sent us prisoners to jail [16 December 1781].

Having no yard, we ware confined in the rooms up stairs. Our prisoners allowence was three quarters of a pound of bread p[e]r day, salt codfish one day and salted horse meat on the next day. The jailor informed us that the soldiers had no better. I could not rellish the horsemeat, therefore I made practice of seling my allowance to the Negros for sugar, which I used with bread and water. In this disagreeable manner I lived. Our boatswain thought to rule us in prison as he thought fit and as he did in the schooner. He was one of the seven Englishmen, all seamen, that run from the *Royal Oak* before

mentioned. One day he undertook to flog me. Though I was young, I engaged him til some of his old shipmates, finding I was two smart for him, one of them came behind me and nocked me down. One of his old shipmates that had been on board of the manawar with the whole of them, and the ablest amongst them, being unwel, and laying on his bead [bed], was looking at the treatment that I received from them. He jumped up and came to me and swore if I did not flog the boatswain he would flog me. He stood my second, and at it we went. In about ten or twelve minutes he gave it up, and the rest was afraid to say any more, as they found my second, call'd Jack, was my friend. Afterwards we had quietness.

Jack was an able man and a good seaman. He shamed sick to get to the hospittal. In a few days he got liberty to work on board the merchant ships. One day a Brittish man of war came into the roads and let go hur anchor. She was called the *Blind Russel,* 74 gun ship.[5] The capt[ain], going on shore in his barge, spied Jack working on board, came along side, and ordered him into the boat. He went in, and they pulled for the shore. The capt[ain] landed and was giving the coxwain orders to carry the man on board. The capt[ain] was standing on the beach with his caine in his hand, Jack was in the bow of the boat, and leaped on the gangboard, and from thence on shore, and snatched the cain out of the capt[ain's] hand and nocked him down and then took to his heels and run for it, and the whole barges crew after him, crying out, ''Stop him,'' runing through the market place, but the blacks [k]nowing they wanted to press him, cried out, ''Run Massa, run Massa, no ketche, no have," and Jack got into a kain [sugar cane] patch where they could not find him. So the capt[ain] went on board with a broken head and lost his man into the bargain. Jack then came into prison and remained there.

Sometime after, a gurdle coaster [*guarda-costa*] belonging to the island came into the roads and wanted hands. The capt[ain] came into prison to see if we would go with him. We agreed to go with him, if he would take us all, as we intended to take the vessel from him, but he got some intelligence from the gailor, as we supposed, by not coming for us. Shortly after, the *Stag* privateer of Liverpool of 26 guns came in, wanted hands, and six or eight went with him. He wanted me verry much to go, but I could not think of fighting against my country, though I learnt afterwards they fared better than we did. They took several prizes, sent them into St. Thomases, sold them, and got their prize money and went home to Philadelphia in American ships, while the remainder of us was laying in jail.

About this time, in the year 1781, Count Degrass returned from America after the Battle of Chessepeak to the West Indies and fitted out in Martinica [Martinique] for Jamaco [Jamaica] with 15 thousand troops on board.[6] But coming down to St. Kits, they landed their troops aback of the island, and the fleet under Count Degrass came to an anchor in a half moon abreast the town and three batteries and sent a flag of truce on shore to [k]now weather they would give up the town [11 January 1781]. What Brittish troops and melisa [militia] they had were gone down to Brimstone Hill, which had a strong fort on the top of it and no way to come at it, only by starving them out. It is 18 miles from the town of Bastar [Basseterre] and between 2 and 3 miles of Sandy Point or Old Roads. The town submited, and the French soldiers took possession. The French troops surrounded the hill and hove works up and begin to cannonade and heave shell night and day.

When we found the French had possession, we thought we had a right to brake out. Down the stair case was only a thin paticion leading into the kitchen. I, among the rest, being foremast, went out to the dore and stood there. By this time the jalor run down to the French officers of the guard and told them the prisoners was braking out of the jail. They, not [k]nowing but we ware Englishmen and criminals, sent a sarjents guard up. The sarjant, seeing me at the dore, and the jailor told him I was one of them, he gave chase after me with a fixed bayonet. I run up stairs and could not run further. I stood with my back against the wall. The jailor had two daughters, the youngest was nearly of my age, and during the time I was in prison she was parcial to me. She seeing the sarjent in chase of me, she came up with him, he lifting his gun to stab me, when the girl claped her back to my breast and screamed bitterly. The soldier appeared to be in a rage and strove to push hur awoneside. Hur mother coming up, she intorceded for me. By this time all the gaurd was up stairs. One among them was an Irishman. He, finding that we ware Americans, he immediately informed the sarjent. He was then rejoiced that he had not killed me, which certainly would of hapened if the young girl had not interfeared.

The guard remained with us till late in the night, but we could not be let out till further orders. The guard gave us wine to drink and was very kind to us, but the general was at Brimston[e] Hill. There was English prisoners and crimenals in the lower apartments. We ware now in a worse sittuation than before. The English commesary could give us no provisions, and the French could not without orders from the admarel or general, and they were both at Brimston Hill; by that means we had no support, till the French officers, hearing of some Americans being in prison, came up to see us, and learning our sittuation, each of them gave us money to buy provisions. Near three weeks the French officers would come up and give us a small supply of money for provisions. We ware in this sittuation when a Boston brig came in to the roads for a supply of water, being bound homewards. The capt[ain] hearing of us, came to see us, and amediately went down to Brimston Hill to

Battle of 25 January 1782 Witnessed by Nagle

the general and admeral and received an order to take us out of prison. The capt[ain] gave a passage to some of the Bostonions, and the admeral gave them provisions. The rest of us had to shift for our selves. The jailor and his wife, when we ware let out, wish me to remain with them and there two daughters, which I ought to have done for the sake of his youngest daughter saving my life, but hur father puting me in the dungen for braking the gail, I was much displeased with him, but the French officers took me out.

Having our liberty now, and a great number of English ships laying in the roads abreast the town that the French had taken possession of and was fitting them out for France, Wm. Regons and myself was engaged by a French capt[ain] to help fit out a large ship at days works.[7] We being on board at work, the French fleet got under way, having intilligence of the Brittish fleet being out. They went to fall in with them. In about three days after, we saw the Brittish fleet coming down under the Isle of Nevus [Nevis] in shore, and Count Degrass's fleet engaging them out side all the way down to St. Christophers, Bassetarre Roads [25 January 1782].[8] We were then in a great hurry to heave up our anchor and get under way as all the rest did that had hands sufficient.

While we ware thus engaged, a ship that lay next to us with some Englishmen on board began a firing at us to prevent us from getting under way, but we being equal in force, we stoperd our cable, cast loose our guns, and gave them a broad side, which made them silant. Afterwards, we hove up and maid sail before the two fleets got down to us. The French fleet had the English fleet hemed in between them and the island. The Brittish came to an anchor in a close line with springs upon their cables. The French fleet lay off and on, out side of them, so that they ware blockaded in the rhodes [roads]. The ship we ware in run down to St. Astacio [St. Eustatius], but passing Brimston Hill, they hove some shells at us, which nearly fell on board of us, which made us shear off, but we got safe to an anchor.

The next day the capt[ain] paid us for our labour, and we went on board of a schooner belonging to the governor of Martinico mounting 10 guns and about 18 hands besides the officers. We left Sta. Stacia bound to Sandy Point near Brimston Hill. We laid there several days. I went on shore. The store houses ware all open and taking all kinds of provisions and liquors to the army. I entered a large stone building, and hearing a pittiful moaning in a joining room, I entered and saw a stout young molatto man laying on a bed with his thy shot off by a cannon ball. He was on Brimston Hill, but they sent all the wounded down, and he was tended by a French doctor. The French

Marquis de Bouillé, Governor of Martinique

never ceased firing either shot or shells during the night or day for six weeks until they blew up all their magozenes of water and provisions. While the schooner was laying at Sandy Point, I made a practise of walking the deck till 2 or 3 in the morning, crying and fretting for the loss of my parents, never being so long from home before, when 14 or 16 shells would be flying in the air at one time.

The Brittish at length had to caputilate and give up Brimston Hill [12 February 1782]. We were then ordered up to the fleet. In a dark night, we went under the shot of the Brittish line a battle ships and lifted three anchors that they had lost and was not discoverd. In a short time after this, the night [14 February 1782] being very dark, and the French fleet laying off and on, the Brittish sliped their cables, leaving lights upon their buoys, and run down close along shore to leeward and made their escape and was not to be seen in the morning. While laying there, they could not land for the troops, nor go to see for the fleet out side of them, till this oppurtinity accured in their favour, as the French fleet was supperior to them.

We ware then ordered to Dominico [Dominica] with dispatches. We only lay two days in the bay within the fort. Dominico is about halfway between Gaudeloupe [Guadeloupe] and Martinico. It is 28 miles in length

Fort Royal, Martinique

and thirteen broad; the capital is Charlotte Town. We got under way for Martinico, keeping a long shore with a moderate breeze, but coming to a valley, a sudden squall came down on us, which is customary in that island. It laid us down on our beam ends, but the topsail sheets being carried away and foresail and mainsail lowered down, she rightened again. Out of 14 French seamen, the capt[ain's] mate, boatswain, and gunner could not get one up a loft to furl the topsail and main topmast staysel. They beat them up the rigging with handspikes and they crying out, "O, Mundue," which is, "O, God." At length we told the mate, who could talk good English, if they would let them come down out of the riging, we would go up and furl the sales. He told the capt[ain], and he ordered them down. We both then had room to go up and furled both sails. After that the capt[ain] would give us wine, beef, and pork at any time we required it, as we could not eat the beans with oile, in soop, which they ware fond of.

We proceeded on for Martinico. In passing St. Piere, the capital of the island, on the west side, Long'd 61°21'W., Lat'd 14°1'N., we ware board'd

by a boat belonging to the *Holker* Privateer, Capt[ain] Kaine, of Philadelphia. We wished to go on board, but the capt[ain] would not let us go, but promised as soon as the schooner was strip[p]ed, he would produce us a pass port to come down by land from Fort Royal, which lays on the south side, W. [?] Log'd 61°E. Lat'd 14°34'.⁹ Accordingly, we arived, and laying there for orders, the French fleet came in and was fitting out for France.

My companion [William Rigeons] and myself had the privilege of taking the boat and go on shore when we pleased, the schooner laying within hail. During the time we lay here, the anchors was sold, and we rec'd the prizemoney, but how much I do not recollect. One day, being on shore, we came down to the boat to go on board, when we ware accosted by a sailor [Thomas Moody], prayed that we would give him some relief, as he had been three days on shore without any subsistance whatever excepting water. We took him into a wine house on the beach and call'd for as much as he thought fit to eat and drink. He hailed for Philadelphia, was taken by the Brittish and kept him, and then taken by the French, and was on board of one of the line a battle ships laying then in the harbour as a prisoner and had got on shore in hopes of getting on board sum America ship bound home. We agreed to take him on b[oar]d with us and inform'd the mate that he was American and wanted to go to St. Pieres with us to go on board the *Holker*.

Being on shore one day, and putting off to go on b[oar]d again, the three of us, this Thos. Moody by name, a French boat was then landing full of men and officers.

The bowman hailed him, "A, Jack, how you do?"[10]

"Verry well," said Jack.

I said, then, "Jack, you are sold," not dreaming it would be any determent to us.

"O, no," says Jack, "that was my best friend on board."

I said, "I would not trust him."

They landed, and we went on board, but they took notice what vessel we went on board of, we thinking no more of it, but about 10 o'clock at night, to our surprise, a serjents guard came on board us (and demanded the whole 3 of us). The mate told him that he new two of us was a Mericans and belonged to the schooner that was taken out of English prison. The sarjent told him he had orders to take all three of us, and we must go to prison. We packed up our clothes and a few dollars of our prize money, and they took us to prison in the night.

They onlocked a room that was so full that we could scarcely find a place vacant to lay down. In the morning the dores was unlocked, and all hands had the priviledge to go down into the yard during the day. These prissoners were two Brittish ships companys: one the *Iris* and the other called the *Richmund,* taken by the French fleet a few days before the Battle of the Chessepeak and brought to Martinico Prison.

Our allowance was three quarters of a pound of bread and about 3 ounces of meat, but no liquor. We sold our meat to the convicts which was in the same prison but confined below for about 2 Dogs, which is about 2 pence, and a stampee is a 3 halfpence. With this we could by fruit or such other articles as we thought fit. The jailor was very strict in respect of liquor, but you could by as much wine from him as you please, but allowing no other person.

Our chief amusement was the cudgels with baskets on the handels.[11] In the morning, coming down into the yard, I admired these hansome strait sticks with baskets on the handels, and not [k]nowing the meaning of their laying a cross each other, I took one up to vew it, a hundred sailors sitting round on the benches. One young man jumped up from his seat, ketched up the other, and struck me over the head. I returned the blow. He guarded it off. I new nothing about cudgeling, but I thrashed away without any guard, and when he struck at me, I struck him at the same time, which put us much upon a parr, but he soon got tired of this sport and told me I did not play fair and I should guard myself. I told him it was not fair to hit me over the head, a stranger as I was, and new nothing about cudgeling. Therefore we droped the sport, with a hearty laugh among the seamen. However, I practised and soon learnt to play a good stick with my old entagonist.

In a few days after, the French commesary came into the prison, and I informed him of my situation and that I was an American and taken out of English prison. He told me the man that we supported was taken as an English prisoner, if he was American, and supplying him with provisions and suckering [succoring] him made us as good Englishmen as he was a Frenchman, and that was all the satisfaction that I could receive from him. At this time I kept a kind of a journal and had a great many remarks in the taking of the island of St. Christopher and the French and Brittish fleet. The prisoners advised me to destroy it, for fear they should find it with me. As I was put into prison, as supposed to support the Brittish prisoners, they would take me up for a spy, passing for a Merican, as one man had been hung for a spy about two month before. Therefore I burnt my book. I then rought to the American Counsel at St. Piers but never receiv'd any answer.

The Brittish prisoners that laid on the ground flore laid out a plan for making their escape in the night. They lifted a cuppel of boards so that one man could be employ'd diging under the foundation of the wall and then upwards till they came to the pavement in the street where the sentry walked. When it was all completed they ware all to get out one by one, the hole not containing more, as the sentry walked to the other end of the jail. When they ware all fixed, the first one broke down the stones, and seeing the sentry walking towards the other end, he started and got round the corner into the next street. The second, taking his oppertunity, when about half way up the soldier, turning suddintly and sooner than was expected, instantly fired and killed him outright in the hole. The rest had to retreat, and the alarm being given, the one that had got away was taken and confined in the dungion for a long time before he was let out amongst the other prisoners.

The jailor had a trustee Negro, which he put great depenance in, who brought the bread in every day and smugeld liquor in the bag and sell a ½ a wine glass for as much as you would get a quart bottle for. The prisoners were determined to fix him. In the morning when he came in with the bread, they seized the bag and took out the blather and gave it to the jailor. He was so enraged at the slave for spoiling his custom, he ordered him to be floged, and to encourage the prisoners, he made us all stand in ranks and served it all out to us in a wine glass. It went twice round the two ships companies. I remain'd in this prison as near as I can guess about 10 month.

A carteel [cartel] was fitted out, and all the youngest [among them, Nagle] and sickleyest were sent in hur to St. Lucia, keeping the best of the seamen to be sent to France in the fleet, which sailed shortly after. We arived and came to an anchor at Pigeon Island and was sent to b[oar]d the *Prudent*, 64 guns, and remained about three weeks, when we ware drafted [26 May 1782] on board the *St. Lucia* Brig, pink stern, had been taken from the Americans, and made a tender of, mounting 12 guns but pierced for 14 guns.[12]

I cannot describe the cruelty of this manawar, but I will endeavour to give a short sketch. Capt[ain] Brooklin [Samuel Brooking] com[mande]d, who was first leutenant of the *Prudent* before mentioned, and six officers out of the same ship, and seven of us that was draughted on b[oar]d.[13] The second day, one man receiv'd two dozen upon suspicion of broaching a cask of rum. In a few days we pressed 5 more out of a transport, though it is not allowed in the service. When but seven men, we had to hoist a six oard boat in and out, night and morning, for fear of our runing away with her. Nothing was to be done without nocking down and thrashing in every duty that was to be done. As soon as we had pressed hands sufficient to weigh the anchor, we run down to the Canash [Carenage] and came to an anchor at the entrance of it and pressed every man, weather sailor or not, that came into the harbour. We pressed an old man from England, a house carpenter, and the merchant that was to employ him had to pay 30 Lb. sterling for a supernumery before he was let go. On shore we ware dreaded by all merchantment.

The purser [James Parry], one day finding a tin cup of mine that I had rought upon with a sail needle, he enquired of the men to [k]now whoes cup that was. They all new but would not tell, for fear that I would get punished, I being away at the same time in the boat. When we came on b[oar]d, as they came up he enquired whos cup that was. None of them would own that they new whose cup it was. I being in the boat as boatkeeper new nothing of it.

The pusser [purser] thought it strange, at last call'd me out of the boat. "Is this your cup?"

"Yes, Sir."

"Come aft on the quarter deck."

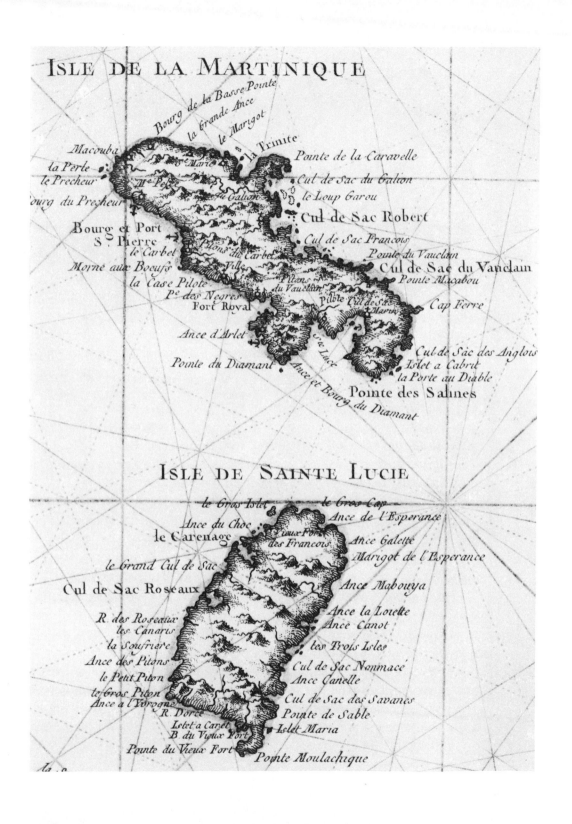

Captain Samuel Brooking

I trimbled, though I new I got the cup onestly. I went aft, where the capt[ain] was sitting by a small table, and the purser giving him the cup, "Is this your cup?"

"Yes, Sr."

"Is this your righting?"

"Yes, Sir."

He calld his steward and desired him to bring up pen, ink, and paper. When it was brought, he desired me to right. I asked him what I should right.

He made the answer, "What was on the cup."

I rought, "Jacob Nagle, Born in the Town of Reading, Berks County, Pennsylvania State, N. America." With my fright and trimbeling I did not right it half so well, but he saw it was the same hand.

"You must act as ships steward under the purser," the capt[ain] replyed. I made answer that I did not [k]now my own allowance.

He replied, "What is the pusser for, but to give you instructions and books."

It hapened well for me, as I was then from under the lash of the boatswain, a meare tirent, and other officers.

A few days after, what apeared strange to both men and officers was, though we ware dreaded as a man of war and cruel usage, a stout young sailor came to the capt[ain] on shore and told him he wanted to enter. He said he belonged to such a ship and the capt[ain] had fell out with him and would not pay him his wages.

"Very well, my man," said the capt[ain], "I will get your wages. There is my boat with 4 boys. You may go on b[oar]d and tell the pusser to give you a bottle of rum to drink my health."

Accordingly, aboard he came, the officers and men staring to see a stout looking sailor coming on b[oar]d by himself. When on board, he call'd out for the pusser, the boatswain and officers gathering round him enquiring who and what he was. The boatswain, more inquisitive than the rest, asked him how long he had been to see. He turned round and told him he had been two days to morrow. The officers all laughed at the joke, and I was sent for the liqur. He would not except of it till I had drank, and then he handed it round amongst the sailors. In a few days the capt[ain] received 70 odd guineas for him and gave it to him and made a boatswain's mate of him, which he did not like.

In a few days we went down to leeward to a watering place for a supply of water. We ware hoisting in the water as the cutter was rafting and towing it off. At noon they piped to dinner, and I served the grog. Luke Arvour, which was his name, sat down on the comings of the main hatch way, where I was sitting, and the capt[ain] on the quarter deck, and the boat was coming off to dinner. Luke said to me, "I am now longanough on b[oar]d this vessel, and you will not see me again, good by."[14] I smiled as I was going below.

In less than three minutes he was overboard like a fish. The capt[ain] hailed the boat that had an officer in her to ketch him and got a musket out of the arm chest and kept firing at him, but whenever he pointed the musket, he would dive and would not come up for 20 yards, and the boat after him. When they came near him, he told the young officer if he offered to lay holt of him, he would hall him overboard and drown'd him. Then he would go down again. The capt[ain] hailed the fort, and the soldiers came down to receive him when he landed, but they ware disapointed. He landed the opposite side of a creek and they could not cross. He made his escape from the whole in the noon day.

We returned to our old ground till we had pressed about 35 or 40 men, then returned to Pigeon Island and heard of the defeat of Count Degrass, 1782.[15] We were then sent to Barbadoes (Barbadoes, eastermost of the Windward Islands, 25 M. in length, 15 in breadth, 70 E. of St. Vincens) with dispatches. Nothing accured on the passage excepting ill yousage. While there, the purser gave me orders to sell bread, beef, and pork of the ships provisions for pocket money for himself. The boatswain [George Douglass], taking notice of it, put me upon my guard and directed me to keep a regular

Carenage Bay, St. Lucia, Looking Beyond Gros Islet Bay and Pigeon Island, with Diamond Rock, Martinique, on the Horizon

account of what I sold and what money I delivered to him, he having a Burbados lady on board which was very expensive. We returned to Sant. Lucia and was stationed to cruse between Pigeon Island and the Dimond Rock on Martinico. Sant Lucia is 22 miles in length and 21 miles in breadth and 21 miles south of Martinico. Every morning, coming to anchor in side of Pigeon Island, and in the morning heave up with a tacle, the fall leading round the deck with snatch blocks, having no capstain or windless. The moment the boatswain blew his call, there must be a full run till the tacle was ablock, and every officer thrashing away, even the capt[ain] himself with his cane when he took the notion, and we scarcely ever had more than 35 men. This was the treatment every day. If the capt[ain] said you was drunk, it was sufficient, if you never tasted liquor. You was brought to the gangway. One of the men had his thum jamed off by the geer block. He tied him up and gave him a dozen before it was dressed by the doctor; another having his thumb jam'd off by a cask, floged him likewise. He floged another for a little ballast falling off the shovel overboard, heaving it into the port. If a boat went on shore for a load of water with an officer in hur, it was seldom to see more come back than one and the officer, which would have to pull the boat on board. He kept the jolly boat for his own use, with 4 little American boys to pul him about, as he new they could not run a way.

We ware sent down to the lee side of the island after smuglers. We run one on shore and left one man [James Nuttal] with hur armed, while the boat went on b[oar]d, and he run away with arms and all. He got up to the Kenash [Carenage], shiped on b[oar]d a vessel bound to England.[16] When about halfway, was taken by American frigate and brought to Guardeloupe [Guadeloupe], from thence to St. Piers in Martinico. We came over as a carteel for prisoners, and he was sent on b[oar]d his own vessel he run from and was nown before he got a long side; was ordered aft and put in double irons.[17] Returning to Pigeon Island, the Brittish fleet lay there.

We ware sent out again to cruise between the islands. About day light, we discovered a brig standing for us. I new her to be the *Holker* Privateer, which I before mentioned. I thought then I would soon be free from those tirants. We beat to quarters. I was stacioned at the brake of the quarter deck.

I said to one of the men along side of me, "You will soon be safe, it is the *Holker*."

The purser heard me. He run and told the capt[ain]. He came to me, "Do you [k]now that vessel?"

"Yes, Sir."

"What sort of a head has she?"

"She has serpant head, but you can scarecely purceive it at a distance."

He looked with his spy glass and swore I was right. She was now nearly within gun shot. He asked me what force she was and what men she generally caried.

I told him, "16 sixes and 90 men."

"Well," he said, "we cant run, we must fight."

She would of had us in 20 minutes more, but a large ship came round the point to windward with all sail crowded, coming down upon us. The *Holker* put about and stood for Martinico, and we bore up for Pigeon Island. We being a dull sailer, she soon came up with us, brought us two. She proved to be the *Jenus*, 50 gun [*Janus*, 44 guns] ship. The *Holker* by this time was under the land of Martinico. We run in and came to anchor.

We ware then ordered by the admiral to run over to Fort Royal as a carteel [cartel]. When as a carteel, we had to put our guns in the hole [hold]. We hove up at dusk and was out side of Pigeon Island catting the anchor. One of the seamen went down and hook'd the cat to the anchor and then droped into the water, unperceiveable by any person on b[oar]d, being

Pigeon Island, with British Ships in Gros Islet Bay, St. Lucia

under sail. He swam for the island amongst a numerous set of shirks [sharks], as the hospittal on the island buried the dead a back of the island where he swam on shore, and then had to swim to the main and travel to the Kenash, where the merchant ships and transports lay. The nex morning he was missed and was supposed to be drownded. In a month after our pusser saw him in the Kenash on board a merchant ship, but he did not fear him, as there was no men of war there.

On our return to Pigeon Island we heard of the *Holker* being upset [2 March 1783]. She was chased by a Brittish frigate, and a heavy squall took her, and Capt[ain] Kaine [*sic*, actually Captain John Quinlan] would not allow any sail to be taken in. She turned keel up. The frigate [*Alemene*] picked up 37 men and the capt[ain] and brought them into St. Lucia.

The cap[tain] kept this deserter, James Nuttle, still in irons. The prisoner beged of me to right a few lines as a pitition to the capt[ain]. I did so, but heard no more of it for two days after, when the capt[ain] ordered all hands to be turned up, and he was brought to the gangway.

The capt[ain] spoke, "You [k]now well the fleet laying hear. If I try you by court marshial, death is your portion, as being a threefold crime; 1sd, leaving your post, then deserted, and taking the Kings arms with you. Therefore to flog you at the gangway is not worth while. Therefore I forgive you."

Although he was so great a tarter in small crimes or even without a crime, he overlooked the greatest, as death would have been the punishment. For instance, the capt[ain] having a cask of maderia wine in the spirit room, and his steward having acasion to broach the cask, found it half empty. He inform'd the capt[ain]. As I kept the kees of the store room, the capt[ain] ordered me in irons without over halling the cask or moving the cask from where it stood against the bulkhead. I could not think how he could suppose me to broach his wine, when I had the command of all the wine and rum in the spirit room of ships stores. Shortly after, the hands was turn'd up, and I was brought to the gangway, tied me up, and ordered the boatswain to give me a good dozen with the cat of nine tails, which I received. After I was punished, the boatswain told me when I received two dozen more I would be a manawars man, and not before. The capt[ain] told me to do my duty as yousual.

The pusser went with me, and several officers that came upon a visit to see the pusser and doctor, belonging to som of the line a battle ships, went into the spirit room, and moving the cask from the bulkhead, we found a worm hole on the bilge of the cask and the bulkhead all stained with the wine. It had run out as far as the worm hole and no further. The gentlemen said it was very evident that it had leaked out. They all went on the quarter deck and inform'd the capt[ain] of the mistake. He told then if I did not deserve it then, I might deserve it hereafter.

The Brittish fleet put to see. The *Genus* [*Janus*], 50 guns ship, laying in the Canash fitting out, had intillegence of a French convoy being to leward of the island, about 40 sail. The *Genus* bent sails and put to see, with all the men of war that lay in St. Lucia.

Genus	50 Guns
Schoon'r *Grosalet*	10 Guns
St. Lucia Brig	12 Ditt
Barbados	2 "
A Privateer	18 "

Those ware the amount of the Brittish. The French, one 74 gun ship, but a good many of the merchant ships were armed, some 12 guns, some 16, and from that to 20 guns. We came up with them about 3 or 4 leagues from the harbours mouth at Fort Royal, Martinico. The first we came up to struck the first broad side. The *Genus* strove to get a long side the French 74, but they made all sail to get in and engaged at long shot. As we learnt afterwards, the most of the French seamen were sick, and water and provisions stowed between there guns, so that they ware not able to come to a regular action. If she had been two leagues farther off the land, she must of struck to the 50 gun ship, but getting under the forts, she got in, and the *Genus* had to leave her. But the fleet had to shift for themselves. Some held their wind for St. Piers, others bore up before the wind. Our best sailing vessels would run a long side and make them strik their colours and leave them to be board'd by the dull sailors which would be a stern. Coming up, we took and maned 14 vessels. Sum was caried into St. Lucia, and those that run to leward were caried into Totolo [Tortola]. We receive'd 13 dollars the first payment, and that was all I ever receive'd, though there was to be three payments.[18]

We still remained in missery on b[oar]d this dungboat of a man a war. When the capt[ain] was out of the ship, the boatswain would call all hands to quarters and exercise us the whole day at great guns and small arms and thrash them for his own amusement till he would be tired himself. Our capt[ain] being prefered, we received a nother [22 October 1782] called Fighting Dundass, and if they ware both in a bag, I could not tell which would come out first.[19] As the black slave said, he was not the chip off the old block, but he was the block altogether, and I beleive worse, if it was posseble. Our employment was still sailing between the Dimond Rock and Pigeon Island every night and morning, as before mentioned, excepting when we ware sent as a carteel [cartel] to Martinico, and return with prisoners, and smugling cordials in boxes of different kinds.

We remained in this situation till 1783, when a frigate came in with a vessel with the packet of Peace on board and brought her to an anchor in Groselet Bay, in side of Pigeon Island, where the fleet was laying. Admaral Rodney finding the peace to be a fact, it was made [k]nown through the fleet [4 April 1783], the sailors cheering through the whole fleet, and hundreds of hats flying in the air and going overboard. Our capt[ain] not being on board, the pusser took it upon him to give the ships company an extry pint of grog. I served it out according to his orders. The other officers were much griped in hearing of the peace. They informed the capt[ain] when he came on board what the pusser had done. Amediately I was put into irons, as he could not undertake to put the pusser there. The malice fell on me, but the pusser

Loss of the Ville de Paris

taking all the blame to himself and making it up with the capt[ain], I was releas'd out of irons.

The next day we rec'd orders to sail for Antege [Antigua]. We arived in English Harbour, we strip'd her, and she was put out of commision. I remained on board that brig of terror in missery for one year. On the 25 of May I was draughted on b[oar]d of her, and on that day twelve months I was draughted on board the *Ardent,* 64, that was retaken from the French with the *Ville de parry* [*Ville de Paris*] and several more on the 11th and 12 of April. She had been hove down twice in English Harbour but still remained verry leaky. We had between 2 or 3 hundred invaleds and soldiers on board. The officers belonging to those troops refused to go in her, being so leaky, but the poor sailors and soldiers were compeled to go and the officers went on b[oar]d the *Ville de Parry,* as they took her to be a sound and large ship. But as God would have it, she was lost in the gale of wind, and we ware saved, as you will hear.[20]

Birdseye View of Plymouth and the Dockyard

We sailed with the *Prudent,* 64, and a seventy four, which was to take us out if we could not keep hur above water. We had Indian pumps between decks, Indien pumps on the main deck, and Bell pumps on the quarter deck, and hand pumps down the main hatchway. They were constantly going, night and day. It took 12 men at each bell pump, 6 at each Indian pump, and lights burning all night between decks. Off Newfound Land, the weather being thick and foggy, we lost the other two ships for three days. We fired minute guns during that time.

On the 4th day we fell in with them again, having a fine and pleasant breeze and a fair wind. Ediston, off Plymouth, hove in sight, and we got in safe [7 July 1783], run into the harbour a breast the dock yard and striped her and got the guns on shore. We had liberty to go on shore till the ship was ready to be paid off.[21]

I went upon liberty, this being the first English ground I ever stood on, and where was it but north corner, Plymouth Dock. I was invited into a publick house, and we had sum beer, but the money was demanded before you got what you call'd for. I thought it very strange. We then went up into

the town and fell in with one of the guners mates belonging to our ship. He invited me and a lad that was with me to take a walk. I agree'd, as I wished to see the town, but I told him I had no money, as I had no credit, being a stranger. He made me answer not to mind that, he would get what we wanted, so we went on. We took a turn through Dock, and then he took us into a publick house and call'd for beer. After we had that, he must have a half pint of rum and some more beer to the value of about 18 pence Sterling. He then desired us to remain there, as he was going backwards. We did so for a long time. I went to look for him, but he was gone. I asked the landlord weather he new him. He said he did not, but he expected that he had left us to pay the reconing. I told him I was a stranger and had no money, but if he would trust me, I would go and get sum. He told me he would, as I told him what ship I belong'd to. We went to the house where my shipmates had taken us, and I inform'd them of the trick I was play'd, and they inform'd the landlord, and he gave me what money I wanted till the ship was paid, and boarded me while on shore. I returned and paid the landlord for what the fellow call'd for and returned back a gain.

When we came in, this fellow was there. I spoke to him in respect of his scandelous behavour before the ships crew that was there. He fell into a great rage and was for giving me a good thrashing. He was a stout built man, and I was but young and slim, but verry active. I told him he should not without a triel, if he would give me fair play.

We all started for the Common, out side of the town, where the soldiers barraks was. As soon as we begin to strip, out came the soldiers, about 2 or 3 hundred, and formed a ring. Two granedeers steped out for our seconds and would not permit the sailors to hav any thing to say to it, and at it we went. He made a heavy lunge at me, but I avoided his blow and ketched him under the jaw. He fell like a log. His second lifted him up carefully, and my second told me to make an offer for the same place and ketch him the opposite side. I took his advise, and we met again, and I ketche'd him on the opposite side, and down he went, and was a considerable time before his second got him up. My second directed me. We met, and I plaid for his ribs till I found an opening. I struck him a cross the nose and cut him considerable, and [he] fell. He then gave up and said he had a nuff. I went to shak hands, but he would not. My second then demanded me to thrash him till he would make it up. I did so, but he soon shook hands without making a blow in return. We then went into a publick house and drank and treated our seconds and then parted. He was so much ashamed to be beat by a striplin, that he went on board and went to the hospittal before I came on board. From the time we entered Plimouth Harbour till we ware paid off was about three week.

Being advised to go to London to get home, I paid my passage with a number more for Portsmouth and there took the stage for London, as the sailor says, ''to see what a 'clock it was.'' I took up my lodging at Mr. Rogers, a public house between the China Ship and Iron Gate, with some more of my ship mates. By this time London was full of sailors. The men of war being all paid off, and the American ships were gone full of passengers from London, and no possibillety of getting work, or a ship, and what few did get work had to work for a shillen a day. Even the men of war that was fitting out for stations would not except of any that was not hail, stout young seamen, and those that had not been careful of their money was then starving.

I had a young lad with me belonging to Canady [Canada] and was paid off with me from the *Ardent*. He apeared so much like me, that all strangers though we ware brothers, therefore we passed for brothers. He was about 14 years of age.[22] We travel'd to Woolage [Woolwich] and Debtford in hopes of getting a ship, but in vain.

One day I ment to take a walk through part of the city, and I gave my watch to my brother, as I call'd him, and though we were both young, I was then about 21 or past, I looked upon myself as his guardien. Though young and unaquainted with the world, particularly in this great matropalis, I gave my brother particular charge not to leave the boarding house till I returned, which he promised. I then took my recriation through the city, in part, and subburbs. In the evening I returned without any thing material excepting my curosity and views in my excursion, but enquiring for my brother, he was not to be found.

I stroled from one public house to the other in St. Catherines and long rooms where all the ladies of pleasure resorted.[23] I fell in with a Merican lady of that discription that came over with an officer. She having seen us both at Mr. Rogers'es, she informed me where he was, with a girl in a house near the China Ship. I went to the house and enquired. There was two men and two wimmen playing cards. They denied that he was there and desired me to go about my business. I told them I was about my business and I new he was there, and I would fetch the constable. They desired me to go. I went home and informed my landlord. He had a young man in his house that was well aquainted with those nany houses, and he profered to go with me. He took a club, and we returned to the house after dark. He desired me to go in and take the candel and go up stairs to a room to the left hand, as he new the girl kept that room, and he would keep the dore, and if any one interupted me, he would soon be with me.

I went in. The wimen of the house and those two bullies were still playing of cards. I went up to a stand that had a candle in a candlestick. I took it up and went to the table where they ware playing and lit the candel, and the man that was with me stood at the dore. By our not speaking, and he having a big club in his hand, they took him to be a constable. I went up stairs and strove to open the dore, but I could not without breaking the lock.

The woman hollowed out, ''What do you want?''

''I want my brother,'' I replied.

''There is no one here but my husband, and he shant get up.''

I made answer, ''Verry well, if he looses any of his property or money, I will have you and the landlady in limbo in the morning.''

Down comes a nother fillow from the second storie, half dressed, and wanted to [k]now what business I had there. I gave him an answer suitable to his question in a verry rough manner, and he went shearing off up stairs, and I went down stairs, [k]nowing I dare not brake the dore open, and joined my cumrad. He told me to warn the landlady that I would make her be answerable for all that should be missing in the morning. I did so, and we went home and went to bed.

In the morning when I awoke I found him a long side of me but without money or watch. I roused him up, and he was then stupid. I enquired where he had been. He inform'd me when I went away a girl came in and enticed him home to hur house, where I came in the evening, and she had got some money from him to get sum phlip and made him so drunk that he could not speak to me when I was there.

"And what have you done with the watch and your money?"

"I do not [k]now." We got up. I went to the house again, the baud being there.

"Now Madam, if you dont deliver watch and money, you shall go before the Squire."

She call'd the girl down stairs. "Do you [k]now any thing of this young mans money and watch?"

"No, I [k]now nothing about him."

"That is sufficient," said I, "but I will convince you better presently," and turned about to go out.

She then got fritened. "Stop," said she, "I will look, purhaps he lost it in the bead," and up she went. In a bout a quarter of an hour she came down with the watch and four guineas, saying she found them in the bed, one guinea short, short of what he had when he went there. The watch was mine but the money was his. I told him he might think himself well off with losing one guinea, as it took part of that to make him drunk and senceless and the remainder he mus of cours allow his loving Dulcana [Dulcinea] for taking care of him, so we took our departure.

Our money getting short, we begin to look out for a ship of any kind. The ship *Sippio*, man of war, was then shipping of men for different stations, laying in the river abreast of Woolage.[24] We went down and shiped on b[oar]d, but when all seamen were overhall'd by the admi[ra]l and capt[ai]n, this brother of mine was sent on shore, being two young, which grieved me, but I was kept, and I never had any intilligence from him afterwards.

We sailed for Spithead. The entered seamon were draughted, and I went on b[oar]d the *Gangess* 74, Capt[ain] Luttrel, one of the Parlement men at that time [28 September 1783]. Laying at Spithead, two 74 and two sixty fours was taking in troops for the releif of Giberalter.[25] We sailed, and on our passage we fell in with a Spanish squadron. The admiral ship was the *St. Trenedad* of 4 tear [tier] of guns, she was then call'd the larges ship that ever was built, and two seventy fours with troops on board, but where they ware bound, I do not recollect.

We arived at Giberalter [29 October 1783], but purhaps it would be requeset to mention the situation of the poor raw soldiers that ware unaquainted on board of a man of war. They ware supplied with beds for the passage, and if not returned, they ware charged for them out of their wages. The sailors beds being small, they endeavourd to make them larger. In the night, they would crawl a long the deck and get holt of a blanket or rug. The sailors would pull, the soldier hold fast and hollow out, but 2 or three to one would gain the prize. Even in day light, the hammocks being stowed on the booms, the topmen would send a hawling line down with a hook, and one standing by, hook on, away it would fly into the top, and whoever owned it was at a loss for his bed when night came on. By the same method, when the pudings ware nearly done, before dinner, in the coppers, they would send a line from the fore top, and one hook on a large pudding, and up it would fly in an instant, and in less than five minutes it would be devored. When they piped to dinner, purhaps six in a mess come to look for there pudding, had nothing to eat, though if detected they would be punished. In the meantime the poor soldiers ware 6 men upon 4 mens allowance. When going for their peas at dinner, with a large bowl full, and the ship rolling, away they went into the see scuppers, and the peas gone for the whole mess. There was no pitty, but all hands laughing at each other. The seamen would go to the steward and get a bowlful of oatmeal and make a cake of it and bake it in the hot ashes till it was done and sell it to the poor fellows for six mens allowance of wine, which was three pints.

We landed those troops at Gibberalter and took in those that ware releived for England. Those men were old soldiers that had crossed the salt water before. Having a good passage, we arived at Spithead and landed the troops [14 December 1783].

We received orders to go into Portsmouth harbour. When winter came on, we struck yards and topmasts. Laying at our morings, we had then little to do excepting supplying the ship with beer and water and that feteague the boats crews had to undergo, towing the liters [lighters] backwards and forwards. The capt[ain] went to London and gave the command of the ship to the first leutenant, Mr. Rio [Edward Riou], a rail [real] tarter to a seamen. He made it his studdy to punish every man he could get holt of, and gloried

Lieutenant Edward Riou

in having the name of a villen and a terror to a seamen. The most frivelous fault, he would make them scrape the anchors in the coldest day in winter, and this was what they called the hard winter in England.[26] He would tie them up in the riging and gag them with a pump bolt till it frose in their mouths. He would muster the ships company on the gangways, quarter deck, and poop in the severest weather in winter. If he saw the least speck of dirt on your shirt in mustering, you was brought to the gangway and floged. The severer the weather, the more he would have all the lower deck ports up, that the wind should fly through the vessel to keep you in motion. There was scarcely a man in that ship but what was punished by him.

One night, he being late on shore, he came down to the beach and took a verry [wherry] to come on board, and he being rapped up in his great cloak, the waterman did not [k]now him. He asked him what ship he wished to go on b[oar]d of. Rio told him to go a long side the *Ganges*.

"And what do you want there?" said the waterman.

"I want to enter," said Rio.

"O, My God, do you want to be murdered? There is one Rio, first leutenant there, the bigest villen that ever God let live upon earth."

"Never mind," said Rio, "put me along side."

Captain Roger Curtis

"I am afraid if he sees us he will sink my boat. I cant go there."

"Go on," said Rio, "I wont be two minutes," and he koaxed him till he got near the ship, when the sentry hailed, "Keep off that boat," it being past nine o'clock.

"Go a long side," said Rio.

"I dare not, for that raskel will sink my boat and flog me in a minute."

Rio then answered, "Aya."

The sentry hailed no more. He run up the commedation lather [accommodation ladder] and went below, pull'd off his great cloak, and came upon deck. By this time the waterman came on the gangway, enquiring for the man that came on b[oar]d. He said he had not paid him for fetching him on board.

"What boat is that?" said Rio. "Where is the raskel that owns that boat? I'le flog the raskel."

"Sir," said the waterman, "I brought a man on b[oar]d, and he has not paid me."

"And dont you [k]now the fellow?"

"No, Sir."

"And dont you think that I am some thing like him?"

"O no, Sir."

"Did you not tell me I was the bigest villen in the world, and every thing that was bad, excepting a gentlemen?"

"Sir, I beg a thousand pardons, I did not [k]now it was you, Mr. Rio."

"Verry well, here is is a shilling for you, and go to my steward and get a bottle of rum. Then you may go on shore."

The waterman was surprised, after calling him every thing he could think of to his face, that he did not flog him, but Rio took a pride in hearing him giving his caracter. But a short time after, Rio was coming a cross the fields to the hard way in the night. He was atack'd by three sailors, and they got him down and cut his long hair off, close to the neck, though he was a strong, powerful man, but they did not hurt him any other way, but he could never discover who they ware that done it.

In the spring, our ship went to dock, refited, and was ordered to Spithead, being nearly three years in commission. Sir Roger Curtise got the command [16 May 1785], and Rio was prefered on b[oar]d of a nother ship.[27] The guard ships, which had been laying at Spithead for the summer, were now ordered into harbour, and those were the ships mentioned.

	Guns
The Duke	90
Golliah	74
Ganges	74
Le Pigasses [*Pegase*]	74
Edgur	74
Hector	74

Going in with a fresh breeze, the *Pigasses* struck aground in the narros nearly abrest of salleport [sally port].[28] We, being a stern of her, had scarcely room to pass her. As we got into the narrows abrest of hur, a squall took us, and carreing on all sail, laid hur down on hur beam ends, that she did not draw so much water. Runing close past the ship aground, the wind from the west, we run clear and run up to our morings at the hardway.

Having but little to do, laying as a guard ship, I belonged to a fast pulling pennice [pinnace], and the officers would send us to the Isle a White [Wight] and smuggle gin and brandy, as the custom house boats could never come up with us before we would reach the ship. Our docter being a close kind of a man, and not being well liked by the sailors, one of our boats crew was determan'd to play him a trick. The doctor made a practice of puting his brandy into medison jars, covered over with parchment with Latin letters on, to smugel on shore to his house. One day he gave us seven large jars to carry to his house. Going on shore with them, this fellow smelt a rat. Getting about half way, he sat down and opened the jar and swore it was the best medison he ever made use of, and then handed it round till it was nearly empty, and caried it home with the rest. The doctor, missing the liquor, complained to the commanding office on the quarter deck. They all burst out a laughing at the joke, and there was no more about it.

I was now near four years on b[oar]d the *Ganges* and often aply'd to the capt. for my discharge, but could not get it, when the *Sirius*, 28 gun frigate, came round from the Downs to Spithead, com[mande]d. by Capt. Hunter and Govener Phillips, bound to Botnay Bay with a fleet of a 11 sail of transports, the *Supply* Brig as a tender, full of men and wimen convicts and soldiers, with provisions and stoers. The Govener having the privilage of taking any men that turned out from the men of war, there was a great number turned out, but the capt[ai]n took his pick, all young men that were called seamen, 160 in number, no boys nor wimen allowed. Seven of us turned out, belonging to the boat from the *Ganges*. I had a mesmate that had been draughted on board the *Golliah* [*Goliath*]; hearing of my being on b[oar]d, he turned out and came on b[oar]d. I was put into the Governors barge.[29]

CHAPTER 4

The First Fleet

INTRODUCTION

I N rather casually volunteering for duty on HMS *Sirius* on 23 March 1787 and becoming part of Australia's First Fleet, Nagle embarked upon the adventure in his life that would have the most far-reaching historical importance of them all. Jacob Nagle's journal is a valuable addition to the literature documenting the voyage of the First Fleet and the early settlement period.

Captain Cook visited the shores of Australia in 1770, on his first voyage, extensively mapped the eastern coastline, and laid the groundwork for this permanent settlement seventeen years later. Actual European discovery, by Portuguese and Dutch explorers, had occurred well over a century earlier, but they had had no inclination to establish a permanent foothold in this very distant land.

It was the American Revolution that indirectly set the whole colonization scheme into motion. Until the humanitarian impulse of the end of the eighteenth century popularized the idea of enlightened penitentiaries for the reform of criminals, the British legal system had never had much use for jails. Prisons were places to lock up disturbers of the peace, debtors, or the dangerous accused until they were brought to trial and sentenced, but "gaols" were not viewed as places of punishment for convicted criminals, if for no other reason than that it cost too much to house and feed the inmates. When a lawbreaker was brought to justice, he was fined, humiliated in some fashion, whipped, or executed, depending on the seriousness of the crime. Or, for many capital offenses, from the early eighteenth century on, there was the alternative to execution of banishment—"transportation" beyond the realm.

The penal system was inexpensive and efficient, but it didn't discourage crime, and seemingly the easiest solution in the eyes of members of Parliament was to stiffen the penalties. Between 1688 and 1820, the number of capital offenses on the statute books rose from about fifty to over two hundred, but judges did not share Parliament's enthusiasm for the death penalty, choosing increasingly to resort to the alternative. Between 1770 and 1775, on average, 1,000 felons per year were transported to the American colonies, where they were sold as indentured servants and were rather quickly assimilated into the heterogeneous mainstream of colonial life.

The American Revolution closed this option, but the wheels of British justice rolled on, not only quickly filling inadequate local jails with sentenced felons awaiting transportation but also prison ships, first along the Thames, then at Plymouth and Portsmouth as well. The "hulks" were introduced in 1776 as a temporary expedient, but by 1786, after Nova Scotia, Central America, Africa, and various foreign countries had failed to emerge as alternative destinations for those sentenced to transportation, the ships were beginning to look disturbingly permanent, dangerous, and expensive.

What the government didn't know about Australia was probably more decisive than what it did in rushing the colonization scheme forward. In August 1786 the decision was made, and within less than a year the First Fleet was under sail. The destination was Botany Bay, which Captain Cook had described in glowing terms as a habitable site for settlement.

Historians of Australian beginnings have debated the motivation behind the colonization, one side arguing that it was a shortsighted decision made purely to solve an immediate criminal justice problem, the other suggesting larger imperial and strategic considerations. In a sense the argument is irrelevant. Once the program was set in motion, participants brought a wide range of purposes into the planning and execution of the enterprise. However unimaginative the governmental officials who authorized the expedition may have been, or even the several generations of bureaucrats who continued to think of New South Wales as nothing more than a dumping ground for Britain's unwanted, there was a form of optimism, a sense of a larger and higher purpose, that took hold of almost anyone who actually went out to the colony. But the 759 convicts had no choice as to whether or not to participate. The noncriminal participants in the First Fleet were all volunteers—marines, sailors, naval officers, transport personnel hired for the voyage, and a few civilian dependents—all of whom had made some sort of wilful, positive commitment to the voyage.

Many of the officers clearly viewed the expedition as an opportunity for career advancement and perhaps fame. Beginning with the Anson voyage of 1740–44, followed by those of Byron, Wallis and Carteret, Cook, and Phipps, the navy had been involved in what were primarily nonmilitary, scientific voyages of discovery. These expeditions had captivated the public imagination, very much as space exploration has excited a more jaded twentieth-century world. The inimitable Joseph Banks, scientific adviser of his era, who had been with Cook in Australia in 1770 and had been particularly high in his praise of Botany Bay as a place for settlement, encouraged the Australian proposal as an opportunity for further exploration and for the discovery of unknown botanical and biological life. The majority of the officers and the intelligentsia in Britain apparently viewed it in this light as well, and there would prove to be a sizable market for the handsomely printed, heavily illustrated journals of the expedition that were rushed into print by Governor Phillip, Captain Hunter, Dr. White, and others, before the colony was more than a year or two old and before some of the authors had even returned to Britain themselves. The participants clearly did not think of the First Fleet as simply boats loaded with prisoners and prison guards.

The positive vision of the entire enterprise, sustained even under the most difficult situations, can be traced in a large degree to Governor Arthur Phillip. A friend of his, Captain John Fortescue, was quoted in a 1791 letter as saying, "Upon my soul . . . I do think God Almighty made Phillips [sic] on purpose for the place, for never did man better know what to do, or with more determination to see it was done." Phillip came from a very humble background, was educated at the charity school at Greenwich Hospital, and was one of the relatively rare individuals to achieve the rank of captain in spite of having begun his life at sea at the very bottom, as cabin boy and seaman, before becoming a midshipman. Although he brought a broad range of talents and experiences with him when he accepted the Australian assignment—linguistic ability, command experience, familiarity with the waters of the South Atlantic, and close friendships in Brazil, where the First Fleet would visit for supplies and where he had served with considerable distinction in the 1770s in the Portuguese navy—his career in the British navy had been undistinguished and slow to develop. He seems to have been a very self-contained individual, unhappy in one brief marriage, and lacking the egotism of most heroic figures, to the degree that his historical reputation has been slighted. But he proved to be a brilliant choice for the Australian mission.

Governor Phillip devoted his whole being to the enterprise, personally overseeing the repair and equipment of the fleet, selecting the voluntary personnel, choosing the route of travel, selecting the site of settlement, and keeping an eye on every detail of the colony's first four years of existence. Considering the odds against the colony—lack of food, a potentially hostile native population, perhaps an even more potentially troublesome convict population within, a woeful scarcity of experienced agricultural workers who could make it self-sustaining, and a complete lack of reliable intelligence about the soil, the terrain, and the coastlines—it is remarkable that it survived at all.

The discouragements in these first years were enough to have easily provoked factionalism and revolt among his officers and the marines, but the enterprise did not fly apart at the seams because Phillip had that rare ability to exercise power firmly but judiciously. In the long run, his greatest contribution was to give the entire enterprise—and, in fact, Australian history from its very beginning—a sense of purpose far loftier than that envisioned by the officials who had authorized it. He envisioned Sydney not merely as the site of a better prison but as the beginnings of a great city, surrounded by productive agricultural land. His conception of Australia was that of an experiment in colonization, not a mere exercise in penal control, and his larger vision was picked up by the other participants. It permeates the diaries and letters that exist from this period, and the idealism survived beyond Phillip's administration to become a positive foundation of the Australian mentality. It did not have to be that way, and with a smaller man, of lesser talents and vision than Phillip, it might not have been.

The cabinet decision authorizing the Australian expedition was made on 18 August 1786, and within two weeks two naval vessels, HMS *Sirius*, 540 tons, 20 guns, and a crew capacity of 160, and HMS *Supply*, 8 guns and 55 men, were activated and the process of selecting crews and officers begun. The two naval vessels and several transports, for supplies and convicts, sailed to Portsmouth early in the new year, and from February until time of sailing, four months later, supplies were collected, ships put in top condition, and the convicts brought overland and by ship from Plymouth. A few additional crewmen were needed for both the *Sirius* and the *Supply*, and Phillip was given permission to accept volunteers from naval vessels in Portsmouth Harbor. Jacob Nagle was among them.

The First Fleet was made up of eleven vessels, the two navy ships and nine privately owned, contracted transports: *Alexander, Scarborough, Friendship, Prince of Wales, Charlotte, Lady Penryhn, Borrowdale, Fishburn,* and *Golden Grove.* Some of the transports were expected to return with cargoes of tea from China after unloading at Botany Bay. The combined tonnage of the entire fleet was slightly under 4,000 and the human cargo approximately 1,500 persons, about half convicts, half sailors, marines, officers, and a few family members and civilians.

The officers for the expedition, in addition to Governor Phillip, were Major Robert Ross, commander of the marines and lieutenant governor; John Hunter, captain of the *Sirius*; Lieutenant Henry Lidgbird Ball, commander of the *Supply*; Lieutenants Philip Gidley King, William Bradley, and George William Maxwell of the *Sirius*. Lieutenant John Shortland was naval agent for the fleet, in charge of the transport vessels, whose captains and seamen were not officially part of the navy or the colony itself.

The fleet followed a route carefully mapped out before sailing, first to Tenerife in the Canary Islands, which they reached on June 3, Rio de Janeiro at the end of August, and the Cape of Good Hope on October 13. Sailing from the Cape on November 11, the entire fleet reached Botany Bay between 18 and 20 January 1788 and Port Jackson on January 26.

Jacob Nagle was one of seven volunteers selected from the *Ganges* who entered on board the *Sirius* on 23 March 1787. He is not particularly informative about his reasons for volunteering, but it would appear that the decision was made with a former shipmate on the *Ganges*, Terence Burne, who had some time earlier transferred to the *Goliath*. Burne came on board the *Sirius* on March 25 and would be a close friend and messmate until he died on the long voyage home, five years later.

The discovery of the Jacob Nagle Journal is an event of considerable importance for the history of Australia's beginnings because it adds both detail and the previously unavailable perspective of the common sailor. Nagle records the fact that he had kept a journal at the time, but that it had been lost, very probably when the *Sirius* went on the rocks at Norfolk Island in 1790. The reminiscences we have here are clearly the products of his memory, and there are a few minor mistakes, a few chronological inconsistencies, which are noted in either the text or the footnotes. We do not know whether he reconstituted the written record soon after the events or only long afterward, but the vast majority of his facts are confirmable in other contemporary sources, and those that are not have the ring of authenticity about them. Nagle, with his gift for narrative and his unorthodox but effective style, has provided us with some of the most vivid pictures of the expedition that have survived.

Nagle was in a particularly fortunate position to observe the beginnings of Australian history because he was not only assigned to the flagship, HMS *Sirius*, but was also a member of Governor Phillip's boat crew. He was able to size up the commander firsthand, he had an unusual amount of contact with officers, and he was one of the select few who took part in the earliest explorations of Port Jackson and Broken Bay. He is the only participant to record in some detail the discovery and selection of Sydney as the site for permanent settlement.

Nagle was a sailor in every way, and he describes the experience through a seaman's eyes. He was a worker, not a decision maker. On shore in Rio he gets drunk and mugged; in Cape Town he jumps ship. In small ways, there is always an underdeck tone to the story as he tells it. One realizes, on reading the surviving record of the First Fleet, the extent to which news and talk circulated throughout the settlements at Sydney and Norfolk Island. Nagle's journal, like all the others, contains a fair amount of rumor and hearsay. The gossip that constantly circulated probably helped to keep the men's minds off their half-filled stomachs in the periods of hardship.

Nagle's journal is also particularly interesting in establishing a connection between an American and Australian settlement. He was but one of six Americans in the crew of the *Sirius* who went to Australia, three of whom listed their birthplace as Philadelphia. The two other Philadelphians left the ship on its first return visit for supplies to the Cape of Good Hope. James Procter of Boston was discharged on 7 March 1791, so that he could remain as a settler on Norfolk Island. John Rowley of Norfolk, Virginia, and John W. Harris, a midshipman from New York, completed the entire voyage. Jacob Nagle is the only American to have left a written record.

WE RECEIVED our wages, and the fleet being ready, we hove up our anchors and run to Sent. Helenah [St. Helens, Isle of Wight] and came to an anchor, the wind being from the westward, on the 10 of May 1787. On the 11th [*sic*, May 13], we got under way, the wind from the eastward, and run through the Neadles and put to see. Our ship being so deep loaded with stores, and having large buttocks, we could scarcely steer her until we got better aquainted with hur. We proceed on with a pleasent breese and a fair wind.

We had now on b[oar]d 160 able young men, before mentioned, picked out for the voige, Capt[ain] Hunter, Govener Phillips, Major Roose [Ross], Leut[enant] Govenor, and a number extra midshipmen going upon perferment, three leutenants, and other regular officers, beside the band of musick, and 3 wimen, but they belong'd to the band. The Govenor thought fit to put us into three watches, as it would be much comfortabler for the seamen.[1]

By the time we got about halfway to the island of Tennereef, our third leutenant having the fournoon watch upon deck, he call'd the boatswains mate to [k]now why both watches was not on deck, and call'd them all aft and ordered the boatswain's mate to thrash them all round, one by one, and told them he would soon have them to the south of the Line and he would then work their hides up.[2] When he begin to flog them, they made a great noise and out cry and begin to be verry rusty. The capt[ain] and Govenor hearing the noise upon deck, came up to see what was the matter. The ships company informed the capt[ain] of the treatment they received and told him if this was the usage they ware to have, it would be better to jump overboard at once than to be murdered in a foreign land. The capt[ain] gave Mr. Maxfield [*sic*, Maxwell] a severe setting down and desired the men to go below and the watch to go to their duty.

Capt[ain] went down to the Govenor and informed him of the behaviour of Mr. Maxfield [Maxwell]. The Govener ordered every officer on board the ship to appear in the cabin, even to a boatswains mate, and told them all if he new any officer to strike a man on board, he would brake him amediately.

He said, "Those men are all we have to depend upon, and if we abuse those men that we have to trust to, the convicts will rise and massecree us all. Those men are our support. We have a long and severe station to go through in settleing this collona, at least we cannot expect to return in less than five years. This ship and her crew is to protect and support the country, and if they are ill treated by their own officers, what support can you expect of them? They will be all dead, before the voige is half out, and who is to bring us back again?"

So he dismist them and would not allow any officer, boatswain, or his mates to carry a stick to strike any man with. In a few days after, in the morning, the hammocke were piped up, and a mishipman, Mr. Hornsby [sic, Ormsby], ordered the armorer's mate to carry his hammock up.[3] He said he could not directly, as he was doing a job for the capt[ain], but if he would wait a little, he would carry it up, but he would not wait, and struck him, and nocked one of his teeth out. The man went on the quarter deck to the Govenor and capt'n and maid his complaint.

The Govenor was very angrey, after giving such puncktual orders for any officer not to strike a man. Mr. Hornsby [Ormsby] was call'd up on the quarter deck. The Govenor repremanded him severly and told him he would break him if he ever atempted to give such another offince. He ordered all hands to be turned up on the quarter deck. He spoke to the midshipmen, one and all, and told them when he was midshipman they had to carry their own hammocks up on deck, and in lew of having a barber, they had to tie and dress one a nothers hair themselves, and he thought that they were no better than he was. He then turned to the ships company and told them if he found any man to carry up a midshipmans hammock or cot, he would amediately flog him.

In a few days after he discovered one of the men fetching one of the midshipmens hammock up and stowing it on the quarter deck. He call'd him and asked him whose hammock that was, [k]nowing it was not his own, being made of fine canvis. The man told him it belonged to a midshipman. He call'd the boatswain and ordered the hands to be turned up for punishment. He had him tied up and told the ships company that he was determened to flog every man that disobayed his orders, but as the capt[ain] and Mr. Bradley, first leutenant, plead hard for him, and being the first offence, he forgave him, but desired him not be guilty of such another offince, as he was determened not to look over it any more, and dismist them.

We hove in sight of the town of St. a Cruze, the island of Tennereef, on the east side on a bay of the same name (Long'd 16°26′W., Latt'd 28°27′N.). We entered and came to an anchor [3 June 1787] with the fleet for refreshment. We hoisted the barge out, and the Govenor went on shore. We all went up to a wine house and got some wine during the time the Govenor was gone, but he coming down sooner than we expected, the boats crew all run for the boat and left me pay for the wine. I gave the woman a guinea to change, and she gave me the change.

I made a spring for the dore, puting the change into a seal skin pouch and then into my pocket. The second spring was on the sil of the dore, where an old woman stood beging. The third spring I made I claped my hand into my pocket for fear of loosing my pouch, but it was gone. I was positive she had got it. I turned round and told the landlady I had lost my pouch. She took charge of the woman, as there was only three of us there in the house. I then run down to the warf, but the boat was gone on board. I then returned amediately to see after my pouch, having two guineas with change in it. The landlady had got hur into her beadroom and searched her and found the pouch in side of her shift aback of her neck. If she had not striped hur naked she would of not found it. She must of been a most dextorous hand in whiping it out of my pocket the second jump I made, when I had scarcely put it in. The landlady gave me the pouch with the full contents, and I went down to the boat, as they had returned again from the ship, and the Govenor excused my not being in the boat.

A few days after, one of the transports parted there cable and drifted to see, having no sails bent. The Govenor sent us in the barge to help hur in. She was full of wimen. We bent hur sails and brought hur to an anchor.

While laying here, the bumboats had the privilage of coming a long side the transport to sell their produce. The convicts got holt of the soldiers buttons and transform'd them into English shillings and sixpencies and passed a great quantity to the bum boats for their traffock before they discovered that it was bad money. They came to the Govenor and showed the coine, but he told them they must abide by the loss, as they ware people already condemned by their country for that trade, therefore they could not receive any satisfaction.

In about ten days, the fleet being refreshed and all complete, we put to see [10 June 1787] and made St. Jago, intending to put in for stock, but having light wind and calms, we drifted to the sotherd of the harbour. When the breeze sprung up, we stood on, making the Equ[atoria]l Line. We fell in with a small vessel that was bound to the coast of Africa. The master of the

*Governor
Arthur Phillip*

vessel informed us he had been drove a cross the Line seventeen times by headwinds during that passage. In passing St. Thomases, on the Line, we had heavy rains and sultry weather with heavy thunder and lightening.

When making Rio Janeiro [6 August 1787], we came to an anchor between the smal islands out side of the Sugar Loaf, and the Govenor sent in a boat to the Vice Roy, or Govenor, for admittance for the fleet to enter the harbour, which was granted. We then hove up and went into the harbour, the fleet all laying in side the large fort call'd the Castle of St. Cruze on the north side of the harbour. Govenor Phillips having been a commedore in the Portegees service, he was highly honoured by the Vice Roy, and the guards at the pallace always had to attend at the steps, at the landing of his barge, and attended to the pallace.[4] The prisoners ware supplied with boat loads of oranges and provisions on board every transport, beside laying in stores and provisions as was thought necessary for a long voige. There is a beautiful fountain in the pallace square that supplys both the town and shiping with exellent water. It is brought from a mountain laying south of the town. A great number make a living by carreing water for the inhabitance.

At this time no person was permitted to land without a purmit or a soldier with him. We had a sarjent to attend us, as a protection that no one should mislist us, but he would not walk about the town with us, as our curiosity led us to see it. He, finding we had money, wished to set in the punch houses all day. We acquainted the Govenor. We ware then permitted to go where we pleased without any guard, though they ware ordered to protect us where ever we should be insulted.

One evening two of us got into a grog shop, and he was a tailor likewise. He apeared to be verry much taken with us, and a verry hansome young woman being there who was verry farmilliar with me and asked me home with her, I excepted the offer and had walked one square, arm in arm, and my comerad following me, up came a Portegee with a great cloak on and pushed me away from her, but I would not let go my holt. He drew back and drew his sword and was raising his sword over his head to make a cut at my head. At that instant a soldier turned the corner, drew his sword, and guarded the blow he was going to make at me, and a nother soldier with him. The solders abused him and threatened to cut him down for medeling with me, but the fellow begged their pardons and said I had taken his wife from him. The soldiers sent him and hur about their business and told me she was a poota, which is a whore. I thought I was well off to be clear of them. We took the soldiers to a punch house and treated them for the service they had done me. We parted in good friendship and we went down to the pallace square to see if the boat was there, but the Govenor was gone on b[oar]d and left us behind. We then went into the market place, and we ware both purty well seized over, laid down on the benches, and fell a sleep. In the morning when I awoke, the Govenors barges cap that I wore was gone, my hankerchief off my neck, and what money I had about me was gone. The cap was silver mounted, with a large silver plate in the front with the Portegee coat of arms stamp'd on it, with Portegees letters or charictors on it. It happened well that I did not wake, or death would of been my portion as I understood by the Govenor afterwards.

In the morning Mr. King, second leut[enant], came on shore and took us on board. The commanding officer enquired of the Govenor what was to be done with us, expecting we would be ordered into irons. When he was inform'd that we ware on b[oar]d, he said he was glad to hear we ware alive and desired we should be sent to our hammocks to get a sleep, as we would be wanted in the barge at 9 o'clock.

The Govenor often landed in different parts of the town, round about the skirts, because he did not wish to trouble the gauards, but land where we would, we could see the soldiers runing to wherever we landed and parade under an arest for him. He landed on a small island abrest the town where was once a gold mine, but now a dock yard for the navy with store houses and magizeens and fortified all round. There is another island farther off to the north with a hospittle, which the Inglish hired for their sick, and two more island to the east of the town, though small, is fortified and soldiers kept in them at all times. We lay here six weeks to refresh the prisoners, soldiers, and seamen and repair our riging. We then put to see again [4 September 1787] with a pleasent and prosperous breeze, stearing for the Cape of Good Hope.

On our passage, one of the seamen, having a piece of beef towing over board, in the evening a devil fish came and laid holt of it, and having a harpoon on board, it was hove into him. We slung him and hoisted him in with the yard and stay tacles. He was allowed to way upwards of eight hundred weight. Some of the seamen tried how he would eat, but it did not prove palatable.[5] On the passage one of the men struck a flying fish with the granes [grains][6] that measured 18 inches from one tip of the wing to the other, which was the largest that any man ever had seen on board the vessel.

On this passage to the Cape of Good Hope, the prisoners on b[oar]d one of the transports [*Alexander*] made an attempt to rise and take the ship, but being detected, they ware brought on board of us [6 October 1787]. The

Govener tied them up and gave them a severe floging and then sent them back to their respective ship in irons, which made them submissive during the voige.

At length [14 October 1787] we arived and entered into Table (Cape Town Capital stands on the W. side of Table Bay, Long. 18°23'E., Lat'd 33°56'S. To the SE of the town are the vineyards which yield the Constantia wine, the castle on the east, Amsterdam Fort on the w[est]. Table Mountain comes with a decent to the town; The Shugar Loaf and Lions Rump is on the point west of the town close to the see shore) Bay to refresh, take in water, and more provisions, and stock, and plants for Botnay Bay. We took in 6 cows, 2 bulls, one horse, and a number of sheep, goats, and poltry. In six weeks the fleet put to see [13 November 1787] with a pleasent breeze, standing to the S.E.

It might be worth mentioning that while at Rio Janaro, in a strong gale of wind a pigeon was blown off from the shore and lit on b[oar]d of us. We cut his wings and let him run on the quarter deck, and when at the Cape of Good Hope, laying in Table Bay in a strong S E wind, an other pigeon was blown off and lit on the cat head and purmitted hurself to be taken; cut hur wings and put it with the other. They hapened to be a pair, he and she. When their wings grew, they would take a flight from the ship in the wide ocion but would return to the ship again, and by those two pigeons all the bread [breed] sprung from on Norfolk Island, which was numerous when I left it. The Leut[enant] Governor had pigeon houses built for them, but they would visit and go on board the rack [wreck] of the ship dayly, looking for food.

On our passage between the Cape and the south end of Vandemons Land, we had the trade winds and pleasent weather. When we got about half way on the passage, the Govenor thought fit to devide the fleet into two devisions, some of the fleet being dull sailors. The *Lady Pennereen,* that was full of wimen, would have all sail set with steering sails set a low and aloft as long as she was able to carry them without carriing hur mast or yards away, while our ship, the *Serious,* would have our topsails lowerd down upon the cap. Therefore the Govenor took all the best sailing ships, which was about one half, and went on board the *Supply* Brig [25 November 1787], and left Capt[ain] Hunter with the remainder of the fleet, expecting they would arive in Botnay Bay along time before us and be ready to receive us at our arival.[7] They maid all sail and was soon out of sight, we proseeding after them as fast as possible till we got round the south end of Vandemans Land. We then lost the trade winds.

We then had to stand to the north of the east side of the island for Botnay Bay, which lays in Long'd 151°28′E., Latt'd 33°50′S. We ware struck with a sudent white squall in the middle of the day [11 January 1788] which laid us down upon our beam ends. Taking in sail, she rightined. The main topmast staysail being hall'd down, I run up to pass a gasket round the sail. I gumped on it to ride it down. The wind blew so powerful it blew me off like a feather, but ketching one of the leastings of the foresail that blew out, it brought me upright, and I fell with my backside on the bit head without being hurt. The officers seeing me fall, from the quarter deck, came runing forward, expecting I was kill'd, but recovering myself, I run up the lee riging and furled the sail. Every ship in the fleet received some damage in that squall.

We arived in Botney Bay about the latter part of January as near as I can recollect [21 January 1787], as I lost my journal. We ware eight month on the passage from the day we left Spithead in England till we arived in Botnay Bay or there abouts.

When we entered the bay, the Govener and his squadron had only arived twenty four hours before us, though they ware all the best sailing ships.[8] The next morning, all the ships laying at a single anchor, we out boats and went on shore with the Govenor and a number of officers. We landed on the south side of the bay, where we found a fine run of water. We begin to clear out the run, being full of leaves and lims of old trees. I, getting into a deep hole, I hall'd up a spunge from the bottom bigger than my head, which I gave to the doctor [Dr. John White]. The natives came down to us and apeared as though they did not aprove of our viset. When we ware going on board, the Govenor attempted to be very friendly with them, but they came with spear in hand and a bark shield. When we ware all in the boats excepting Capt[ain] Ball, they begin to be mischievous with him, but he took one of their shields and set it up against an old stump of a tree and fired one of his pistols at it, which frightened them when they heard the report, but much more when they saw the ball went through the shield, which cooled their passion.[9] We went on b[oar]d.

The Govenor wished to see Port Jackson before any improvement was made in Botnay Bay. Three boats was got ready with three days provisions to go round to Port Jackson, a number of officers, and sum marines. In the morning [22 January 1788] we started, it being about five leagues by water, but we found afterwards it was not more than 5 or 6 miles across by land.

We arived in the afternoon and run up Middle Harbour to the westward

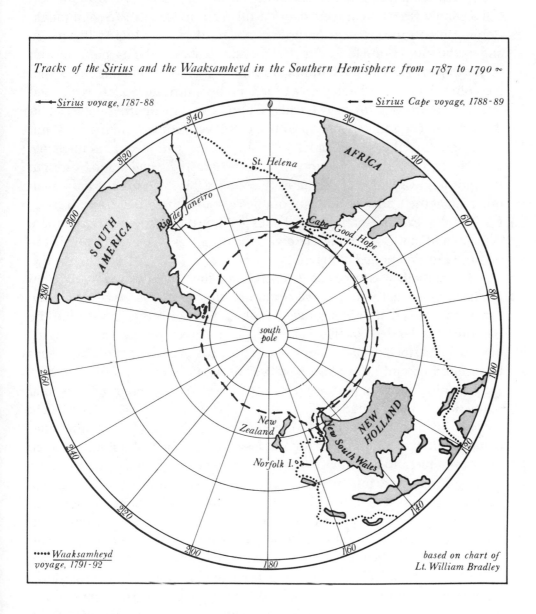

Tracks of the _Sirius_ and the _Waaksamheyd_ in the Southern Hemisphere from 1787 to 1790 ～

◄— _Sirius_ voyage, 1787-88   ◄- - _Sirius_ Cape voyage, 1788-89

••••• _Waaksamheyd_
voyage, 1791-92

based on chart of
Lt. William Bradley

and then a sircular round to a bay on the north side, which Govenor Phillips call'd Manly Bay, and survey'd round till we came into the S.W. branch. Coming into the heads of the harbour on the north side is a high clift of rocks, and on the south side a low point, but rocks, and abreast the harbours mouth on the opposite side of the harbour is a high clift of rocks and flat on the top. It coming on dark, we landed on a beach on the south side and there pitched our tents for the night. This was call'd Camp Cove. The marines were put on there posts. The sailors were variously employed, some kindling fires and some shooting the seen [seine] for fish, others getting out utentiels for cooking. By the time we got our suppers, was late in the night, and by four in the morning we had every thing in the boats again, and on our oars, with one man at the lead sounding out of one cove into the other, Capt. Hunter, Mr. Bradley [sic, not present on this expedition], and the master taking a draught and of the soundings, likewise the distances. We eat our breekfasts on our seats and pulled all day.

The harbour was large and extensive, and the Govenor anxious to get to the head of the harbour, but we could not, but we got as far as where the town is now, called Sidney Cove, about 7 miles from the entrance of the harbour. We landed on the west side of the cove. A long shore was all bushes, but a small distance at the head of the cove was level, and large trees but scattering, and no under wood worth mentioning, and a run of fresh water runing down into the center of the cove. The Govenor, officers, and seamen went up to see it.

I being boat keeper, I had to remain in the boat. I hove my line over, being about 4 or 5 fathom water along side of the rocks. I hal'd up a large black brim [bream] and hove it into the stern sheets of the boat. The Govenor coming down, verry much pleased with this cove and a situation for a town, he was determined to settle in this cove. Coming into the barge, he observed the fish I had ketched and asked who had caught that fish. I inform'd him that I had. "Recollect," said he, "that you are the first white man that ever caught a fish in Sidney Cove where the town is to be built."

We could not remain longer than three days for the want of provisions. Therefore we returned the next morning to Botnay Bay. The next day [26 January 1788] the fleet got under way and sailed to Port Jackson, which lies in Lattitude 33°50'S., Longitude 151°28'E., and run up to Sidney Cove. The *Sirius* Frigate came to an anchor in the stream abreast the cove, but the transports and *Supply* Brig run in to the cove. There was a small island in the stream, a sollid rock about 5 or 6 hundred yards from us, which was

Port Jackson, 1788

afterwards called Pinchgut Island by two prisoners being condemed to remain on it upon bread and water in double irons and no boat allowed to land on it excepting from the Govenor (this was for the killing a goat belong to the minister).

The troops landed and pitched there tents, and convicts to clear away the ground. The Govenor had a frame canvas house brought from England, and that was set up on the east side of the run of fresh water at the head of the cove, and the Leut[enant] Govenor, Major Ross, officers, and troops encamped on the west side of the run of water. In the center, the men and wimen were incamped on the west side, but the wimen by themselves, and sentries placed through all the camp, likewise a guard on the Govenors side. Eight of us that belonged to the Goveners barge pitched our tent by the water side on a rock near the landing place and the boat in view. The convicts ware amediately employed in cutting down timber and clearing to build log houses for the officers and soldiers on the west side, and fencing in ground, and the wimen employed carreing the stones away into the corners of the fences.

We ware then employed [28 January 1788] with the Govenor, survey-ing the remainder of the harbour, and a boat from the ship with Capt[ain] Hunter and Mister Bradley, leut[enant], beside soldier officers and Dr. White, head serjint.[10] We landed on a point on the south side of the river about 3 miles above the town, which was call'd Point no Point, to cook dinner. We had a large iron pot on the fier boiling some fish, when one of the natives came in his bark canoo and landed. The Govenor gave him a small looking glass. He admired it equal to a monkey. He would look in it and put his hand to the back of it to feel the person he saw. He then came to us, and looking wishfully at the fish that was boiling up in the boiling water, and signefied to me that he wanted some of them, I made a motion to him to take them. He very readily put his hand into the boiling water to take out the fish, but to his great astonishment he gumped, he run, he hollowed, and away to his cannoo, put his hand into the water, then paddle. It is impossable to describe the anticks he cut. We laughing, the Govenor was surprised, and enquiring what we had done to him, I informed him, which made them laugh as hearty as we did. He paddel'd off and left us.

We finishing our meal, we proceeded up the river till we came to the flats, which is shoal water, about or near a mile to the head of it. The Govener made a settlement at the head of it, call'd Rose Hill.[11] From the entrance of the harbour to Rose Hill was call'd fourteen miles, and Sidney Cove about half way. In that distance it contains coves and branches all the way up to the head of the river, both on the north and south sides. In my belief I should suppose Port Jackson to hold nearly all the ships in England.

When we ware not employed with the Govenor, he would send us a fishing with a seene or hooks and lines for the use of goverment, which would be sheared out. After the Govenor and officers, the fish would be served out to soldiers and prisoners in rotation. Our customary method was to leave Sidney Cove about four a'clock in the after noon and go down the harbour and fish all night from one cove to another. We have made twenty three halls of the seene in one night and not ketch as many as would fill a bucket, and other times, in one or two halls, falling in with schools, that would be sufficient to fill our stern sheets. We then would make a fier on the beach, cook our supper, and take our grog, lay down in the sand before the fire, wet or dry, and go to sleep till morning, though we would be often disturbed by the natives heaving there spears at us at a distance, and being in the night, it would be by random. In the morning we would return, take the fish to the Goveners house, where they would be sheared out as far as they would go.

Jacob Nagle's Will,
Sydney, 29 May 1788

In the Name of God Amen I Jacob Nagle Seaman belonging to His Majesty's Ship Sirius, Captain Arthur Phillip Commander Number on the Books, 177, being in bodily Health, and of sound and disposing Mind and Memory, and considering the Perils and Dangers of the Seas and other Uncertainties of this transitory Life I do for avoiding controversies after my decease I make, publish and declare this my last Will and Testament in manner following, that is to say First I recommend my Soul to God that gave it, and my Body I commit to the Earth or Sea, as it shall please God to Order, and as for and concerning all my worldly Estate: I give bequeath and dispose thereof as followeth, that is to say All such

Wages, Sum and Sums of Money, Lands, Tenements, Goods, Chattels and Estate whatsoever, as shall be any ways due owing, or belonging unto me at the time of my decease I do give devise and bequeath the same unto My beloved Friend Terence Burne Seaman Onboard His Majesty's said Ship

And I do hereby nominate and appoint the said Terence Burne my sole

Executor of this my last Will and Testament, hereby revoking all former and other Wills, Testaments and Deeds of Gifts, by me at any time heretofore made. And I do ordain and ratify these Presents, to stand and be for and as my last Will and Testament Revokable for me & in my Name In Witness whereof to this my said Will, I have set my Hand & Seal in

Port Jackson New South Wales the Twenty Ninth Day of May in the Year of our Lord One Thousand Seven Hundred and Eighty Eight And in the Twenty Eight Year of the Reign of His Majesty King George the Third over Great Britain &c.

Signed sealed, published and
declared in the presence of

Jacob Nagel

J. Hunter 2d Capt.

W. Keltie Master

*Native Australian Sketched by
Captain Hunter*

On one of these excurcions, one night shooting the seen [seine] at the head of Middle Harbour, as we supposed, and shifting a long a rising sandy beach towards the north side, we found a narrow entrance, and going over the bank of sand, we discovered an other branch runing to the westward, full of coves, though we ware as far as this beach when surveying with the Govenor but did not discover the entrance of this branch. When we return'd, we inform'd the Govenor, and he came down, and it was survayed likewise.

All this time they ware building storehouses for the provisions and stores that was brought out for the use of the country. The provision store house for the soldiers and prisoners was on the west side near the Leut[enant] Govenors house, and the officers and soldiers had their log houses built forming a street. As soon as they ware ready, the store ships begin to discharge. When they ware discharged and refited, they sailed for different parts of India.

The *Sirius*, having the stock on b[oar]d, laying at the entrance of the cove, we landed the cattle on the east side, being a flat point, and all the other stock that was for the settlement. While laying in the stream, the natives would come a long side in their bark cannoose with amazement, and putting there hands on the ships side with wondering surprize to think what it could be made of.

Whatever excurcions we went on with the Govenor, he endeavoured to naturelize them, and giving them clothing and trinkets, and would not purmit them to be mislisted by any means, though he run many risks of his life by them. When we would be shooting the seen and came a cross a school of fish, and the natives see us, they would come down with spear in hand and take what fish they thought fit until we could get them into the boat and push off. The Govenor would not allow us arms to defend ourselves, for fear we would kill them in our own defence, but informing the Govenor of the risk we run by the natives both day and night, he sent his orderly sargent with us as a protection.

A few days after we had been robed of our fish, we ware shooting the sean in a larg cove opposite to the cove that we had been robed of our fish. One of the natives came over in his bark cannoo and scemed verry friendly. We new him to be one of them that robed us on the other side. The sargent had put his gun up against one of the trees with the catrige box hanging to the gun and took a walk up the woods. I took a catrige out of the box and poured it into his hand. He admir'd the grains of powder, and having a stick of fier in the other hand, which they generally carry with them, I motioned to him to put the fire to it, which he did, but the flame, smoke, and the powder flying in his face and the burning of his hand, he gave a spring and a hollow that I never saw equeled and run to his cannoo and put off, sum times padling with one hand and then the other until he got to the other side. The laughter and noise alarmed the sargent, and wanted to [k]now what was the matter, but we did not tell him till some time afterwards.

The begining of this settlement we ware put on short allowance, six men upon four, as provisions would be short, and not [k]nowing when a fleet would arive from England. The Govenor had a lighter built for carrying timber from up or down the river and fetching shells for lime, and sand, or whatever might be wanting for building. When we ware not otherwise employed with the Govenor, we had to tow the lighter up and down the harbour and load hur with timber, beside a boat which was built, pulling 16 ores, with shoulder of mutton sails, to go a surveying. Therefore eight of us had three boats to take care of, and employed acasionaly in all of them.

We went in this boat and two 6 oard cutters with the Govenor to Broken Bay (Broken Bay form'd by Hawksbury River Long'd 151°27'E., Latt'd 33°34'S.) which is call'd 16 miles by water.[12] We pulled 16 oars, beside the coxswain, and rrom [room] for about 10 sitters with provisions and water. The Govenor, officers, and marines in each boat, having no wind, we had to

North Arm of Broken Bay

pull all the way. Ariving there, we surveyed the beaches, took the distences and the soundings in both branches and purticulary where the barr lies across from the island on the south side a cross to the main on the north side. In the south west branch we landed on a small island with lofty trees and no under wood, but like a grass plat, but it was so numerous with smal birds call'd parrekeets that we could scarcely hear when we spoke to each other. We saw some very large fox bats.

A considerable way from the heads, on the S.E. side, we discovered shelves of rocks over each other in a small cove, of a considerable highth, three of them, each of them about 12 feet in highth from each other, beside the rock on the surface of the ground on top, and a strong run of fresh water decending from one shelf to the other and so on till it came down into the salt water.[13] On every shelf it was entierly flat, and by the constant run and fall of the water from every shelf, the rocks was wore away in the form of a bason on every shelf. As that remained full, it run off to the other. I suppose it to be about 60 feet from the top to the surface of the salt water at the bottom, whire is an iron minneral spring, and on the top entierly level.

In the N.W. branch we landed on the west side of the harbour, where the river that was called Hoksburry [Hawkesbury] River enters into the bay. Here we dined, but first shot the seene. We ketched the largest mullet I ever saw at this place. Dinner being ready, they turned too. Doc'r White said to the Govener, "I am amazing fond of those mullet." The Govener, being in a jokus youmer, answered him, "So I purceive, for you have eat six of them as you say, and we must allow that the least of them weigh three pound, and by calculation, the whole must weigh eighteen pounds," which created a deal of sport and deversion among the officers and likewise the seamen and soldiers. Though we ware not dining with the Govenor and officers, we ware all in one cluster, that whatever passed was heard by the whole.

When dinner was over we pulled a short distance up Hoksburry River, and it was observed that when the flods came down this river, that it must rise to a great highth, as we could see large timber laying in the crutches of large trees about 36 feet from the surface of the ground, which would be dangerous to settle on the lower ground upon the account of those flods.[14] We ware about ten days surveying this harbour and then returned to Port Jackson. Likewise, we surveyed Botney Bay (Botnay Bay, Long'd 151°21'E., Lattitude 34°0'S.) until we could go no higher up the creek with our boats, which was not above a mile from the head of the bay. There is a numerous kind of beautiful small birds, white cockatoos with yellow top nots and black ones, some swans, curloos, the eagle, falkon, bustards, patridges, etc. The Govenors hunter shot a bird with short wings which he only flutters with. He stood seven feet when upright on his feet. They can run faster that a horse or a hound. He was call'd a cassowary. There is pillicans, and ducks, and

Mullet

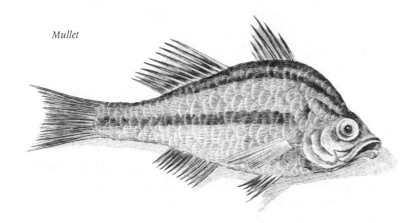

"The Kangooroo"

Cassowary

different kinds of animals, but the kangoroo is the chief. They leap on the hind legs which is very long and supported by a strong tail. There fore feet is quite short. The she have a fals belly, which the young go into when in danger. They leap 20 or 30 feet at a leap. Some have been shot of two hundred weight. The native dogs are of a fox colour but larger, though I never heard one bark. Their tail is rather bushey.

The natives here are the most miserable on the see coast I ever saw in any island. They have some huts of bark, but when the w[eathe]r is cole [cold], they go over to the weather side of the harbour in there bark cannoos and get into the caves or hollow rocks. They always carry fier with them to make a fier at the entrance or otherwise in the middle of the cave. Their chief living is on fish. I have seen them have a yellow root, but it was so noicious and slimey that I could not bear it in my mouth. We have seen them when we would hall in the sean take up a fish and put their hand behind their back with it, and we pretending not to see it, they would turn round and walk away and still keep their hand behind them in full vew to us all looking at them. We observed they all wanted one tooth and a joint of the little finger. They have a hole through the grissel of their nose which they can put a bone or small stick through, lighking to a spritsail yard. There is some of them tall, but slender bone and ill made. The men have bushey beards and large mouths but good teeth. If they ketch fish, they stick the guts in their hair. They make their lines of the stuf that grows round the beach cabage tree, which is very strong. There fish hooks is made of shells in the shape of a new moon and fastened to the line. They can heave a spear 4 or 5 hundred yards. They have clubs pointed at both ends and a hole in the middle to hold by, with a bark shild on the arm for close quarters.

We ware down in Manly Bay with the Govener [24 August 1788], three boats of us, and laying off from the beach, we saw an action between two parties. The one as we supposed was from the interior. They fought on the rising ground nearly in front of us as we lay in our boats. They fought spear in hand with great dexterity for nearly an hour, when the interior party apeared to gane the victory, the others having to retreat, with there wimen and children screaching and hollowing at a dreadful rate till they ware out of hearing, and we returned to town.[15] It was always the Govenors studdy to cultivate and naturelize those natives as much as posseble. We had a girl [Abaroo], the Govenor clothed and kept hur at the hospittal with Doctor White, as he wished to get an insight of the language.[16]

By this time the fleet that came out with us ware all gone. It would not be amis to mention, while the fleet was laying in the cove, the capt[ains] of these transports had ventures and liquor to dispose of. One of the convicts [James Daly] by some means got a half guinea, and filing it up with some other mettal, brought it to one of the capt[ains] to barter for liquor and other articles, and told him he could find more gold dust when oppertunity served. It was amediately rumord that gold dust was found, and it came to the Govenors ears. He must either tell where he found it or be punished. He said he would show them. The boats ware ordered to be ready, and down the harbour they went [24 August 1788], but he could not find any. He was brought back and made to confess the truth, and when all was found out, he got a severe floging for making fools of the public.[17]

The Kings Birthday was drawing on. The *Supply* Brig was sent out to some of the islands for turkle [turtle] and return with some which was sheared out as far as it would go. Two of the prisoners, before mentioned on Pinch Gut Island, was forgiven and taken off by the Govener. About this time the cattle we brought with us were all missing in one night, and not to be found, though a search was made upon all directions, but we learnt afterwards, in the year 92 they ware found runing wild and greatly increased through the interior.[18]

Three boats of us ware ordered to be ready [25 November 1790] to go down the harbour with the Govenor, Dr. White, Capt. Johnson, and a number of other officers, armed, the Govenor intending to take some of the heads of the natives to natrolize them. We went down and landed in Manly Bay. The natives came to us, and we ware very friendly, and the Govenor apointed the two that ware to be seized and put into the boat. One was called Bennelong, the others name [Colbey] I do not recollet, the two head warriers of the tribe. When the signal was given by the Govenor, the boats crews seized them and carried them into the boats in an instant. The spears begin to fly, the officers and sum marines firing upon them, but loosing their chiefs, they ware verry resolute, but retreating in the bushes, they hove their spears at random, and Capt. Johnson kept up so steady and quick a fier upon them that we got off with both the warriers and brought them both to town. The Govenor kept them both in his house till he had a small house built on Cattle Point on the east side of the cove. They ware both sent to England afterwards, and one died on the passage, and the other returned again.[19]

In one of these excurcions the Govenor had nearly lost his life on the North Branch. A spear that was hove from the natives went through his right breast and came out behind [7 September 1790]. The doctor not having materials with him to stop the blod, he dare not take the spear out, but cut it off, and it remained in him till we pulled the boat to Sidney Cove with all our might. The Govener bore it with the greates patience, and as the docter rought according to his directions, he made his will and settled his affairs, not expecting to live, while we ware pulling him up in the boat. As soon as we arived, the doct'r drew the spear out of his body and stoped the blod. Though it was unexpected, the Govenor recovered.[20]

The natives now begin to be troubalsom. Being down the harbour in the six oard cutter, when pushing off from the shore, a number of spears, one went through the coxswains right arm. I was standing a long side the foremast. A spear struck the side of the mast and it slanted off, or it would of went through my body. The coxswain recovered of his wound. The natives

Bennelong

ware now so troublesome that we ware allow'd a musket in the boat, as we ware constantly up and down the harbour. The Govenor's two storey stone house was built by one of the convicts, which I beleive he received his liberty for his labour and good behaviour.

The collony being short of provisions, and no certainty of any ships ariving from England, the *Sirius* begin to fit out for the Cape of Good Hope. As soon as she was ready for see, we had to go on board.

We sailed [2 October 1788] to the sotherd and eastward, round Cape Horn, having fine weather. One day we ware surprised to see land, as we supposed. The whole ships crew came on deck to view it. The capt[ain] and first leut[enant] brought their charts on deck and over halled them; could not find any land near us by the charts or their reconing. We did not apear to be more and [than] 3 or fore miles off, and we ware standing right for it. The lead was ordered to be hove, but no bottom. We could see the surf roling on the beach, the trees, and hills, in some places like yellow clay, other plases brush and woods and farther in the interiour apeared to be high mountains, and while gazing at it by all hands, it begin to vanish away and proved to be Cape Flyaway.

One night, before we made the Cape, our third leut[enant] having the watch, Mr. Maxwell, which was heretofore mentioned, having a stiff quarterly breeze, he begin to set all sail that he could crowd, and at 12 o'clock when the watch was call'd up, begin to set the steeringsails, though the wind was freshening and blowing harder, till the ship lay down sufficient to heave the capt[ain] out of his cot on the cabin flore. The capt[ain] got on deck in his shirt and begin to take in sail as fast as posseble till she was under snug sail. He asked Mr. Maxwell what he was doing. He told the capt[ain] he would "tip all nines to see weather the *Siriuses* could riger again for a set of dam'd raskels." The capt[ain] finding he was delarious, ordered a nother officer in his watch.[21]

We made the Island of Terrelde Fuego, the sothermost part of South America, Long't 69°14'W., Latt'd 56°S. The island was covered with ice and snow. We kept our Chrismas going round the Horn. We passed 37 islands of ice during the passage round, besides flat ice, which is the most dangerous in the night. We had nearly run into a large field of ice, but bearing up before the wind for several hours, we clear'd it. The whale was so numerous at one time that we could not count them, and with there spouting they often wet us on deck.

Going round the Horn this passage, the ships company was taken with the scurvey till we had but 13 in the watch with the carpenters crew. I was caried below three times in one night, but I done my duty the next day. Some died in sight of the Cape of Good Hope, or Table Bay. The wind being scant, and we could not fetch into Table Bay, we fetched into Pinquin Island [Penguin or Robben Island] and came to an anchor [2 January 1789]. The docter went to town and braught a quantity of fruit on board to be served out to both sick and well, for even those that were doing there duty, when biteing an aple, pare, or peach, the blod would run out of our mouth from our gums with the scurvey. The next day we run up to Table Bay and mored ship. By Capt[ain] Hunters orders and at the assistance of the docter, we ware supplyed with the best of provisions the Cape could afford. Mutton and vigatebles was the most suitable for the scurvey, and the capt[ain] allow'd us to send for as much wine as we thought fit to make use of, the ships company recovering daily, till we were all well and harty. We shiped hands in lew of those that died in the passage.

I belonged to the large cutter which went dayly for water, commanded by a midshipman, and when going on shore, he would take the liberty to thrash us whenever he thought proper, which we new was not allowed by the Govenor or Capt[ain] Hunter. One day going on shore for water, he begin upon the whole boats crew with his ratan with out any provecation whatever, and being a striplin not more than 15 years of age, I told him we would not be treated in such a manner by a boy. When we got on shore, five of us out of six left the boat, not intending to return any more. The other four never did return.[22]

One Lewis was with me, and walking through the town, we agreed to stick to each other if attacted by any officers. We had not walked a square, on the corner of a nother street we fell in with one of our masters mates, Mr. Brien [Bryant], but the moment Lewis saw him, he darted away frome me like a dog. Mr. Brien stoped, and I stoped. He asked me if I was not going on board. I told him, "No, Sir." He having his side arms, I was upon my guard. He told me the capt[ain] had sent for me to come on board particularly, "and your mesmate that you have been with so many years is now on shore looking for you," and advised me to go down to the warf. In the mean time he steping towards me, I stood on my guard. He purceived that I ment to defend myself. He told me he had no intention to strive to force me, but hoped I would go and see my mesmate [Terence Burne]. I told him I would. I went down and found him. He was glad to see me and told me the capt[ain] had sent word by officers and men to tell me to come on board, and "Now I hope you wont leave me."

While on the warf, an officer that had been on shore, did not [k]now that I had left the ship, asked me if I would go up to the market and by him sum garden stuff, as he could not go himself. I told him I would, and he gave me money. While I was gone, down came Mr. Brien and asked if I had been there. The officer told him he had sent me to market to by sum garden stuff for him. Mr. Brien call'd my mesmate and sent him after me, telling the other that I had been away 10 days, and if he comes a cross that raskel that was with him, he will purswade him away and your money two. I was about half way down when I met my mesmate. He laughed and said Mr. Brien expected you was gone. We came down and delivered what I went for and gave him his change. He said he expected I was gone. I told him I would not of took his money if I ment to stay behind.

We went on board; the capt[ain] was on deck. He asked me what reasons we had for leaving the ship. I inform'd him of the whole. "No wonder, Mr. Bradley, loosing our men, when our young officers gives them such abuse against my orders." He confined him to his cabbin for three weeks and told me to go to my hammock and get some rest.

We took in our cargo and stock and put to see again [20 February 1789]. We had not gott round the Cape before a N.W. gale came on and blew a most tremendious and a mountanious see, that we could not scud, though we had as fair a wind as could blow, all sails being furled except three foul weather staysails. Laying two for 21 days, the wind begin to ceace a little. We got her before the wind, which caried us into the trades, we then having pleasent w[eathe]r till we came to the south end of Vandemons Land.

The capt[ain] thinking to give a wide birth to the five Sunken Rocks, we got nearer the land, and a gale coming on from the sotherd, till we ware under a reefed fore course in the night, and so dark you could scarcely [k]now the next man to you, the see flying over us and the pumps going, though she did not leak, and the hatches battened down, but the look out forrod cried out "Land a head." We then had to ware ship and stand to the westward. In about an hour there was land a head again. We then had just room to ware again. Though dark it was, we could then see the surf beating over the rocks, and apeared higher than our mast heads. We found now that we ware imbayed, and a heavy gale, and a heavy see rolling in upon us, and nothing but high clifts of rocke under our lee. The capt[ain] ordered close reef topsails to be set and loosed the mainsail and set it. He said she must carry it, or capsise, or carry a way the masts, or go on the rocks. The men at the lee pumps were standing to their nees in water and every man in his station. If she had not had a spar deck upon hur, she could not of caried the sail without filling hur gun deck, the see flying over us under such a press of sail, standing on, expecting every moment the masts to go over the side, and I dont suppose their was a living soul on b[oar]d that expected to see daylight.

(About half an hour before day light) she struck upon the reef, a sand bank that run as good as two miles to windward of us. She lay motionless for the space of two or three minutes when a most tremendious see struck hur under the quarter and hove hur over the reef and a way she went in full sail and smooth water, the reef keeping the heavy see off. We carried a way our fore top gallant mast and split the uper part of hur stem and lost the figure head. At day light it fell calm, and the ship lay two streaks to port, or on the left side, our backstays and riging all carreeing away, with the sails flaping to the mast, they ware so strained by the gale. We turned too to righten the ship by putting as much flower as we could on the opposite side between decks; spliced the riging. Through Gods assistance, we ware saved, where we had no hopes but in him.[23]

In a few days after we got into Port Jackson [9 May 1789]. There was great rejoiceing for our arival, as they were very short of provisions and supposed our ship to be lost. We sent the cargo of flower on shore and put in to store. Our third leut[enant], Mr. Makwell [Maxwell], got so raving that he was sent to the hospittel under the care of the docters. Our ship now lay in the entrance of the cove.

About this time, there was a discovery made of the provision store being robed. There was eight of the prime soldiers and best caractors in the rigment laid a plot and had a key made by one of the blacksmiths, a convict, by the means of making stiff clay morter and taking the key out of the dore when oppertunity served and having the mold of it. The convict made it, and when one of them was sentry in the night, the rest would come and rob the store of liquor and what provisions they thought fit, and the settlement upon short allowance, till one night by opening the dore, the key broke and left the piece in the lock. The provisions being served out once a week to the prisoners, which was on Saturday, when the store keeper came to open the dore he could not enter the key. He gave information, and the lock was taken off, and the peace found in the lock. By that means it was discovered the store was robed. The storekeeper had often suspected, but could not be certan, as there was always sentries at the dore, night and day.

The alarme was given, and one of them being sentry at the Leut[enan]t Govenors dore, and expected it would be discovered, he sent into the Leut[enant] Govenor and informed him he had something of importance to relate to him; he suspecting what it was, and had him relieved. He discovered the whole affair and gave their names to the Govener as a Kings Evidence. He informed him, one night before they had a frollick and got drunk; one of them having a falling out with the rest, he said he would discover; they beat him; that he died in a couple of days, and when buried, they went to his grave with a kag of liquor, in the night, and sat on the grave, and stuck a bayonet in to the grave, and renewed their oath not to discover. By this John Hunt turning Kings Evidence, they were all tried, condemed, and hung, though there was great application made to the Govenor to save some of them, but he said if he saved one he must forgive all, and that was out of his power, to do justice to his country.[24]

Some time after this, one of the wimen [Ann Davis] stole some wet clothes, and was condemned and hung [23 November 1789]. She strove to bring a free man in guilty that belonged to our ship that was on duty on shore, it being proved by a number of witnesses that he was innocent and new nothing of it. Other wise she might of been saved, as the Govenor left it to Capt[ain] Hunter, but he would not for give her, and when brought to the

Australian Convicts

gallos, leading her by two wimen, she was so much intocsicated in liquor that she could not stand without holding her up. It was dreadful to see hur going to aternity out of this world in such a senceless, shocking manner.[25]

We took the ship down to Elbow Cove [19 June 1789], about two miles from Sidney Cove on the north side, to refit the ship for see service. We cut down timber and made a frame along side the rocks and filled it up with rocks, then leveled with earth. The ship could lay a long side the warf in five fathom water. We discharged everything out of her and put 28 riders into hur, which made hur as strong as wood, iron, and copper bolts could make hur.

While laying in Elbow Cove refitting, Mr. Hill, a masters mate and a fine officer, undertook to walk up to town [ca. 6 November 1789] on the north side without any arms excepting a small dirk as side arms and was missing. It was supposed sum natives from the interiour had came a cross him and taken him with them or killed him. When he was first missed, we supposed him to be lost, and fired guns, but never had any account of him.[26] Likewise our sail maker [Peter White] went a hunting and lost himself [12 July 1789]. We fired minute guns three days, but he had got round the head of the branches that he could not find the way back. He could hear the guns, but when coming to the branches of the rivers he could go no farther. He lived on the birds he killed. He had strayed away north of Manley Bay. The Govenor, Capt[ain] Hunter, and a number of other officers being on an excursion to Broken Bay by land, on there return hearing a gun fired, which he often did, they expected some one was lost and firing in return, they fell in with him and brought him to Manly Bay, where we ware apointed to meet the Govener on that certain day with the boats. They new then what the guns was fired for, and we ware amazed to see the sail maker with them, but he looked bad and distressed. We took them in and returned.[27]

The ship being refited, we returned to Sidney Cove [7 November 1789], where the *Supply* Brig lay. Our third leut[enant], Mr. Maxwell, before mentioned, was put into a house in the hospittle garden, and a man to atend him, being leunatick, received a draught from England to the amount of 70 guineas, and in his fits he got holt of a how [hoe] and buried them singly all over the garden, saying he would have a good crop of guineas the next year.[28] When the docter discovered what he had don, they endeavoured to find them, but the garden being dug, they could not find one third of them.

One of the convicts, a Negro [John Caesar], was guilty of several crimes. At last he got holt of a musquet and amunition and run away into the woods [ca. 24 December 1789]. It was dangerous to strive to take him, being both ignorant and verry powerful and strong. However he was at last taken [30 January 1790] and put in double irons and tried for his life and condem'd. But the Govenor talking with him and enquiring what he thought would become of him when he had to die, he laughed and seemed to rejoice, saying he would go to his own country and see his friends. The Govenor could not think of hanging such an ignorand creature and pardoned him.[29]

CHAPTER 5

Around the World

INTRODUCTION

S T R A N G E as it may seem, the infant settlement at Sydney Cove was not two months old before it embarked upon a colonizing effort of its own on Norfolk Island, more than 1,000 miles east of the Australian mainland and some 700 miles NNW of yet unsettled New Zealand.

The lush but uninhabited island, particularly notable for its majestic Norfolk pines, had been discovered, named, and briefly explored by Captain Cook in 1774. Cook had the misleading good fortune to visit on one of the rare days in the year when the wind was not churning up waves that normally break dangerously across a coral reef surrounding the island on all sides, obscuring the few channels that make safe landing possible. Cook noted rich vegetation, including what he thought were vast quantities of natural flax, abundant fresh water, and plentiful fish along the shores. To British officials, towering pines gave them visions of a much-needed supply of masts and spars, and flax suggested a source for cordage; thus, when instructions were drawn up for Governor Phillip in 1786, the occupation of Norfolk Island was included as a high priority.

Lieutenant Philip King was assigned by Phillip to establish a British foothold, and King and twenty-two colonists, fifteen of them convicts, embarked on the *Supply* on 15 February 1788. Along the route they discovered and named Lord Howe's Island and Ball's Pyramid, both mentioned by Nagle, and after some difficulties in getting close enough to the island to disembark, the entire party came ashore on 6 March 1788. Captain Cook's vision of the island as a fruitful source of naval supplies would never materialize—the pine proved to be too brittle for masts, the natural "flax," not flax at all and unsuitable for rope—but the soil was rich and the land healthy, and gardening and fishing gave greater promise of self-sufficiency in the first two years than was the case at the larger settlement on the Australian mainland. The *Supply* shuttled back and forth between 1788 and early 1790, bringing some supplies, new convicts, and marines to Norfolk Island and taking back what were prematurely optimistic reports from Lieutenant King.

Since the initial landing in January 1788, the *Sirius* had made the one expedition for supplies to the Cape of Good Hope described in the last chapter, but food was becoming again dangerously short by early 1790. Neither gardening nor fishing had been sufficiently productive at Port Jackson, and no new vessels had arrived from England. Governor Phillip decided to send a third of the convicts, with two companies of marines, from Sydney to Norfolk Island and then intended to dispatch the *Supply* directly to the Cape again for supplies and the *Sirius* to England by way of China. It was a desperate gamble that did not pay off. The *Sirius,* with Nagle aboard, and the *Supply* left Port Jackson on March 6. On the 19th, while off the Norfolk Island shore, awaiting favorable conditions for landing supplies, the *Sirius* was caught by a sudden shift in wind and tide and was swept onto the reef. The colonies lost their one sizable vessel, Norfolk Island inherited not only the convicts and the marines but some eighty crewmen from the *Sirius* to feed, and the plans for resupply from the Cape and communication with England were rendered too dangerous to attempt with only one seaworthy ship left.

The annals of almost every colonial settlement, true at Jamestown and at Plymouth in America a century and a half before, include a "starving time," and the Australian and Norfolk Island settlements faced their bleakest prospects between March and June 1790. On the island, the "mount pitters" or "mutton birds," the capture of which Nagle describes in such vivid detail, made the difference between survival and starvation.

Jacob Nagle's account of life on Norfolk Island in this trying period is exceptionally valuable. Major Ross was a difficult man to get along with, and a degree of ill will developed between the lieutenant governor and Captain Hunter. This actually worked to the advantage of Nagle and his fellow sailors by providing them a greater degree of freedom than was enjoyed by the regular colonists. Governor Phillip was something of a puritan at heart, but on Norfolk Island, from the beginning, it was acceptable practice for officers and men to take convict mistresses. Nagle describes "Irish Town," where the crew of the *Sirius* set up a temporary community of their own, keeping house with their female companions.

At Port Jackson, relief of a dubious nature arrived in June with the appearance of the *Justinian,* a supply vessel directly from England, and three shiploads of new convicts in the *Neptune, Surprise,* and *Scarborough.* This Second Fleet is notorious in Australian history. The masters of the vessels withheld foodstuffs from the convicts in order to sell them at profit on their arrival, contributing to the death of 273 and sickness of 486 of a total of 1,038 on board. For the existing colony, though, it provided sufficient supplies to get them through until harvesttime and ended the most discouraging period of Australia's early history.

The *Surprise* and *Justinian* arrived at Norfolk Island in August 1790 with much-needed supplies, and on February 12 the *Supply,* having sailed to Batavia and returned with a rented Dutch ship, the *Waaksamheyd,* picked up the majority of the crew of the *Sirius* and brought them back to Port Jackson, from which they reembarked for England in the Dutch vessel on 27 March 1791. In spite of the hardships, a majority of Nagle's shipmates would have preferred to have stayed behind, attracted presumably by the promise of the land, others by new friendships and ties of affection with new "wives" and children. Nagle was not among them. He was a sailor through and through, and he was by now incapable of staying in any one place for more than a year or two without dreaming of new expeditions and new adventures.

The return trip of the *Waaksamheyd,* which took slightly over a full year to complete, had all the excitement Nagle could have wished for. Up to this time, the eastern portions of the Pacific Ocean had remained relatively unknown and infrequently visited by English navigators. The Spanish went to great lengths to protect the western coast of South America from foreign intrusion, and they conducted their own trade with Asia through Central America and Mexico to Manila, establishing no regular trade routes or important ports south of Lima. The Portuguese and Dutch had established trading outposts in the Spice Islands and Asian mainland in the late sixteenth and early seventeenth centuries, which the British East India Company made rather vain attempts to compete with, but in all these cases, the approach was from west to east, around the Cape of Good Hope to India and Southeast Asia. When the *Waaksamheyd* set sail from Port Jackson in 1791, the crew had little more to guide them than the charts of Captain Cook and other mid-eighteenth-century English explorers, the accounts of the return trips of the transports in 1789, a Dutch sea captain who trusted his very fallible judgment more than navigational instruments, Captain Hunter's knowledge of the experiences of the *Supply* on its voyage to Batavia the previous year, and the luck of the prevailing winds and tides.

On the route out to Australia, the First Fleet had traveled from west to east, taking advantage of the prevailing winds of that direction in the Southern Hemisphere. The same winds did not favor the *Waaksamheyd* on the return voyage. An intended stopover at Norfolk Island proved to be impossible after three weeks' effort, and the ship pursued a meandering, east-to-west course through the Solomon Islands, the straits between New Britain and New Ireland, northwest to the coast of Mindanao in the Philippines, and then south through the Makassar Straits separating Borneo and Celebes to Batavia, present-day Djakarta, on the western end of Java. The vessel was repaired and resupplied, the Dutch captain and crew put ashore. Unfortunately, the British crew became infected with what apparently was a deadly form of malaria that had recently decimated the town. Most of the ship's personnel sickened and several of Nagle's shipmates died, including his close friend Terence Burne. From Batavia, the *Waaksamheyd* sailed through the straits separating Java and Sumatra, then through largely open seas to Cape Town, St. Helena, and back to England, where they docked at Portsmouth on 22 April 1792.

Nagle is selective in what he tells us of the long homeward journey. He does not record every landfall, is a little confused in his sense of direction, and entirely off on many of the longitudes and latitudes, which he copied from an early-nineteenth-century edition of Brookes' or Darby's gazetteer (where they are also incorrectly printed). Captain Hunter, Lieutenant Bradley, and Lieutenant Daniel Southwell kept records of the voyage that are more reliable and better informed than Nagle's, but his account provides the particularly interesting contrast of the sailor's versus the officers' impressions of the experiences they endured.

Captain Detmar Smith of the *Waaksamheyd* was obviously a "character." Hunter and Bradley found him stubborn and difficult, and they were both glad to get rid of him at Batavia. Lieutenant Southwell described him as "inhuman," "savage," and "barbarous," and blamed him entirely for the fights with the natives. Nagle, on the other hand, found Smith somewhat amusing and credits the Dutch captain and his Malay mistress with saving the lives of the crew. Nagle, who speaks of "tame Malays" as if they were a form of wild animal and notes that the Duke of York Islanders "are rather smaller than the general run of natives," was a cultural bigot, but it is likely that his attitudes and impressions more nearly represent that of the majority of the crew than their more educated and open-minded officers.

Although Nagle never returned to its shores except in his memory, Norfolk Island deserves a postscript. The colony that Nagle had been a part of survived until 1814, when the remaining convicts were transported to Australia. Between 1825 and 1856, the island was reoccupied, this time as a high-security prison for the most hopeless criminals of Britain and Australia. Substantial stone structures were constructed, some of which survive as public buildings and tourist attractions today. When the prison was finally closed, the island was resettled by inhabitants of Pitcairn Island, descendants of the *Bounty* mutineers, who established a whaling industry modeled after that of New Bedford, Massachusetts. Their descendants remain as the decreasing percentage of "old settlers" on Norfolk Island, which now depends largely on tourism from Australia and New Zealand for its economic well-being. The "mount pitters" are long gone, although they remain on Lord Howe's Island, and the forests of stately Norfolk pines that Nagle saw are reduced to small stands of smaller trees. Two of the cannons of the *Sirius*, which Nagle undoubtedly helped personally to retrieve, remain, facing the site of the wreck that made him a resident of this beautiful island for a brief period in his life.

WE WARE now taking in water and got ready to take in prisoners for Norfolk Island, though I must here make mention the Govenor had sent the *Supply* Brig to Norfolk and landed 16 men with Mr. King, our second leut[enant], as Leut[enant] Govenor and the *Supply* returned. While there, one of the midshipmen going on shore in the jolly boat, he atempted to sail through the surf, and that with a rudder. The men told him the danger, but being head strong, he and the four men were drownded and enter'd the whirl pool through the stoborness of one lad not more than 15 or 16 years of age.[1]

Having men and wimen prisoners on b[oar]d, with provision, and Leut[enant] Govenor Ross, we sailed in company with the *Supply* Brig about the begining of March 1790. We sailed for Norfolk Island. Going out of the heads, we had a narrow escape of loosing our ship on the rocks, being light winds, and a heavy swell setting in for the rocks, but a little more wind springing up, we got out safe to see.[2]

On our passage we fel in with a small island that had not been discovered, which was call'd Lord Hows [Howe's] Island. On the S.W. side is a small sandy bay, very hansom for landing. On the east end is a rocky mount, but the remainder level and hansom grass plats. The island I suppose is about 10 or 12 miles round. The *Supply* Brig left some men and an officer with provisions and water to explore the island and search for water till hur return, but none being found on it, they ware taken off at the east end of the island.[3] At a considerable distance from the island is a rock growing out of the see [Ball's Pyramid] in the form of a monument and to a great highth and ending at the top with a peak, is almost as regular as though it had been built, and with the dung of the see fowl it apears entierly white. There is no possibillity of acending to the top of it.

Having a pleasent breeze, we arived at Norfolk Island about the 18 of March 1790 [*sic,* March 13]. Lay too and out boats and sent the Leut[enant] Govener and his troops, all the men and wimen convicts on shore, the bagage remaining on board.[4] We continuing to lay off and on, as there is no anchorage, being nothing but curl [coral] rock. Laying two all night, and having a strong current that we ware not aware of setting us to the south, at day light we could scarcely see the island off deck. In shore the current is verry strong, runing six hours to the west and three to the east. We making all sail, and the current shifting, we ware up with the island by a leven o'clock in the day and sent the boats on shore with bagage.

Having a fine pleasant day [19 March 1790], with a light breeze off shore, all the seamen that could muster hoks and lines was ketching groopers, not thinking of any danger. At 12 o clock, when thinking of going to dinner, Capt[ain] Ball of the *Supply* Brig hailed us and informed Capt[ain] Hunter that we ware two close in, the swell of the surf having holt of us though it did not brake. Capt[ain] Ball, being at a distance out side of us, purseived it sooner than we did. Immediately we made sail that we could set,

Sirius *and* Supply *at Sydney Bay, Norfolk Island, 23 August 1790*

and a light breeze off shore, but it all availed nothing. The swell was stronger than the wind, and the swell still driving us in, we let go an anchor, thinking to warp out, but the curl [coral] roks cut the cable the first and second time we struck. (About half past twelve P.M. on the 19th of March, 1790, we struck on the rock.)

We opened the main hatch and sounded the well, found four foot water in hur hold. We ware then about ³/₄ of a mile from the shore and as the rocks cut hur bottom, the ballace and pig ballice fell out, and the heavey surf roling aboard of us, still drove hur further in, but before the swell broke, we got a boat along side and sent Capt[ain] Cooks time peace and two wimen, one being pregnant, on shore. They ware wives to two of the musicioners. They got safe on shore. The capt[ain] then ordered the masts to be cut away. By cutting the lanyards of the larboard riging, and the surf roling a board of us, the masts all went together a long side. When the wimen on shore saw the mast go, they set up such cries and shrieks and hollowing that the Govenor had to send soldiers to drive them off the beach and compel them to remain in their huts. By this time the surf roled heavy against us, but having a spar deck, it sheltered us.

The capt[ain] gave orders to open the after hatchway and stave all the liquor that could be got at to prevent the seamen from getting drunk. We began to secure our clothing in our chests and lash them well with cords and hove them overboard, thinking the surf would take them on shore, but being a strong currant setting to the westward, they either drove to see or into the whirlpool, so we lost all, only what we stood in.

We then got a harsor on shore by heaving a cask overboard with a small line made fast, then a haser with the heart of the fore sty [stay] on it, and a halling line both on shore and aboard to hall it backwards and forwards, with a grating slung to it to sit on. By that means the capt[ain] and sum men and officers got on shore, or to the reef, which is a good distance from the shore, and from thence the boats took them on shore. The harser was made fast to a large pine tree and houve tought by our capstain, and on the reef was made a triangle with our fier booms that went on shore to keep the harser as high as posseble on the reef. Four men could sit on the grating at one time, but when they ware halling them to the reef, they would be under water a considerable time, when the surf was roling in over them to a great highth.

Mr. Bradley, first leutenant, and a number of us more remained on b[oar]d all night, under the spar deck, the surf roling on board so heavy during the night that we expected she would go to pieces before morning, and she did so in hur bottom, which drove hur nearer the shore and slewed hur round, with hur head to the eastward. But her upper works was as strong as wood, iron, and copper bolts could make a ship, being well fitted in England for the setelment in the country. We put 28 rider into her of the country oak, copper bolted, in Port Jackson, which saved us, or otherwise nothing could resist so tremendious a surf as there is round that island. The lanyards of the starbourd riging being cut, the masts and sails drifted on shore, and on the 20th, the remainder of us and leutenant went on shore.

We ware then fully employed cutting trees down to build a barraks for men and officers to live in, some employed preserving the sails and riging that drifted on shore, and others thatching the barraks with rushes. We ware now as near as I could understand about 700 on the island, sailors, soldiers, and men and wimen convicts, including the officers.[5] Some of our officers returned to Sidney in the *Supply* brig to inform the Govenor of our misfortune.

The Govenor, not [k]nowing what time a fleet would arive from England, sent the *Supply* Brig away to Betavia to take up a vessel and load hur with rice for the colloney.[6] In Sidney they ware 6 upon 4 as usual, but ours was quite different. Leut[enant] Govenor Ross was a merciless commander to either free man or prisoner. He laid us under three different laws: the seamen ware still under the naval laws, the soldiers under the millitary laws, beside the sivel laws and a marchal law of his own directions, with strict orders to be attended to for the smallest crime whatever or neglect of duty.

We ware now ordered to get on board the *Sireus,* as many as could, to save all the provisions we could. There was thirteen of the best swimers and a masters mate got on b[oar]d. When the tide was half ebb, the men could work on the reefe, and we on b[oar]d would send it on shore to them by harser and hawling lines. We cut away the stern to make a port to sling the casks, and when the flod tide begin to rise on the reef, they had to leave it and go on shore in the boats. We on b[oar]d then had to get the casks out of the hold upon the gun deck, and those in the hole, up to there neks in the water, both night and day, so we had no rest. By the time the tide had ebbed on the reef so that they could stand to receive the casks, we had to send them on shore and then endeavour to get at all we could for the nex tide, both night and day, during our labour, to save all the provisions we could.

The harser was carried away. Whenever we hove a cask over board with a line to go on shore, the current would heave it out to see or into the whirlpool, and we laying so far off, the Govenor and Capt[ain] Hunter could not let us [k]now what we ware to do. Therefore the officer concluded that Wm. Hunter and myself should toss up to [k]now which should atempt to carry a letter on shore to Capt[ain] Hunter, as we ware allowed to be the two best swimers, and it fell to my lot. The letter was put into a quart bottle and slung under my arm. I had the end of the dipsey line, which I was to take on shore if I could. I went down the stern lattur, and as there is always three following seas, or surfs, I waited for the first heavy surf and then followed it. I swam with all my might, when the next see rolled over me. I found the line was foul of the curl [coral] rock. I hung by it a conderable time. I new the danger I was in, the current very strong, setting in for the whirlpool, which was not more than 400 yards farther to the westward. The Govenor and capt[ain] was on the beach, present. They ordered a coble to be lanched, but

Captain John Hunter

no sooner than she was lanched into the surf, she was stove to pieces and the men hove on the reef. They ordered a larger coble to be launched. I was holding on at this time. They hallowed out from the ship to me to let go the line. When I found the line could not be cleared, I let go and swam with all my strength and got on the reef before the second boat got over the reef.

They carried me over to the Govenor and capt[ain]. I broke the bottle and gave him the letter. He appeared to be much surprised and said he never saw a man swim with so much power and strength as I had done. I told them I knew the danger and had great reason for it. "But now," said the capt[ain], after reading the letter, "the difficulty is to [k]now, how we can let them [k]now how to act?" I told him I would carry a letter on board. He said he thought I had run a great risk of my life already and wanted to [k]now how I ment to get on board. I told him I would go away to windward and go through the surf and come down with the current to the ship. I receiv'd a letter in a bottle, and slung it, and went about a quarter of a mile to windward, and a number with me to see me get through the surf. I waded in till I see a heavy surf coming and dived under and held on till it was past, then swam on and dived under the second, till I got in the swell where it did not brake. I hove myself on my back, and the current took me down very quick, the men on board standing ready to heave ropes with boling nots [bowline knots] to me, and hall'd me up.

In delivering the letter we found we could do nothing till slack water excepting hoisting up provisions, till slack water. We got another harser on shore and continued to send all the provisions on shore that we could get at. The bread was all spoilt with the salt water. I think it was about 14 days we ware employed on b[oar]d and then left hur, though we that could swim often went on b[oar]d by leave of the capt[ain] and get copper off hur bottom to make kettles, as we had lost all our pots, likewise small tom-mehocks, which was brought out for the natives, proved useful to us to cut down cabbige tree. Hur bottom breaking out, and the surf beating her in, she got so near the reef that we could wade to hur bows at low water. In about 5 or 6 month we got hur guns out, all excepting one that fell overboard when first castaway. They ware all put in a tear (tier) alongside of the flag staff.

Our ships company not being satisfied living in the barraks that we had built, they begin building huts near the beach, which was call'd Irish Town, and the most of them had wimen to live with them, and everyday they had to produce a bundel of rushes to the overseer as their days work, for thatching of houses.[7]

We ware one day employed in cutting sum trees down upon the ridge of the hill near the town, each one cutting a tree, and I was at one of the lowermus. When my tree was about two thirds through, the third tree from me fell and hit the other and they both fell against mine. I did not [k]now which way to run, but I run a few stepts, when I was nocked down senceless. The men coming to my assistance, they draged me out from under the tree, dead by all appearence, and carried me to town to the doctors. They cut my stocking jacket off, which I had on, and bled me in different places, which brought me two. One lim had struck me a cross the shoulders and another broke my jawbone and bruised in different places, but as God protects us, one large lim broke off and entered the ground 4 or 5 feet, which kept the body of the tree from me by 2 or [3] feet which saved me from being mashed in the ground, but thank God I recovered in about 6 or 8 weeks.

The Govenor and capt[ain] though[t] it best to cultivate and make gardens, and the prisoners cleared a large piece of ground on the side of the hill, next to the town, was sowed with wheat, and the gardens with what seed could be got. The ground is rich and black soil. We ware put upon a pound and a half of flower and a pound and half of bran, mixed together, and a few ounces of meat for seven day, but in six weeke the meat was gone. But good water from Mount Pit runs to the eastward past the town on the south side, and a nother branch on the north side, forming a beautiful

Mount Pitter or Mutton Bird

caskade or fall of water from the level of the ground, down a considerable highth to the beach and runs into the ocion. The powder that we saved from the ship was buried for safety, as there was no use for powder on the island.

When we first landed, the gannetts, a see foul, appearingly as big as a goose, would come open mouthed at you, but distroying a good many, they lef the island. But the princible see bird that resorted and bread on the island was call'd mount-piters and mutton birds. The mount pitters were about the size of a pigeon but fuller in the body, with a hawk bill and webb footed. They bread in the vallies at Mount Pit, the ground being entierly underminded by them. Every evening, over head like the chimley birds, with a great chattering, as soon as dusk, they drop to the ground and look for their holes. These birds, seemingly as God would have it, was the saving of us, as it was the chief living we had while they lasted, beside the wild mountain cabbage tree that growed on the island.

Our method of living while we could forage was thus: we would first get pine nots, which was plentiful, and split the pine for torches, one small one to seek the birds with when on the Mount, and one large one to bring us home with. We would go out in the afternoon and reach the Mount by dusk, I suppose about 4 or 5 miles up hills and down steep vallies, having the trees marked all the way. If we once got out of the foot path and the marks of the trees on our return, we would have to remain all night. When we arived at the Mount, we would nock up a fier and wait till the birds begin to fall. There would be sailors, soldiers, and convicts, to the amount of 50 or 60 of a night. By calculation there would not be less than 12 or 14 hundred destroyed of a night. When they begin to drop, we would go down into the valles, and the more we hollowed "ho, ho, ho," the birds would come runing, crying out "ke, ke, ke," thinking it was their mate or their young, and by that means every man would take home what he thought sufficient in his knapsack, which would be from 20 to 30 at least if not more. When completed, every man would light his torch and set out homwards, all in a line, as the path was small, and in this season of the year was heavy rains. By the time we got to the town, would be about 11 or 12 o'clock at night, all wet and muddy. Coming down the hill, it was equal to a lumenation, 40 or 50 torches all in rotation, one after the other, until we decended to the foot of the hill into the town and disapeared.

In respect of the mutton birds, they ware rather smaller than the mount pitters. They breed all over the island, having holes under ground. The method we had to ketch them was with a hoe and a sharp pointed stick. When we found a hole, hollow out "ke, ke, ke," and if the old ones were there or the young when hatched, they would answer you, crying out in the same manner and runing to the entrance of the hole, and if you missed ketching holt of him, he will run back again. Then, the way the sound of him was, you run the sharp stick down into the ground, it being like a soft mold, and clap your mouth to the hole and hollow, he will answer, and so on. By that means you will dig over him, and the ground being soft, it falls in and stops his holes up. You then ketch him.[8]

There was but few land birds on the island eccepting quail, a few parots, parrokeets that fed on the wild red peper, and some wild pigeons of the same colour as our tame pigeons, but we reduced them a great deal before we left the island. We never found any kind of wild beasts on the island, snakes, or todes, or any thing that was venemous during the time we ware on the island. The wood that groes on the island is in general pine, and they grow to a mazen highth and thickness. One tree was found, though but short, the top being blown off and sprouted out again and hollow, which missured 25 fathom round, which is 150 feet round. We ware a considerable time employed in cutting down trees and sawing them for masts and spars for shiping, but we found they ware not serviceable, as it was white pine, brickel and worm eaten, but useful for building houses. There is a good deal of faron tree, which is good to feed hogs, and great quantity of mountain cabbage tree, but when we left the island it was very scarce. There was fields of wild

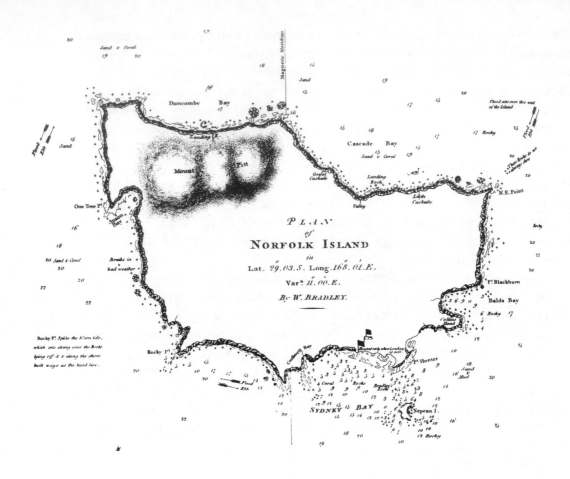

rushes that growed in the vallies that was supposed would make excelent
flax, as some was manufactured and sent to England.[9]

The first farm that was culivated was in a valley near the town called
Arthurs Vale. They found some wild benanoes on it and expected they
would turn out well by cultivation. We had two cobels built by our carpen-
tors to go out a fishing when the weather would purmit. The groopers was
plentiful at the west end of the island, but the misfortune was we could not
go out through the surfe unless it was a very calm day and without wind.
Sometimes it would be five or six weeks that we could not attempt to go out,
and when we did, the moment a breeze sprung up on that side of the island,
the flag would be hoisted, which was to come in amediately, or otherwise
the surf would rise so quick and high that it would be unpossble to come in,
and then we would have to go round the island on the lee side, which would

be verry dangerous. It was remarkable, the grain that was sowed when in the blade was chiefly destryed in one night with a blast of wind that came from the see. The grain was covered with a catepiller which eat the blade up. Though all the wimen were employed to pick them off, it availed nothing. They ware so numerous that we did not get the quantity that was sowed.

About this time the Govenor issued out orders that no man dare kill a bird at Mount Pit, unless a punishment, though he had a convict which he sent dayle to the mount for birds who discoverd one of our seamen that had killed two or three, and Govenor Ross punished him with two dozen. Through his tyranicale behaviour, Capt[ain] Hunter and him did not agree while on the island. He would not allow the soldiers or convicts to go a forigin and wished the capt[ain] to prevent us likewise, but as the Govenor claped sentries on the roads which led round the island, that no one could go any where without a pass, the capt[ain] ordered Mr. Bradley to give the seamen a pass whenever they call'd upon him for one. At this present time one of the convicts was fishing on the rocks, was taken off by the surf, and drownded. The Govenor then applyed to Capt[ain] Hunter to prevent the seamen from fishing a long shore. He told him his men were like spaniel dogs—if they fell in they would crawl out again, and he did not wish his men to starve while there was any thing to be got by foreging round the island.

On one evening 4 of us was sitting in my hut. We ware all mesmates and considering the situation we ware in at that present time. I think it was of a Thursday evening. On the next Saturday our last provisions was to be served out, which was but one half barrel of flower, to be served out amongst 700 souls. The birds ware destroyed, the cabbage tree likewise all gone, and as for fish, it was very uncertain, and even then, when we could go out and ketch fish and brought them in it would not supply one quarter of the number. We allowed our selves to be in a reched situation.

The next morning at day light, which was on Friday [Saturday, 7 August 1790] as near as I can recollect, I walked out on the beach a back of my hut. I cast my eyes around on the ocion, and then, to the westward of the island, I discovered a ship close under the island, coming down along shore, pasing the S.W. point. My heart leaped within me. I run for the flagstaff, where I new Mr. Bradley would always be at daylight.

I hollowed out, "Sail ho! Sail ho!"

I coming up to Mr. Bradley, "Where is she?"

"Coming round S.W. Point."

By this time she apeared, coming down under easy sail. We then

Justinian *and* Surprise *Arriving at Norfolk Island, 23 August 1790*

discovered a second sail in the offin. By this time the whole town was alarmed. We amediately launched two boats, being fine weather and little wind, and went out to them. They proved to be from Sidney Cove, with supplies of provisions and some convict wimen. We boarded the ship that I first saw along shore. She was call'd the *Surprise,* which was as such to us. The capt[ain], understanding our sittuation, treated us extreamly well, gave us a hearty meal and some grog. The other ships name was the *Julean* [*sic, Justinian*]. We then took in sume beef and went on shore.

We continud discharging as fast as posseble, the convicts standing ready to receive the boats when landing upon the account of the surf doing ingory or staving the boats. We launched all the boats we could muster and among the rest the large cutter belonging to the ship that I been in from the time we left England with the Govenor. Mr. Bradley took me out of hur at this time and put me into a new coble to assist in stearing her through the surf. We all went out, loaded the boats, and had some wimen, three in our boat, and two and an infant in the large cutter. By the time we returned, the surf had ris considerable. The large cutter being a head of us, we lay aback of the surf, waiting for hur to get in, but the surf fill'd the cutter and stove hur all to pieces. One of the seamen, William Hunter, got holt of the woman and child in hur arms and got them on shore safe. Six seamen, one woman, were drownded, boat and five went into the whirlpool. Two quartermasters was got on shore and buried on the island. What was surprising, those two men, petty officers and good seamen, always dreaded being in a boat.[10] Our coble came in the next three following surfs after them and came in safe, though the surf had risen considerably.

The next I was put into a yawl, 5 ores, being small and low on the water. She was not fitting for a surf, but necesaty required it. Coming in with 4 casks of beef, the stearsman run hur on a rock that lay in the middle of the chanel, going stern on, and she being a Dutch bilt boat and very strong, it did not ingure hur. We all jumped out for fear of the following surf. We swam to the shelf of rocks that leads into the whirlpool. Being low water, we got on the shelf of rock, out of the suction. If it had been higher tide we would not of had any chance. By this time the surf was gone past and the boat was not filled or upset. I jumped in again and swam to the boat. Another came to my assistance. We got hur into the channel before the next surf came and got hur in safe. We continued discharging at all oppertunities till we got all on shore, and the ships took their departure for India.

We now found ourselves comfortable, being on full allowance, and I know a great many of the seamen would rather have staid on the island than to come away.[11] It was rather singular, though the hardships and want of provisions, while on this island, a leven months and seven days, there was neither man, woman, or child died a natural death, excepting one old woman 70 or 80 years of age.

Norfolk Island, Sidney Bay, is on the south side of the island, Long. 168°12′E., Latt'd 29°4′S., Mount Pit, 12,000 feet high, the cliffs in most parts round the island is 240 perpendicular. (Some books says good anchorage and ells [eels] in the runs of water), but in anchorage there is a mistake.[12] It is iron bound all round, with curl [coral] rock and a heavy surf, and all ships while I remained on (the island) had to lay two, or off and on while dischargeing or taking in, and as for the two branches of water, from the foot of Mount Pit, runing east, one on the north and one on the south side, we never new of an ell [eel] or a fish during our time on the island. Ansons Bay

Governor's House, Port Jackson, 1791

on the west side goes down with a deap decent until you come down to a small sandy beach and full of rushes from the top to the bottom.

The *Supply* Brig arived to bring the *Siriuses* crew to Port Jackson. We embarked [11 February 1791], and having a pleasant passage, we arived in Sidney Cove [27 February 1791]. All the ships crew landed and made there residence in the Copper Hospittle till further orders. At the same time the Govenor, capt[ain], and officers were consulting about buying the snow [*Waaksamheyd*] from the Dutch capt[ain] to bring the officers and men to England. The Dutch capt[ain] demanded 800 Lb. sterling for the vessel, but they supposed the topmasts ware not so good as they ware, and having no timber fitting for masts, they thought it best to hier the vessel to carry us home and save a good deal of provisions in the country. Therefore the Govenor took hur up for Timore, expecting to reach there in six weeks, belonging to the Portegees, at the rate of three hundred Pounds pr. month.

For the time we had been on short allowance on Norfolk Island we receiv'd 3 or 4 dollars, I am not certain which, though it was scarcely worth mentioning for what we suffered.

The Govenor understanding that a number of the ships company wished to settle in the country, we ware all ordered over to the Govenors house to inform himself who was most fittest for farmours. The whole ships company turned out excepting about ten of us, Terence Burn and myself being of that number that did not wish to remain. However, the Govenor found there was but few that could expect to improve in the farming business. Likewise it required seamen to carry the vessel and officers to England. Out of the whole crew he permitted ten or a leven seamen and three marines to remain as setlers, and it was directed so as to send their wages out to them in whatever they might think most fit for their situation in the county. Likewise there was a few draughted on b[oar]d the *Supply* Brig, as she was to remain in the country till further orders.

The remainder of us, officers and men, were sent on b[oar]d the Dutch snow [*Waaksamheyd*], I believe 85 in number. Besides our crew there was 30 Dutch sailors and some tame Malays that belonged to Betavia. We ware at this time as passengers, though we ware put into waches, as it made it more convenient below, however having our wood and water and what provisions the Govenor could allow us for six weeks, expecting to get to Timore.

We sailed [27 March 1791], the first month 6 men upon 4 mens allowance. We steared to the sotherd, and when we got off Vandemons Land we found the wind continued from the westward, and we beating for three weeks in vain, we bore up and steared to the notherd and eastward for the Middle Passage.

Finding our vessel a dull sailor, our capt[ain] asked the Dutch capt'n [Detmar Smith] how she sailed. He made answer, "O, she go eight nots."

"O," said our capt[ain], "that is verry well for a merchant vessel."

"O, yes," said the Dutch capt[ain], "but when she g'dat, it must blow damd hard," which we found to be true afterwards.

In leaving Port Jackson we brought Mr. Maxfield [Maxwell], third leutenant, on b[oar]d, before mentioned. Laying in his cabin in a dreadful condition, constantly delerious and unsencible of anything whatever, and in the three weeks he died [13 April 1791] and was buried in as genteel a maner as could be expected at see.

We steered our course till we made the Isle of Pines [23 April 1791], South Pacific Ocean, to the south of New Caledonia, Long'd 167°38′E.,

Latt'd 22°38′ South. This island apears very handsome at a distance, the land being very low at the south end, and the trees lofty, it apears like a fleet of shiping with there masts vissible only. Coming close in with the land, the capt[ain] wished to pass between the high land which lay to the north which was call'd the New Hebades, but runing close in with a fresh breeze and finding no channel, we had to beat out again with great difficulty and got round New Caledonia. In those climates, we generally having light winds, and our vessel being a dull sailor, we seldom went more than 3 or 4 miles an hour.

The next [14 May 1791] we hove in sight of was a groop of islands call'd (Admiralty [sic] or) Solomons Ilse [in part named Lord Howe Group by Captain Hunter]. We counted from the mast head upwards of 30 rocks or islands, Long'd 146°22′, Latt'd 15°37′N.[13] In passing, four cannoos made an atempt to come up with us, but there was only one that got along side. The canoo was made out of a large tree seemingly burnt out, with out rigers formed thus

which bearing on either side the cannoo, could not upset. The cannoo was large and heavy but the men in hur ware remarkable large and well made, of a bright colour, with their long hair put up very neat on top of their heads. The least of them stood 6 feet, 1 or 2 inches. The Prince, as we supposed him to be, sat in the middle but yoused no paddle. He had a large bloom of coloured feathers on his head, apeared to be about 18 or 19 years of age, and taller but not so stout as the rest. They gave us coca nuts and wanted us to come to their island, but having a fair wind but light, we proceeded on our voige, and they ware almost out of sight of there island, but they padled that heavy conoo with such strength that they sent hur through the water at the rate of 6 or 7 miles an hour. In passing these islands in the night, at daylight we saw a sand bank a stern of us which we must of run over in the night at the time of high water without perceiving the danger we ware in.

We saw a number of islands at a distance that I cannot tell the names of them. We made the island of Georgea, then New Guinea, north of New Holland. It was the intention of Capt[ain] Hunter to go through Endeavour Strates, which devides New Holland and New Guinea, but the winds did not purmit us. Thefore we run between New Brittain and New Ierland. Being in

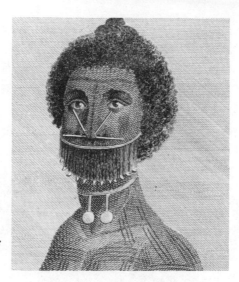

Lord Howe's Islands Native

want of water, we run down along shore of New Ireland, intending to stop at a watering place that is laid down in the chart, but we mised it. We run so clost that our yard arms almost tutched the bows [boughs] of the trees and could not get soundings with the hand lead, and when we hall'd off between the two islands we sounded with the dipsey lead and found no bottom.

We discovered a small island [22 May 1791] which lay between New Britton and New Ierland which we run down to. New Ireland is verry high land. We did not land on it. New Brittain is also high, but runs with a decent to the see shore. We could see beutiful vales, which appeared to be clear of wood and cocoa nut trees. When we got near the small island, which the capt[ain] call'd Duke of Yorks Island, the natives came off to us in canoos. There was about 30 canoos in numbers, some 2, 4, 6, 8, some more in each cannoo.

We signified we wanted water and gave them a kag. They padled for the shore all in a body, and when they begin to paddle they begin with a song, crying out, "E, E, E," till their breath was nearly expended, then crying out like a dog, "Woo, woo, woo," and so on. They continued till they came to the island. In a short time they returned with a kag of water.

We run close to the island and run down along shore until we purceiv'd a small cove which we entered and let go our anchor in 16 fathom water along side of the beach, which was right up and down, like a wall. We then got a harser from the stern a shore to keep hur from swinging, as there was not room for hur to swing in the cove. We sent our casks on shore. On one

Waaksamheyd *at Duke of York Island*

end of the beach was a small run of fresh water. We dug a whole in the sand and sunk a kask, that we could bail the water out and fill the casks, but when we begin to dig the sand up, the natives would fill it up again. It apeared as though they intended we should not have water.

We had two boats, one with casks and men to fill them and a masters mate, Mr. Brien, on shore with them, he having a gun. The boat I was in lay off from the shore about 15 or 20 yards to cover them, being eight of us with muskets. As there was a hill or rising ground right over the men filling water, the natives could heave rocks down upon them. Therefore, we laying off, we had a full view of them and could protect the men below at work. Mr. Shortland, mast'r mate, had the command of our boat. We ware looking at the natives clearing away the leaves and bushes on the hill to make room for their slings, and an old Chief came down on the beach about a hundred yards from the men on shore; Mr. Brian had his gun ready for him. A cannoo came along the beach towards us, and two canoos came round the point towards us and a stern of the vessel. Capt[ain] Hunter and the Duch [Dutch] capt[ain], observing their motions, eased off the stern harser and lay broad side to the shore. We mounted 16 six pounders. We could see a town of huts a short distance from the beach back in the woods. There was a great number of natives on b[oar]d when we came on shore. When they see us put the muskets in the boat, they laughted at them, taking them for fighting clubs, and thought there slings and spears ware far supperiour to our weapons.

They ware now ready to attact us in four different quarters and waiting for the Chief to fling the first stone, which he did, after whirling his sling for a short time. We ware ordered not to fire until he hove. Fortunately the Chief missed Mist'r Brian, but in lew of firing at him again, he turned round to see weather it had hit any of the men behind him. But it was not the case with us in the boat. We took good aim, with a rest, and gave them a full volly on the hill and likewise on the beach. Those in the canoos would of injured us the most, but the boat being Dutch built and verry strong, fended off the stones they hove out of their slings, though they made dents in the gunel of the boat a quarter of an inch deep, but sciming the stones along the water, all hit the gunnel of the boat, which saved us. No sooner than they found out the virtue of our clubs, our guns I mean, that produced fire, smoke, and thunder, as they took it to be, there was not one to be seen on shore. At the same time, as soon as they saw us attacted, they begin to open a broad side from the ship and hove the shot over the town. One canoo padled over towards New Ireland. I suppose they ware half a mile off, when they fired a round shot over them, to let them see that we could reach them. When the shot whisled over them, they fell in the canoo, but looking up again and seeing the shot strike a half a mile the other side of them, it hove them into such a pannich and amaze that they laid in there paddle and sat motionless. The natives that were on b[oar]d jumped overboard and swam on shore. When firing over the town, one of the shot hapened to cut a cocoa nut tree down, with one of the natives on top of it getting cocoa nuts. He was not hurt, but so frightened that he could not move from the spot he was in.

Those natives are rather smaller than the general run of natives, of a yallow cast, but well made. They have hogs, fowls, and breadfruit, with West Indies produce. The time we had completed our water and was on b[oar]d, they came down to the beach with green boughs. We went on shore with Capt[ain] Hunter and the Dutch capt[ain]. When we landed they presented the green boughs to us, which we receiv'd. They then begin to gather cocoa nuts and put to the amount of nine hundred and odd into the boat and gave us sugar cane. As well as we could understand by their motions we killed seven of them, which two of them I saw myself on the hill, the first fier we made.

One of them came to me sitting in the boat to give me some sugar cane. I, turning round, acsidentaly laid my hand on the musquet, which terrified him in such a maner that he fell down in the water which was nea deep. I laid holt of him and helped him up alongside the boat and patted him on the shoulder to passefy him. He made motions to me that we came from the clouds, pointings up in the elements, supposing our guns to be thunder and lightening.

After peace was made, they came a long side again as friendly as ever. What asstonished us was that such ignorant poor souls should put so much confidence in us when they thought we ware so powerful. The chief articles they admired most was bright buttons, bits of coloured cloth, perticularly bits of silk was great ornaments. There canoos ware hansom, turning up at each end, like a new moon made of peth wood. Too of them I see carry one of these canoos, 16 or 18 feet long, up into the woods when not wanted. There spears were hansome, ornimented with a bloom of feathers of all colours on the top of them. We had no oppertunity of seeing there wimen.

This small island apeared level and rich. At the eastermost end there is two mounts call'd the Two Sisters with a vulcaney on the top. It might be proper to mention, when we made peace, they brought two small dogs as a great present, but so vicious that they had to gag them, which was excepted of, through friendship, and in return the Dutch capt[ain] gave them a hound slut, which they seemed to adore. They tied a string round hur neck and danced round hur with great joy and led hur up to the town. I realy beleive the poor slut had more wisdom than all that was around hur, which gave us reason to think they worshiped dogs. Likewise we took notice that they always went into the water to do their need, as we supposed they held the earth as sacred. Before we had the distrubance, some of our men went upon that business. They hove stones at them. We now had a supply of water, though it was brackish, and could get no other.[14]

We put to see [27 May 1791]. New Britton laying in Long'd 152°19'E. and Latt'd 4°0' South, this island is about 4° south of the Line. We runing to the eastward [*sic*, westward], through the Straits, continuing to have light winds and moderate weather, the nex islands we passed was call'd Solomons Islands [*sic*, Admiralty], 3 in number, S. Pacific Ocion, Long.

169°28′W. and 10°5′S.[15] In passing, 2 of there war boats came off to us in a hostile maner, with a stage fixed upon two cannoos. On this platform the fighting men stood, with men in the bow and stern to paddel. Two of them followed us and came within pistol shot, turning up their backsides at us, and was inclining to engage us but a heavy squall coming on, and they being a long distance from the shore, they ware more afraid of the bad weather than they ware of us, as they did not [k]now the danger they ware in, so they made for the shore as fast as they could, which proved well for them, as our guns was well provided with round, grape, and canester shot, but the capt[ain] did not intend to ingure them unless they fired upon us.

We stood on our course, finding the winds continued from the westward, and we getting into an easterly current, we found we ware drifting to the E. in lew of getting to the westward. The Dutch capt[ain] worked by plain [plane] sailing and was expecting to make some of the Spice Islands every day, but Capt[ain] Hunter and Mr. Bradly worked their day works by lunar observations. They found we had drifted 700 miles to the eastward in 26 days, and we having no provisions on board but some rice that we got from the Dutch capt[ain], which was a half a pint pr. day in the husk, and when cleaned it would not amount to more than three half gils pr. man, Capt[ain] Hunter advised him to run a cross the Line into North Lattitude. He did so as far as 13°N. Latt'd. We then got out of the easterly current, but stil having westerly winds, we ware now much afraid of starving, no islands to the eastward of us, and contrary winds from the west.

We then bore up for Manela [Manila], but in a short time the wind shifted and headed us again.[16] We then attempted to run for China, but we had not stood on for China 12 hours when the wind headed us again. It apeared wonderful, whatever course we attempted to make a port, the wind would head us. We then fell in with a heavy gale from the westward [26 July 1791].

In the night, blowing very hard, a compasant came out of the see and wint up the riging and went out on the topsail yard arm. One of the men followed it, but fell off before he could get to it. Old seamen allows it denotes a heavy gale of wind. It apears like a star or a candel at a distance, but supposed to be a bluber that comes out of the see.[17] The next day, by their observation, found we ware in a current that drifted us at the rate of one degree against the gail of wind in 24 hours to the westward, which was the course we wanted to steer for the Straits of Me Cassa [Macassar].

We then got in [11 August 1791] amongst the Spice Islands and came to an anchor at a small island [Balut Island] which pretended to be subject to the Dutch goverment at Betavia. The name of the island I do not recollect, but they ware at war with a larger island that lay about 3 or 4 leagues to the nothord. They had several guardle coasters which cruised round their island. We begin a trading with them for rice and tobacco, which we ware in great distress for. With a piece of iron hoop a foot long, you could get a large Melay foul. The Dutch capt[ain] had some silk pieces that he was intending to trade for rice, goats, tobacco, and fowls, etc. We sent our casks on shore for water.

In the mean time the King of the island with his general and other officers came on b[oar]d in his own vessel, pretending to come a trading in a friendly manner, and two of his guardly coasters, one on each side and one a stern. They caried several swivels and two pounders.

The King and his Chiefs wished to purswade the capt[ain] to weigh anchor and come round to the town, which lay on the east side, and he could lay in safety and be acomedated with every article that he might want, but the Dutch capt[ain] suspecting there tretchary, sent a boat to sound and discover the chanel and found it full of sunken rocks and no passage, and when we got on them, they could do what they pleased and destroy us all at their pleasure.

While getting our water on board, the ships company was trading with them for tobacco, fowls, and sego, and the capt[ain] had received 900 weight of rice and a few goats. About this time there was between 2 and 3 hundred on board in pretence of trade. The Dutch capt[ain] had a Malay girl sitting on the quarter deck which he kept as a miss, and she was very fond of him. She, understanding the language, heard by there discourse when they found we would not go round to the town and be led into the snare that they had planed, they ware then determined to massecree all the whites on board. Of us, was 85 Englishmen, officers and men, 30 Duchmen and 16 tame Melays under Dutch goverment, 16 six pounders, and plenty of small arms. At this junkture, one of our men had been left on shore at the watering place and was coming off with the Kings son and sum goats. We had them hoisted in the large boat. The girl informed the capt[ain], and he sent the mate below for an armful of cutlashes. The general drew his dirk half out. The decks being full of Melays, they done as he did, having there eyes on him, but the King thinking it was too soon, his son not being on b[oar]d, stoped his arm.

At that moment the mate hove down an armful of cutlashes. Both capt[ains] ketched up a cutlash. The King finding they ware discovered made a spring on the gunel of the vessel and from thence into his boat and

Fight between Waaksamheyd *and Natives at Balut Island*

the general with him at the same time. Capt[ain] Hunter and Capt[ain] Smith made a blow at each of them but mised them. The King, when in his boat, drew a poisoned spear and hove at the capt[ain], but struck the bull work. When the general half drew his dirk and the King stoping him, I was not three yards from both of them. The first cutlash I got holt of was rusted. By this time the ships company was alarmed and flying to arms. Though the deks were full of Melays, and all armed with dirks, and seeing the King and general fly, they all jumped overboard and swam to the canoose, which ware numerous, laying off waiting for the massecree. The masters mate, Mr. Shortland, having a fusee in his cabin, jump'd up as the bowman was atempting to cut the painter and shot him dead. The moment he fell, the bowmans mate jumped up and cut the painter. Mist'r Shortland fired several times at that fellow and could not hit him.

The Kings boat was pulling away from the vessel by this time. The two guardlecoasters cut their painters and drifted a stern with the current, [k]nowing we could not bring our great guns to bare upon them, but we got 12 or 14 men with muskets on the poop, playing on them till they ware out of reach. In the meantime our guns was playing on the Kings boat that had his head officers on board. This boat could not sink. The hull was built of

Batavia

pine or seador and hur upper works, covered over, were made of bamboo. We sent our 6 pound shot through and through hur bottom till she fell on hur side. They hoisted Dutch colours all the time. We shot the colours away while she lay on hur side drifting, as they could not pull their oars, but they hoisted their colours again. Their cannoes full of men took the Kings boat in tow and took hur in. When the firing first begun, the Kings sons was within five hundred yards of the ship, with the goats, and one of our men with him that was before mentioned left on shore. He [k]nowing by the firing that they ware discover'd, he jumped overboard and swam to one of there boats. This man took to the paddle and pulled a long side.

In the scirmige, the Kings boat laying disabled, the Dutch capt[ain] asked us to go with him and bring hur along side. I jump'd into the yall, a five oard boat, mand and armed. As we ware shoving off, Capt[ain] Hunter came to the gangway and spoke to Capt[ain] Smith and beged of him not to go, they being so numerous, and if we had the Kings boat in tow, they would kill us all with their poisoned spears. Beside, the boats would gather round us and over power us, only six in number. Therefore he took the capt[ain's] advice and went on b[oar]d.[18]

After this fray was over we hove up our anchor [14 August 1791] and made sale to the westward, not thinking it safe to lay there any longer. The night before this hapened, it might be proper to mention we maned our 6 oard cutter, and Mr. Bradly with some more officers went to an island about

Onrust, Batavia Bay

9 or 10 miles from the vessel to endeavour to ketch some turkel. While on the island, about 12 o'clock at night a rainbow commenced like four rainbows of different colours, which officers or seamen had [n]ever seen before at that time of night. We took it as a token of a gale of wind. Having found no turkel, we left the island and hurried away for the ship. We had not got half way before it blew a smart gale, the wind from the N.W. We could nearly lay up for the ship but we was compelled to carry on, till we caried away our mainmast. We then carried on with our foremast sail and got out our oars, one man bailing, and the boat half full of water. We at length got on b[oar]d before the highth of the gale commenced. It blew amost tremendious, and the see in continuel foam. We must of perished, as the boat could not have remained above water half an a hour, when the hight of the gale commenced, and by next morning it moderated.

We now standing to the westward, heaving pleasent w[eathe]r, in a few days [25 August 1791] we made the entrance of the Straits of Macassar. Celebes and Bornio forms the Straits, Long. 116° to 124°E., Latt'd from 1°30'N. to 5°30'S. In entering the Straits we saw three Melay vessels standing for us on the Bornio shore, but not likeing the looks of us, they sheared off again. These Strates is very shoal in many parts of it, and see the sandy bottom. Snakes are numerous swiming about. Out of curiousity we caught them with a bucket. Having light winds, we ware some time getting through the Strates.

Ariving at Betavia, and wanting refiting, we went [29 September 1791] to an island calld Henroost [Onrust, or Kapal Island] where all the Dutch India Men refit. We had one man died on this passage from Port Jackson.[19] This vessel we came in belonged to the Dutch Govener, and being to refit, the Duchmen ware discharged and Capt[ain] Hunter took charge of the vessel.[20]

Batavia City is the capital of the island of Java and all the Dutch settlements in the East Indies in general. The city is hansome built with white stones. The canels [canals] in the principal streets are planted on each side with evergreen trees. The canals have drawbridges that can be lifted every night, that you cannot go out of one street into the other, though it is the most unhealtyest place I ever was in. A great number of the inhabitance are Chinamen and Malays. During the seven weeks we lay here, it was computed, on shore and aboard the Dutch Indiman, which are 64 gun ships upon acasion in war time, ware four thousand seven hundred that died. When we arived we had not a sick man on board, and when we left it, we had not a well man on board. We had our vessel covered with arnings [awnings] from stem to stern. Neither did we atempt to work from 8 in the morning till 4 in the afternoon. The see breeze comes in about 9 o'clock. The principal ailments was a swelling in the bowels, the other a pain in the breast. One of the soldiers told me, having small pay, they had chiefly to live on the fruit of the country, which gives them the flux and takes them off.

Allegaters are numerous. We ware informed a short time before we arived a barges crew, a leven men in number, going over the bar, was capsised on the flats and devoured, the allegators halling them off of the bottom of the boat, and no other boat dare go to their assistance without runing the same risk. The water from the rivers is verry bad, being salt peter ground. We had to boil our water in rice or barley, and then being so hot, it was like phisick to us when we had to drink it. Their Indimen lays out side the barr like a roadsted. There is a strong fort abreast the shiping, but it is at two great a distance to protect them from an enemy. The Duch are cruel to the Malay slaves. They wark them in the heat of the day without mercy, and if they die, heave them overboard like a beast.

While we lay hear the cap[tain] allowed us fowls, the beef being two strong for us, but having so many sick, we let them run about and took the first that come to hand. We lost several men here and one in Bantom Bay which had been a mesmate of mine [Terence Burne] for nine year in two ships. I must observe the capt[ain] never pravented any from drinking liquor while laying here, and those that would not drink any were the first that died, and others [who] would set and drink on the forecastle every night ware the helthiest men on board. Batavia, Long. 106° 51'E., Latt'd. 6°10'S.

We sailed [20 October 1791] for the Cape of Good Hope and had a good passage, but the ships company was verry sickly. One seaman died as we entered the Bay. As soon as we come to an anchor [17 December 1791], we sent all the worst of the sick on shore. We had to hist them over the side on gratings and when on shore taken to the hospittal in waggons. We that remain'd on b[oar]d was allow'd all kinds of vegitables and what wine we pleased to send for on shore. While laying here the chief of the ships company recovered, but we had to leave about 12 behind us. As I larnt afterwards the chief of them died at the Cape.

While laying here [20 December 1791] a south easter, which is common almost every day, blew so hard that we draged our anchors near half way to Pinquin Island, about one mile and a half, we then laying so open to the see, that we should of foundered at our anchors. Being bass cabled, we had to cut and run out to see with our yards and topmasts down. We then hove two till the gale ceased. In two days we got in again, but having neither anchor nor cable, the *Swan,* 20 gun ship, sent hur boats on shore and fetched off a large anchor and 18 inch cable.[21]

A few days before we sailed, the ships company, what was on board, recovering, and being in good spirits, the capt[ain] being on shore, Mr. Bradley, first leutenant, gave the ships company a frollick, being rejoiced to think we ware so near England after five years absence. Mr. Bradley giving us as much as we pleased to drink and carousing on the quarter deck and dansing and shouting and so great a noise on board of us, the capt[ain] of the *Swan,* man of war, thought there was a mutiny on board of us. It was then about dusk. Sent a boat with men and officers a long side to [k]now what was the matter. Mr. Bradley came to the gangway and desired them to come up, but they said they could not, but he handed liquor to the officers and we supplyed the men, and Mr. Bradley informing them of the frolick. They all drinked hearty and laughed till we sent them back nearly as well intoxicated as we ware on board.

In about six weeks [18 January 1792] we sailed for St. Hellena, as the seamen terms it "rolling down to St. Hellena," 1200 miles west of the Cape, always having a fair wind in those lattitudes. Being a dull sailor, we ware about ten or a leven days when we made the island, or Diana Peak, and we run down a long shore under the batteries and let go the anchor [4 February 1792] on the bank, abreast Jamestown, in a valley between two hills which is both fortified, one of them call'd Lather Hill, with a tear [tier] of guns and a tower, the shiping laying under it, another battery level with the see, and a half moon battery over the landing place where the shiping is supplyed with excelent water, but being a surf they have to back the boat in to land on the steps, two or three at a time, two cannon fronting the landing place. Every Indiaman is compeled to leave stores on the island on their homeward bound passage. Makeral is plentiful, some beneta, and albacore. They are the chief fish that is cought here. There is a great number of wild goats amongst these high clifts. Water crises [watercress] is numerous, the shiping make use of it, being holesom for the scurvey. Since that time this island has become the residence of the Emperor Napoleon. He was landed October 16th, 1815. Died on the 5th and was intered on the 9th of May, 1821, aged 51 years, eight months, and 20 days, born at Ajaccio, in Corsica, August 15th 1769.[22]

In about a week [23 February 1792] we sailed for England. We passed the island of Ascension, a barren island. There is wild goats, and it is resorted for turkle, 600 miles N.W. of St. Helena, Long'd 14°18′W., Lat'd 7°40′N. We made no stop, having pleasent weather.

Nothing accured till we arived in the Chanel of England. Having a fair wind from the westward, runing up Channel, in the night we fell in with a Brittish frigate cruising in the Chanel. They informed us that the *Supply* Brig, Capt[ain] Ball, had passed up Chanel the day before, which we had left in Sidney Cove when we sail'd, and did not sail for six month after us, and enquiring if we had arived, and being inform'd we had not, they supposed we ware lost.

The next day we run through the Needles with a stagering breeze. Came to Spithead and run into Portsmouth Harbour and came to an anchor [23 April 1792] close to Common hard and made fast to the morings. It may well be supposed of what remain'd of us, officers and men, out of 160 young, able men which was before mentioned, 37 of us returned that sailed from Spithead. The remainder came on b[oar]d at the Cape of Good Hope, which amounted to 84 or 85 in the whole number, and being chiefly on short allowance of provisions for five years absence. In a few days we striped the vessel, and she was delivered up to the owners consinement according to his directions from the Duch Govenor. This vessel could of been bought for 800 Lb. in Botnay, or at least in Port Jackson, but by foul winds and currents we ware 13 months on the voige. At 300 Lbs. pr. month, came to three thousand nine hundred Lb. for the voige beside our provisions.[23]

We were sent on b[oar]d the *Duke* [28 April 1791], ninety gun ship that lay abreast of Common hard as flag ship, til orders should be received from London to pay us off.[24] In a few days after [4 May 1792] we ware paid off on b[oar]d the *Duke* and distributed, and I received the check from Capt[ain] Hunter for my mesmate [Terence Burne] that died, which had been sent from the Summerset House in London out to us in Port Jackson, signed by the capt[ain] and officers according to the will and power we made to each other during our absence from England.

CHAPTER 6

London

INTRODUCTION

J ACOB Nagle spent no more than six months of his life in London, but from the summer of 1783 until the fall of 1795 it was his home port. On his first visit he recorded the fact that he had taken his "recriation," walking "through the city, in part, and suburbs," probably meaning that he had made at least a brief excursion through the central city itself and some of its more elegant western residential areas. But Nagle's real home in the metropolis was the East End. That summer he had boarded at Mr. Rogers's public house, "between the China Ship and Iron Gate," just to the east of the Tower, and in 1794 and again in 1795, he lived at Mr. Goodall's boarding house on Tower Hill. Neither establishment was of sufficient note to make the directories at the time or the histories of public houses of later date, although "Mr. Goodall's" was apparently a perfectly respectable place of lodging. The same could not be said for many nearby establishments.

Jacob Nagle's London stretched from Billingsgate Market, just west of the Tower of London, to Wapping on the east, and out Ratcliffe Highway, also to the east, and north, through what was then rural country to Stepney. He knew the dens of iniquity between Ratcliffe Highway and the river, in St. Katharine's, and had at least some acquaintance with the waterfront across the river, from Southwark to Deptford. The Thames was the center of his environment, as it was of London as a whole until the rise of rapid public transportation would transform it into an impediment to, rather than a vehicle of, public conveyance. The Tower and the river itself are timeless survivals of his world, but very little else remains today, and in fact, very little remained even a half century after Nagle was there.

St. Katharine's, the area just east of the Tower, was probably London's worst slum of the eighteenth century, containing a large population crowded into decrepit housing and dangerous alleys and courtyards. Crime and prostitution were widespread. To the east of St. Katharine's, the riverside was built up with warehouses and businesses, but inland there were still open spaces. Ropewalks, gardens, and open fields separated Whitechapel, Wapping, and Limehouse from Stepney, and these communities still had separate, distinctive identities of their own. The Isle of Dogs remained an uninhabited pasture, and Blackwall and Poplar, the center of activity for the East India Company, were entirely set apart from London.

The one common denominator of the entire area was involvement in, or a livelihood based directly or indirectly upon, Britain's vast maritime industry. There were a few sections of respectable housing for captains and officers, at Well Close Square and Prince's Square, but most of the inhabitants in the communities to the east of St. Katharine's were dockworkers, shipbuilders, customs inspectors, ropemakers, and active and retired seamen, generally solid citizens of limited means and often short-term residency at any one address.

Just as the honest occupations of the area had a distinctive maritime cast, so did the shadier activities. Ports and docks, where cargoes of immense value have to be inspected, unloaded, perhaps repackaged, and reshipped by cart or by small boat, handled along the way by many people, always have promoted crime. Nagle's journal is a rich source on the ingenuity and the widespread nature of petty theft and smuggling operations on the part of sailors and captains. Private cargoes, not on bills of lading, could be smuggled in duty free if customs agents or lumpers could be paid off to look the other way, or if they could be dropped off the side of the vessel on the slow passage up the congested Thames, to be retrieved by "mudlarks" who would return them for a fee. The methods of hiding or stealing cargo were innumerable, and the East End of London, which Nagle frequented, being outside the city limits, was where many of the landsmen involved in illicit trade resided and where deals, payoffs, and illegal sales could be quietly arranged in an atmosphere approving of such transactions. The volume of illicit trade was immense. In 1784 William Pitt estimated that well under half of the thirteen million pounds of tea consumed in Britain had entered the nation legally, and this was but one of many products that were smuggled in or stolen along the way, a good percentage of it along the Thames.

The other vices for which St. Katharine's was particularly known were of the more human but equally dangerous variety, aimed at parting sailors with their pay in the quickest possible time. They tended to be willing partners in the process, by the nature of their occupations inexperienced in handling infrequent and momentarily large wage payments and anxious to enjoy all the pleasures of equally infrequent shore liberty on their first night in the city. Ships of up to 800 tons could navigate as high up the river as London Bridge, larger vessels as far as Greenwich and Deptford on the south side of the river, or the East India Company docks at Blackwall on the north. Because of the tremendous volume of traffic and the narrowness of the channel, incoming ships could often take days to work their way upriver from Gravesend to their moorings. Passengers and unneeded crewmen would often disembark and come up by land, arriving in the city by way of Ratcliffe Highway. Either way, whether by land or from the docks, the pubs, the "long rooms," and the whores working out of rooming houses along the Highway and throughout St. Katharine's were inescapable. From the point of view of the navy or the East India Company, the area served a purpose by quickly impoverishing seamen and keeping them in the vicinity where the crimps and press crews could expeditiously commit them to future voyages.

With the construction of the great docks, the whole area changed rapidly soon after the time Nagle was there. The West India Docks on the Isle of Dogs, East India Dock near Poplar, and London Dock at Wapping were all constructed and put in operation in the first decade of the nineteenth century. St. Katharine's Docks were built in the 1820s, obliterating much of the neighborhood Nagle had gotten to know on his "cruises." Ratcliffe Highway retained its seamy reputation well into the present century, but suffered particularly destructive bomb damage during World War II and never regained its former, tawdry character. By the last quarter of the twentieth century, with the changing nature of international transportation, the advent of the container ship, and the development of modern docking facilities well below the city, the port of London as Nagle knew it no longer exists.

WHILE BEING in Gosport I boarded in South Street with an old shipmate that kept a public house, and a number more of my ship mates. The first day of May we all took a walk out of town to go amayin, as is custamery, early in the morning to gather flowers in the fields and drink milk punch. On our return we fel in with two hansome young ladies walking towards town. I fel into discourse with them till we came to the Sign of the Belflore. We all went in to have sum milk punch. I asked the ladies in to refresh themselves. They sat down in the parlour and we in the bar room. I brought them some punch but they would not except of it, but they would except of lemanade which I brought them. We then took our departure for town.

On our way I took the liberty to ask one of them if she would purmit me to see hur home. She said she had no objections, as I had been so obliging. When we entered the town, my comrades took a nother course, and hur sister as I understood lived in a nother part of the town, and we walked on to a place call'd the Back of the Buildings which is the hansomest part of the town. She invited me into a most elegant furnished room. She understanding that I came from Botnay Bay, she was inquisitive in respect of the country and invited me to take a glass of wine. Shortly after I took my leave to go to dinner. In parting she invited me to tea in the after noon, which I excepted of the invitation, and returned to my boarding house, had my diner with my shipmates, and passed the after noon till four a'clock, then returned to the invitation. When I arived she was waiting for me, but no company as I expect'd there would be. We had our tea and passed the afternoon very pleasent and became very farmiliar with each other. She found a bead [bed] that night, and I remain'd til morning and by invitation stoped to breekfast, then took my departure. Ariving home, my landlady by some means had information where I had been, took me a side, and told me to be aware of myself, for she was a maried woman and hur husband an officer on b[oar]d a seventy four laying in the harbour. I thanked hur for informing me that she was a maried woman.

About a dozen of us ware on our rambels in Gosport. Went in a public house where some of my shipmates boarded. While they were drinking and discoursing I was talking with the landlady at the barr, and observing a pair of large stufed gloves on the shelf, I asked hur what they ware for, as I never had seen boxing gloves before. She smiled and handed them down to me. Hur husband was watching me, he being call'd a prime boxer. I put one on. He steped up and took the other. "Now," he said, "you must pay a forfit of a crown bowl of punch or box with me." He [k]nowing I had money, I thougt it was imposition, and he being a light man, but smart and active. In the barro[o]m there was a fier place with a large pot boiling meat for dinner. I told him I did not value a bowl of punch, but I would not pay for fear of boxing with him. "Well, you must come on then."

My landlord and all the rest of my shipmates were looking on. He came gumping up to me and a squareing at me. I ketched him on one side of the head and nocked him into the fier place and durted his clothes and singed his hair before we got him out, the whole company full of laughtur. He got into a great rage, striped for a fair box. I strip'd and laughed. My landlord [k]nowing me in the *Ganges* 74 and took him a one side and told him to drop it as he would have but little chance with me, so he came to me and made it up. I told him I had no intention to hurt him, neither did I think I could with them stuffed gloves on. We had some more to drink and took our departure.

Wm. Hunter, myself and a number more took stage for London, and one of them brought his girl with him as she wanted to go to London. In the night the stage stop'd for super. The table all ready, they all sat down to supper excepting myself and Harry Ackin [Henry Hacking, quartermaster on *Sirius*] which this girl was with, us two not wanting any but call'd for a couple of rummers of hot, being cold in the night.[1] Calling for the reconing, the landlady sharged us for supper. She said if we came into the room it was sufficient weather we eat or not. Hearing what she said, when the landlayde was going backwards and forwards, this girl having two large side pockets, she cut large chunks of cheese, ham, breat, sasages, till hur pockets was full, and we all laughing. She had sufficient towards daylight as we felt grubish for all hands on the coach, which was about eight or nine of us, so I think the landlady lost deal by hur two shillings that she thought she had gained.

Ariving in London, I boa[rde]d on Big Tower Hill at Mr. Goodall. I often amused myself in going to the plays and opparas with Wm. Hunter, which had been a mesmate during our hard voige. His parents living in Shard [Shadwell?] Street, near Wapping Church, his stepfather then being one of the 12 Masters of the Navy, Mr. Hunter introduced me to his parents, and often din'd with them.

London Waterfront near Tower of London

Mr. Hunter coming down to see me one after noon, Mr. Goodall having one of the actors living in his house, proposed to take an excurcion to the play that night, which was agreed on. Mr. Goodall was to prepare and have a hackney coach in the evening. Our company was to be Mr. Goodall, a capt'n of troops belonging the East India Company, Mr. Burley and his wife, pusser [purser] of a man a war, Wm. Hunter, and myself, which was 6 in number. We ware all to sup at Mr. Goodalls after the play was over. Mr. Goodall received tickets for the boxes, 3 shillings each.

In the evening, the coach being ready, we all started. Ariving at the playhouse, the croud was numerous. Mr. Goodall gave us warning to secure our pockets. We entered the stair case, which was very broad, but so throng that it was difficult to squese along, but Mr. Goodall and Mr. Hunter led the van along side each other, the pusser and his wife next to them, the capt. and myself bringing up the rear, keeping close together. There hapened to be a great big bussen gutted gentleman got a long side of me, and being so much scrouged, he would come bump up against me. I claped my hands to my side and my elbo sticking out would lunge against his ribs, made him cry out, "You hurt me verry much, Sir, with your elbo." "I cannot avoid it, Sir." Therefore he sheared off from me as much as possible. About half way up the stair case, a scamp in the crow'd got holt of Mrs. Burleys silk cloke and pull'd till the ribben broke and was flying off hur sholdiers into the croud, when I, being behind her, purceiving it, I got holt of it, and he let go, for fear of being detected.

At length we got up where we delivered our tickets for the boxes, but the genleman that received the tickets observed that I had a short round-about on, and that I could not go into the boxes without a long coat. Mr. Goodall observed it was first cloth and finer than his coat. He allowed that, but it was a rule. "Well, Sir," said I, "lend me your coat till I come out again." It created a monstrous laugh amongst the croud. "Well," said Mr. Goodall, "we will all go into the one shilling gallery." Therefore he lost twelve shillings by my round about jacket.

We went to the gallery and seated our selves in a row on one bench. When they begin to act, there was a lady with a large bonnet on sitting in front of Mr. Goodall and me that provented us from having a vieu when they ware acting. Therefore Mr. Goodall spoke to her very politely if she would be so good as to pull hur bonnet off, the [that] we might see, but she would not take any notice in what he desired hur. He having a light kain in his hand, he touched hur on the shoulder several times, but would not take any notice. There was a number more behind us that ware discomoded by hur large bonnet. Mr. Goodall finding she would not take it off, and beside it being against the rules in the playhouse, he took his kain and put the end into the loop of a floroshing ribben behind and twisted it round and hove the bonnet clean off hur head. The cap, being pined to the bonnett, went with it, and hur head was as bare as a plucked fowl. There was such a cruel laugh and uproar in the gallery, made them stare from all quarters of the playhouse. The lady being elegantly dressed ketched up hur bonnet and cap and got out of the playhouse as fast as posseble. The play being over we returned and suped at Mr. Goodalls and then parted for the night.

The next day I made a search for a Merican ship to get home. There was but one ship bound to Philadelphia taking in passengers. I went on b[oar]d and spoke to the mate. He said if I would wait, the capt[ain] would be on board shortly. The capt[ain] coming in b[oar]d, I went to him, but he said he was full of pasengers and he could not take me under ten guineas and work my passage, and his stearage pasengers paid only five Pound that never was on salt water and no benefit to the ship except as lumber. The mate and seemen was mad to think he should ask me that price and work as a seaman. I was determined not to give it and went on shore.

Finding one of my shipmates [William Beard] on my rambels, he had engaged a vessel bound home to Leath, and she was not going to sail for a few days, and we must have a cruise. We first started down to Debtford to see our old shipmates, the *Supply* Brig laying there and was not paid off.[2] Having a little sport with them in Debtfort, we return'd again.

Being only about three mile, we walked, and on the road he informed me of a trick he was played no great distance from where I boarded, in Ratlif [Ratcliffe] high way.[3] He said he fell in with a hansome young girl and she took him home to a small room, well set off with furneture. He new he was purty well intoxacated but he said he had not more than about three guineas with him, and while there he recollected he had some more to drink, but when he awoke he found his pockets empty. When he asked hur, she said he was drunk when he came there, and she could not tell weather he had any money or not excepting what money he had gave hur to get some liquor with. Therefore he thought it was not worth while to say anything about it, but he new she had some stow hole about the chimbley. It came in to my head we could ketch hur in hur own trap.

"Bill," said I, "if you can show hur to me and the house, I think I will ketch hur."

"We can easy do that," said Bill, "going along towards Tower Hill, in passing you go into the Public house oppisate and you will see me go in and I will ask hur to come over to take something to drink, but we must not pretend to [k]now each other."

Coming through Wapping, we met Will'm Hunter and he came with us. Going into the public house Bill Beard left us and I informed Bill when Beard came in with a girl not to take notice and not to [k]now him while she was there. Presently in they came, sat in a box by themselves. She was a smart looking girl as he had said. We then walked out and walk towards Tower Hill. Shortly after, Bill came to us. "Now," said I, "we will try that lovely lass and see how hur pulsepeats by tomorrow morning." We passed the afternoon together and promised to meet the next day about eight o'clock.

I went to this house with about two guineas in my pocked and som silver to cut a flash with and at the same time apeared to be well siezed oover. There was a number of girls there. I sat down on one of the benches and called for a pot of phlip and the girls around me. I paid for the phlip, letting

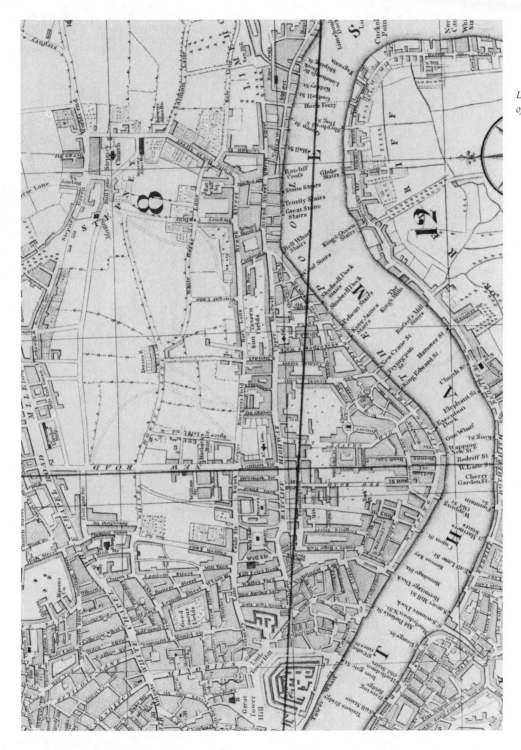

London East of the Tower

them see I had both gold and silver. I took one glass and passed it round amongst the rest of the girls. I asked this girl where she lived. She informed me across the street and said if I would go home with hur she would give me a good bead, as I was rather in liquor. I took hur advice.

We went to hur room. She said I better go to bed. I told hur I wanted a pot of phlip and then I would go to bed. She agreed to that, thinking if I was not drunk enough she would make me so. I gave hur a shilling. She went for the flip. I took the candel and over hall'd the bricks in the firehath. I found one loose in the second teer, in the back of the chimble; I lifted it up and saw some gold, and a watch, put the brick in its place.

By the time she returned, I was sitting on the bed with my clothes off, excepting my pantaloons which I had my money in. She handed me a large tumbler of flip. As soon as I tasted it, I found there was double allowance of rum and well sweatened. I drank some and pretended I could not sit up any longer and laid down. I suppose it was about 10 o'clock. She put the light out and laid down. About 12 or one a'clock she begin to hug me to see if I was sound, but having no life in me, she got up, overhalled my pockets, and stowed a way all she found, and turned into bed. In the morning I pretended I did not [k]now where I was, and when half dressed, I asked hur to fetch some bitters. She went over. In that time I took all in the whole [hole] and put into my pockets, and by the time she returned, I was dressed and took my bitters and told hur I would see hur in the evening. She thought then that I had not missed my money, and we parted.

I went home. After breckfast Wm. Beard and Wm. Hunter came. We went into a private room, and I begin to examin my prize, which contained 11 guineas, 5 half guineas, three Spanish dollars, 1 watch, one set of gold earrings with bobs, three broaches, and six brest pins. "Now lads, we will go and see our lady. She dare not take the law of me. She [k]nows she had robed us both, and we will see weather she has missed hur property, and return all excepting our own money."

We agreed and started. We came to hur room, went in without nocking. She sat on the bed crying, expecting I had taken the property before a justice, and knowing that she had robed Beard and me, Hunter being dressed in long clothes, took him to be a constable.

I sat down a long side of hur, and purceiving she was nearly fainting, I said, "Liddey, dont be fritened. It may not be so bad as you may suppose if you tel the truth in what I am going to ask you before this constable."

She trembled and cried again, "O, for Godsake forgive me."

"You are already forgiven, only pasefy yourself, and answer my question." She said she would.

[Nagle] "Did you not take 3 guineas from this young man?"

[Lydia] "No, he changed one for some drink."

[Nagle] "How much did you tak[e]?"

[Lydia] "2 guineas and about 17 or 18 shillings."

[Nagle] "Well, are you willing to pay him that money?"

[Lydia] "Yes, Sir, if I had what I lost, but I have nothing left but sume change that I have in my pocket."

[Nagle] "Well, how much did you take from me?"

[Lydia] "Two guineas and some silver."

"Now, here is your property, before this gentleman." I gave hur all I had taken. She gave Beard his money and paid me what she had taken and said I was the best friend she ever fell in with and said I have saived hur from the gallos or transportation and promised she never would take any thing in a clandestante manner again and would insist on my taking the wach as a present from hur. At length I excepted of it before witness and [she] beged the favour of us all three to come in the after noon and take tea with hur. We promised we would. We parted and met about four.

Coming to the house, we found Liddy ellegently dressed, full of glee and good youmer. We enjoyed a pleasent afternoon with hur. She said she hoped I would come and visit hur whenever opertunity served. I promised I would and we parted. During the time I was in London I had a good many excursions which would be two tedious and take up two much paper, therefore I pass them over.

The next day the three of us was taking a walk down to Waping, and going into the Red Lion, we fell in with two young men that had been paid off from a man of war, and falling into discourse, they said it was dull times in London, and they thought they would go to Ostend, as they understood there was a Merican Indiaman laying there that wanted hands. I told them I wanted to go home, as I was American, and if they ment going, I would go with them, which was agreed on. Therefore we would provide for the passage.

Wm. Beard, which was in company, was to sail two day after this for Scotland.[4] As he found I was going away he proposed to me to come to his b[oardin]g house in the evening. I promised I would. I then went with Bille Hunter to his father and mother to wish them farewell. After a repast I parted with Bille and his parence. I went home and desired Dr. Goodall to lay in

JACK in a White Squall. Amongst Breakers—on the Lee Shore of St CATHERINEs

some liqur and some provision as a see stock to put into my chest as I was going to Ostend in a few days and I did not expect to be home that night.

I went down to Wm. Beards boarding house near Iron Gate and found him there expecting me. We sat a while.

"Now," sid Bill, "you saved me near three guineas which I never would of got if it had not been for your scheme. We must have a cruise this night, as I expect to sail to morrow or next day."

We started and went through St. Catharines, joaking and sporting with the ladies as we went a long, crossing Big and Little Tower Hill into them street and from thence to Billinsgate, but before we got there we went into a genteel inn and call'd for liquor.

In siting down in a box there was a smart well drest soldier in his uniforms and side arms sitting. We asked him if [he] would take a glass with us. He said he would and drank.

He said, "Lads, dont think I want to impose on you, I will be my shot as wel as you," and pull'd out a handful of silver. He inform'd us he belonged to the Kings Guards and "I am upon a cruise as well as you are, and if you have no objections, I will go with you."

All being agreed we went into Billinsgate before mentioned. We call'd for a half pint of rum and sat it on the table. The soldier went to the bar to pay for the liquor. Beard had acasion to go out a dores. I sat waiting for them. A fellow sitting by the fier with a hankerchief tied round his jaws and crying out, "O, o, o" and moaning at a great rate, while I looking at the people at the bar and waiting, this fellow whiped up the half pint and drank it off. Turning round, I saw the half pint was empty. I turned to this fellow still moaning with his elbow on his nea, and his hand on his jaw. "You raskel, how dare you drink that liquor? Il heave you into the fier place." He stoped moaning and jumped up, and three or four more at the bar came flying at me, when, Beard just coming in, the soldier drawing his sword made a shlash over one of their heads. They skamperd off like lightening. I told them the circumstance. "Well," said the soldier, "we must be off, for there will be twenty of them scamps here shortly and we will have no chance with such a number of them." So we started and went into a jenteel house on Little Tower Hill and passed the evening till the young soldier bid us good night.

We call'd for a super and then went to bed. Bille, being a little over the bridge, he took one bed and I took another. We fell a sleep. In the morning when I awoke Bille asked me if I new anything of his money. I told him I did not. He searched the bed, hove all the bed clothes on the flore, and nothing to be found. I was much conserned, no one being in the room but our two selves since the girl left us with the candle the night before. He said there was 25 guineas in a silk hankerchief. I expected he must think that I had the money, I having a belt round me at the same time of 35 guineas. He had give it up, and I was dressing myself to go down stairs, when he was going to heave the bed and bedding on the bedstead again. I took notice of a mat laying on the bed cords that had not been moved. I hall'd the mat off and there was the hankerchief laying on the crossing of the bed cord and all his money in it. He said he had [k]nown himself to stow things away that he could not recollect what he had done with them. I was rejoiced that the money was found. We went home. His vessel being ready, we took the parting glass, and I went to the Red Lion and met my two comrades. We then went to Billinsgate and found a hoy bound to Dover, was to sail at 9 o'clock the next morning. We went and got our chest and bedding on b[oar]d to be ready in the morning. We apointed to meet at 7 o'clock.

I went to see Liddy and informed her I was going to Ostend. She wished me to stay with hur till we started, and then I went and settled with my landlord for my board and see stock and then returned. We passed the evening very comfortable. At seven in the morning I joined my comrads and we went down to the hoy. Being two early for starting, we went into a public house to have some bitters. There I mised my belt with 35 guineas sowed up, having money about me besides for use. Well, thinks I, Liddy had done me with all my [k]nowingness, but I told them to remain till I return'd. I run up as fast as I could. Coming to the hous, she was looking out of the window and seeing me she new there was something the matter. When I came up stairs she asked what was the matter. I said nothing but went to the bed, which had not been made up, hove the covering and sheet back, and there laid my belt, had got loose from around me in the night. She asked me if I had mistrusted hur. I said I could not tell till I return'd to see. She cried. I pittied hur. I gave hur two guineas. She refused, and I made hur take it, bid hur good by, and started back to my shipmates.

The hoy being ready, we went on b[oar]d and sailed for Dover. She was loaded on deck up to the boom so it could swing clear. When we had got our chest and bedding down the forecastel, we came up on deck.

I took notice of three hansome young girls amidship on the oakum. I supposed them to be from sixteen to nineteen. I sat down alongside the youngest as I supposed and fell into discourse with hur. She informed me they ware going to Dover on a visit to see some aquaintance. I found in the course of the day they ware in a poor sittuation. There was no room below excepting where our chests and bedding was. They had no provisions or clothing to keep them warm during the night, excepting their thin silk cloaks, and having a head wind, I new we could not arive in Dover under three days at least. As for our selves, we ware well provided. Being full of cash, we laid in a good stock for a cruise. I pittied the poor lases. I spoke to my comrads and we brought them our Flushen great koats, and I gave mine to this lovely maid that I first discoursed which made them warm and comfortable. By this time it was getting late in the after noon, and having a nother passenger which was a labouring man bound to Dover, and he complained of hunger, I told him to put the kittle on the fier and we would give him as much as he would eat, which he did with pleasure, and we provided our young ladies with a pleasant and agreeable meal of tea, ham, cheese, and cakes, but liquor they declined. Through our generous and desent behaviour, they became more sociable and free with us. As for the young lady that I paid most attention to and endeavour'd to oblige in everything I could, she informed me the next youngest was hur sister and the elder a first cousin.

The wind continuing a head and the tide leaving us, the next day about noon we came to an anchor at Sandown Castle close to Deal. Therefore we agreed to go to Deal and take stage for Dover, as the vessel could not arive till next day. Therefore I informed the ladies that we would take them round in the stage in safety that afternoon. This fine girl put hur trust in me and gave me hur hand with a hankerchief that contained a round sum of gold and silver. When in the boat hur sister was following, but the elder would not come and insisted they should not go, but remain on board. We all endeavoured to purswade hur, but she would not, so the two sisters told me as she was the eldest they did not wish to go without hur. I told them it lay entirely to there own opsion and I helped them out of the boat one after the other, and I handed hur hankerchief to hur with hur money.

We went on shore, got a dinner, and went in the stage for Dover. We arived in the evening and put up at the Sign of the Griffin. The next day the hoy arived about 10 o'clock and we ware there ready to go on board to get our baggage out. I was discoursing with the young ladie, when down came a coach and four on the warf. This young damsel new the coach and burst out

Ostend, Belgium

in a flod of tears. "O," said this lovely girl, "if I had taken your advice in lew of my cousin I should of been safe. Now we are ketched. That is my father and brothers."

They came to the hoy and ordered the ladies out and eyed me verry much. Seeing me discoursing with his youngest daughter, asked the capt[ain] weather we came on b[oar]d with the ladies. The capt[ain] informed him we ware entierly strangers to each other, anymore than being very kind to them. "Not having any provisions or anything to keep them warm in the night, they supplyed them with everything they could desire. They took them into the inn on the key [quay] to get breckfast before they started for London."

After sending my bagage up, I walked toward the dore. The young lady saw me. She got up and was meeting of me to speak to me, but before we reached each other, one of hur brothers run and turned hur into the room and shut the dore. The truth was, he was a rich merchant in London, maried the second wife, and she treated these girls with great cruelty, and they laid the plan to run away with a small bundel each and what cash they could muster. Accordingly they hapened to take the same boat for Dover that we had engaged.

On the next day the packet was to sail for Ostend. Dover is a hansome small town with a fine mold [mole] for the shipping, clear of all bad weather. The next day we sailed in the packet and arived at Ostend on the following day. We landed and took up our quarters on the key at Mrs. Kelleys. Ostend is a fortified town in Flanders full of canels [canals]. Large ships can enter the canel into the town at high water. It lays 10 miles west of Bruges, 22 miles N.E. of Dunkirk, 60 miles N.W. of Brussels, Long'd 3°1′E., Lat'd 51°14′N.

This American ship, beforementioned, was laying here, bound as was reported to Philadelphia. Being in want of hands, we shiped with the capt[ain]. I now expected once more to see my native place, but while fiting out, the capt[ain] went to London. In about a fortnight we had the ship ready for see, and we taking our cruises through the town at our pleasure. The capt[ain] ariving, but unfortunately for me he had reciv'd orders to go to France for a cargo upon a nother voige. Therefore we all three left the ship, meaning to return to London, but one of my comrades fell sick and could not go with us, and being low in pocket, I paid a months board for him and gave him a trifel in cash. He went by the name of Thos. Nash. Bill Williams and myself paid our passage, which was a guinea, and find our selves for London.

The day before we sailed, Mrs. Kelley call'd me into hur private room, and a nother fine looking woman sitting there, informed me that this ladys husband was now fighting against the enemy and was draughted as a milishaman, and not being able to pay the rent in hur husbands absence, the landlord was going to sese all hur goods for the rent, and asked me to assist hur in getting hur goods on board in the night. I told the sircumstance to my comrades and they came with me about 10 at night, took down the bead-steads, lash'd them and beads, lashed chests of drawers and desks, secured them with bed cords, and had all hur best furneture on board that she wished to take by two o'clock in the night. As for hur mahogany chairs and sofaies [sofas], we took to Mrs. Kelleys, as she bought them to assist hur in getting to London.

The next morning we sailed and the poor woman left the key under the dore. We had not got more than halfway a cross the Chanel, standing for the Downs, when a gale came on and blew tremendious from the S.W. They had but four men belonging to the brig, therefore we gave them our assistance both day and night, and with all our eforts we ware very near getting on quik sands, but getting hur under snug sail, as much as we could carry on hur, we weathered them or none could be saved. They could not of worked that vessel quick anough to clear the sands if we had not been on board, which the men allowed themselves.

In 48 hours it cleared off and the wind came round to the nothord, which was a head wind, to run up London River. Therefore we had to work tides work and come to an anchor whenever the ebb begin to make. In three days we got as high as Woolage, then had to come to an anchor. Us two being passangers, we wanted to go on shore and walk up to London, as it was only 5 or 6 miles, but the capt[ain] insisted we should help to take the vessel up, having a head wind and light handed. I told him if he would return half the money we gave him for our passage we would stop, but he was two covetous to do that, for his own men said he was a real miser. Therefore on shore we went and walked up to London.

We went up to Lydea before mentioned. She apeared rejoic'd to see me, and we had supper with hur. The next day, the brig ariving, we went on board and got our chests and bedding on shore and left them at the Red Lion in Red Lion Street. Coming down Ratlef high way, I saw the lady that I helped away from Ostend. She was glad to see me and dined with hur. I remained in London about three weeks, and finding no Americans ships to suite me and having information there was one laying at Portsmouth, I took stage and went to Portsmouth, but the vessel was gone.

CHAPTER 7

Run to India

INTRODUCTION

*E*UROPE had undergone a revolutionary political transformation since the spring of 1788, when Nagle embarked for Australia, and he returned to a world about to plunge into more than two decades of almost continuous warfare. In the very week that the *Waaksamheyd* anchored at Portsmouth, France had declared war against Austria. A mob attacked the Tuileries Palace on June 20, and the French Assembly, declaring a state of national emergency, began the process of raising an army.

Britain would not formally enter the war against France until early in 1793, when Louis XVI lost his head and French military success in Holland posed a direct threat to Britain itself, but it required no unusual farsightedness on the part of the Admiralty in the summer and fall of 1792 to realize that the time would soon be at hand when its fleets would have to be in readiness. Plymouth, Portsmouth, and dockside London began to hum with a level of activity and expectancy they had not felt for a decade. To man the ships that were being brought to a state of readiness, press crews became increasingly active.

Jacob Nagle, every bit the able-bodied sailor in terms of both experience and appearance—possessing an agile step and a cocky, tough demeanor, and clothed in sailor's trousers and a roundabout coat—was the kind of catch most sought by press gangs, and he was grabbed in early August 1792. Nagle would spend much of the rest of his maritime career evading, or attempting to evade, the long arm of the British navy, and his journal is a marvelous document of the system in action.

The impress system for manning the British navy has historical roots that go back to the time of the Magna Charta. While by the eighteenth century a long process of evolution had transformed the theories and forms of British government, there survived a bit of the spirit of the nobles at Runnymede in the back benches of Parliament, distrustful of any central, permanent government and any system of taxation that made the king and his ministers capable of action independent of specific, parliamentary approval. At the end of the seventeenth century there had been serious debate about the necessity of maintaining a standing army in peacetime, and even at the end of the eighteenth century there was a group of parliamentary opponents to any measure that would enhance the central administration and require taxation to keep it going. This tradition to a large degree explains the longevity of impressment as a primary method of manning the navy as late as the Napoleonic Wars, well after the system had been rendered inadequate to the international responsibilities that Britain had accepted with the growth of trade and empire.

In the modern sense, eighteenth-century Britain did not have a permanent navy. There were administrators and dockyards, ships and upkeep expenses, and hundreds of inactive officers on half pay, but there was no full-time corps of active officers or seamen. When a ship was put into commission, officers and crew were hired for that ship and for that tour of duty. When the tour was over, if not turned over to another ship, officers went on half pay and sailors were paid off and dismissed from the service. This theoretically minimized the dangers of a paid, professional armed force in peacetime and saved the expense of unwanted sailors. The drawback, when there continued to be ships that needed men with experience, was that it became regularly necessary to find seamen after a cruise and also to find ways to either entice them again to volunteer their services or force them to do so. The British public of the eighteenth century feared and disliked press crews, but they had not yet come to accept the alternatives, which were either general conscription or sufficient taxation to support a permanent, salaried navy.

The ambiguous public and political attitude toward impressment spilled over into the workings of the system as well. Impressment was legally but begrudgingly recognized in British common law and operated within ill-defined limits. Individual towns and cities, at various times in the eighteenth century, successfully prohibited pressing within their jurisdictions. Men of property, in the unusual cases when they were caught in the press crews' nets, could buy their way out. Local magistrates, when a case involving impressment came before them, frequently sided with the prey rather than the predator, going so far in some instances as to prosecute and imprison press crews themselves. Although in times of unusual military crisis press crews were known to go after men who had not previously served at sea, this was unusual because it involved risks to themselves and it secured men likely to be rejected by ships' officers, denying the captors the bounties they received for producing acceptable crewmen. The primary targets and victims of impressment, then, were men between sixteen and forty-five who had been to sea in some capacity previously, men who had the necessary experience to make good sailors and who lacked the political influence likely to impede the process. Certain occupational groups involved in maritime activities were legally exempt—naval dock-workers and shipbuilders, merchant ship apprentices, pilots, seamen on outgoing trading vessels, and "ticket men" who had been given "protections" from the press by the Admiralty or by parliamentary enactment.

The two primary theaters of operation for press crews were at sea and in coastal areas on land. From the navy's point of view, impressment at sea had the advantage of assuring them of experienced, qualified sailors. During the Anglo-French War, between 1793 and 1815, it was a rare occurrence that a merchant vessel could make it up the Channel or into a West Country port without being stopped by men-of-war or by cutters manned by press gangs. Sizable percentages of merchant crews, unless successfully hidden in carefully prepared "stowe holes," were forcibly removed and "volunteered" for an outward-bound naval expedition. By law, a sufficient crew had to be left to get the ship into port, but this could be provided with ticket men brought out for that purpose, or by regular sailors who would then be picked up after the merchant vessel was brought to anchor.

Beyond coastal waters, naval impressment rested on questionable legality. It was widely practiced in the vicinity of British naval installations such as Jamaica or Halifax, illegally in many cases but at such a distance from courts of redress as to offer the pressed seamen little hope for justice.

It was fairly common for naval vessels to take men from East India

Company ships in distant waters, where the necessity was obvious. The company was highly dependent on naval protection of its fleets and would rarely make an issue of it. On the high seas, whether from British or foreign ships, naval vessels tended to be selective, primarily taking British subjects or sailors who had formerly served in the British navy.

On land, the impress was entrusted to a captain, in charge of a particular geographical district, and lieutenants, each of whom commanded a gang of either seamen or paid bullies. They would round up potential sailors and bring them to the "rendezvous" at a tavern, close to the water, where the recruits could be enrolled and quickly put aboard ship or on tenders that would transport the victims to ships in need of crewmen. The Admiralty paid officers additional bounties for impressment work.

In spite of all the legalities, it was physical force, combined with a degree of ingenuity and good judgment, that made impressment an effective source of manpower. The trick was to catch a would-be recruit when he least expected it and in situations where he was outnumbered and could be physically detained without attracting public attention and support. Spies were paid to point out potential victims and places where they could be easily taken. Taverns were watched and street corners along well-traveled routes manned at times of the evening most likely to produce results.

For a seaman, the alternative to impressment was to volunteer, and the advantage of doing so was that the recruit could choose his ship and would receive a bounty. In the 1790s, Parliament also passed two Quota Acts, whereby each county or city was required to produce a certain number of seamen, in actuality an early form of conscription, but one that provided the volunteering seaman with generous bounties.

In the years covered by this chapter, 1792 to 1796, the war with France became a serious business, and the efforts to man the expanding fleets became increasingly intense. Nagle goes into no detail but says that in August 1792 he was "pressed" and sent on board the *Hector*. He devotes less than a page to his service on board the ship, although in fact he served seven and a half months, most of it moored at Portsmouth or Spithead. While he was on board, the *Hector* served as the place of imprisonment for the ten mutineers of HMS *Bounty* during their court-martial, and the four men actually hanged went from the ship to the gallows, undoubtedly in Nagle's presence.

After a brief cruise in the Channel, the *Hector* helped stop an incoming East India Company vessel and impressed its entire crew, then assigned sailors to take the vessel into port. In such situations, the navy exercised the right to transfer crewmen from one vessel to another without consulting them, and by way of HMS *La Nymphe* and HMS *Scipio*, Nagle and his fellows were transferred to HMS *Brunswick*, from which he deserted on 26 April 1794.

Nagle tells us very little about his desertion. Much of what he does say or at least suggest is incorrect, but there are enough facts in the log books to make reasonable guesses as to what occurred. The British government at this period was placed in the somewhat awkward position of officially supporting two "navies," the regular service, and the East India Company service, which had a fleet of dozens of ships sailing to and from India and China under the full protection and encouragement of the Crown, which profited greatly from customs duties paid on the immense tea traffic. It had taken over the company's military and political responsibilities in India in the previous decade.

Officially, relations between the Royal Navy and the East India Company navy were supportive and amicable. In reality, particularly as the war with France made it necessary for the Royal Navy to double and triple its fighting force, intense rivalry developed between them for seamen. Nagle's journal provides rarely encountered documentation of the almost treasonable lengths to which the company's captains would go in order to maintain their crews, encouraging and paying sailors to desert the Royal Navy and helping them to evade impressment.

The log of Captain John Harvey of the *Brunswick* notes that on the morning of 27 April 1794, the ship was anchored at Spithead. It was part of Admiral Howe's fleet, which was gathering its vast convoy of merchant vessels for sailing that afternoon. A lighter was dispatched to take some empty casks into shore. Jacob Nagle and William Pyke were among the men assigned to the duty. The log of Captain Alexander Gray of the *Rose*, an East Indiaman bound for Madras and Calcutta and one of the merchant ships making up the convoy that Admiral Howe was about to escort out of port, notes that on April 23 the "Captn. & 2 officers went ashore to get men." Captain Gray undoubtedly offered sizable bounties, and he was eminently successful, picking up twenty-one seamen, two servants, and two quartermasters, all of whom came on board on the morning of April 27, just before the fleet sailed. The perfect timing suggests that Captain Gray was an old hand at encouraging naval desertion. "Jacob Nagle" does not appear on the crew list, but his alias, "Jacob Lincoln," does, based upon his grandmother's name. Undoubtedly many of the other twenty-five names were equally fictitious.

What is somewhat intriguing is that William Pyke, the seaman who deserted with Nagle from the *Brunswick* on the 27th, reentered the *Brunswick* on 21 June 1794 and was honorably discharged three weeks later. Nagle, by this time, was well on his way to India, but it suggests that there may have been extenuating circumstances, possibly that the *Brunswick* had to obey the admiral's sailing orders earlier than expected and that Nagle and Pyke were actually left behind. For the sake of their longevity, they may both have been lucky, for after escorting the merchant vessels to their respective shipping lanes, Admiral Howe's fleet would encounter the French in one of the first major sea battles of the war, "The Glorious First of June." The *Brunswick* suffered considerable damage and its captain was mortally wounded. Nagle eventually heard about it, and whether or not he had intentionally left the vessel, it had the appearance in retrospect of running in the face of danger. When he began relating his career in America, forty years later, with no one around to contradict him, it undoubtedly eased his conscience to gloss over the facts. Those portions of his journal that do not actually record events which he witnessed are printed here in *italics*.

Nagle's voyage to and from India took fifteen months. The British nation had been on a war footing when he left, but it was in a near panic when he returned. In the interim, a scheme had been set in motion to land a group of French émigrés at Quiberon Bay, in Brittany, to establish a pro-British foothold on the mainland that could be expanded by rallying defectors from the countryside, and perhaps then landing British troops. The first contingent sailed on June 17, and by July 10 the fort guarding the bay had been secured and some 4,000 Royalists had gathered. The British began raising troops for the follow-up expedition under the earl of Moira, and orders were issued for 7,000 infantrymen and 2,400 cavalry. Then disaster struck. The French Royalist forces were badly divided between two commanders and between those who had crossed the Channel and those from the countryside. On July 16 they were beaten in an engagement with Republican forces. On the 19th some of the troops that had come from England deserted, and the remainder were massacred by the Republicans, to a man.

At the very moment the *Rose* arrived in the Channel, news of the disaster at Quiberon Bay had reached England. Meanwhile, British troops were assembling for the second invasion. It was this heightened atmosphere of disaster on the one hand, and the excitement of raising troops on the other, that Nagle and his party encountered as they marched overland from their landing place at Long Reach to London, armed with pikes and pistols, and avoiding the main roads until they reached the enclave of the East India Company at Poplar and the city limits of London, where the army was not permitted to force men into the service.

Once in London, although he had escaped the army, he had to protect himself against the navy, and he did so by volunteering for the *Gorgon,* a ship that was fitting out and could not possibly be ready to sail for a month or two. With protection in hand, he could move freely around his London world. His encounter with the young prostitute provides not only a fascinating glimpse of social conditions in London at the time but also a statement of Nagle's decidedly pre-Victorian but humane sense of morality.

He then encountered the "lively hansome" Miss Pitman, daughter of a boat builder from the Isle of Wight, who lived near St. Dunstan's Church in Stepney, whom he married, and by whom he would have "children" before her and their untimely deaths from yellow fever, in Lisbon, seven years later. There was a brief but sharp economic depression in Britain at this period, which hit the shipbuilding industry particularly hard. The Pitmans soon moved closer to home, at Portsmouth, where Nagle would occasionally and briefly see his wife over the next few years.

Perhaps in the euphoria of his marriage, Nagle made the mistake of walking with his wife from Stepney to London without his protection one night and was grabbed by the press crew and taken before the captain of the district, who by coincidence happened also to be his future commander on the *Gorgon*. There are several letters of Captain Terrell surviving from this period in the Admiralty archives, discussing impressment, and they not only show his abilities but completely explain his actions with regard to Nagle.

If Nagle had remembered to keep his protection with him, the press crew would not have bothered him. Captain Terrell found St. Katharine's to be a particularly troublesome area. He was convinced that the East India Company was in league with local magistrates, landlords, and shop and pub owners to frustrate naval impressment. He most strongly advocated two rules to be followed in recruiting in the vicinity: unless the man has a protection on his person, detain him; get the recruits immediately on the tender in the river and transport them to the fleet quickly. Nagle fell afoul of both maxims. Terrell surrounded himself with an audience of friends at the rendezvous in the tavern near Iron Gate, and to have made an exception for a volunteer on his own ship would have contradicted his stated policies and been seen as playing favorites.

Nagle had deserted from his immediately previous duty in the Royal Navy, technically a capital offense, although normally excused when the offender reenlisted before being caught. Since Nagle was smart and rarely did anything without a reason, it is probable that his show of defiance, jumping on the table and brandishing a knife at the press crew, was staged entirely for Captain Terrell's benefit, to make him want Nagle as a "man of spirit" and at the same time to throw a smokescreen over his previous defection from the service, keeping Terrell from asking too many questions. If so, it worked to perfection.

AT THIS TIME the French war broke out (at the commencement of the French war when the King was beheaded), and I having no protection, was pressed and sent on b[oar]d the *Hecktor* [3 August 1792], Capt. Mountague [George Montagu]. We went to Spithead, and shortly after went out on a cruise down Chanel with a nother seventy four [*Hannibal*] which was as commadore, being an older captain.[1] One day a sail hove in sight, and both gave chace. Our ship sailed faster, and we coming up with the chace very fast, but our consort was left behind. We got so near that we could discover she was a French 44 gun ship, and should of come up with the chace, if the commedore had not made our signal to return. Therefore we had to give up chase. In a few days after we lost our consort and fell in with two frigates that came bareing down upon us. In rounding two we split all three topsails. We turned too, getting them down and other sails up to bend, but before we ware complete they ware along side of us, but they proved to be English frigates.

The next day [22 February 1793] we fell in with the *Ganges*, East Indiaman, brought hur two, and press all hands out of hur and put a leutenant and 45 men on board to carry hur into port. I being one of the number, we run into Falmouth and lay there for a convoy to take us to the Downs. In about three weeks the *Lee Nymph* [*La Nymphe*] frigate camc in. In a few days we got under way with about 40 sail for the Downs. In two days we arived safe at an anchor abreast of Deal. A pilot came on board with 40 ticket men, which is protected from the press gang, to carry the India men up to Long Reach, where at that time they mored the vessels and discharged the cargoes. Our leutenant went to Portsmouth to his respective ship but us 45 seamen they would not trust. We ware sent on board the *Lee Nymph* to assist in fitting hur out for see till there was an oppertunity to send us round to Spithead. Capt'n Purlew [Pellew], capt[ain] of the *Lee Nymph*, made applycation to the Admaralaty to keep us, as we ware all call'd prime seamen and his ship was poorly maned, but he could not have his wish.

In about three weeks we ware sent on b[oar]d the *Le Eagle* [*L'Aigle*] Frigate, and went round to Spithead. Ariving there, our ship had sailed for the West Indies and had received a draughtt of men from the *Brumswick* [*Brunswick*] by order of the Amerality.[2] Therefore we ware sent [3 April 1793] on board the *Brumswick* in their stid. Capt[ain] Harvey was very much pleased with us, as we ware allowed to be choice men, and those they had sent on board the *Hector* were the worst of his ships crew that they could pick out. We ware well treated and had liberty to go on shore in turns. We laid at Spithead about four month. We then received orders to go round to the Downs and returned again to Spithead. We then sailed and joined the fleet at Tarbay Bay [Torbay] under the command of Lord How[e].

In a few days a signal was made to weigh anchor and the fleet put to see, down Chanal. We run off Belile on the coast of France. We fell in with the French fleet, 23 sail, and we had seventeen. The signal was made for chase, but the wind being light, and heavy ships, we could not get too them. It fell a dead calm all day. One French ship laying to leeward and nearest to us, our signal was made to go down to hur. The *Brumswick*, being flat bottom, sailed best before the wind, but we could not get to hur. In the mean time, a small American ship came through both fleets and was boarded by both and informed us that the French were on two different parties and did not wish to come to an action if they could get away. We lay in this situation till night came on, but the French fleet getting a breeze of wind in the night, by day light we saw them going round Belile to windward 3 or 4 leagues. Being out of reach, we crused about again.

A few days after, a frigate hove in sight, and a signal was made for a general chace. Some of the ships coming up with hur, she hove all hur guns overboard and what loose spars was on deck, which made hur sail worse than she did before. But she hove too, proved to be a Spaniord, which was not at war with England at that time, but took us to be the French fleet, as they ware at war then. A short time after we fell in with a heavy gale off the

The Thames, Looking toward Long Reach

Lands End of England, but nothing accured perticularly excepting loosing a few spars. The gale seaceing, the fleet run in to Tarbay [Torbay] and lay for a while ketching mackrel, but one squdron was always out at see.

At length Lord How[e] had information of a French squadron being out, expecting to meet a fleet of East Indiaman home ward bound. We then sailed down Channel in pursuit of them. I beleive we had about three or four and twenty sail of the line.

We crused for sum time when one morning we purceived a leven sail to windward of us coming down upon us which we took to be the East Indiaman homeward bound. Likewise the French took us to be the same, but when they came within about three leagues, they purceived what we ware. They amediately hall'd their wind, and we ware all this time close upon a wind, formed in two lines.

Amediately a signal was made for a general chace. Every ship crowded all the sail they could set, and having a good stiff breeze, the *Russel* 74, the *Belleroughen* 74, and two or thre more, beside two frigates that were a head of the whole fleet coming up with them. The French commedore was in an 84 beside eight more ships of the line and two frigates, the two French frigates being the hindmost all this time. We cleared our quarters for action, expecting we would take the whole squadron, being so much supperior to them. The breeze increasing and our ships nearest the enemy carreing on, one of them caried hur three topmasts over the side and several more lost different topmasts and yards. One of our frigates coming up with the sternmust of their frigates began to engage hur. The French admaral being in the fastest sailing ship droped a stern to save his frigate, which made our frigate drop a stern after receiving a broad side from the eighty four. The chace continued and night came on, both the enemy and us standing close upon a wind with our larbourd tacks on board. It being dark, some time in the night we lost sight of them, we still standing our course til morning but they escape'd and was out of sight.

We then crused a while and then put into Tar Bay [Torbay]. Remaining there for a time, we sailed for Spithead. At this time a fleet of merchant men were collecting to sail to different parts of the globe. This hapened in the year 1794. The Brittish Chanel fleet under Lord How[e] being ready for see and to protect such an amence quantity of merchant men down Channel, we got under way from St. Helena at the east end of the Isle of White [Wight], the merchant men runing through the Needles from Mother Bank, Gilkiker, and Spithead. In this convoy there was allowed to be 800 sail of India men and merchant men, and every convoy was allowed a man of war to protect them on the respective voige.[3]

Lord How[e] and his fleet sailed out side of the convoy next to the French shore, 25 saile of the line.[4] Out of them was 7 three deckers and two eighty gun ships and 16 seventy fours. We had a fine fresh breeze from the eastward, passing all the small harbours, sailing down Chanel. The merchantmen came out and joined the fleet from Tarbay [Torbay], Plimouth, and Falmouth, and the grand fleet remained with the fleet to the Lands End of England, the convoys then stearing their course for their respective ports wherever they ware bound to.

Lord How[e] [k]nowing the French fleet was out, cruising about till the 28th of May at 8 or 9 in the morning in Latt'd 47°33' N., Long'd 14°10' West, the rival fleets discovered each other about one time. The wind blowing fresh from the S.W., accompanied with a heavy rough see and the French having the weather gage, Lord How[e] continued his course, while the French admaral Villaret Joyeuse endeavoured to keep a regular order of battle upon the starboard tack. About noon, How[e] made a signal for a general chace. Neare the close of the day, the headmost ship came up with the sternmust ship, Revolutionere, *a three decker, 110 guns, the* sternmost ship in the French line. But Admaral Pasley in the Belleroughen 74 having hur topmasts disabled, Lord Hugh Seymore Conway in the Leveathen 74 came up and received hur fier, which was tremendious, and by the time it was dark Capt'n Parcer in the Audacious 74 came up and faught hur at the distance of a half cable's length, but without any effect on either side. The French having 26 sail of the line and the English 25, they remained in sight during the night on the starboard tack, the French still to windward.

In the morning on the 29 the French wore from van to rare [rear] and edged down on our line a head to engage the van ship of the English. Admarel How[e] taking advantage of so favourable an oppertunity renewed the signal for passing the enemys line and sucseed in gaining the weather gage while the enemy ware repassed by the Belflour and two other three deckers in atempting to cut off the Queen and Royal George, both three deckers. At length the French tack'd again by signal and after a distant canonade stood away in order of battle on the larboard tacks, followed by How[e] having the weather gage. The second day action proved equally unsettled as the former, and a thick fog came on during the night and the greatest part of the next day prevented the renewal of the engagement.

In the mean time Neilly joined the French fleet with a rainforcement of three line a battle ships and two frigates. He, being commander in chief, they remained in line of battle till morning. Lord How[e] seeing time for breekfast, made the signal for it which made the French beleive they wished to decline the engagement, but they ware mistaken. In half and our [hour] Lord How[e] steared close a longside the French admarel with the signal for close quarters, about 9 or 10 in the morning. In about an hour and a half the French admiral seing a number of his ships disabled and one about sinking and six struck, or taken, and his own ship greatly slaughter, he made all sail and the rest followed him, and the Brittish ships were so much racked [wrecked] that they had a nuff to take kare of what they had and repair their own ships to get into harbour.

In the Brunswick Capt[ain] Harvey lost his thy [thigh] with a cannon ball. He lived to get into Portsmouth and see his family. He was much regreted by the whole ships crew. Our masts being gone, we fell out of the line and two ship on us. Capt[ain] Harvy's brother that commanded the Ramalees run up and took the fire off one, and the other was sunk. She fired hur upper deck guns when the lower deck guns were in the water. We that ware dismasted were toed in by the rest to Portsmouth with 6 prises.

Our Capt'n buried and the ships company draughted, I got on shore, run away [26 April 1794] on board an Indiaman call'd the Rose, a ship of 801 tons bound to Bengall. Being a fast sailing ship, we run to Madrass in 4 month [arrived 3 September 1794]. Some part of the passage we had good wind and fine w[eathe]r; we lay there about a week and discharged some articles. This place is an open roadstead and a heavy surf. In landing, ships boats are not fit, having boats for that purpos. Fort St. George is close to the beach. It lays in Log'd 80°25′ East, Latt'd 13°5′N.

We sailed for Bengall, but while laying [10 September 1794] here 4 of us made an atempt to run a way. The boats all being on the booms excepting the jolly boat, about dark the hands ware turned up to hoist the boat in. As soon as she was at the gangway, we jump'd in, sent the boys up that had been in hur, and droped a stern. The officers crying out, "Hall up that boat, you raskels," "Aya" was the answer, till we got a stern, then we took to our oars. The chief mate, finding what we ware at, begin a firing at us. One hollowed out, "Fire a way." We new they could not bring a great gun to bare on us, and we ware soon out of musket shot and out of sight.

We made then for the shore, but we got aback of the surf. The wind blowing right on shore, we found it was no use to atempt to go through such a surf. We saw a ship that lay in the offin ready for sailing. We new she was a country ship. We then pull'd for hur. In our absence they hailed a nother ship and got a six oard boat, the 2d mate, boatswain, carpenter, guner, and 2 more petty officers with arms, and made for that ship, [k]nowing she was going to see in the morning. They had got on board before we hove in sight. Being on b[oar]d, there boat was on the opposite side that we could not see hur. Not suspecting, we asked for some water which we stood in need of, pulling so hard. The capt[ain] said if we would come up, he would give us some grog. We went up.

As soon as we got on the quarter deck they all surrounded us and the second mate claped a pistol to my brest. "If you move an inch, I will blow your brains out."

"Sir," said I, "if I had a pistol, purhaps you would not be so bold."

The capt[ain] ordered the steward to give us grog, which he did. They went in the cabin to take a glass. A young lad told me if we had come 20 minutes sooner, we would of been safe, for they had a stow hole for that purpos and wanted 4 seamen for see cunnes, which is to stear the ship. The boatswain [John Hardy] being a American said he was sorry I should atempt to runaway as I was so much liked by the officers. I told him it was done now.

The mate desired us to go into the cutter, which we did, and wanted us to pull the cutter. We told him we would go in the jolly boat and pull hur aboard, but he would not allow it, knowing we could pull away from them in the jolly boat. Therefore we told him we ware prisoners and we would not pull in the cutter. Therefore two had to pull the jolly boat and the rest the cutter. It being moonlight by this time, we got on board.

The chief mate being raging mad, put us in double irons, but while the guner was getting the irons I saw the steward coming out of the cabin, and I being very thirsty, I steped over to him and beged he would give me a drink of water. The mate coming out of the cabin at that time with a drawn cutlash and seeing me on the larbourt side, where he had put us on the starbourd side, he made a slash at me and hit me on the left shoulder, but being nearly on the flat I was not much cut, but bled a good deal and broke the sword in three peases. "Well, Sir," said I, "there is a time for all things." The bolts was ready and each of us had two shecold [shackles] on with a long bolt, and then the bolt stapled down to the deck amidships on the quarter deck. The next day we ware shifted on the poop in irons and none of the crew or mesmates allowed to come near us.

That night a ships boat came a long side to see some of our officers. 5 more got into hur and stowed themselves away in the bottom of the boat. It being dark, they ware not purceived till they got on board the other ship, but in the morning they ware brought back, being a Company ship, and put in irons with us. What hurt their feelings was we ware call'd prime men, one boatswains mate, one quarter master, one gunners mate, two capt[ains] of the tops, and the rest forecastle men out of the nine.

I beleive we ware three days in irons, when the capt[ain] come on board. We ware all brought on the quarter deck. The capt[ain] not wishing to punish us gave us a lecture in respect of our conduct. When he was going to pronounce the word that he forgave us all, one Jack Robinson, American, burst out a laughing before the capt[ain's] face, which enraged Capt. Gray in such a maner that he ordered us all to be floged. I got a leven lashes, which was the least, and the rest from one dozen to two dozen. We ware then dismissed.[5]

We ariving in the Bay of Bengall, the pilot came on board and the schooner went a head, the sands shifting so often that they have to keep the lead agoing a head of the ship in the schooner, and by signals, if not water enough, comes to an anchor. Coming up to Dimond Harbour, in the evening it came on to blow and rain like a herican [23–24 September 1794]. The rest of the Indiaman that was laying there was laying at morings, but laying at a single anchor. Our cable parted. We let go another and shortly after an other,

Calcutta Sedan Chair

and they all parted. We then let go the sheet anchor with a good new cable. We then bent the spare sheet anchor to a cable that was caried away before. In the dead of the night, blowing a herecan and raining heavy and as dark as pitch, having to steer the vessel at a single anchor, the bore coming down from the River Ganges with that force that apearantly nothing could withstand its tremendious force, at length the new cable gave way. Two men being stationed in the head with a lanthorn cryed out, and we let go the last anchor and the old cable, the men in the head directing the man at the wheele when the current would give hur a shear off to keep hur head direct for the anchor. We found we ware not more then 15 yards from the quick sands. If that cable gave way our ship would of been covered in a few hours, but as God would have it, the last anchor and old cable rode it out. In the morning it fell moderate, and that day we got all our anchors again.

We mored ship, struck our topmasts, and striped hur and got our yards fore and aft ready for refiting. During the time we ware discharging and receiving a cargo, 8 men and the boatswain were employed refiting the riging ready for see. When the India men ware nearly ready for see, we had the launch fited out for the ships company to go up to Calcutta by turns, which is called 80 miles from Dimand Harbour. When we reached Calcutta, we rec'd our two month advance and had our three days cruise.

I fell in with two ladies that new me, had made there escape from Port Jackson.[6] They were rejoice'd to see me and invited me home. I was astonished to see the grand situation they ware in, sedans and chairs at all calls.

Anchorage off Fort St. George, Madras

They treated me very hansomely, I suppose that I might keep my tounge to myself, as they kept no company excepting mates and capt[ains] of ships or those that apeared as gentlemen, though sailors when there are all gentlemen. The weather being hot, they must have a sedan with two Negroes to carry them wherever they wish to go and a boy a long side to fan them. The men that carries you for the day get a half crown, and the boy is well satisfied in getting the cowries that you get in changes when you by any article. Those cowries are shells, 80 of them is a penny, beside whatever shop they bring you to they recive some cowries from the storekeeper for bringing him the custom, so by the evening they think they make a good days work.

Calcutta is a sickley place. Fort William lays on the western arm of the Ganges, 100 miles from the sea, in the Bay of Bengall. Calcutta is 1030 miles N.N.E. of Madrass, Long'd 88°28'E., Lat'd 22°23'North. Fulton is three miles above Dimond Harbour, which did formerly belong to the Duch, where there Indiamen formerly laid, and the mouth of the Ganges is above that on the opposite shore. The river up to Calcutta is but narrow but deep water, but

Sailors Entertaining the Passengers

the English Indiamen go no higher than Dimond Harbour and the cargoes is brought down in boats for that purpose.

We being ready for sea, the number of ships I do not recollect, we had two ladies on b[oar]d of the first rank in Bengall which sent 300 sheep on board for the ships company, like wise 3 buffalow, they having a supply of poltry, as many as the vessel could take on board. After sailing [8 December 1794], in about a week we fell in with a smart gale of wind, and in the night a packet brig that was with us was missing in the morning, but we had a pleasent voige to St. Helena, having fresh provisions and extra grog almost every evening through the generosity of the ladies. To entertain them, Capt. Gray would have the ships company to dance the Irish trot whenever we had fine weather.

When a riving in St. Hellena [18 March 1795], the brig we mised in the gale arived there as soon as we did, though she was a dull sailor, but a fleet of ships will always make more delay than a single ship. We lay here 4 months [*sic*, 2 months] waiting for a convoy and then sailed without, we having now

Jamestown, St. Helena

seventeen sail of Indiamen, and the smallest was the *Rose*, which I was in, and we mounted 32 guns. While laying here, we had a deal of sport in boat rasing and frolicks on board different ships every night, Sunday excepted.

At length [10 May 1795] we sailed for England with a prosperous and pleasent breese. When we got on the coast of Ingland, we stood well to the westward and made Ireland, meaning to put in there, but making the land we saw seven sail bearing down upon us [17 July 1795]. We took them to be a French squadron as we had intilegence they ware on the lookout for us. Immediately the oldest capt[ain] belonging to the Company ships in the fleet made a signal to form the line, which was done and that so close under each others sterns that the line could not be broken without they run on board of our ships, but we hoisting the Companies colours, they hoisted English. They came down and spoke the Commedore and inform'd they ware cruising to protect us and likewise to prevent us from going into Ireland to smugel. They pressed 4 men out of each ship.[7]

We then made sail for the Channel of England and having a fine moderate breeze from the westward we fetched round Cilly Roks and bore up Channel. When we passed the Isle of White [Wight], runing for the Downs, we ware brought too [22 July 1795] by the *Dimond* Frigate and boarded us and pressed 23 men out of us, the rest being stowed away amongst the cargo. Coming into the Downs we had to come to an anchor, and 27 of us which the capt[ain] and chief mate wished to save from the press we ware put down amongst the cargo. The men of war sent all their boats along side to press all they could find, but they dare not open the hatches, and all the rest were pressed excepting us 27.

The pilot coming on board with 45 ticket men after dark, they begin to heave up the anchor, but those landlubers new so little about it that they could not get under way. We having some inveleads soldiers on board, the chief mate came down to us to come up and get the ship under way. We put on the soldiers jackets and hats, run up aloft, and cleared away the riging, sheated home, and hoisted the topsails and got hur underway in sailing trim, then went below. The ticket men seeing the activity of us swore we ware not soldiers, and we being shy of them for fear they would give information. While in the whole [hold] we ware supplyed with provisions and grog by our officers.

When we got up to the Lower Hope [25 July 1795], the capt[ain] seeing two large men of war laying farther up, the capt[ain] sent the chief mate to let us know how to act. They lowered the boat down and hall'd hur along side. Likewise he borrowed a boat from another vessel.

Amediately the signal was given, the 27 of us jumped up on the quarter deck and laid holt of a crow bar and pretended to brake open the arm chest which was left open for that purpose, the capt[ain] and mate crying out, "Men, what are you about?" We made no answer, but took a brace of pistols with 24 rounds of catrages and a cutlash each of us and went into the boats and pulled away for the shore. A revenew cutter purceiving us stoped us to overhall for smugled goods. They took chiefly what we had, but did not get all. The capt[ain] hailed the officer and beged he would let us go, as there was three men of wars boats after us. He let us go and we pulled for life. By the time we landed and got on the bank, we paraded in the medow. They ware close to the shore by this time and seeing we did not run but determened to fight, they lay on their oars and looked at us for awhile, then returned to their ships again. We got on the road for London. In a half an hour after we fell in with 10 sailors armed with harpoons, and we joined company.

We coming to a small village, we ware informed that 30,000 regular troops ware incamped at the Lower Hope within three miles of us, and the light horse being on the road had orders to take all sailors that they came a cross, and one of them undertook to pilate [pilot] us a cross the country clear of the high roads.

After refreshing our selves we started. When about half way we had to take part of the main road, but before we got out of it again we fell in with about fourteen light horse beside the capt[ain]. We immediately paraded close a long the fence with our pistols cocked in each hand. When they came abrest of us, they stoped. The harpeners hove there harpoons over there heads, shining like silver. The capt[ain] enquired from whence we came. We informed him. He discours'd with us a considerable time. The solders vewed the harpoons over their heads as they sat on there horses, and seeing us so well armed, 47 in number, he told us he did not wish to trouble us and rode off.

When getting within a mile of Popler, we fell into the main road again and met a general going to camp with six or seven servents attending him. He stoped us to enquire what news from India and what ships had arived. He very genteelly wished us safe to London.

We, ariving at Popler, we gave our pilot a silk hankerchief a peace, which was 27, worth 5 shillings sterling each. He was well pleased and said he had made a great days work. We refreshed our selves at the first public house. We ware informed there was four press gangs in Popler. We sent for two coaches and started for London with the harpeners on the top of the coaches, and going through Popler we kep a continuel firing till we came to the subburbs of London, then discharged all our arms before we entered the citty, as the press gangs are not allowed to press within the citty. At this time it was expected that Bonepart would invade England.[8]

We delivered up our arms to the Company at the East India House. In a short time the capt[ain] got us our wages. I remained at the White Swan for a few days, not daring to go out of the citty without a protection.[9]

I sent a few lines to Mr. Goodall on Tower Hill. He came to me and took me to his house. He being aquainted with the press master, went to him. It was agre'd I should come over in the evening and he would be there. Accordingly I went into the public house which was only three dores from my boarding house. The gang sitting there, I enquired for the capt[ain] of the press gang. They stared at me, seeing a sailor dressed in India gingams and sattin enquiring for their capt[ain]. They directed me to the stair case, and the landlady showed me up with a light. When I entered, he knowing my business, he told me it would be necessary for me to hail for some man a war in the river that I enter'd for. He said the *Gorgeon* [*Gorgon*] 44 was laying at Woolage [Woolwich] fitting out and would not be ready for see under two month as a Kings storeship. Therefore he gave me a protection as belonging to the *Gorgeon*. I thank'd him and went down stairs.

There was two livers of the place playing a game of draughts. I stood looking on and one beat the other till he gave it up, a pot of beer a game. The winer asked me if I would take a game. I told him I had no objections. For the good of the house we plaid. I beat him. The gang standing round, I told them to drink as it came in. The other trades man wished to try me. I beat him. The gang then begin, and I beat the whole gang which in the whole in the barroom was 12 and had all the bear [beer] in. "Wel," said I, "as I have not been beat, I will have my pot in," which made a purty hearty laugh amongst them all, but the gang thought that would not excuse me, expecting I might have no protection, but not being alowed to over hall me in the house, but when I bid them all good night, they follow'd me and wish'd to [k]now weather I had a protection. I went in again and showed it. They had no more to say. I went home. I then could go wherever I pleased. The gangs [k]nowing me, they seldom overhall'd me.

One evening, going up Ratlif [Ratcliffe] high way, I sept'd [stepped] into a public house and caled for somthing to drink, and sitting at the same table where two young girls were sitting, supposing they belonged to the house, I fell in discourse with one of them I supposed could not be more than thirteen. I asked hur if she was the landlords daughter. She said, "No, Sir, but I live close by." I had drink'd my beer and was going out. She asked me if I would see hur home. I was surprised, but I told hur I would if she would show me the way. She got up and we went out.

She took me up a lane and entered a house where there was an elderly woman sitting a mending some cloking. They asked me to sit down. I observed the old woman was droping a tear. I asked hur what troubled hur mind. She said she had lost hur husband about two months ago and she had no one to help hur but hur daughter and was comp[elle]d to do what could not be helped. I felt for hur and expected they ware in want.

I pretended I wanted something to drink and I felt hungry. I asked hur daughter if she would fetch me some. She said by all means. I gave hur a seven shilling peace and told hur to go to a cook shop and get some cook'd victuals. I told hur to bring a half pint of rum and a quart of beer and the rest in provisions. She took a cloth and some materiels with hur. In hur absence I had some conversation with the old lady in respect of London being so great and popular a city why there was not assistance given to the poor. She said there was in some cases, but it requird friends, and then there was many hundreds in London pereshing for want. By this time hur daughter return'd with all that was required. I took a glass of grog and eat a little, and gave me pleasure to see them eat.

After supper I ment to bid them good night, but the daughter would not purmit me, and likewise hur mother wish'd me to stop as it was late. We went up stairs and I laid down, when she pulled hur gown'd off, which was clean and deasent, but hur shift was nothing but rags. It hurt me to see so lovely a young girl so much in distress for the want of some assistance, and I found by discourse it was to support hur poor mother.

In the morning when rising, I gave hur a half a guinea and told hur to get a couple of shifts. She cried and took me round the neck. I went down stairs and the old ladie was there. I bid hur good morning and she return'd the complement with chearfulness. I presented hur a guinea and told hur it might be of service to hur. She seemed stagnated, and I told hur purhaps you may never see me any more and bid them both good morning. I always thought I never done a better job in my life for the good of my own soul.

When in London before, I got aquainted with a family [that] lived near Stepney Church, though they came from the Isle of White [Wight] abreast of Portsmouth Harbour. I took a liking to a daughter of Mr. Pitmuns, a lively hansome girl in my eye, and maried hur. She had three brothers that I was aquainted with before.

Being at her fathers house, we took a walk down street. Then I proposed walking up to Tower Hill to Mr. Goodalls. Coming along towards St. Catherine, we saw the gang in chase of a sailor. Passing us in the dusk of the evening, the last of the gang purceiving me, came up to me, and asked me who I was and wanted to [k]now whether I had a protection. I told him I belonged to the *Gorgeon* at Woolage and my ticket was where I was going to on Tower Hill. He begin to make free with my wife and I nock'd him down, and a nother coming up, I made him stager, but a number gathering round me and a midshipman of the gang, I told him I would go where he pleased but not to allow his vagabons to insult my wife. He said they should not. Then I walked on with them, and my wife with me.

They took me to Iron Gate where the randevoos was.[10] As soon as I entered I sent my wife up to Mr. Goodalls to bring him down, as I hail for the

Stepney Church

Gorgeon. I was then brought up stairs before the pressmaster. There was several capt[ains] there and a number of ladies. The capt[ain] of the *Gorgeon* [Edward Tyrrell] being one of the company, desired the pressmaster to let him overhall me, as I hail'd for his ship, before I was brought up. I was well dressed in silk jacket, waiscoat, and India gingums. When I apeared they all took there vew of me, both ladies and officers.

"Well," said the capt[ain] of the *Gorgeon*, "what ship do you hail for?"

"The *Gorgeon*, Sir, laying at Wollige."

"Are you aquainted with the capt[ain]?"

"No, Sir, I would not know him if I met him in my dish." There was a loud laugh with the ladies and gentlemen.

"Well, how came you to enter for the *Gorgeon* particularly, not [k]nowing the capt[ain]?"

"I can inform you, Sir. Mr. Goodall, I believe, is a friend to me, and I board in his house since I new London, and Mr. Burley, belonging to the *Gorgeon*, which boards there and I believe is pusser [purser] of the ship, inform'd me the capt[ain] was a fine man and by going in hur I could remain with me wife for a short time as she is not ready for see."

By this time my wife return'd and told me Mr. Goodall was up in the citty. "Well," said the capt[ain], "you must content yourself for the night on board the tender. I am capt[ain] of the *Gorgeon* and I will come and see you in the morning."

"Sir," said I, "will you tear me away from my wife no sooner than I am maried to hur, and she is here now, and if you send me on board the tender this night I wont go in your ship, I will go aboard the largest ship in the navy first."

The ladies endeavoured to interceed for me, but the capt[ain] said he was afraid to trust me without security and Mr. Goodall not being at home. I desired my wife to go and stay with Mrs. Goodall for to night and come on b[oar]d the tender after breckfast.

Going down into the barroom, the gang being all there, I asked the landlady for a pint of beer. "No," said the gang, "we cant wait, you must come a long. Dont bring any beer."

I gumped on a table in a box next to a window fronting the street and drew my knife. "The first raskel that comes in reach of me I will be his death." Some run out and bared the windows, came and locked the dore.

The midshipman run up stairs to the officers. Down came Capt[ain] Terrel. "What's the matter?"

"These raskels," said I, "wont allow me a pint of beer, and I am famishing with drought."

"Madam, fetch him some beer. You raskels, how dare you refuse him that privilage!" The beer was brought.

I sat down and drank my beer. "Now I will go with you."

After going out of the house towards Iron Gate Steps, there was one of each side of me, some a head and some behind me. The two that was a long side of me, I nocked them both backwards, but the fellow behind hit me with a club which stagerd me. The capt[ain], hearing the noise, hollowed out of the window, "You raskels, if you hurt that man I will flog every man of you."

By this time they had all got close round me and got into the very [wherry], which is a boat in common in crossing the river or elswhere. They placed themselves all a round me. My intention was to jump over board and dive a mongst the ships in a strong tide. They could not have found me, but they kept fast holt of me till they got me on board.

The steward demanded me to give him somthing to put my days allowance in. I had nothing. He took my hat and put bisquit and chees into my hat, then on locked the bars and put me on a stair case that led me into the hole [hold]. Coming to the bottom there was a demand for a shilling to drink. There was about 14 prest men. They had a candle burning, and the liquor was soon got by a halling line from the upper deck. I discoverd an old shipmate that had run away from the *Brumswick* and was pressed again. I put my bisquit and cheese on a platform that was made to lay on, having no apetite for eating, but in less than five minutes there was not a crum to be foun, and when I laid down to take a nap, they would be draging at my close [clothes], which ware large Norway rats that ware so numerous and ravenous you could get no rest for them.[11]

The next morning Capt[ain] Terrel came on board, and I was call'd up on the quarter deck. He asked me if I would go on board his ship. I told him through the treatment I had received I did not care where I went to, and I was American. He new he could not get me, as I was pressed on board the tender, unless I entered particularly for his ship, being a Kings transport, and I would be sent on board some line a battle ship. He told me he took a great liking to me, and if I would go on board his ship he would let me come up to London till the ship was ready for see. Likewise he would get me the large bounty which was then allowed for seeman. I new if I did not except of that offer, my portion was a three decker at the Nore, therefore I agreed. The whole sum amounted to 35 Ld. sterling.

The next day I went down in the tender that took all the prest men down to the Nore, but I was not put below as the rest ware. Coming to Wollige [Woolwich], we hail'd the *Gorgon* and a jolly boat was sent, and I came aboard and went on the quarter deck and enquired for the commanding officer. He came up and told me he had just received a litter from the capt[ain] to let me come up to London amediately. I received a ticket.

Boat Carrying Seamen and Friends from London to the Nore

My wife being with me, the boatswain, being a Merican and his wife being on board, they invited us to dinner, and after dinner the leutenant maned the boat and took us on shore. Took stage and arived in London, went to my boarding house, and from thence to hur fathers. Hur father was about moving to Portsmouth. His son being a ship carpenter, and he a boat builder, he thought he would do better there with his son.[12]

By the time my liberty ticket was out, the capt[ain] send for me, and Mr. Goodall went with me, he boarding on Little Tower Hill. When we arived we ware introduc'd up stairs and a great number of capt[ains] in the navy ware there. My capt[ain] was much pleased with me and asked for my ticket. I gave it to him, and he backe my ticket, week after week, till I did not wish to remain any longer, and every time he sent for me, he treated me very hansomely in whatever I chused to drink.

During this time Mr. Smith, that I came home with in the Indiaman, sent the pusser [purser] after me, he going capt[ain] of the same ship, that if I woud desert, he would send me into the country till the ship was ready for sea and give me 10 Lb. sterling pr. month. I told the pusser I new the danger and death would be my portion if caught again, therefore I would not atempt it.[13] After being a month in London, I returned on board.

CHAPTER 8

The Mediterranean

INTRODUCTION

W H E N the *Gorgon* set sail from Spithead in November 1795, with the unspectacular responsibility of delivering masts and naval stores to Gibraltar, Jacob Nagle embarked upon one of the most unusual and eventful cruises of his career in the Royal Navy. Under normal circumstances, when a sailor signed on a ship and sailed from England, the voyage would last a year or two. He would serve with essentially the same officers and men throughout the cruise and return to a British port when the ship needed repairs and refitting of a more serious nature than could be performed at sea or in visiting ports of call. On this voyage, Nagle would serve on two different ships and under four captains; he would be away from home for two and a half years.

Nagle never provides a full explanation of why he found duty on board the *Gorgon* distasteful. Perhaps there was a continuing personality conflict with a lieutenant who attempted to bring him up for court-martial before they left Deptford; possibly he had problems accepting the supervisory responsibilities of his position as assistant quartermaster or the close scrutiny by ship's officers that came with the job. Whatever the reason, Captain Terrell obligingly transferred him to the

Blanche in late April 1796, when the two ships were briefly moored together at Corsica. The navy frowned upon the transfer of individual men or officers, but the practice was not unusual. The problems that may have existed on the *Gorgon* would prove to be small in comparison to those he would have quickly found on the *Blanche*, whose captain, Charles Sawyer, had made several blatant homosexual advances to young men on his ship, and had lost effective discipline in the process.

Sawyer's activities had first come to light in June 1795, at a time when HMS *Blanche* and HMS *Meleanger* were in company. Captain George Cockburn of the *Meleanger*, later noted as the man responsible for burning the government buildings in Washington, D.C., during the War of 1812, had assembled the men from the two ships who were aware of whatever incident had transpired, and there was a mutual agreement to cover up the whole matter. Unfortunately, in June of 1796, Sawyer began calling young men to his hammock late at night, making small talk, asking that the light be put out, and then taking hold of them "about the privates." He also permitted a degree of insubordination on the part of a coxswain and one of the midshipmen, presumably his sometime lovers, so that he effectively lost control of the vessel. The first lieutenant requested a court-martial and Captain Sawyer counteracted with charges against most of the officers on board. To Cockburn, who was now one of Nelson's protégés, the whole matter was deeply embarrassing but skillfully handled. Cockburn submitted to the court correspondence between himself and Sawyer that clearly convicted the captain by his own words, and after sufficient testimony to corroborate the sordid episode, the court dismissed him from the service. The record of the entire proceeding survives in the Admiralty records at the Public Record Office. Nagle was not personally involved in the scandal, but everyone on board had been affected in one way or another.

Sawyer was replaced by Captain D'Arcy Preston, who seems to have been energetic and capable but did not hold the post for long. In January 1797, Commodore Nelson transferred him to the *Dido* and put Henry Hotham on the *Blanche*. Whether he deserved it or not, Hotham had a reputation as a stern disciplinarian, and the crew, according to Nagle, staged a minor revolt, until Nelson himself intervened. The incident is not recorded elsewhere in the official log books or captain's or admiral's correspondence, but it is highly probable that it did occur.

At this particular period there was a tremendous spirit of unrest among the seamen of the British navy. Food supplies were low and rations had been inadequate. In doubling the size of the navy in wartime, many landsmen had been brought into the service and many persons against their will who were not accustomed to shipboard discipline. In 1796 and 1797 a remarkable number of petitions began coming in to the Admiralty from sailors, requesting and demanding better food and pay and even replacement of unpopular officers, and the officials in London for a while vacillated between answering some of the demands and dealing firmly with them. At this very time, Jervis's fleet in the vicinity of Gibraltar was rife with discord. The following year, when both the Channel Fleet and the fleet at the Nore mutinied, the navy reacted swiftly and harshly, but until then, there was an impulse on the part of some captains and admirals to appease the men, to cover up activity that would reflect poorly on their disciplinary abilities, and to hope that the problem would go away. Nelson had replaced Preston with Hotham while at Elba, far from the main fleet, apparently without previous approval of Admiral Jervis. They were in a critical situation. Neither Hotham's nor Nelson's careers would have benefited from provoking a serious mutiny, if it could be avoided, and there was no need to make it a part of the official record. Hotham retained command of the *Blanche* for a year until it arrived back at Portsmouth, at which time the crew petitioned the Admiralty to leave the ship.

In terms of Nagle's career, what makes this tour of duty particularly unusual was the extent to which he was at the center of action. Like many career seamen, he had the good sense to stay away from the large ships of the line, and except for two brief terms of service on the *Hector* and *Brunswick,* and the portside duty on the *Ganges,* all 74-gun ships, he spent his entire active career on frigates and sloops, vessels that could not stand up to the broadsides of the battleships in fighting formations or serve quite as long or effectively in blockades. Ambitious officers made an effort to ship on the larger vessels; this was where one was most likely to be involved in the great sea battles where laurels were won and promotions rapidly achieved. On the ships themselves, with large complements of both men and officers, internal promotions were possible. For the sailor, on the other hand, the worst conditions of the navy were to be found on the large battleships, while on the frigate or the sloop, relations between crewmen were on a more personal basis.

Circumstances beyond Nagle's, and even the British navy's, control placed the *Gorgon* and the *Blanche* in the middle of a rapidly changing situation in the Mediterranean between the spring of 1796 and the spring of 1798. In order for the reader to make any sense out of the seemingly haphazard wanderings of Nagle's ships, it is necessary to outline as clearly as possible what was happening.

When the *Gorgon* arrived at Corsica in March 1796, the British seemed to have effective naval control of the Mediterranean. Through a series of alliances made shortly after the war had broken out in 1793, Britain had obtained the neutrality of France's neighbors, Spain and Portugal to the west, the Italian states bordering the Mediterranean to the east. The English had been forced to evacuate Toulon, the French naval base on the Mediterranean that Admiral Hood had taken with the help of Royalists, but in 1794 they had established British sovereignty over Corsica, giving them a naval and trading base from which they could keep open the vitally important sources of naval supply and trade at Leghorn and Genoa. Admiral John Jarvis arrived at Corsica in November 1795 to take command in the Mediterranean, and he succeeded in establishing a very effective blockade of Toulon that kept the French fleet bottled up in its own harbor.

Just as the *Gorgon* arrived and Nagle was transferred to the *Blanche*, the situation began to deteriorate. Napoleon launched his brilliant Italian campaign in March from Nice, working his way toward Italy, defeating the Austrians at every engagement and turning the Italian states, one after the other, against the British. The British community at Leghorn, an important source of much-needed naval cordage, had to be evacuated in June. Britain's rising star, Commodore Nelson, took possession of Elba and established a blockade of Leghorn in July, in which the *Blanche* played a part, but Genoa began to waver. On August 19, Spain and France signed a treaty of alliance, and on September 8, Spain declared war on Britain, bringing her very sizable and hostile fleet into play at the western end of the Mediterranean.

The British ministry was forced to change completely its naval strategy, and it decided to abandon positions in the eastern Mediterranean and to concentrate all efforts on propping up Portugal. Corsica was evacuated in late October and stores were removed to Elba. The blockades of Leghorn and Toulon were raised, and Jervis's fleet sailed in November, establishing its new base at Lisbon amid general apathy on the part of the Portuguese themselves.

There was one more assignment before the complete abandonment of the eastern Mediterranean was complete, and that was the evacuation of the garrison and the stores at Elba. The task was assigned by Jervis to Nelson, and the two vessels selected were the *Minerve*, with Commodore Nelson and Captain Cockburn aboard, and the *Blanche*. It proved to be an adventuresome trip, and because Nelson was involved, it is the one action of Nagle's career that receives mention in general naval histories of the era.

The two ships set out from Gibraltar on December 15. On the 20th, off Cartagena, they encountered two Spanish warships. The *Minerve* took on the *Santa Sabina* and, after inflicting heavy casualties, forced its surrender. Its commander, who was brought on board, was Don Jacobo Stuart, a great-grandson of England's onetime King James II, who was treated with the utmost courtesy and exchanged. The *Blanche* had taken on the other vessel, the *Ceres*, but before she made a capture, additional Spanish ships appeared, then an entire fleet.

The *Santa Sabina* was recaptured with Nelson's prize crew aboard, before they had been able to transfer any additional prisoners, and the *Blanche*, aware sooner than Nelson of the near presence of the fleet, separated and attempted to decoy the ships away from the *Minerve*. Nelson arrived at Porto Ferragio, Elba, on the 26th, wondering what had become of the *Blanche* and a little annoyed that the ship had not helped him to save his prize; the *Blanche* arrived on the 29th.

Nelson carried specific orders to evacuate the garrison at Elba, but its stubborn military commander, J. Thomas De Burgh, although accepting the wisdom of the withdrawal, refused to move until he had received direct orders himself. Nelson waited at Porto Ferragio until the end of January, perfecting arrangements for the withdrawal and leaving Captain Thomas Fremantle in charge. The *Blanche* was left, and Nelson quickly returned to Jervis's fleet, where he performed heroically at the Battle of St. Vincent on February 14. De Burgh finally evacuated Elba on 17 April 1797. Fremantle's fleet of forty-five vessels was met by Nelson on April 21 on their return, and they arrived safely at Gibraltar in late May. The final period of Nagle's cruise on the *Blanche* was boring in comparison—at times participating in the blockade of Cadiz, at other times lying off Gibraltar, taking supplies to the fleet. It lasted nine months, but Nagle devotes only two pages of the journal to it.

Admiral Jervis took a very tough line in regard to the wave of insubordination that had infected the fleets in the previous two years, and his solution was to make public examples through highly visible executions. At the end of June, Captain Shuldham Peard, of HMS *St. George*, one of the ships besieging Cadiz, brought two seamen up for trial for homosexuality. The men were declared guilty and sentenced by the admiral to death. The crew petitioned the captain for leniency, and the two men carrying the petition were accused of planning to seize the ship, which may or may not have been true, and were sentenced to execution. It was these two men, John Anderson and Michael

McCann, whose execution Nagle witnessed from the deck of the *Blanche* on Sunday morning, 8 July 1796, as the *Blanche* prepared to leave for England. It is not surprising that it made a considerable impression on the ship's crew. Had it been Jervis, rather than the more sympathetic Nelson, on the scene at Elba a year and a half earlier when they stood up to Captain Hotham, a number of them would have shared a similar fate. On 29 June 1798 the *Blanche* returned to Portsmouth for repairs. Nagle had the opportunity to see his wife for the first time in two and a half years and probably an eldest child for the first time. Whether or not all the crew members succeeded in getting off Captain Hotham's ship is uncertain, but Nagle managed to ship on a vessel that would provide the high point of his entire naval career.

THE SHIP [HMS *Gorgon*] was loading with masts and stores for Giberalter and the Island of Cossico [Corsica] where the Brittish fleet made there randevoos in Farensa [Fiorenzo] Bay. At length we sailed for Spithead and the capt[ain] made me a petty officer, which was a boatswains mate. That I did not like, but I refused the birth, but Capt[ain] Terrel told me I must do my duty as such or he would flog me, which he was no slouch at, though he was always a friend to me.

While laying there the boatswain was confined to his cabin and I was ordered to do his duty. One evening I was ordered to hoist the boats in. I turned the hands up, and I was on the gangway, seeing the boat hooked on. At that very time my wife came a long side. I asked the leughtenant to purmit my wife on board. "No, Sir, she shal not." I turned round, vexed and savage. Having a rattan in my hand which I was compelled to carry, it being broke, I hove it overboard and the silver call I hove into the waist to the boatswain, as it belonged to him.

The leutenant taking notice what I had done, as soon as the boats was in, he called me aft and told me to prepare for a court marshial, heaving my stick over board and the call into the waist in such a disdainful manner. The

St. Fiorenzo Bay, Corsica

capt[ain] coming on board, he informed the capt[ain] and demand a court marshal. I was call aft before him and the capt[ain]. I informed the capt[ain] that it was not with any dirision to my commanding officer that I had done either. The rattan was broke in too and useless and as for the call, it belonged to the boatswain, and he asked me for the call, and I hove it down to him. The capt[ain] asked the boatswain weather he had demanded the call of me. The boatswain, knowing the danger I was in, and being American, he said, "Yes, Sir, I did," which was greatly in my favour. He plead for me till he got cooler, which he could of tried me weather the capt[ain] thought fit or not, but the capt[ain] told me to beg his pardon, which I did, if he thought it was out of derision, that I beged his pardon, and he apeared to be satisfied.

Now a three decker and some more men of war beside a fleet of transports being ready, we sailed [11 November 1795]. On the passage, we fell in with a gail of wind that parted the fleet, but they all arived safe at Giberalter [28 November 1795]. We discharged part of our stores, then sailed and ariving in Corsico [3 March 1796] and came to an anchor in Ferensa [Fiorenzo] Bay without anything hapening worthy of notice where the fleet was laying and supplied them with riging and spars. We ware then sent round to the west end of the island to Ajacco, (where Bonaprt was born). Cossico lays between 8° and 10° E. Long'd and 41° [and] 43°N. Latt'd. On the south it is separated from Sardinia by the Strait of Bonifacio; to the east the Tuscan; north the Gulf of Genoa; west, opposite the coast of France and Spain, 158 miles from N. to S., from 40 to 50 in breadth. A ridge of mountains devide the island in two parts, N. and South. The capetal is Bastia.[1] When we ware there it was taken from the French and the English had possession. Bastia [is] 70 miles from Leghorn.

We came to an anchor in a bay [21 April 1796] within the town and found the *Blanch* Frigate laying there. At this time the Corsekons were verry troublesome to the English. Abreast of where we lay was a large stone building with a high wall around it and a run of fresh water runing past it into the bay. The wimen went on shore to this creeke to wash for the officers and men, but we had to send all the marines on shore to guard them or they would of taken all the clothes from [them].

The marines was paraded in a file abreast the house. Our first leut't and a midshipman went with there fusees into the next field to shoot some birds. The Cosecans ware laying in ambush in sight of us on board. One Cossican came to them and took both their guns from them, and showing them the men that ware laying ready with their rifels to fire at them if they resisted and then walked off with there guns and left them to come on b[oar]d empty handed. As soon as the wimen and marines got on b[oar]d they got into the large stone house, up stairs and begin to fire at us upon deck which made it dangerous to walk the deck till the capt[ain] ordered the six pounder on the forecastle to be got ready, and we boared the house and walls and nocked one corner of the house entierly away. They then thought it time to leave the house and not to trouble us any more.

A few days after there was information given they ment to storm the town. Our ship laying abreast the valley where they had to pass to go up the hill to the town, that we rake the valley from one end to the other with round and grape. Our guns being cast loose, and a spring on the cable, laying broad side to the valley, when the signal was given, about 9 o'clock at night we opened our broad side with a constant fire.

Though I was capt[ain] of the gun, the men not being all there, I fired the 12 pounder that I was at and got to the mussel [muzzle] of the gun to receive the catrige and ram it hom, when the second thought struck me the gun had been laying a long time loaded. I handed the catrige back to the man and took up the worm and screwed it round two or three times and halled it out with a blaze half as big as my head and shooked it overboard. If it had not been ordain'd, I should have went to see what the Casacans was about and not to return any more. But keeping a constant fire, they retreated and made no more attempt while we lay there.

Bastia, Corsica

The capt[ain] dining on board the *Blanch* frigate, and he new I did not like my sittuation on acount of what hapened before, he sent for me, and I was brought into the caben. Capt[ain] Sawyer seeing me gave one seaman and one landsman in my room. I came on board [24 April 1796] the *Blanch* Frigate.[2] We then sailed for Farensa [Fiorenzo] Bay and joined Commedore Nelsons squadron [27 May 1796] along the coast of Genoa from Wille Frank [Villa Franca] up to Leghorn.

We run into Genoa in the *Blanch* and came to an anchor alongside a Spanish frigate of 36 guns and we 32 guns. In swiming we would intermix among each other and being in a neutral port we ware not allowed to trouble each other. In a few days we sailed and left hur there, not being in a youmer for boxing.

The next day we made sail (Genoa Citty, capital of the province of the same name, it is situated at the bottom of a little gulf partly on the declivity of a pleasent hill defended on the land side by a double wall in circumfrance about six miles, 62 miles S.E. of Turun, 299 miles N.W. of Rome) to joine the squadron. Bonapart at this tim[e] was coming up a long shore driving all before him, having no army against him exepting the Austrins, making a vissit to Rome. Coming to Vardo, they gave up the fort to him without any opposition. This fort is on a high hill that projects out into the see and is allowed to have 365 guns and morters in it. After passing Vardo, the road leads a long shore for Genoa. Nelson having information that his [Bonaparte's] army was to pass that night along the road close to the water, he brought his squadron to an anchor [1 June 1796] close in shore, with springs on our cables, 2 sixty fours, 4 frigates, a twenty gun ship, and 2 sloops of war. We lay there during the night, but Boneypart having intilagance took a nother road through the fields and was past in the morning. We then hove up our anchors and cruised a long shore.

In a few days the *Blanch* went to Leghorn [13 June 1796]. I belonging to the capt[ain's] barge, we ware on shore, and the capt[ain] and several officers. They suspected that two of us ment to leave the ship. Making a search, they found us, took us on board with the capt[ain] as prisoners about 12 o'clock at night and put us in irons, but the next day forgave us, and by two o'clock the French light horse came into the town.

Early in the morning the French begin to fire at us, but the guns from the batteries could not reach us by 15 or 20 yards though their guns was chock'd so that they could not recoil. We lay about half a mile within the malora. We lay still and washed our decks down as is usual in the morning.

At 8 o'clock we piped to breckfast. During this time, finding they could not reach us, they got a long gun from a tower on the S.W. side of the town and brought it to the nearest battery to us and begin to open upon us. The very first shot went over us a quarter of a mile.

Immediately the hands were turned up to weigh anchor [3 July 1796], got under way, and begin to beat out, having a head wind from the westward. Our vessel being light, we fell to leeward and having to stretch a long shore past all the batteries, they kept a continual fire upon us and we returning the salute till we ware out of reach of their guns which was not less than two hours. We then steered a long the Genoa coast and fell in with the squadron [6 July 1796] we belonged to and inform'd Nelson of the French being in Leghorn. We ware then sent to inform the fleet off Taloon [Toulon] under the command of Adm'l Jarvice [Jervis] and returned again to join the squodran.

We then crused a long shore day and night. Purceiving two brigs and a gun boat laying in a small bay abreast of a small village under cover of a tower that mounted eight thirty two pounders completed for firing hot shot, about a leven o'clock Nelson made the signal to enter the bay.

We ketching a light breeze of wind, we run in within half musket shot of the shore [7 September 1796], but the wind dying away and fell dead calm, we lay like a target under their guns, boath great guns and small arms, and Nelson and the squadron could not get in to our assistance. The shot from the tower being hot shot, therefore one watch was employed with fierbuckets and the other half at their quarters. We receiv'd one shot abreast the fore magizene and set us afier, but supplying it well with water till we could clear away below and cut it out, as fortune favoured us the shot was two large to fall between the lineing and the ships out side plank. If it had been smaller it would of fell down under the magizeine where we could not get at it and would of blown the ship up; a nother shot set the heel of the main topmast on fire, but we got that out before it ketched the sails. Another shot struck us on the quarter and set us on fire, entering the gunroom. All this was done in the space of 30 minutes.

Captain Sawyer made a signal to Com'd. Nelson to purmit us to engage, but he anull'd the signal which was luckey for us. If we had been engaging, what with the fire and smoke, we should of not seen where we ware on fier until it would of been two late to put it out. I was stationed as capt[ain] of the 5 gun from forward, abreast the chestree. A hot shot entered the chesstree and passed the back of my neck. Having tied hair, it cut and singed my hair without doing any more damage to me. The men ware all laying down at there quarters according to orders excepting myself. The officer of the deck coming along at that moment ordered me to lay down, and by stooping my head, the shot entered which would of beheaded me completely. The same shot wounded an officer with the splinters, 5 or 6 yards off, and I being abreast of it, receiv'd no damage. It kill'd some fowls in the hen coobs [coops] a midships and entered the spare topmasts on the booms and broke the iron wenches [winches] that we pump ship with into pieces.[3]

All this time we had sent our boats to bring the brigs off and gun boat. The men had left them, but they ware hard and fast ashore and a continuel fire upon them with musketry from the shore, and having several wounded, we left them. After laying in this situation for the space of three hours and no breeze springing up, Nelson made the signal for all boats from the squadron. They came in and took us in toe. As soon as they found they ware taking us in toe, they quit firing at us and began firing at the boats, but it was in vain, the boats being low on the water and in constant motion. They took us out without the loss of a man. It was surprising we had no men killed, except some slitely wounded.

In this maner we cruised a long the coast. Beside the squadron we had two gunboats that was taken by the squadron: one was a small galyot that mounted three (3) long 24 pounders, the other was a small schooner riged boat with a long brass eighteen pounder. Those two sneaked a long shore in the day time, to give information. Then at night Nelson would send in boats to cut them out.

At this time the French had command all a long the coast. Coming off Ville Frank we stood off from the land till night, then stood in and hoisted out two boats from each ship and went in with muffeld oars, the galyot gunboat being in before us. As soon as we discover'd hur we made for hur in two divisions, it being verry dark, but she saw us and was well prepared, hur guns being loaded with grape and canister. Coming up about 15 yards from hur, they hail'd our com[andin]g officer. Finding there mistake, answered the countersign, which proved well for us. We then pulled a long shore under the forts, so close that we could of fired at the sentries with our pistols. They having fiers and lanthorns and we being in the dark, they could not purceive us till we came to the mold [mole], thinking to fetch out some of the best of the shipping, but we found it locked. We then passed the town and took a cirkle round the bay. We then spied some boats. We made for them and boarded with cutlashes, making such a clattering with the weapons they cried out for quarters, expecting death in a moment, but they proved to be poor fishermen. We went on and left them.

The next we spied a ship. We came up with hur and boarded hur in three divisions. She was full of men. They were resolute though they had no arms. We had to drive them down the hatchways and tumbled some of them down to clear the deck. They took us to be Turks. She proved to be a French ship full of Austrons [Austrians], prisoners to the French, but when they found we ware English they did rejoice, and afterwards a great number entered on board of Nelsons ship.[4]

By this time daylight was apearing, and it came on to blow a smart gale from the westward, but we could sea no ships. We up hellem and put the boats before the wind under close reef foresail. [K]nowing the ships must be to the eastward, our boat being a yall and the smallest boat in company, we had to lower our reef foresail halfway down. Being a heavy following sea and the boat very low, it took 3 and 4 hand abailing the water out. In about one hour we saw two sail laying two and by the time we came up to them we discovered our own frigate about 3 leagues ahead of us, therefore we stood on, and in a short time we came a long side with the boat half full of water. We hoisted the boat in and we ware order'd to our hammoks after we had some refreshment.

Horatio Nelson in 1795

Some time after, runing off Vardo, we discovered a French sloop of war mored close to the shore and gunboats laying round hur under the heavy fort over hur masts heads. As soon as dark came on, Nelson ordered eight boats from different ships with two marines in each boat, beside the boats crews, armed, and an officer, his first leutenant, commander. We pulled into the eastermost part of the bay and pulled a long shore, one boats painter fast to the other in a line, with our oars muffled til we got within about 15 yards of the vessel, when a gunboat that lay within us let fly an 18 pound shot over the center of us. The sentry on b[oar]d the brig was so much fritened that he could not utter himself when he attempted to hail us. If the gunboat had not kept a better lookout than the brig, we would of been on board in less than three minutes, but being discover'd, the commanding officers orders was to cast loose and run. Our leut[enan]t was for boarding, but it was two late. We pulled out for the offin. The batteries on the mount opened upon us with grape and canister, and droped round us like hale, but as God would have it a dark black cloud came over the mount at that momint which compel'd them to fier at random. It was surprising how we could escape without a man being hurt. Before we ware from under their guns we met a vessel coming in, but she proved to be no enemy. We returned on board.

The Commodore sent the *Blanch* to blockade Leghorn. We run in side of the melora and came to an anchor, not to purmit any vessel to go in or out. We took several vessals which had French property on board in nuteral bottoms. Nelson came in in the *Capt* [*Captain*], 74 gun ship, and came to an anchor a few days, then run out and went over to the island of Elbow [Elba], run in to the harbour [10 July 1796], and they surrendered with out a shot being fired.

Our squadron at different times would come and lay at Leghorn with us, till being short of provisions we sailed for Farenza [Fiorenzo] Bay in the Island of Cossico [Corsica], where we found Adm'l Jarvis and his fleet. While there the capt[ain] and first leutenant fell out, and they ware both tried by a court martial on board the flag ship, and the proof being so strong against Capt[ain] Sawyer, having a fondness for young men and boys, that he broke from ever serving in his Majesties service [18 October 1796]. We then receiv'd a young capt. [D'Arcy Preston] till further orders and was ordered to see with all new officers, crusing for the Spanish fleet.

A few days after, came on to blow a fresh gale from the westward, About 10 P.M., being dark, we fell into the middle of the Spanish fleet. We up helam and kep the ship before the wind to the eastward, the enemy beating to the westward. They begin to make signals by lights and sky rockits. Discovering that an enemy was in the fleet, and we runing the gantlet through them, three sail gave chase after us. At day light they found we had the heels of them, gave up the chase, and return'd.

We endeavoured to get into Farenza [Fiorenzo] Bay to inform the adm[ira]l, but that night blowing very heavy, our main riging gave way from the mainmast head. By getting takles up to support the masts till we got sum harsers secured over the mast head and set up, we saved the mast. The nex day we got into Farenza Bay. After the court marshal being over, our first leutenant and all the officers returned to the ship excepting Capt[ain] Sawyer.

We ware sent over to Leghorn for cattle, which we could get by smuglin off in the night, along shore, and likewise fresh beef, though the French had possession.[5] In returning, being about half way, we saw a very great elumenation towards the island of Cossaco [Corsica] but could not emagin wat it might be, but when ariving in the bay we ware inform'd a French three decker that had been taken by the English was burnt to the waters edge. We went out again and went into Genoa for a few days and sailed again. The Brittish troops were sent on board the transports and evacuated the island of

Admiral John Jervis

Cossaco [Corsica] and went to the island of Elbo [Elba], which had been taken by Nelson, and we went to that port, where Com'd Nelson was then laying in the *Manerva* [*Minerve*] Frigate.

We ware then ordered to joine the fleet. Bonaparte had then left Leghorn but kept the ports in possession, excepting the island of Elbow which the Brittish troops had possession of with the transports. Jervice and his fleet sailed for Giberalter, and we joined them. We had a good and pleasant passage, but the night before we got into Giberalter we fell foul of the admiral ship [1 December 1796] and carried away hur fore yard without doing any damage to our selves.[6] Our capt[ain] in the *Blanch* Frigate was a nephew of the admirals. He ordered him out of the fleet and make sail for Giberalter, which we did the next day.

The fleet under Jarvis went off Cadis and blockaded the Spanish fleet, which was laying there. Nelson in the *Manerva* Frigate and the *Blanch* was ordered up the Straits again to the island of Elbow [Elba] to convoy the transports and troops down to Jiberalter. We sailed [15 December 1796] with a pleasant breeze in the after noon. Sailing a long the Spanish shore we fell in with a Spanish coaster [19 December 1796] runing a long shore. We brought hur two and boarded hur. She was loaded with bales of silk, but overhalling hur log book we found there was two Spanish frigates crusing off

Cathergeen [Cartagena]. Nelson ordered 7 bails of silk to be hoisted out of hur for a drink for the sailors and let hur go and amediately made sail and ordered our capt[ain] to go a head.[7] As the *Manerve* that he was in was the fastest sailer, he kept a stern. Nelson gave orders as soon as we should sea the frigates to heave two till he came up.

It had been now dark a considerable time. At length we spied a sail a head laying two, and we hove two till Nelson came up and spoke, as by this time we purceived the other a beam of us with a top light. Nelson stood for the commedore [*Santa Sabina*] and we for the other [*Ceres*]. Before we got to our antagonist Nelson was a long side of the commedore and poared a broad side into hur and killed 36 men on the quarter deck, beside the capt[ain], first and second leutenant, beside what was slaughtered on the main deck and forecastle. The third leutenant made an apemps [attempt] to fight hur, but in vain. They struck and Nelson took possession [20 December 1796] and put 30 men on board and took hur in tow. Nelsons ship mounted 36 guns and the Spanish ship 48.[8]

In the *Blanch* we ware not idel [idle]. We run as close along side as we could without runing on board of hur and gave hur a broadside fore and aft. We played so hot upon them, they run from there quarters. The second broadside we shot ahead and laying a cross hur bows, raked hur fore and aft and carried away hur fore topgall[an]t and royal stays. Rounding two under hur lee, we gave hur another broad side. Hur topsails and colours all came down by the run. When they did fire there guns they ware in such haste that there shot all went over us.

We ware boarding hur when we spied a 74 gun ship and two frigates close a board. We up boat and made sail. We hall'd our wind, having the weather gage. They all stood for Nelson. He, having the frigate in tow and seeing the 74 close on board, cut and run, at the same time gave the seventy four a broad side, and the 30 men on b[oar]d the prize gave hur a broad side and then struck. When taking possession they all gave chace after Nelson.

We huging our wind, which was from the westward, they supposed us to belong to the convoy which we new nothing of till daylight, when we found our selves in the midst of a fleet of merchent men of Spanish bound into Cathegen [Cartagena]. Nelson then had the 74 and 5 frigates in chase of him. Nelson made signals to us, but we dare not answer them. We remained quietly till night, then droping out side of the fleet and stood over for the Turkish shore and towards morning stood for the Spanish shore and run up a long shore. By that means we escaped, for we ware out of trim and could not

Porto Ferrajo Bay, Elba

sail as she generally had done. Nelson out run them all excepting one small frigate that could come up with him, but he got two long 18 pounders out of the gun room ports and two out of the cabin windows and two on the quarter deck, which was 6 long eighteens. When she would come about half gun shot, he would bore hur fore and aft. She would then drop a stern. By that means he escaped and got into the island of Elbow [Elba] three days before us, which made him doubtful but what we ware taken. When we came to an anchor Nelson came on board and ordered the capt[ain] to beat to quarters, and as we ware in a line before our guns, he came round the decks and shook hands with us as he went along and telling us he was rejoice'd to find that we had escaped.

At the time we fell in and engaged these two frigates there was four frigates in company, though we ware not aware of it, beside 28 sail of the line laying at an anchor within three miles of us, beside three frigates that ware in the convoy. The 30 men that had been taken was caried into Cathejene [Cartagena] and the Spanierde treated them well and sent them back and Nelson returned there prisoners. They gave an acount: the frigate that we engaged was brought in by two frigates, slung with harsers, one frigate on each side to keep hur from sinking. The day before they took an English transport and those men were on board at the time we engaged them. They said the Spanish officers run several men through with their swords, driving them to their quarter.

In a few days Nelson sent us out upon a cruise off of Taloon [Toulon]. One morning about 10 A.M. we spied too sail to leeward. We bore down upon them. They both made sail, but one out sail'd the other. We coming up alongside, she struck hur colours. They ware a French 20 gun ship out of Toloon bound for Corsico [Corsica]. She had about one hundred men on board and a great number of wimen and Bonaparts baggage, but by sum means or other he was detained and sent them off without going himself.[9] Therefore he saved his bacon for that time, but his bagage and clothing as I understood was sent back to him. The other ship got away.

We maned the prise and took the men out but left the wimen on board, sending hur into the island of Elbow [Elba]. While on the passage, a gale of wind came on. She was cast a way on the east end of Cosico [Corsica], but none lost, but our men ware made prisoners, but our seamen endeavouring

Spirit of Rebellion on HMS Blanche *in 1795*

to save the wimen and being kind to them while under their charge, when they ware in prison the wimen would be coming every day to supply them with the best provisions they could get, beside the allowance they ware allowed.

We still remained on a cruise off Taloon till we receiv'd orders to return. When we arived and came to an anchor we found the *Dido* Frigate laying there of 28 guns, and their capt'n being an older capt'n than ours, was commisoned to take our ship and our capt[ain] to take the *Dido* in his place. Capt[ain] Hothom [Henry Hotham] bearing the name of such a tarter by his own ships crew, that our ship mutinised and entierly refused him. He came on board [7 January 1797], had all the officers armed on the quarter deck and all hands turned aft to hear his commission read at the capstain head. They all cried out, "No, no, no." He asked what they had to say against. One of the petty officers replyed that his ships company informed us that he was a dam'd tarter and we would not have him and went forward and turned the two forecastle guns aft with canester shot.[10]

He then went in his boat on board the commedore and returned with the com[modore's] first leutenant. When on b[oar]d he ordered all hands aft. The ships company came aft. He called all the petty officers out, which ware call'd by name, and pareded them in a line on the quarter deck. "Now, my lads, if you resist taking Capt[ain] Hotham as your capt[ain], every third man shall be hung." The crew flew in a body forward to the guns with match in hand, likewise crowbars, handspikes, and all kinds of weapons they could get holt of and left him, Capt[ain] Hothom, and the officers standing looking at us. They consulted for a moment and returned on b[oar]d Commodere Nelson.

In the space of half an hour the Commedore came on b[oar]d, call'd all hands aft, and enquired the reason of this disturbance. He was inform'd of Capt[ain] Hotham's caractor, which was the reason that we refused him.

"Lads," said he, "you have the greatest caracter on b[oar]d the *Blanch* of any frigates crew in the navy. You have taken two frigates supperiour to the frigate you are in, and now to rebel. If Capt[ain] Hotham ill treats you, give me a letter and I will support you."

Amediately there was three chears given and Capt[ain] Hothom shed tears, and Nelson went on b[oar]d his ship. All being ready, the troops were all sent on board the transport and we sailed [18 April 1797] for Giberalter under the convoy of Com[madore] Nelson [*sic*, Fremantle] in the *Manerve* [*sic, Inconstant*] Frigate and the *Blanch*, Capt[ain] Hotham, and two kings

Inner Squadron, Blockade of Cadiz, 1797

ships, transports, but they having no guns excepting on the uper deck. We had pleasent w[eathe]r. Getting a little to the westward of Taloon, we fell in with three line of battle ships which was sent to meet and protect the convoy, as part of the Spanish fleet lay in Taloon. We arived in safety at Giberalter [24 May 1797].

In a few days [6 June 1797] we joined Jarvises fleet off Cadis. Jarvises fleet lay at an anchor out side, then Nelson with a squadron of seven sail of the line lay in side of them, and we ware stationed within the whole, laying off and on from one shore to the other, all hand at quarters during the night with the hatches laid over that no one was allowed to go below, and let us stand on the one tack or the other, we would have a shot or a shell flying over us during the night. The reason was to keep the gun boats off from anoying the line of battle ships. The gunboats would come a[nd] lay off and keep firing at the ships laying at their anchors, but when we ware in side we could cut them off, but the bateries on either shore could fire at us. We remained on this station about a fortnight, then we ware releived and sent over to Algiers for cattle for the fleet, and when returning with the cattle, we ware ordered to take the out side station as a look out.

One morning at 4 A.M. [24 June 1797] we saw a sail coming bearing down upon us with all sail she could croud. When drawing nearer we could purceive she mounted 24 guns. We beat to quarter and when they came close to us they hoisted jack, insign, and pennant, Spanish colours. We up English colours and gave hur about 6 or 7 guns nearly at one time. Amediate she hall'd hur colours down. They took the fleet inside to be the Spanish fleet and we as a look out ship. We took hur into Adm'l Jarvis and was made fast a stern of his ship but never received anything for hur. She was a rich loaded ship from the River of Plate, South America, which Jervice put in his own pocket.

Shortly after [15 July 1797] Nelson sailed with a squadron of frigates to take St. a Cruse on the island of Tenereef, but we ware detain'd from his squodron to take the station off Cape St. Marys to the north of Cadis.[11] We remained there about a month [*sic,* a year], and then ordered to the fleet to receive our orders. On the day we ware laying two to receive our orders, which was to sail for England, the inside devision of line a battle ships was engaged by the gunboats, the other division had their penant up at the mizen peak for prayers, and the other division had the yellow flag hoisted, a hanging of two men, all at one time on a Sunday, and we receiving our orders, made sail, and put into Lisbon, water'd ship, and sailed for England.

We arived [11 July 1798] and went into Portsmouth harbour and the *Blanch* was ordered into dock for repair. As soon as she was striped, the ships company rought a petition to the Admirality wishing to be draughted, as we did not like the capt[ain].

CHAPTER 9

Prizemaster of HMS Netley

INTRODUCTION

*I*F THERE ever was the perfect marriage between sailor and ship, it was the combination of Nagle and the *Netley*. The ship, a new sloop of somewhat unusual design, was placed under a lieutenant who had never had command before and never would again; it served far from any memorable theater of the war and was a part of no major battle. Yet, during the period Nagle served on it, the *Netley* was one of the most successful ships in the Royal Navy.

The *Netley* had three keels for the sake of stability, not unusual for vessels of its class but sufficiently odd on the coast of Portugal, where it saw much of its service, to earn it the nickname of "tres keelus." The unusual feature was that it had a "sliding keel," a retractable centerboard, so that it could cruise close to shore, getting over sandbars and reefs more easily than most vessels. The sliding keel was not a particular success. A careless seaman jammed its winch on its first Portuguese cruise. By the second cruise, it leaked badly, and the captain had it removed. But the vessel itself had exceptional sailing qualities that Nagle rhapsodically praises. It was flat bottomed, could overtake any ship it came up with, and could be propelled effectively by sweeps (oars) in a dead calm. The ship had 16 guns, among them the relatively new carronades, with 24-pound shot, which possessed far more weight and destructive power than the long guns that such a small vessel could have carried. The normal complement on the ship was sixty crewmen, but at times they had well over one hundred prisoners on board.

The ship's first commander was Francis Godolphin Bond (1765–1839), a very interesting, exceptionally capable, but relatively unknown figure. His father was a naval surgeon and his two brothers and one of two brothers-in-law were navy men. Of greater interest, Captain Bligh of *Bounty* fame was a half brother of his mother. Bond apparently entered the service at age nine as a surgeon's assistant or captain's servant, became a midshipman in 1779, and achieved the rank of lieutenant in 1782. He became a first lieutenant in 1791, in which capacity he accompanied Bligh on the second breadfruit voyage in the *Providence*.

It is hard to understand why Bond seems to have been stalled at the lieutenant's rank quite as long as he was, and it is entirely possible that his greatest liability was his relationship with Bligh, who, although exonerated in the *Bounty* court-martial, was the object of a defamation campaign afterward by the Christian family, which found a sympathetic audience, even among fellow naval officers. Bond had helped Bligh write a defense in 1794, but, privately, Bond had a fairly low opinion of Bligh and had found him imperious and a bit paranoid in the course of the *Providence* voyage. Bond's own unusually humane treatment of his crew, which Nagle describes in interesting detail, may well have been in part a reaction to all the qualities in Bligh that he found distasteful.

Nagle served on the *Netley* from 28 July 1798 until 26 June 1801. Bond immediately appointed him quartermaster, and off the Portuguese coast, when the ship was making captures almost daily, Nagle was frequently assigned to take prizes into port. He thrived under the responsibility, and the whole spirit of this section of the journal suggests that it was the most rewarding period of his life.

On its first cruises, the *Netley* served as part of a small fleet off Le Havre, stationed there to keep an eye on French ship movement in and out of the harbor. It was somewhat unusual to assign a sloop to such duty, but Nagle's journal, combined with the ship's logs, and confidential records of the Foreign Office, make it clear that the ship was there primarily as a vehicle of a highly confidential spy network between London and Paris.

Nagle mentions that the ship frequently put Royalists ashore and would pick up spies late at night. The logs are entirely silent with regard to spies, but Bond's logbook has a seemingly innocent entry on 19 September 1798 that "Sir Sydney Smith came on Board," when the ship came back to Portsmouth for repairs after the engagement of August 20 at Le Havre. Sir William Sydney Smith (1764–1840) was a remarkable individual, captain in the navy at the age of nineteen, spy, naval adviser to the king of Sweden, and a brilliant commander in a sloop off the coast of France in 1795–96. He had been captured at Le Havre in 1796 and imprisoned in Paris, but had made a daring escape four months before visiting the *Netley*. There is not enough correspondence to know exactly what the nature of his involvement had been, but apparently, while stationed off Le Havre and then while in Paris, he had helped to organize a network of spies who transported intelligence from Paris by way of paid couriers. The spies in Paris used code names; agents knew the identities only of their immediate contacts; financing was apparently provided by secret government funds, entirely off the record, and the object was at least in part to spy on the regular spies. Smith apparently worked out a highly secret arrangement with Bond to maintain spy contacts, which we know about sketchily only by the fortunate survival of a couple of letters in the Public Record Office.

In December 1798, the vessel came into Portsmouth for four months, sailing on April 13 with a convoy of merchant ships to Oporto, Portugal, which became its primary base of operations for the years Nagle served on board. It was a most unusual assignment for a vessel of the Royal Navy. Technically, Captain Bond reported to the commanders of the main British fleet based at Lisbon; in reality it was not a standard naval operation at all, but a response to political and economic pressures brought to bear on the British ministry. Bond may have been only a lieutenant, but the career of the *Netley* was obviously of particular interest at the highest level of Pitt's administration. Bond sent most of his operational reports directly to Evan Nepean, secretary of the Admiralty, who in turn made certain that most of his detailed letters describing the *Netley*'s successes were published in the *London Gazette* or *The Naval Chronicle*.

The group that wielded such political pressure as to influence the assignment of the *Netley* was the English Factory of Oporto, a rather tightly knit association of British merchants resident in Portugal who controlled the port wine industry. The origins of the wine trade between Britain and Portugal go back far enough to be lost to historical memory, but by the seventeenth century, the English palate had developed a particular affection for the distinctively rich wine of the Douro

Valley. The trade was important to the Portuguese treasury, and during the eighteenth century, various measures were enacted to define clearly Douro wine and to ensure both its uniqueness and its quality. Port wine was not entirely unknown to other cultures, but it has always been essentially a British enthusiasm, aged in casks of distinctive British construction, and traded almost exclusively by expatriate British mercantile firms. William Pitt is reported to have consumed three bottles of port a day, and by the late eighteenth century it was well ensconced as the proper drink of English gentlemen, whether they be Dr. Johnson and his admiring circle at the coffeehouse, or the officers of the Royal Navy in the cabin of the admiral of the fleet, toasting the health of the king. There was an emotional and physical interest in keeping the trade with Oporto free of difficulty that went beyond the very considerable monetary benefits to the Crown. In addition to the wine business, Oporto and nearby ports imported great quantities of English and American grain and fish from Newfoundland, most of it carried in British ships. Oporto and a few smaller ports such as Viana were the points of international commerce, to which coastal vessels brought local products and carried imported goods up and down the coasts.

The trade of this region was sufficiently rich and its geographical location close enough to Spain and France to attract privateers and pirates. To the English eye, unaccustomed to the distinctive styles of coastal vessels of Spain and Portugal, it was difficult to tell which were honest fishing and trading craft, and which were predators. The *Netley* capitalized on the confusion itself, having the ability to camouflage its military function by closing its ports and changing its rigging to that of a fishing lugger.

Captain Bond was an intelligent and daring commander, and the cruise must have reminded Nagle of his privateering days on the *Fair American.* Once the ship had got the feel of the coast, the number of prizes they took was phenomenal, and there was a constant need to take ships and prisoners into port, to Viana, Oporto, or Lisbon, depending on where the capture had been made. The ship had prize agents, in both Oporto and Lisbon, who were responsible for selling enemy ships and cargoes or returning recaptured vessels belonging to friends or neutrals for a percentage of the net worth. The log books confirm the fact that Nagle was away from the *Netley* almost a third of the time Bond commanded the ship, taking the captures into port.

On shore, particularly at Viana, Nagle developed close friendships with Richard Allen, the vice-consul there, and some of his friends. A couple of years earlier, Allen had incurred the wrath of the British navy in transmitting intelligence on the fortifications of Vigo's harbor that had proven to be highly inaccurate when Admiral Samuel Hood attempted an abortive landing expedition. Allen was probably going out of his way to make amends.

The Admiralty publicized the successes of the *Netley* as widely as it did to satisfy powerful mercantile interests at home by showing that the government was concerned with keeping trade routes open. Inevitably, this success would bring a promotion to Bond, and on 11 December 1801 he received notice of his appointment as captain. By regulation, only lieutenants could command sloops, and on 18 January 1801 he turned the ship over to Lieutenant James Mein. Bond was assigned on 1 July 1803 to the Sea Fencibles, militialike forces organized to defend the coasts of Great Britain, under Nagle's other former commander, Arthur Phillip. He never again was given a ship, but he lived long enough to achieve the rank of rear admiral in 1837 and died at his hometown of Exeter two years later.

On the *Netley*, for Nagle, the situation deteriorated immediately upon Bond's removal. Probably any officer would have seemed poor by comparison, but correspondence surviving in the Admiralty files supports Nagle's portrayal of James Mein as small-minded. Nagle jumped at the opportunity to transfer back to the *Gorgon* in late June 1801. The ship had been dispatched to take troops to Egypt and to transport invalids back home after the Battle of Alexandria.

For Nagle, Egypt was a new and interesting destination, but in spite of the fact that his abilities were highly regarded (he served first as quartermaster's mate, then as quartermaster, and then, according to the ship's paybooks, in the capacity of a midshipman), his thoughts were on getting back to his family. The cruise home proved to be gruesome, with both passengers and crewmen dying almost daily, and the ship had to go into quarantine on its return. The invalids were disembarked at Portsmouth in December, and in February the *Gorgon* sailed around to Woolwich, where the company was discharged on 19 April 1802, just one month short of twenty years after Jacob Nagle had stepped on board the *Prudent* and become a British sailor.

IN ABOUT ten days after, orders came to draught our ships crew. The most of them were sent on board the *Le Tigat*, 84 gun ship, and Capt[ain] Bond came on board, being aquainted with the first leutenant, and had a pick of choice seamen and their recommendations from the first leut[enan]t to the number of 45 seamen. She was a new constructed schooner with fals keels. We ware sent on board [28 July 1798], laying at Spithead.[1]

When we had received our wages for the *Blanch* we sailed [2 August 1798] for Haverdegrass [Le Havre-de-Grâce], but that evening we came to an anchor at St. Hellena and the capt[ain] having the hands all sent aft to station them, he call'd them all in rotation excepting three of us, which was nearly on the first of the list. When they ware all station'd, I said to the cap[tain], "You have forgot us, Sir."

"No, I have not," said he. Pointing to Donalson, "You are to act as boatswain and Covington, you are to act as guner," and as for me, I was chief quartermaster and afterwards prize master and third in command. I kept the first watch, and a beautiful night, the men laying about the decks, the most of them "sowed up," as the sailors terms is, and bottles of liquor between the guns on both sides.

In the morning, washed the decks down and got under way and arived off Haverdegrass to assist in blockading four frigates and four sloops of war that lay in the mold [mole]. We provented all vessels from going in and took all that attempted to come out.

One morning two gun boats a coming a long shore, they mounted 8 thirty twos and 24 pounders each. We gave chace. They finding we ware coming up with them, they run on shore on a sand bank. We followed them till we got aground, but having fals keels, we drew 16 feet water and when we lifted our keels, they drew 10 feet forward and a leven aft. Therefore after boaring them for a half an hour with our 24 pounders, we lifted our keels, hove a bout, and left them there.

At every spring tide there would be 6 or 7 frigates to joine us, as the

French frigates could not come out at any other time. Sir Richard Strawen [Strachan] was the commodore, which the sailors call'd Mad Dickey.

At Haverdegrass there is three forts, one round the town, one large battery on the north side, a good highth from the level of the water, and a four gun battery out side towards the point. The mold [mole] for the shiping is inside of the town, on the River Seane [Seine]. It lays 45 miles west of Rowen [Rouen] and 112 N.W. of Paris upon the English Channel, Log'd. 11° E., Latt'd 42°29'N.

The commedore having a French young gentelman on board of note, which had been taken prisoner, and meaning to send him on shore, lowered the cutter down and sent him to be landed with a flag of truce, but no sooner than the boat got under there guns they opened a heavy fire from the foregun battery on them till they shot all there oars away and lay there like a target, and still continuing there fire, meaning to sink the boat, the commedore then made our signal to go in and fetch the boat out. We run in under the four gun battery and hove two and opened our broad side with our 24 pounders and made the rocks fly over there heads as thick and coming down upon them that they had to leave the battery. We then took the boat in tow and brought hur out.

Shortly after, on a Sunday morning [19 August 1798], Mad Dickey ment to give us some amusement. At 8 o'clock he made the signal to go to breckfast, at 9 o'clock to go to prayers, and a little before noon, the signal was made to go to dinner. About one o'clock he hoisted a flag for action and our signal to lead the van, and we went a head.

There was 2 frigates, our schooner, and a bum ship, but the other frigate did not come in, as he thought it was not proper to have his men killed and of no service. However we obey'd the signal and the commedore followed us, the bum laid off, and a long the beach, from the town to the large battery, laid 47 gunboats in a range. We run in with the schooner till we brought all the gunboats in a range, between us and the fort, and raked them every broadside, and what shot went over the gunboats would go into the fort. The frigate could not come in so far as we ware, and finding our heavey mettal so warm, that they nearly neglected the frigate to fire at us till the water apeared like hail around us with grape and canister, one thirty two pound shot struck the muzel of one of our 24 pounders and disabled the gun and kiled and wounded five men, and the capt[ain] wounded in the thy.

We engage'd two hours and fifteen minutes when Mad Dickey made a signal to put about and stand out, and as soon as we ceased firing, the French

quit likewise, though we ware still under their guns. I beleive they liked our room better than our company, though we never fired a shot into the town, as we new there ware none but wimen and children. The men of the town and the seamen ware all in the batiries and gunboats. The frigate received no damage excepting hur riging, the bum ship laying at so great a distance that she received no damage, though she could heave hur shells into the fort.

As soon as we ware from under the enemies guns, the com[modore] sent his docktor on board to assist in dressing the wounded. Our masts being wounded, we had to fish them. The next day we ware ordered to Spithead for repair. We ariving [21 August 1798], run into harbour and our schooner went into dock and the capt[ain] and wounded went to the hospittle.[2]

In about a month we ware ready for see with new masts, and Capt[ain] Bond came on b[oar]d from the hospittle. We sailed again [18 September 1798] for Haver de Grass and remained on that station for two months. During this time we had some French men going backwards and forwards as spies, and we would land them in the night and when they wanted to return they would make a few small fiers according to the signals they would agree on and then send a boat for them when they had the information they required and then send them to England, but the French having some information, a cutter that was with us landing one of them in the night, and the French laying wait took the boats crew as well as the spy, but the spy they hung on the first tree, but the crew and officer ware made prisoners of.

During this station, in the winter was very severe, we came a cross a

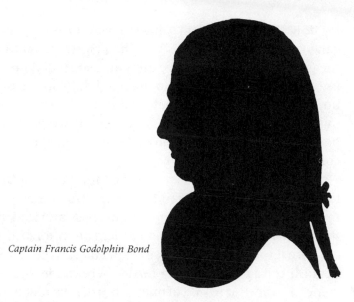

Captain Francis Godolphin Bond

decked boat which pretended to be a fishing boat, as we did not mislist [molest] them, but overhalling hur we found both men and arms and brought hur with us to Spithead. Laying there awhile and being ready for sea, we receiv'd orders to take a convoy to Porto Port in Portangal [Portugal] and afterwards to remain on that station till further orders from Cape Finister, to the lattitude of Lisbon.

After getting the convoy safe into Porto Port we cruised for one month, chased and spoke a great number of vessels, but all proving to be neutral vessels or English. At length on the 1st day of May, early in the morning, I kept the capt[ain's] watch. The capt[ain] came on deck, and we fell into discourse. I inform'd him it was surprising to me that we should cruise on that coast so long without falling in with privateers or vessels taken by them. When cruising in the *Blanch* Frigate we fell in with a great many, but always being off the land so far in the frigate, they would fetch into the small harbours before we could come up with them. While discoursing, the man at mast head cried out, "Sail ho."

The capt[ain] made answer, "Where abouts?"

"Right to windward." Turn'd the hands up and made sail as close as she would lay. In a short time we ware a longside the brig off of Mount Vigo on the point of the see shore and the entrance of the River Commenia [Miño], which devides Spain and Portangal [Portugal]. She proved to be an English brig [*Black Eyed Susan*] taken by a French privateer.

While putting men on b[oar]d we saw a schooner [*L'Egyptienne*] coming down upon us with all sail set [1 May 1799]. We being riged like a Dutch galyot, deceived them. This was the privateer that took the brig, but when she got so near as to purceive our guns, she hall'd hur wind, but it was of no use, for we could lay closer to the wind than any vessel I ever saw. She then up hellem and clap'd hur before the wind. We ware then alongside in 15 minutes. They stood to there quarters till we gave them 3 or 4 of our 24 pounders. They all run below, leaving the French capt[ain] to hall the colours down.

While getting the prisoners on board we saw a Dutch galyott [*Wohlfort*] to windward, and understanding by the Dutchmen that they ware taken by the privateer, we sent the schooner in chase and took hur. I went on b[oar]d the brig with 5 men and we took them all into Porto Port.

In a few days we put to see again and run off Vigo where the French and Spanish privateers generally made there randevoes. Sometimes we would come to an anchor in side of one of the islands in sight of the privateers laying and looking at us and water our vessel and wash our clothes and dry them. There lay at one time a French 24 gun ship and 14 small privateers. We got underway and run in within gun shot and they would not come out to atackt us.

One day we observed a schooner coming a long shore towards the battery, abrest of the town, and we run hur a shore, and got our boat out and got hur off, but finding nothing in hur excepting ballast as we supposed, we tared hur decks and set hur on fire in several places. The boat had not reached the schooner before she blew up, having a number of barrals of powder under the ballast for the fort that we ware then laying within gun shot of.

We saw a nother small privateer laying inside of the fort, a front of the town. We maned our boats and sent them on board. The fort opened upon us, and we on them, but our 24 being much heavyer than there mettle, and what went over the fort tore the town down, therefore they stoped firing at us. We then ceased firing but brought the privateer out and took hur with us into Porto Port.

There was such a number of privateers on the coast that we ware falling in with some almost every day. In one day we took a leven priveteers and retaken vessels. In that number was three Portegee Brazeal ships, and a Spanish privateer of 16 guns came down to sea what we ware, and we took hur, but having no men to put on board of hur, we had to let hur go. We had then but 17 men on board with the marines. We runing down amongst the

Oporto, Portugal

fleet, she made sail again and went off, we having at the same time 132 prisoners on board, but they had no way to come on deck, excepting by one scuttle and only one could come up at a time, and a brass 4 pounder pointing down the scuttle loaded with musket balls, and a sentry with match pistols and cutlash, every man being armed with pistols below or aloft.

At length Capt[ain] Bond agreed with the French capt[ai]ns to make a carteel of one of the vessels that was in ballast to take them into Vigo on conditions to purmit hur to return to Portoport, which they did with honour. In getting our prises into Lisbon, the master, being in one of the Brazel ships, got inside the Burlins and was lost, but the men were saved.

Coming out again we took a lugger [*L'Esperance*] of 8 guns, 4 swivels, and a long brass 9 pounder off of Vigo [22 December 1798]. I was sent on board to take hur into Porto Port, but while with the *Netley*, a fleet hove in sight to the sotherd. We stood for them, but a heavy frigate stood out from among them and gave us chace. I prepared my large lugs to keep hur before the wind upon one mast so that hur sails would not all be of any use to hur, but the *Netley* being to windward, the frigat luffed up for hur and the frigate being a French bilt ship made us jubus [dubious], but Capt[ain] Bond kept his wind till they gave him a gun, and the *Netley* returned the salute, then hoisting his colours, bore down upon him and ran under his quarter. She proved to be the *Manerva* which had been taken from the French.

I made sail and stood in for Porto, where this convoy was bound to. The frigate spoke me and inform'd me I must take charge of the convoy, which was a bout 40 sail. I inform'd him I had but 5 men onboard. He told me if acasion required to take a seaman out of each ship. Likewise he gave the pilot orders not to take me in till the convoy was all safe over the bar, and then the frigate left us.

The *Netley* was then gone on a cruise. The winds being unfavou[r]able, we lay off and on, day after day. In about a week we saw a lugger standing in for the convoy from the sotherd. I aplyed to the capt[ain] of the convoy for men to go and engage the luger, but there was not a man that would turn out. Therefore I stood out of the convoy and maid sail for the luger, but when they saw me, they up hallom afore the wind. Then I hall'd to the wind for the convoy. In about 10 days they all got in except our selves.

On Chrismas Eve, coming on to blow from the N. West, I stood off the land. In the night, laying too under the mizen lug, I fell in with a schoner. Laying two, hailing hur, I found she was from Lisbon bound to Viana with codfish. They took us to be an enemy by our lug sails and a privateer, but when they found we ware English and belong'd to the *Netley*, or "trees kealus" as the Portegees call'd her, [k]nowing we ware guarding there coast from the privateers, they ware rejoiced, and the capt[ain] told me if I would lay two by him, he would pilot me into Viana in the morning if I would follow him, which I agreed to.

About three A.M., blowing heavy, our mizen lug went overboard, mast and all. We got it on b[oar]d and lay two under a close reef mainsail, we being well to windward of the harbour. At daylight the schooner bore up and I followed him. We entered through the chanal and was in side the reef, standing a long shore with a leading wind, but before we reached the mouth of the harbour, the wind choped round to the N.W. and headed us, and the heavy surf roling over the reef, and not having room to ware, there was no way to escape but to plump them on shore. The schooner [*L'Esperance*] run on the beach amediately and I up helem and run under hur lee, it blowing, raining, thundered, and lightened a most tremendious that day and all that night. The English Counsel, Mr. Allen, came with a gard of soldiers to protect the vessels from being plundered. We pitched tents with our sails and got the guns out and provisions that was not damaged and even the masts we got out of hur, but the schooner was totally lost and went to pieces before morning, and all hur cargo was drifted away and no more to be seen of hur.

When the Counsal had sold what was saved out of the luger it was allowed that there was not one hundred Lbs. lost by the lugger, and by the report of the Counsel to the capt[ain] I receiv'd great praise for my conduct when ariving in Porto Port from the Counsel and likewise from my commander when the *Netley* arived off the barr.

Mr. Allen, Vice Counsel, paid every attention both to me and my crew. He had a country seat on the subbords of the town, that we lived in and some more that had been taken in prises and caried into Vigo in Spain and was purmited to travel to Viana by land, and the Counsel put them under my command, being supperior with the rest of the prize masters.[3] While under the Counsels charge, I got aquainted with a genteel family within a few dores of us, and it was his wish that I would come and make his house and family as I would my own. They wished me to sleep in their house. At every evening, if I would not be there, I was sent for unless I was with the Counsel. I could not at that time understand any Portegees, excepting by our motions and behaviour, but I, upon that coast, had the privilage from Capt[ain] Bond to chuse one or two men that I was well assured I could depend on. Therefore I had one, and he understood the Portegee languige perfectly. This gentleman was well a quainted with the Counsel, where we had been several times before in respect of my duty.

This gental[ma]n had two sons, but the eldest was a young officer in the army, about 17 years of age, and bold in his temper. His mother was a lovely woman and of the most kind and afable wimen I ever was in company with, even before hur husband, but he was one of the most kindest, free hearted men I ever met, for the most part of the Portegees dont purmit their wives and daughter to be amongst stranger, unless it is some particular friend that they may introduce you to their family. But this I must say upon oath, though I was not aware of any mistrust or any temptation whatever, but that lovely woman gave way to hur own inclinations and was determended to be folse to a true and loving husband, which I loved and respected while I ever new him. Even hur sun, that had no suspicion, if he and me walked out after night, she would give him the greates caution that I should not be hurt by the soldiers taking there rounds in the night, though I caried my side arms and pocket pistols as well as they did, but no sooner than he gave the contersigne they would walk off and leave us.[4]

One day hur sun invited me and my linkister [interpreter] to ride out into the country upon an excurcion. We stop'd at a wine house and took a little refresment. In our return, about two miles from town, he took a small whissel out of his pocket and begin to blow it. I understood before that it was a signal. I begin to be a little doubtful of him, and seeing two men on horse back came riding out a wood towards us, I put myself in a posicion of defence and my comrod likewise. The young officer burst out a laughing and when these men came up he told my linkister they ware friends and I need not be under any apprihension while we ware together. In entering the town we stoped at a very genteel house and introduced me to a hansome young woman and told me that was to be his intended bride. They treated us to some good wine. We then returned home.

We had now been about a month in Viana. By consulting with my linkister, I thought it best to prepare for Porto Port, as I wished to get on b[oar]d. There was 12 men in all, beside myself. The Counsel gave me the money that was allowed for the men, beside money I drew upon my agent in Porto, which was Sq[uire] Cazy. This gentl[eman] and his wife understanding that we ware going away the next morning, he came with us a cross the river and after landing, walking up the road, we came to a church, and who should I see but his wife and a servent girl with two baskets, one with provisions ready dressed and the other with wine, and desired us all to come into a large porch and regale our selves before we went any farther. We then started on the road, and while walking about a mile, she fill'd my pockets with amons [almonds], raeaons [raisins], and different kinds of dried fruit, unpurceiv'd by him. Coming to the foot of a hill, we parted and arived in Porto the day following.

Shortly after the *Netley* came off the barr, and we went on board. Runing off Vigo, we fell in with an English brig taken by a Spanish privateer, but she was in ballast. I was sent on b[oar]d to take hur into Porto, where she had been bound to for port wine. When I came off the bar and was runing in, the fort fired me off, thinking we ware load'd and not water sufficient for a loaded vessel, but being light there was water sufficient as the head pilot inform'd me afterwards. The wind being dead on shore from the westward, I had to hall close to the wind to get off shore as fast as I could.

It conn[ti]n[ue]d on to blow hard from the S.W. I found the ship was making water fast. I found by three Spaniards, prisoners I had on b[oar]d, that she had receiv'd some shot between wind and water, and we could not find out where the leaks was. We kept one pump constantly going. By 12 o'clock in the night it blew a gale with rain. I got hur under close reef topsails and foresail, but carreing away our fore and aft mainsail, I then took in the foresail and fore topsail and laid hur two under the main topsail. She then lay two very well, but the ballast in the whole was sand and nothing to prevent the sand from washing to the pump. It would choke, though we pumped a great deal on deck, and while lifting the pum[p] to clear it and put it down again the leak gained on us. We then got both pumps agoing, but they soon choaked again. In lifting the larboard pump, as we had the starbourd three of four times, we found it was splised, therefore it was useless. In bending an other mainsail and lifting the one pump so often, that by daylight she was two thirds full of water, but the gale had luled a good deal, but the ballace washing about begin to heave hur on hur side, or on hur beam ends, I found there was no hopes of saving the vessel.

We got a six oard boat out, and in hoisting hur out in a hurry we lost three oars, but with great difficulty we got hur under the stern. We could not get either bread or water, being below. I allowed we ware about ten or a leven leagues from the high lands of Viana. I found it time to leave hur. They all got over the stern by a rope, excepting a Portegee boy and myself, which was the last, and he begin to cry. He understood the Spaniards was going to cut the painter and leave us behind. I having a brace of ships pistols in my belt, I drew one and told them I would kill the first man that let go the rope till the boy was in the boat. I hove another rope over the stern, and while they ware receiving the boy, I was down likewise.

I went aft and took charge of the boat. I kept hur before the wind and as the see fell I edged in for the land. All our crew in the boat was 9 in number: 3 Spanish prisoners, 3 Portegees beside the boy, ware friendly with the Spanish at that time, the capt[ain's] son which was left on board, being sick, and myself. We puled with two oars and steared with the other. We continued all day and all night in that situation. In the morning before day light we ware within 3 or 4 miles of the shore. They became so weary that they hove the two oars across the boat and fell asleep. I endeavoured to encourage them, but all in vain. I found the boat was nearly as full of water as we had left the ship, and as I had not before mentioned when we ware about 500 yards she was under water.

The men sitting on the seats asleep, I laid my stearing oar in and turned to bailing till I had got hur nearly clear of water. I then roused up the Portegees and they assisted to clear the boat entierly. They took fresh courage. We got in shore about 4 o'clock P.M. but could not land, the surf being very high. We pulled a long shore till we made the entrance of Comenia River, a Portegee fort being there, and night coming on, I was determened to risk it through the surf, beside I understood by the Portegees that the Spaniards wanted them to land on the north side, under the Spanish fort, beside, for the want of water and nourishment, we ware nearly helpless. I up hellem and away we went. The Portegee soldiers looking at us, they came on the beach to receive us, but the boat struck a rock that lay under water, which we could not see, and stove hur to peaces, and we ware left a floating in the surf, nearly helpless. The soldiers came in to their necks in the water and brougt us out, but they put us into the fort, not [k]nowing weather we ware friends or enemies, but the Portegees that I had with me inform the commander who we ware, and knowing the *Netley* protected there coast, he took me to his own room. I having money, I gave him a half joe and he sent two soldiers to a public house about a mile off and brought a feather bead, wine, and fowls for the capt[ain] of the fort and myself and a good supply for the few soldiers that ware there and the men that ware with me, which refresh'd us very much that night.

In the morning the commander inform'd me that we must go to Commenia to be overhall'd and give information from whence we came, which was four miles out of our road. However we started with a guard, and ariving there, was overhall'd by the Squiers, and all being rectified, they gave me a passport and a small sum of money to take us to Viana, which was 4 leagues. That evening we arived in Viana. Being acquainted with the Counsel, beforementioned, I applyed to him. He informed me there was a capt[ain] of a vessel had been taken by the Spanierds and was then on his way to Portoport, and if I could make it convenient, we could both start in the morning, and he would find mules for us both, and inform'd me where I would find the capt[ain] in the morning.

I took my departure from the Counsel that evening and went to see my old friends, which I have heretofore made mention of. Ariving at there habutation, they ware rejoiced to see me, and supper was provided, but he purceiving my shoes was torn in traveling, without saying anything to me, he went out and brought some new shoes to fit me, he supposing that I had lost everything and moneless [moneyless] (by the acount they had received), which was true excepting money. When the shoes was fited he then went into his bedroom and brought out a bag of money, opened it, and would insist on my taking as much as I thought proper. It was all silver and gold. I refused and told him I had money, but he would not be satisfied till I show'd him nine half joes, beside what I had spent. Then he apeared to be satisfied. He would not receive any money for the shoes and likewise when I was in his house before mentioned would not receive any money from me. I then having two watches about me, I beged he wout give the one I gave him to a

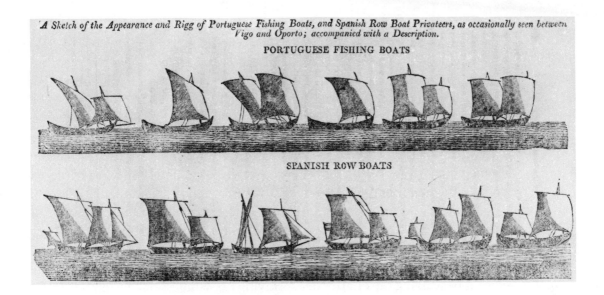

watchmaker to clean it, as it had got wet in the boat, and to keep it till I sent for it, being then valued at 25 dollars. He promised he would, but it was not my intention ever to send for it after the kindest treatment I could receive from my greatest friends.

We had an excelent super, but I must confess my felings was hurt by the conduct of his wife. He served my plate upon his left hand and his wife on the right, then serving himself. His wife observing, according to hur opinion that he had taken the preference to himself, she took hur fork and put the prime piece into my plate and put what he had put into my plate into his plate, which would apear very singular in many parts that I had travel'd at that time, however it all pased as kindness to a stranger, which it apeared to me that it pleas'd him in hur so doing.

The young officer, being present at supper, was to escort me before daylight to the place where the capt[ain] was to be ready. We had not went above half way to the main street when two soldiers came up to us drawing there swords. We both drew, but he steped forward and cried out "Leguardo," and they seeing him in officers uniforms, they run and was soon out of sight. We went on and found the capt[ain] preparing. The young officer being aquainted with the family, we remained till daylight, ful of friendship and mirth. We took our departure. The Counsel had a flat and the mules with a man to bring them back. We cross'd the river and arived in

Porto about 9 o'clock that night, which is call'd 10 leagues, but cruel, bad roads, rocks, sands, swamps, and rivers, where a horse could not go.

I remained sum time in Porto til the *Netley* arived and then went on board. Laying off Vigo, we fell in with a brig of sixteen guns bound into Vigo, taken by a French cutter mounting 18 long 18 pounders. She proved to be American brig [*Nymph*] from Philadelphia bound up the Straits. This was in the year [26 March] 1800. I was sent on board to take charge, though the capt[ain] when taken was left on board. He told Capt[ain] Bond that the French cutter was crusing for the *Netley* in the latt'd of Lisbon. I was ordered to take the brig into the first port that would be most convenient.

I run off Porto barr, came to an anchor, and having but a light air of wind and the pilots would not atempt to take a vessel in without being high tide and a favouable wind, beside having a boat a head with a ketch anchor, I then begin to lift my anchor, having but 5 men with myself, and the capt[ain] walking the quarter deck. Having no windless or capstan, we had a leading takle to the quarter deck, and when the takle was a block we had to stoper the cable till we fleeted our purchase. In the meantime, being calm, I had my topsails hoisted to the mast head, the fore topsail crased aback to heave hur head off shore, and the main topsail to shiver the wind. We pulling with all our might to get the anchor to the bows, I observed the swell was drawing us in shore.

I said to the capt[ain], "Will you give us a pul till we get the anchor to the bows?"

"No," said he, "but if you get my vessel on shore, I will blow your brains out."

It inraged me. I let go the fall, and the four men held on and took a turn standing, looking on. I run to the armchest and took out a brace that I had loaded myself and steped on the weather side where he was. "Now, Sir, I am ready. Is your pistol loaded?"

"Yes."

"Then lay holt of it, or walk down into the cabin. I will let you [k]now that I command this vessel." He said no more but walked into the cabin. We turned too and got the anchor up, cated [catted], and fish'd, and secured. We ketched a breeze, sprung up from the N.W., and kep away for Lisbon.

In the evening he came on deck and apeared to be very sociable. I overhall'd the guns to see weather they ware in order, as there was a great number of small privateers lurking about the Burlins, a few leagues to the N. of the rock of Lisbon. Laying near the entrance on the north side of the river

Tagus, it is a remarkable high mountain, 22 miles west of Lisbon, Long'd 9°35'W., Lat'd 38°42'N., and Porto port lays in 41°15'N. L'd, Long'd 10°W. by account.

On the passage the capt'n was very desirous I would run away and he would take me as his chief mate. When we got into Lisbon I saw his deception and put no trust in him. Whin we came to Bellam Castle we had to come to an anchor till further orders. In lifting our anchor he went and got some more men to help us to take the vessel up. When coming to an anchor, our agent came on b[oar]d. The capt[ain] demanded an order from me to the Counsel to pay those men, thinking he would trick me. The agent told me to give it to him and the Counsel would laugh at him. I gave it to him. He then required me to go with him. I did so and went to the Counsel. When he gave it to him, and he looked at it, the Counsel looked at me, and we both laughed. The Counsel told him if he hired a hundred men he would have to pay them, as one eighth goes to the vessel that retook hur from the enemy. The Counsel laugh'd and I laugh'd and he bit his lips with anger, and I thought I was about square with him for his trickery to me. The brig was delivered up to the capt[ain], and shortly after the *Netley* came into Lisbon. I went on board.

In a few days we put to see and run off Vigo. Cruising, at about 10 o'clock A.M., we ware standing to the south, we discoverd a sail standing for us till she could make out that it was the *Netley*. We ware in the rig of a galyot chiefly, but in 20 minutes we could be a schooner, but they had been deceived so often by us that the sight of us was a dred to them, but this was the cutter [*La Légère*] that the French capt[ain] told the Americans he was cruising for the *Netley* and wished he could meet us, but now when she perfectly new what we ware, she halled hur wind, standing to the north to get into Vigo. We put about and stood after hur, but we still kept to leeward betwen hur and the shore. The wind being light, they got their swepes out. We then got our sweeps out and in a dead calm we could pull the *Netley* three mile in an hour. She proved to be the same vessel before mentioned.

We ware prepared and had our (boarding) nettings up, knowing hur force, which was 18 long 18 pounders and one hundred men. Our force was 16–24 pounders and our full compliment was 60 men, but by taking so many vessels we often had more. We sailing faster than the cutter, we came up alongside of hur. They ware for boarding, but our boarding netting being three quarters of an inch and nearly up to the catharpens [catharpins], which made it very difficult, the French got into the riging and netting to cut away, but we being prepared with cutlash, pistols, and boarding pikes, beside we had a brass 4 pounder we could ship fore and aft with musket balls that they dreaded. Being close quarter, our great guns was not used except an oppertunity served. Likewise, we could fier our guns twice to there once, there guns being long.

In the smoke I purceiv'd the French capt[ain] drawing a pistol from his belt to fire at our capt[ain] that was giving command. I drew a pistol at the same time and let him have the contents. At the same time a stout Frenchman made a blow at me with a large hanger, from the netting, but the man behind me saw the blow and covered my head with his boarding pike, which was cut that it fell and the bare pint struck me in the head and I fell, but the man ketch'd up the pike and run it into his body and he fell between the two vessels. I recovered in a few minutes.

They finding they could not board us, and there capt[ain] slain, and our small brass piece made a scattering on their decks, they found it in vain and struck their colours [29 May 1800] in less than 30 minutes. We had no men killed but a good many wounded. What was kiled on b[oar]d the cutter we had no purticular account of, as some went over board, but a great many wounded.

We cleared the decks and repaird the riging and took hur into Lisbon. We refited and refreshed the crew. The cutter was sold into the Portogees service as a man of war.

We put to see again. Runing off Porto we took a Spanish lugger. I went on board, and in going to Lisbon, the *Netley* in company, we took two more, and the *Netley* going on a cruise, left me in charge of them. I took them in, and laying there under the charge of Mr. Lynes & Gill, our agents, Mr. Lynes had bought a privateer schooner that had been taken, and I laying in one of the luggers, close two hur off of Buckeys Stairs, about the center of the town, which is a square where the gentry generally walk and meat [meet] upon acasion on the River Tagos. Mr. Loynes wished I would "give an I," or take charge of the schooner, as well as the rest, having only one old man on board, a Portegee, and all hur powder on board.

One forenoon, being on board my own lugger with the men and one of the prisemasters belonging to one of the luggers, we purceived the flames and smoke coming up the main hatchway. I jumped into the skiff and asked who would follow me. They, knowing the danger, refused, till one man by the name of Wm. Grimes came with me and a bucket. We got on b[oar]d as fast as posseble. The merchant ships that lay all around hur wore away their cables to the klinch, [k]nowing she had a good deal of powder in and expecting she would blow up every moment. We got on board, and the old man was sitting before the fire in the hatchway and the bulkhead all in a blaze. There was the lazareet between the magazeen and the fire, which was not more than 10 or 12 feet.

The oul man, as soon as he saw me, cried out, "O, munta frees," and rubing his hands, which was that he was very cold.

"Yes, dam you," said I, "you will be hot a nuff presently," jumping down the hatchway, with a crowbar in my hand, and stove away the bulk head, as he kept heaving water wherever I stove down the bricks and boards. Some bricks in the fireplace had been broken, therefore the bulk head ketched fire on the opposite side. We got the fire out but could not be certain. I hailed the nearest ship to send there boat to take the powder out of the schooner, but the mate told me he could not get a man to go. I inshured him there was no danger.

At length one of the men came with the mate in the lanch [launch] a long side. I broke open the magazeen scuttle and took out 14 whole and half barrels of powder, several boxes of hand granades, several boxes of muskets catriges, and boxes of glas handgronades, which are to heave by hand, where you see them most numerous for boarding. I took it all on b[oar]d the lugger, which I was in myself and would not allow any fier on b[oar]d while I had charg of it. If she had been blown up there would of been a great distruction both by the houses on shore and the shiping laying roun about hur. I went to the agent and inform'd him, but he had the news before I inform'd him. I and my comrad receiv'd great aplause for our conduct, but I had a new suit of clothing spoilt for my labour. Shortly after the *Netley* came in and Capt[ain] Bond was inform'd by the agent of my conduct in saving his vessel and a number of lives, which gave me a great deal of privilage both on b[oar]d and a shore.

The *Netley* being complete for see we all went on b[oar]d and put to see. After passing Fort Julian, which stands on the north side and west end in entering the Tagos up to Lisbon, we fell in with a Portegee fishing boat. They inform'd us there was a Spanish privateer laying under the fort at an anchor with an English brig they had taken the same day. We run in shore and by this time it was dark. We saw both schooner and brig. We lowered the boat down, armed, and boarded hur as we run under hur stern. When we had possession we lufed up for the schooner. I was order to be ready with 25 men to jump on board as soon as we tutched hur sides. The anchor was let go the

Belem Castle, Lisbon

moment we tuched hur main chains, head and stern. We jumped on board. Some run below, and some that did not got wounded. We cleared the decks. The officers run down in the cabin. I told them to remain there and they would not be hurt. I claped a sentry on the dore, and we cut the cable and made sail out to see, and the *Netley* hove up hur anchor and followed us.

In the morning we fell in with a fleet of Portegee merchantmen under convoy of an English 24 gun ship man of war and a privateer of 16 guns. The privateer had seen the Spanish schooner the day before and was afraid to engage hur and supposing she and the *Netley* was coming to take the convoy, begin to fire at us by whole broad sides, and we could not fire at hur without damaging or hurting some of the merchat men, till the *Netley* made sail and spoke the commedore. Then they ceased, but there shot was at random and done us no harm, excepting cuting our riging. We went in with them and our prises. The Portegees thought to take them from us, as they ware taken under there forts, but we took the privateer out in the night and sent hur to England. The English privateer lay below Bellom Castle and would not come up to Lisbon for fear of our captain.

We put to see again and run to Porto Port and went in as soon as we came to an anchor. We ware inform'd that a French privateer of 14 guns had come off the barr and had taken an English brig that lay under the fort. Being

British Factory House, Oporto

loaded, and not able to get hur in till the tide served, therefore the Portegees new they would have to pay for hur. Being taken under cover of there guns, they sent out a Kings lugger mounted 12 twelve pounders to retake the brig. Being heavyer mettal than the Frenchman off Viana, she came up with them. The privateer engaged the luger and in a quarter of an hour took the luger. The next day we ariving and hearing of the event, the capt[ain] got under way to go out, but the pilots said it was unpossible, as the wind was due west and right into the harbour, and the channel too narrow to beat out over the barr. The capt[ain] was determend to take hur out himself and he beat hur out. The pilots said there never was the like done before over that bar.

We stood to the nothord, but the wind died away almost calm. The capt[ain] seeing a fishing boat within gunshot, we fired a 24 pounder over them and they came a long side amediately, [k]nowing the *Netley*. We took the men on b[oar]d. The master and myself with 25 men took to the oars and pulled all night to the nothord. We had no other arms but pistols and cutlashes. By daylight we ware off Viana and saw the brig in the offin. The *Netley* had ketched a breze of wind in the night and had got farther to the nothord than we ware. The lugger was close in shore, but the wind was very light. We made for the brig and came up with hur and boarded hur. I rem[aine]d on board with 5 men and 9 Spaniards. The master went to the *Netley* and from thence to the lugger, pulled up a stern and boarded hur, but they could of kill'd every man if they had fired, but they said they new the *Netley* would take them, and if they had fired they expected no quarter from us. The privateer had got off Vigo, and seeing hur prizes taken she was glad to get in hurself. We took the prizes into Porto Port. Capt[ain] Bond and ships company agreed to make the lugger a present to the King again, and I having charge of hur, I received a letter to deliver hur up to the Kings officer when he came on board, which I did according to my orders. We went out again and fell in with a Sweedish ship that had been taken by the Spaniard. I was sent on board and took charge of hur, though the capt[ain] and mate were left on board.

About 10 o'clock the next day, having light winds and fair weather, coming in with the bar off Porto Port, distance about 5 mile, I purceived a French privateer schooner boarding every vessel that was coming into the bar, and an English man of war of 24 guns was laying at an anchor without the bar and took no notice of hur. At the same time a convoy of Portegees vessels was to the sotherd of harbour, distance about 5 or 6 miles. The Frenchman was now coming to board me, but when about half way, they purceived a vessel standing out to the westward from the convoy. The Frenchman new hur and amediately called them back again and got the boat in and made sail. I amediately new hur to be the *Netley*. This French schoon[er] was supposed to out sail anything on the coast, which made hur so daring with the 20 gun ship, but the *Netley* having such a name made them jubus [dubious] of hur. The *Netley* was coming up with hur very fast. When we ware going over the bar, about 9 o'clock P.M., the *Netley* got with in gun shot, and to the Frenchmans misfortune, shot away the head of hur foremast. Then she was amediately a long side of hur. They struck and was brough[t] into Porto next morning.

In a few days I returned on board, and we put to sea. Cruising off Laguardo we saw a schooner coming down upon us before the wind, and we were then in the rig of a Dutch galyot, which I before mentioned we could be in the rig of a schooner in twenty minutes, and when our ports were closed and caps on the muzels of the guns they could not purceive we had any till they got near us. This schooner had a French sailor on board that had been taken by us twice before. He inform'd the French capt[ain] that we ware the "trees keelus" as they call'd us, having three keels, but the French capt[ain] thought he new better and said we ware a Sweedish galyot, as they ware very comon then on the Portegee coast trading from Hollond. However they came down so close that they could purceive we had guns but not at any great distance with the spy glass. They hall'd their wind. We then made sail. In a short time we ware abrest of them. They up hellem and claped hur before the wind, but all would not do, we ware amediately along side of hur and they struck their colours.

The Frenchman that we had taken before got up on one of the guns and cried out, "Capt[ain], how you do." We all new him.

The capt[ain] asked him why he did not [k]now the *Netley*. He replyed, "Yes, Sir, I [k]now de trees keelus. De capt[ai]n no belief me. I tel him many times. Now he tink so two."

We got the prisoners on b[oar]d and this Frenchman went to the capt[ain] and told him he must stay on board the *Netley*. The capt[ain] asked him if he wanted to enter for the *Netley*. He replyed, "Yes, Sir, I go no more from de trees keelus. He take me tree times, I must stay here." Therefore he remain'd on board. Som tim after, we retook an English ship from New-found land which had been taken by the Spaniards. She had seven thousand kentals [quintals] of kodfish on board, and in sending hur into Lisbon, this Frenchman was one sent in hur. In going in in a gale of wind the ship was lost and all hands perished excepting this Frenchman. He got on shore and left Lisbon, and we never heard of him afterwards.

The *Netley*, though a man of war, having such excelent yousage on board from Capt[ain] Bond that we could at any time get as many seamen out of the merchant ships as he wanted and would not except of them unless they ware good seaman, I being on shore waiting for the *Netley* to come off the bar at Porto and having orders from the capt[ain] to enter some good seam[en], and when they had intilegence, there ware more came than I would except of, but I took 28 men and a good many of them ware mates and boatswains of merchantmen, and when I came on b[oar]d we had more men than we wanted. Capt[ain] Bond runing into Lisbon in my absence had entered some there. In a few days after we fell in with a gansey [Guernsey] privateer that had all hur men pressed by a sixty four and had not men sufficient to take hur into harbour. Capt[ain] Bond gave him the priviledge of having any of the new hand if they chewsed to go, but all he could get was one Sweed and a boy.

Capt[ain] Bond took a delight in making his ships company comfortable, and when in harbour as much liberty as could be expected. He could not bare to punish men at the gangway, but he contrived a collar of one inch plank to ware round there necks with a large padlock for any certain time, which they dreaded more than floging. Likewise for lighter crimes was a scarlot cap full of black tossels hung all over it. When any strangers came on board, these men that had them on would sneak a way below for shame.

We fell in with a Merican ship that had lost hur masts and hur side stove in, which made hur so leakey they could scarcely keep hur free. We sent men on board and carpenters on board, tared a tarpolan, and ocam [oakum] over it, and nail'd it well over with boards, which stoped the leak considerable, and took hur in tow and caried hur into Lisbon where she was bound to. She belonged to the notherd.

On our cruises there was two privateers hove in sight, a cutter of 18 guns, the schooner of 16 guns, and we gave chase after them. Coming up, we run betwen both of them with our colours hoisted. The cutter fired two broad sides, great guns and small arms, and then made sail. We having the schooner under our lee, when the cutter made sale, he gave hur one 24 p[ounde]r, which dismounted one gun, killed one man, and wounded several more. At the same time the capt[ain] gave me orters to give the schooner a gun, which I did and split hur stem. The men left their quarter and the capt[ain] hall'd the coluurs down. We sent the boat on board and brought the capt[ain] on board. They proved to be English privateers from the Isle of Ganzey [Guernsey]. They new we ware an English man of war, but they expected we would press there men. As luck would have it, they done us no harm excepting cutting some of our riging. We took one man out of the schooner, not as we wanted him, but to certify as a witness. The capt[ain] rought to the Admiralety and there was strict orders sent to Gernsey that the capt[ain] of the cutter was never more to have command of a vessel out of the port, if known.

We then run north as far as Cape Finister and was laying two, close under the Cape, sounding, and the capt[ain] was taking the remarks of the Cape, of a thick foggy morning [13 August 1800]. All of a suddent appeared a verry large ship in the fog. We up hellem before the wind, but coming to vew hur with the spy glass and counting hur port, we found she carried only 24 guns. We hall'd our wind for hur. She hoisted hur Spanish colours. When we got a long side we up English colours and gave hur three or four of our 24 pounders. They finding our mettle so heavy, they run from there quarter and struck there colours.

We boarded hur. She proved to be a fine packet [*La Reyna Luisa*] from South America bound to Spain with a good quantity of Kings money on board. She had two capt[ains] and a Spanish general on b[oar]d. Mr. Buchan, master, took charge, he being my suprior officer, while I took the officers on board. When we ordered the men into the cabin and overhall'd them, we found a good quantity of dollars, half joes, doubleelons, 7 lb. bars and 14 lb. bars of gold. We overhall'd the men twice and found as much with them the last time as we did the first. We found doubleoons sowed in the soles of there stockings, 2 deep, from one end to the other. All the money we found was among the men and officers and some bars they hove overboard. The General got away with 4 gold bars, as the Spanis[h] capt[ain] inform Capt[ain] Bond afterwards. We brought hur into Lisbon. She had a great quantity of curious articles on board such as curious mats, wild fir skins, one of them was so butiful, dimond cut of different colours and not more than three and a half square, it sold for 38 dollars on b[oar]d the *Netley* Schooner. She had on b[oar]d 30,000 neats tongues dried, ostrige feathers in stands, length about two feet and about 40 in one stand, and 45 pigs of tooth and egge, beside a great quantity of goods in boxes which I cannot give an acount of. The ship was a fast sailor. The Spanish capt[ain] inform'd us that two English frigates had chased them three days and could not cetch them. When the prisoners were sent on shore, I remain'd on b[oar]d the Spanish ship with the men I had with me.

Having some business on shore I landed at the lower end of the town [Lisbon] where the ship lay and walked up to town, but being two late to go to the ship, about 10 o'clock at night I went down to Buckleys Stares to go on b[oar]d the *Netley* that lay off in the stream. While standing at the foot of the stairs, next to the water, calling a boat, two men came down the steps behind me. One, raped [wrapped] up in a cloak, clap'd a small sord to my brest. The other, behind me, had a Portegee dirk and put the point of it to my side. I had no arms, neither would they allow me to put my hand into my pocket for fear I had arm. They took my gold watch, a silver chain purse, and about forty five gold dollars and even some copper in my jacket pocket. I had a large gold ring on my finger which they did not observe. They then left me. I went up the steps when they ware at a small distance to see where they went to, but when they see me follow them, they gave chase after me. I took up a large street, [k]nowing if they came up with me they would kill me. I run for life. Coming to a large brick building that was broke down, I run into the back side of it and covered myself with bricks and the dry morter. When they came up, they looked all round, both in side and out and then discoursed together and went off. I lay there till day light, for fear they might be

Anchorage at Lisbon

watching me. When day light apeared, I got up and brushed myself as well as I could and went and got some refreshment and went on board. The next day I received two hundred Pounds [sterling], therefore I only regreted the loss of my watch, though I had others at the same time.

We went out, and standing to the nothord we saw a schooner at a long distance off. We made sail and was coming up very fast with hur, when to our surpris she hove two and took in hur sale when she was above two leagues off. Coming up to hur, our capt[ain] asked him what he hove two for.

"O, I [k]now de trees kealus. No can run away, so I stay," which made all hands laugh.

We took hur into Lisbon. Ariving, Capt[ain] Bond received a Letter of Preferment from the Board of war. It was a severe cut to the ships crew. Capt[ain] Bond wished to take me with him, but not having a nother ship apointed, he could not take me with him.

Ca[ptain] Mean [James Mein] took com[mand], both proud, hauty, and severe [18 January 1801]. We took some prises under his command, but one in purticular I would wish to mention. Off Vigo, out side the islands, we took a Spanish merchant ship. They finding the ship would be taken, they out lanch [launch], armed themselves, and put some boxes of money in the boat and pull'd away for Vigo. Coming up with the ship, we out boat, a six oard boat, and put the brass four pounder into hur, which had a slide fixed for that purpose. The capt[ain], in the room of putting an experient officer in the boat, he put a midshipman about 12 or 13 years of age to take com[man]d. The cutter, though only six oars, soon came up within gunshot, and giving them a few shot, they lay two for the boat to come up, which they did, in the room of making them return back by keeping at a distance, as they could of done. The boy run along side the lanch. They had 18 or 20 men well armed and only 7 men and himself. They amediately shot the bowman as he laid holt of the lanch with his boat hook. The boy cryed, and the six men gave up, and they took them into Vigo with the boat. We took the ship into Porto and then returned to England to refit.

Runing up the English Channel in the night, we fell in with some Tarbay [Torbay] fishing boats, and Capt[ain] Mean turn'd the hands up and made sale after them and cleared away for quarters. The poor fishermen thinking we ware a French privateer strove to get away and made all sail. Capt[ain] Mean ordered me to be ready with 4 men to b[oar]d the one we was coming alongside of, which we did. I found 3 poor fishermen on b[oar]d, unarmed and fritened almost to death, till they discovered what we ware. I searched the vessel, found nothing but nets and fishpots. I hailed the capt[ain] and informed him she was nothing but a Tarbay fishing boat. He was so angry that he would not lissen to me, but ordered me to follow him to Portsmouth. The next morning he took us on b[oar]d and pressed one of the men out of hur and let hur return.

We arived in Portsmouth [20 April 1801] and refited and I had the pleasure to see my wife and hur father and mother. In about six weeks, being refited, we had orders to return to our station on the Portagees coast. On our passage, off Cape Ortangal [Ortegal], we spied a large ship, and seeing she was a vessel of force, we took hur to be a French privateer of 34 guns upon two decks which we had heard crused off there. We bore down upon hur, but she proved to be the *Gorgeon* [*Gorgon*], 44 gun ship, bound to Egebt [Egypt] with light dragoons and there baggage—the ship I had belonged to before mentioned.

Capt[ain] Ross, who commanded the *Gorgeon*, was very intimate with our capt[ain]. Going on b[oar]d, Capt[ain] Ross beged the favour of Capt[ain] Main to let him have a quartermaster as he was in great need of one, which he promised he would if any of us would go. Coming on b[oar]d, he call'd us aft and inform'd us, but the other two would not agree to go. Therefore I turned out [26 June 1801], being aquainted with some of the officers and men, and in an hour afterwards I went on board with the capt[ain] and was received very friendly by the capt[ain], officers, and men and purticularly those that were on board when I left hur in Corsico to go on

Malta

board the *Blanch* Frigate. We ware both bound to the sotherd and kept company till we came off the coast of Portangal [Portugal] and then parted.

We stood on for Giberalter. Coming off Cadis, we fell in with a Brittish sloop of war on a cruise. About noon [30 June 1801] we saw a small privateer a head of us. She maid all sail she could crowd to get into Cadis, but the *Gorgeon* being a verry fast sailor, we soon got within gun shot and shot hur foremast away. We gave hur in charge of the sloop of war and stood on for the entrance of the Straits.

The next morning, being in the guts mouth of the Straits, we discovered nine sail of the line of Spanish and French two and three deckers, besides two frigates, stretching a cross from Jiberalter to the Algerene shore. We having a fair wind up the Straits, and being to windward, we hall'd our wind. They beating up for us, we huged our wind till dark, and having no other way of escape but to take chance and run the gantlet through the squadron, it being very dark, we up hellem and put hur before the wind and run through the center of the fleet with all sail that we could croud. And the wind freshening, we caried on, expecting every minute when the mast would go over the side. One of their frigates spied us and made a signal and bore up a long side of us, but seeing lights on our lower deck, she halled off, taking us to be a line of battle ship, but we had no guns on the lower deck, but 700 light horsemen and their baggage. We hove the log three times over and she was going at the rate of 15 nots, or miles an hour. The capt[ain] not beleiveing it, he hove it himself and found it so. The quartermaster at the wheel cried out to be releaved, not being able to stand there any longer. I was then call'd, he being there four hours. I remained there four more, till I was so weak I could not remain any longer, and the capt[ain] was doubtful who to trust. At length the boatswains yeoman releaved me. At daylight we found we had run them out of sight. The young man that I releaved was about 28 years of age, having strained himself, died in two days after. This same squadron Nelson fell in with laying in Algers some time afterwards and took and distroyed the chief of the squadron.

We stood on our course till we arived in Malto [Malta], which the English had possession of at that time [13 July 1801]. After refreshing the troops and taking in water, we sailed for Boko [Aboukir] Bay on the entrance of the Nile. We arived [24 July 1801] and landed the troops and their baggage. The Brittish and Turks was then blockading Alexander [Alexandria] by see and land, five or six sail of the line laying off the harbours mouth and the army laying on the sands on the back of the town, which acasioned a great number of sick and likewise a great number got blind by the heat and dazlin of the sands. I having charge of a lanch [launch], and taking stores to the camp, the beach master pressed us to carry stores to Carravensa Bay, the second branch of the Nile, and while there, the French arived that was taken at Caro [Cairo] and sent on board the transports to be taken to Taloon [Toulon]. I observed while there the French had some very handsome Turkish wimen with them, going to France. In about 12 days we ware purmitted to return to our ship again.

In about two month our ship took in sick, wounded, and blind. We then sailed [12 August 1801] with the transports and put into Malto [Malta] to refresh the sick and wounded [31 August 1801], but they ware dying every day. I having charge of the watering boats, before day light we would have to carry them out side of the harbour, sowed up in a hammock, and heave them overboard, as it dare not be known or otherwise they would of put us in currenteen [quarantine]. While we lay there, the *Enterprise*, American schooner, came in to refit, having had a sharp action with three galles [galleys]. They sunk the whole three of the galles with the loss of 16 men. When we [were] watered and ready for see, we sailed with the transports that was bound to Toloon with the French prisoners that was taken at Cairo.

We having a pleasent passage, after leaving the transports we put into

Majorco [Majorca] to water and refresh the sick and wounded [23 September 1801] that remained and then sailed with some other transports and arived at Jiberalter [28 October 1801], and in a few days we sailed for England. On the passage we lost our first leutenant [Thomas Gillispie], who died. He was a fine old seaman. Ariving at Spithead [7 December 1801] and having such a number of sick on board, we were put into currenteen [quarantine] for six weeks and laid at Gilkicker for that time. Our currenteen being out, we sent all the sick and wounded on shore.

It was shortly expected to have a peace with France, and they discharged a number of seamin that they thought would be of the least use. I offered a seaman 20 guineas to take my place and brought him on board, but the capt[ain] allowed he was not fit for my duty and refused him. Shortly after we ware ordered round to Debtford. I was at this time doing the duty of masters mate and was offered a masters birth on b[oar]d the *Minnetar* [*Minotaur*], 74 gun ship, but expecting a peace, I refused the offer before Capt. Ross of the *Gorgeon*. We arived at Debtford [4 March 1802], and in a few days the news of peace arived which acasioned the greatest elumenation in London I ever saw. We ware then sent to Wollage [Woolwich] to strip the ship, and put hur into dock. We went down and strip'd hur. While laying there I went to Portsmouth, having three days liberty from the capt[ain], and returned with my wife. In about 10 days after we ware paid off [19 April 1802] at the dock yard.

*Illumination in London
Celebrating Peace of 1802*

CHAPTER 10

Merchant Seaman

INTRODUCTION

O N   B O A R D both the *Netley* and the *Gorgon,* Nagle had served as quartermaster. He notes in the journal that just before his tour of duty on the *Gorgon* was over, he was offered but refused an assignment as master of one of the ships of the line. These were signs, perhaps, of growing maturity on his part, but also an indication of his advancing age. In 1802 he was forty-one years old, serving alongside sailors who were in their twenties and younger. He had a wife of seven years, living with her parents in Portsmouth, with whom he had spent less than six months since they were married, and he had children. Captain Bond had been about his own age, but Lieutenant Mein was not only fifteen years his junior but unappreciative of Nagle's talents. The Peace of Amiens was signed on 27 March 1802, and though it would last for little more than a year, for Nagle it provided a convenient opportunity to leave a service that was not much fun anymore.

Nagle was something of a stoic; perhaps some of the hurt of thirty-odd years had lost its immediacy when he sat down to write the journal, but one can read between the lines a certain loss of purpose in his life as a result of the personal tragedies he experienced in 1802. His intention, obviously, was to take his wife and children back to the United States, which he hadn't seen for twenty-one years. He had never communicated with his family and undoubtedly had visions that things were as they had been before he left. He brought his family up to Deptford, where they briefly took a room and waited for a ship to Lisbon.

Once they reached Lisbon, things went badly from the beginning. He learned that Lieutenant Mein had cheated him out of prize money. He was victimized by a landlord. He took the case to court and won, but lawyers' fees swallowed up the funds the court awarded him. And then the real tragedy occurred: Lisbon experienced a terrible yellow fever epidemic in 1802, and his wife and children died.

Because there had been newspaper stories indicating that the yellow fever had broken out in New York, an embargo was placed on shipping to the United States. Nagle appealed to the consul in Lisbon, William Jarvis, recently appointed by President Jefferson, and was able to get passage to Norfolk, Virginia, arriving probably in late summer of 1802. He then shipped with Captain Tice on the *Success* to Philadelphia. New but less unpredictable shocks awaited him there, where he was able to make contact with a sister and learned that both his parents were deceased. After a brief voyage to Richmond and Norfolk, he embarked on a trip of several months to visit his relatives in Pennsylvania and Maryland before returning to Philadelphia and taking up the occupation of merchant seaman.

In some ways, the journal during his twenty-two years as a merchant sailor is a little misleading in terms of commentary versus chronology. As one might expect, he devotes more text to eventful than to uneventful voyages and skips many of them altogether. He had a tendency to stick with a captain he liked until the ship needed repairs or until he got the urge to see another part of the world.

In 1805 he signed on the *Science,* a brand-new and rather elegant ship, a precursor of the passenger liners of later years in the century. To Nagle, whose shipping career had been spent in roughly furnished and crowded lower-deck accommodations, the mahogany woodwork, separate cabins, and mirrors were a wonder, and perhaps a little silly. In terms of his thinking, Nagle never really made it into the mainstream of the nineteenth century.

I TOOK a whery and got my chest and bedding in the boat and went up to Debtford and took a room for ourselves ready furnished till we could suit our selves. We remained in Debtford about a month when I fell in with a Portegee schooner bound to Porto Port. I paid our passage and in about a week we sailed [late April 1802] and the schooner came to an anchor at Gravesend to be overhalled at the customhouse to see that she had no more than hur propor crew on board, excepting about 40 Portegees officers and sailers that had been picked up at see, there ship being burnt by chefortus being stowed in the whole [hold]. I came from London in a boat and remained on shore till they ware overhalled and when going on board I joined them with my wife. I having no protection to produce, they would of stop'd me, as no seamen ware allowed to leave England, excepting what was on the ships books and compliment for the ship. However we sailed and came to an anchor in the Downs. A gale came on from the westward and we lost all the anchors but one, which was let go with a kedge, and it rode the gale out. If they had give way we should of perished on the quicksands. We made a signal of distress. A boat came off from Deal, but they would not bring off an anchor untill the capt[ain] would give them 50 guineas, and went on shore again, but as God would have it, it fell more moderate by next morning, but the wind continued to the westward. We got under way and put to see down Channel with a beating wind. In three weaks we fetched into Plimoth, being out of provisions. We got a supply. In two days the wind shifted. We sailed and had a pleasent passage and arived in Porto.

I went on shore and received some prize money from Sq[uire] Casy, which was our agent for the *Netley* Schooner. While I was with Capt[ain] Mean [Mein] he made another agent, and I went to him, I being a five shearman [share man]. My prize money amounted while with Capt. Main to about 39 guineas, as the agent inform'd me himself, and Capt. Mean rec[eive]d it in pretense he would deliver it to me when I arived in England, but I never receiv'd a cent of it. I then took passage in a Portegee schooner for

Lisbon and we arived safe. I went to Mr. Loyns & Gill in Co., which was agent, and receiv'd 45 half joes.[1]

I hired a room for the present and got aquainted with one Mr. More who kept a hotel, a most notorious villen though I new it not, pasing for a Merican. I resorted his house, and he finding I was flush of money and no American ships being there that was bound for America, he intised me to take a small house that he had rented, which to my sorrow I laid him down 13 half joes for the rent for six month, two small rooms and a kitchen backwards, on the second storie. I had not been more than two month in this house, and thought I was doing tolebarable well, when Mr. John More sent a fals bill to me of 80 crowns in his debt for board and at the same time I did not owe him one farthing. I sent him word I did not owe him any thing. He then sude me. I then found out by a Portegee gentelman that he had rented the house to me for six month where he only had the house for four month and in debt for the rent. My property was in danger of being seized for his rent, but applying to the owner, he assured me he would take no advantage, but insisted I should sue the villen to recover my money, which I did. In about a month we had our trials. Though I could not speak the language, my loyer won both causes by my having a linkister, though he had me before two different judges and then had to return what was due to me, though in feeing the loyer it cost me as much as I receiv'd. But as it often hapens, one trouble seldome comes alone. At this time my wife and children took the fever, and in the space of six weeks I was left alone.[2]

I then sold the remainder of my time for the house and sold the chief of my goods, and applying to the American Counsel, Mr. Jarvice [William Jarvis], which was then in Lisbon, and got on board of a Merican ship [June–July 1802] that had been dismasted in a gale of wind coming from Amsterdam in the east sees, bound to Norfolk in Virginia.[3] The second mate leaving the ship, I acted as such, though I receiv'd no pay, being a cabin passanger. In about three weeks we sailed and having pleasent w[eathe]r and nothing very purticular till we got within the gulf, and we had not sounded with the dipsey line, we laying drifting in a dead calm. The chief mate and myself were observing the water was pailer than the real seawater. I went into the main chains and hove the hand lead. It hapened to fall upon a sunken rock and the vessel laying along side of it. I found it to be quarter less twain, which is only 10 feet and a half. I inform'd the chief mate. By the time he call'd the capt[ain], the ship drifting, I had seventeen fathom water. We ware then allowed not to be more than seventeen miles from the land, but

Virginia Pilot Boat

being hazy and foggy w[eathe]r, we could not see it. As I have understood out of Norfolk, by the pilots, that rock has been the loss and distruction of many lives and vessels. I was going myself out of Philadelphia in a schooner bound to Havana that was going before the wind and struck on that rock and every soul perished and I had two purticular acquaintence on board, but I was not ordain'd to go with them. A breeze springing up we stood in for the land and got a pilot on board and arived in Norfolk. I went to a boarding house and sold off the remainder of my effects that I brought with me at auction, then took passage with Capt. [Richard] Tice for Philadelphia and arived safe there.[4]

I went to Third Street, between Archstreet and Raystreet [Race Street], and enquired for Mr. Carr, where he formerly lived.[5] I found one of his daughters living in a private apartment by hur self named Susan. She was surprised to see me living, being away 24 years and accounts given by seamen that new me in the Straits that I was dead, and he, one of them, was at my burial as my youngest sister informed me at my arival. My parents being gone, I learnt I had three sister living through the country. Susan informed me that hur brother James lived in Dock Street and kept an open house. I went to Dock Street and found Mr. Carr. I then boarded there. In a few days after my youngest sister Polly arived out of the country, and having information of my arival, found me at Mr. Carrs. I went with hur to Mr. Harts, who was maried to Betsey Lincoln, first cozins and rais'd in our family.[6]

I shortly after took a voige with Capt[ain] Tice to Norfolk and Richmund in Virginia and return'd with a load of cole [coal].[7] Ariving in Phila[delphia], I receiv'd a letter from my unkle in Reading, wishing me to come to Reading. Therefore, by enquiry, I fell in with three men belonging to Reading. We took koach as far as Jarmantown. We then concluded to walk. We stop'd after dark at a public house and got supper, where I fell in with Polly Deweas, an old playmate when young in the town of Reading. We traveled all night, but before I got to the Trap I gave out and could not keep up, but that evening I got to Potsgrove and found one more had given out.[8] The other two went on. We remained there all night and hired two horses the next morning and arived in Reading before the other too.

I remained in Reading with my unkel about a week and received a small legacy that my Grand father had left me that lived in the Swamp.[9] I then

Philadelphia

started for Sunsbury with two wagons and ariving there I found my Ant Kiger [Geiger], a sister of my fathers, hearty and well in health, and several relations of hur suns and daughters living in Sunsbury and round about that part of the country.[10] In a few days, sitting at dinner with my ant and some of hur suns and daughters, taking our repast in pleasentry and mirth, there was a mesenger sent to me across the Suskehannah from the Ferry. My Unkel Younkman coming from Lancaster, hearing of my arival, stoped and wished me to come over amediately.[11] By the consent of my [aunt] and hur children, I amediately rose and crossed with the mesenger. My unkle was rejoiced to see me. After taking a glass of mathiglam, we started in his chaiz for Younkmans Town, which is called 18 miles.[12] We arived in the evening, and supper being ready, we sat down with my ant, a sister to my Ant Kiger. My sister Sally living a cross the street, hearing of my arival, came over, but when she saw me she could not tell whether I was hur brother or not, being young when I was taken prisoner, sailing out of the city of Philadelphia. She was then maried to Mr. John Webb and had three children.[13] After rising from supper I went home with my sister. A short time after we took an

Philadelphia Waterfront

excurcion down to Hagers Town in Merreland to our sister Ann, which was maried to Mr. McCardal, and remain'd there a week and then return'd to Younkmans Town.[14] To make short, I remained amongst my relations about four month and then started for the city of Philadelphia in the month of November.

In a few days after I arived, I shiped in a ship called the *Old Tom*, Capt[ain] Smith, bound for Vigo in old Spain with a cargo of ingeon [indian] corn and from thence to Lisbon in Portangal [Portugal], we having a good passage to these two different ports without anything remarkable excepting gales, which is common on the wide ocion. We discharging our cargoes, took in a cargo of wine for Philadelphia, with some salt. We had a pleasent passage till we got into the gulf and fell in with a heavy gale from the eastward, but rec[eive]d no damage, but our capt[ain] sold part of our ships provisions to a privateer in Vigo, therefore we ware supplyed at three different times by vessels we fell in with by small quantitys, and the last supply was a buisquit a day for 21 day, and one young sailor eat what he had in half the time and must of perished if we had not broken a small piece off of our allowance each of us, by that means he had equal to what we had, but ariving in Philadelphia [29 March 1803], the mate informing the merchant, the capt[ain] was turned out of the ship.

In a short time after I shiped in the *Roseana*, Capt[ain] Brown, for Orleans in ballace [ballast]. We sailed and made the whole in the wall [Hole-in-the-Wall, Abaco] and run through the Behemes [Bahamas], in side the Island of Cube [Cuba], and made the Belees [Belize] and got up to [New] Orleans and took in a cargo of cotton and horns for Liverpool. Sailed, but got a ground on the bar at the Belees, drawing 14 feet water. With carreing anchors out, we got hur off and had a pleasent passage to Liverpool. Discharged and took in salt for ballace [ballast]. On our return we fell in with a heavy squal from the N. E.. We kep hur before the wind till we had time to take in sail and get hur snug and by that squal, runing before it, about noon we saw a schooner upset. We run down to hur, lowered the boat down and went a longside and took the capt[ain], mate, and three men from hur, but had nearly lost the boat and ourselves. The schooner was from Philadelphia, b[oun]d to France with coco and sugar. They had been two nights and three days on the rack [wreck] from the time she capsised. They cut the masts away and then she rightened and floated on the surface of the water. The suger in the whole [hold] was hur heaveist cargo and by that melting she did not go down. The steward was drounded in the cabin and one man died on the quarter deck, which was hove overboard. The quarterdeck and forecastel was above water, but they had to lash themselves to keep the see from washing them overboard. When we came a long side, the sherks [sharks] was numerous, ready to receive more pray. They had a bag of coco and a cask of water which was lash'd on deck. There bodies ware raw with the rope lashed around them. We scarcely had got them on board, and the boat hoisted up, when another gale came on. If we had been one hour later they must of perished. Our capt[ain] and crew done all we could for them and brought them to Philadelphia. On the passage we saw several racke [wrecks] broke to pieces and floating on the water; we picked up one boat, but noboddy in hur and brought hur with us.

While in Philad[elphi]a I remain'd with my sister and first cousen for about three weeks.[15] I then shiped in a sloop [*James*] bound to the West Indies com[mande]d by Capt[ai]n Hazard and part owner of the vessel and cargo, which was provisions of different kinds, besides poltry such as ducks, fowls, and turkeys, to the number of 1700 and odd. We ware bound to Bartholames, but falling to leeward of the island, we run down to St. Acruise and sold part of the cargo, put to see, and run over to St. Thomases, which lay abreast of it, and sold the remainder, took in sugar and coffee and put to see.[16]

It being winter time on our coast, the N. westers prevailed. We would have a fair wind for four or five hours, then chop round to the westward and blow us off again. We got our main topsail yard and main yard down upon deck, our mainsail spliting almost every day, and repairing it, till it got so small that we could carry all our sail in the strongest breezes of wind, blow high or low.

We got out of bread and meat. The capt[ain] had four shoots [shoats] in the pen to use on the passage, but in one night they ware all drownded. The next morning the capt[ain] desired they should be hove overboard, but a sailor and myself agreed to skin two of them on the quarter deck and cleaned them and put them into a pickel cask for our use. Though we had plenty of coffee and sugar, it did not satisfy hunger altogether. In a few day the capt[ain] applyed to us for some of our "drownded pork," which he then confessed went down very sweat. We fell in with a Yankee schooner and the capt[ain] inform'd them our sittuation and offered them sugar and coffee if he would give us a small supply of bread or whatever he could spare, but he would not, and stood on his course. In a few days after, the wind favouring us, we got off Cape May. A pilot boat came to us. Informing them our

St. Thomas

situation, the pilot came on b[oar]d with a hankerchief ful of buiskuit and a large codfish fresh that they had caught a few hours before. We turned to cooking and had a glorious meal. We had not been sixty four days from St. Thomases on our coast in the dead of winter, which is not more than 10 or 12 days run in fine weather. In two or thre days we arived in Philadelphia [4 April 1804].

In about two weeks I shiped with Capt[ain] Tice before mentioned in a new schooner of his own [*Eliza*], bound for [New] Orleans. We made the whole in the Rock [Hole-in-the-Wall, Abaco], where we take our departure from. We then run down through those small rocky island, but coming to the N. end of the island of Cuba (it touches the Trophic of Cancer, on the E. Side, 20°20′N. Latt'd, on the entrance of the gulf of Mexico, 700 miles in length and about 60 wide, extends from 74° to 85°18′W., Long'd, 85 m[iles] N. of Jamaco [Jamaica] and Havanah is the capatal of the island), we runing in side between the main and the island, we pass Havannah and keep out of the gulf and made the Belees [Belize]. We ware three weeks getting up to Orleans, which I beleive by account is not more than two hundred miles, though at that time it was call'd a short passage.[17] We took in a cargo of cotton, and having what supplyes was requeset, we sailed.

Getting over the barr at the Belees [Belize], we had a strong breeze from the N.W., keeping hur about a point free for the gulf, which sets to the nothord. Getting a boom takel from forrod to hook to the main boom, the man got into the lee main chains and fell over board. We hove the vessel up into the wind, though a strong breeze, which endangered our masts being caried away as we ware then going about 8 or 9 nots an hour. We amediately cut away the lashings of the boat, being secured, and lowered the boat. A brotherinlaw to the man which was overboard ketched holt of a peace of the lashing which was greasy to slip down to the boat which was in the water, but missing the boat, overboard he went. Immediately the chief mate and myself strove to hall the boat up to get into hur, but the see runing high, being a strong breezs, she got under the counter and filled. However, we got hur along side so that I could get into hur. We having 9 passengers on boa[r]d, they would insist on having a rope fast to me, for fear I should be lost likewise and only being four in number beside the capt[ain] and mate, the pasengers thought they would all be lost as they new nothing concerning the working of the ship. They held the rope so fast that I was in danger of being mashed to pieces between the vessel and boat with the rise and fall of the see till I call'd out to the capt[ain] to make them let go the rope. The two men that was overboard swam very well, but the see runing very rough and short, it soon smothered them, and before I could clear the boat of water, they both went down and we lost sight of them.

We then hoisted the boat up again and secured hur and made sail with two hands before the mast and capt[ain] and mate. We got into the gulf, which sets to the nothord, and having two topsails we ware not sufficient to wark all the sails. Therefore the capt[ain] desired me to go up and send down the main topsail yard, likewise the main yard, which I did, and having a favourable wind, with the current, we reached the Capes of Deliver [Delaware] in 10 days, but being about the begining of January [1805], the river was entierly frose up as the pilots inform'd us. We took a pilot on board from Cape May, and while at breekfast our cable parted and we got aground before we new that she was adrift, through the pilot not attending to the deck, but having a fresh breeze from the S.E., we loosed the fore topsail and sheated it home and hoisted hur fore and aft sails, which hove hur down on hur beam ends, which made hur draw less water, and she shot off and we steared for New York. But being bitter cold weather, we had to releive the man at the hellem every hour, and being frose up forrod, we all lived in the cabin. Having a good breeze, we reached Neversink in about forty eight hours. We got up above the currenteen [quarantine] ground, but the ice came down in such large flakes that we got entangled and had nearly been caried to see again. Finding we could not get up to New York, we bore up and run into the currenteen wharf and made fast on the lee side of the wharf. The capt[ain] and pilot went to Philadelphia and we remain'd six weeks there, when the capt[ain] returned and brought his old pilot with him that was born in the town of Reading by the name of Hoos Nagle [Hoosnagle?], where I was born myself.

We sailed for Philadelphia. Nothing purticular accured till we got up the river as high as New Castle, when the ice came down in such large flakes that we could not keep in the river. However, by the oconomy of the pilot, we made shift to get a long side the warf at Markus Hook and made fast, but a sloop that was a stern of us was so much cut with the ice that the capt[ain] and crew left hur with the boat, being nearly full of water, but a number of pilots went off and brought hur into Newcastel and they got a selvage for saving the vessel and cargo, though a great deal was damaged. We lay there about 10 days for the ice and then got up to Philadelphia, which is call'd 18 miles by land.

I sail'd several trips with Capt[ain] Tice that I make no mention of, not being any thing purticular.[18] I remain'd about three weeks in Philadelphia, when I fell in with a mate of a vessel belonging to Hudson, up the river at New York, and the capt[ain]s name was Hudson, who gave me a passage round to New York. We had a pleasent passage, and I landed near the hay scales on the north side. Having never been acquainted in New York at this time, I had a recommendation to Mr. Cooms [sic, John McCombs] from a friend of his in Philad[elphia]. He lived in Grinnige [Greenwich] Street and receiv'd me very kindly. He was a gentelman of good property and respectable caracter. He had the over looking of all the paving in New York.[19] He made me aquainted with his brother in law, Mr. Moneypenny, that kept a grosery but no boarders excepting aquaintances, where I remain'd about three weeks, when I shiped in a new ship call'd the *Ciance* [*Science*] bound for

London [sailed 1 January 1806]. She was chiefly intended for passangers, though she had likewise a cargo of pitch and tar and turpentine, but hur cabin was entierly for ladies, and hur steerage equally as well set off as the cabin. They were both set off with mahogany and fixtures of looking glass that you could see yourself, look which way you would. The gentlemens cabins in the stearage were 16 in number and eight on each side of the dining table and numbered. The cabin for the ladies had fine cabenet work for the china, and closets ware superior. They could sit in the beds and cabins and vew themselves, look which way they would, but we had but few passengers outward bound, being the first voige.[20]

Capt[ain] Howard was our capt[ain], being well [k]nown by the sailors in New York, being such a tarter, but at this time he was bound down not to strike a man. The voige before, he had three different ships crews from New York to London and back again. On our voige to Lundon we had four men in a watch besides the mate. We chiefly had a fair or leading winds but squally and heavy rains. The darkest night and the more rain, he would keep you aloft, sending the top gallant yard up and down, one man at the helem, one man up aloft to clear a way the riging, and the other two and the mate to heave the yard up by a crab or capstain that was on the quarter deck. Then the yard must be bore off. When it came to the main top, the one more must go a loft, while the mate and one man attended to their call when high enough and the yard riged, ready for crossing, and the yard crossed. By the time the yard rope was taken off by the men that was aloft, and sheets, buntlins, and clewlines all bent ready for setting the sail, the brave capt[ain] would be standing in the companion to see the sail set. Then he would be abusing the man at the wheel, finding fault with his stearage. When tired with giving abuse, he would go down to his cabin for about 20 or 30 minutes, then come up to see if it rain'd, and if so, too hands must go aloft and send the top gall[an]t yard down again.

This was the situatien during our passage, though winter. There was not a seaman on board that had a dry jacket or shirt til we got into the Downs going up London River. When laying in New York, though winter, he had the ship riged out with royals sciscraper, ringtail booms for water sails to cut a dash, but as soon as we put to see, having nothing but stiff gales and heavy rain, we had to get all these kites, yards, and booms upon deck and then she was two krank to carry sail in the weather we had.

A few days before we entered the Chanel of England, being a new ship, she made a good deal of water, and I was coming from forward to releave the pum[p]. Being to windward, a heavy see struck hur on the weather beam. The lachings of the spare topmast gave way and jamed me fast against the boom and nearly smothered me with the see. The capt[ain], standing in the companion, saw what situation I was in, call'd out to the chief mate, which was a smart and powerful man. He ketched up a handspike laying a long side the mainmast and prised the spars off so far that I clear'd myself, but as God pleased I had no bones brok, but brused in the thies. With the same see one of the men at the lee pum[p] was carried over board, the vessel giving a heavy lee lurch, and sending to leeward as he ris, he got holt of a lanyard that had got loose and floting off from the vessel, which belonged to the topmast backstay, and halled himself into the main chains and got on board. When in the Downs we ware 27 days from New York, but when this man was overboard it was doubtful weather she would rise again, being so krank. When we arived, we went into London Dock according to custom.

We discharged the cargo. The ballace [ballast] we had in was not sufficient to keep hur upright. We had to support hur with luff takels to the wharf till we got 10 ton of ballace more in hur hole, besides what we took in at New York. Now being in dock, the capt[ain's] treatment was not forgot during the passage. In the first place the chief mate left the ship, and the seamen followed. As for my part, I was determened to leave her, but my chest and beding being aboard, I waited till she hall'd along side of another ship to go out of dock. I new the capt[ain] must cross this vessel to go on board and I laid wait for him. While discoursing with the mate of the other vessel, the capt[ain] apeared. I stood by the mainmast til he came across. I then stop'd him and demanded my chest and bedding. He asked me if I was not going in the ship. I told him I would not unless he gave me my see stores. He said he would not till we got down to the Nore in the Downs. I then demanded my property. He then gave his consent and left me. I went on board and got out my chest and bedding. I then went to a boarding house till I could suit myself.

In a few days after I fell in with the mate of the *Hope*, belonging to Philadelphia. He inform'd me they had lost the chief of their hands, as they had been smuglin some of the cargo, and [k]nowing they would loose there wages when they arived, therefore they left the vessel. He was very desirous for me to go, but I was doubtful in that case what the capt[ain] might be. The mate offered me 18 doll[ar]s in advance. I had a nother seamen with me, but we concluded not to go.

PLATE 1 *Philadelphia*

PLATE 2   *Basseterre, St. Christopher*

PLATE 3   *Brimstone Hill, St. Christopher*

PLATE 4   *Sea Battle between Hood and de Grasse off St. Christopher, 25 January 1782*

PLATE 5   *Plymouth Harbor*

PLATE 6   *HMS* Sirius *in the Harbor at Rio de Janeiro*

PLATE 7   *Broken Bay, Australia, March 1788*

PLATE 8   *HMS* Sirius *Encountering Icebergs on Voyage to Cape of Good Hope,*
14 December 1788

PLATE 9   *Capture of Bennelong, 25 November 1789*

PLATE 10   *Wreck of HMS* Sirius *at Norfolk Island, 19 March 1790*

PLATE 11   *The Thames near the Tower of London*

PLATE 12 *Fight between HMS* Brunswick *and* Vengeur, *1 June 1794*

PLATE 13   *London from Greenwich Park*

PLATE 14   *Johann Schmidt Portrait of Lord Nelson*

PLATE 15   *Porto Ferrajo, Elba*

PLATE 16   *East India Company Dockyards, Blackwall*

PLATE 17 *Chinese Court Questioning Crew of the* Neptune *at Canton, 1807*

PLATE 18   *Lisbon, Portugal*

PLATE 19   *Bahia, Brazil*

PLATE 20 *Rio de Janeiro*

CHAPTER 11

Voyage to China

INTRODUCTION

IN 1806, a war was still in progress between France and England, but Nagle turned forty-five that year and was beyond the age where he had to worry about being impressed. He could again risk going to London. Captain Howard of the *Science* had proven to be a difficult man to sail under, and apparently thinking back to the Australian voyage of fifteen years earlier, Nagle "concluded to take a voige to the East Indies once more." Sailings from England to China were commonplace for the East India Company, but this particular trip had more than the normal share of adventure and drama.

Nagle got off to a bad start by allowing himself and a shipmate to be victimized by a "crimp." The landlord of the White Swan Tavern, near East India House, seems to have specialized in recruiting men for the company's service, undoubtedly with official approval and cooperation, because of the desperate shortage of seamen. The landlord would provide food and drink, cover a few debts, and perhaps advance a little money in return for the company's advance money or a lien on some or all wages. The navy and press crews had a particular hostility to crimps, because they encouraged desertion, and by the early nineteenth century the crimps were wary of being taken to court. In this case, Nagle and his friend unwittingly signed away their advance money and a portion of their wages, their entire pay if they happened to die on the voyage. Nagle stood up to the system and beat it, but for average sailors, this was one of the many ways they were kept in a state of constant indebtedness, and for the East India Company and merchant vessels and privateers, it was one of the primary methods of getting seamen.

Nagle had sailed with the East India Company in the *Rose* in 1794–95, an 800-ton vessel typical of the company's fleet throughout most of the eighteenth century. The *Neptune,* however, was of a style introduced in the late 1780s, of 1,200 tons burden, which by this time had become the standard for the fleet to China, able to carry an immense cargo. The *Neptune* sailed in February from the East India dock at Blackwall to Portsmouth, and at the end of April, set off with a large convoy of Indiamen, a crew of 149, and close to 400 passengers, troops for the Cape of Good Hope, military dependents, and native Chinese. It stopped at the Cape, disembarked the 47th Regiment of Foot and took on board the 30th Regiment, and sailed for Penang, which it reached in October and where it took on a cargo of betel nut and spices for China.

The *Neptune* entered the Canton River on January 14 and began the delicate process of working up to the anchorage at Wampoa and satisfying the many regulations imposed on the trade by Chinese officials. To minimize potential trouble, only half of the crew of any ship was permitted to land at Canton at one time. Fellow crewmen of Nagle's were there on February 24 when trouble developed. Richard Standring, one of the men, was apparently stealing handkerchiefs in Hog Lane. When the Chinese shopkeeper protested, the drunken sailors started a riot, making forays beyond the compound, indiscriminately beating anyone in their way. Leav-a-ting, a Canton native who was wounded in the fight, died soon afterward. The Chinese demanded that Captain Buchanan turn over the murderer. He refused, and the tea trade was stopped for two months. In the fleet's own private investigation, the probable culprit or at least instigator of the fight was identified as Phillip Murray, but the findings were never shared with Chinese officials.

The Chinese next demanded the right to interrogate the fifty-two seamen who had been involved. They did so, and on no more evidence than that he had been wounded, they settled on Philip Sheen as the guilty man and demanded that he be turned over for execution. Sheen was sent to Macao and the demand refused. Permission was given to the rest of the fleet to load and depart, but they would not leave until the *Neptune* was granted the same privilege. Eventually permission to sail was granted, and the *Neptune,* loaded with tea and chinaware, set sail with nine other ships, convoyed by HMS *Lion,* on 9 May 1807. It is hard to say which side won, or what the outcome would have been had the Chinese insisted upon justice. The British, when they heard of the trouble, sent several warships to the area. The mayor of Canton for a time revoked the privilege of shore leaves for sailors, but the trade was important to both sides, and it soon resumed its normal course.

The fleet was dogged briefly by one of the French privateers that at this time made close convoy formations in the Indian Ocean essential. The fleet reached the Cape of Good Hope on 19 September 1806. There the crews learned of the loss of the *Blenheim,* which had impressed sixteen unlucky seamen from the *Neptune.* The *Blenheim,* with Admiral Troubridge on board, and the *Java* had gone down off Madagascar on 1 February 1807 with the loss of all hands, over five hundred of them. For months, there were rumors and hope that the two vessels had survived, and as Nagle relates in a somewhat confusing passage, the admiral's son, Captain Troubridge in the *Greyhound,* was dispatched on a fruitless search.

The *Neptune* had its own problems on the voyage home. The crew had picked up something Nagle calls the "white flux" in China or Penang. The captain's log notes that there were seventeen on the sick list on July 19, twenty-eight on October 9, and by November, on the passage from St. Helena to Britain, men were dying almost daily. East Indiamen were always shorthanded in this era, but by the time this ship reached home waters, it had an able-bodied crew of less than fifty men, hardly enough to work the sails.

Their first port of call was Crookhaven, County Cork, Ireland, supposedly out of necessity, but probably by design. On his earlier voyage in the *Rose,* the captain had attempted an unscheduled landing in Ireland, only to be foiled by British revenue cutters. It was common practice for the captains and officers to ship private cargoes from India or China, and it saved trouble and expensive bribes if they could profitably sell or smuggle them before reaching the East India docks. In spite of its grand facade and enormous fleet, the company was, even by 1806, a sick giant. It lost money annually while its directors, its ship-builders, its captains, and even its sailors were putting their own profits above that of their employer. In 1813 the company's monopoly on trade with India was revoked by Parliament, and in 1833 its trading privileges were withdrawn altogether. When the company itself was abolished, after the Sepoy Rebellion in 1858, the British government had to assume a £100 million debt that had been building for seventy-five years.

After the stop in Ireland, the *Neptune* crossed St. George's Channel and put into Milford Haven, where the sailors had the opportunity to profit enormously from the sale of "smutty" snuffboxes and trinkets. No ship of this size had ever been in the harbor previously. The crew of the ship had been decimated by the disease, and additional crewmen were sent to it from London. The ship finally arrived at Long Reach on 22 February 1808, two full years after it had set out on the voyage.

Nagle then shipped on the *Highlander* of Greenock for New Brunswick. The voyage had the overtones of a Joseph Conrad short story, with a sick captain and a dangerous crew. Nagle saved the ship at one point, punched the most threatening sailors into submission, and then played the role of crew representative in a strike against a penny-pinching owner when they returned to Greenock. But the voyage was a costly one for him. When he saved the ship at Cape Breton by freeing cables to two anchors that had been put out to pull the ship off a bar it had grounded on, Nagle worked in ice-cold water, and he was badly chilled. It was the first serious health problem of the sort that never entirely went away, and one senses that from then on, he never quite regained the physical stamina of his earlier years.

WE THEN concluded to take a voige to the East Indies once more. We both went up to the India house, or at least the White Swan, close by, where they ship seamen for the East India service. We spoke to him. He profered to pay what trifel we owed and send us down to the *Neptune,* one of the largest Indiamen belonging to the India Company. They then lay in Long Reach. He took both of us into a private room to sign the Articles. When laying the Articles on the table, he laid a Power [of Attorney] on the top of the Articles, that if we should die, for him to receive our wages. Neither of us having any suspicion that they ware any more than Articles of the ship which is the regulor rule, had no thought of reading the contents. Therefore we sign'd the papers. He paid the trifel we owed and supplied me with a pair of course stockinge that I expected would be of service to me when coming back in cold weather.

The next day we went down to Long Reach and joined the *Neptune,* where the rest of the Indiaman lay. The ship was then fitting out and had a full compliment on board, but few seamen. In the run of about three weeks the commissioner of the Company came on board to see who was to go the voige or not. The chief mate, Mr. Ribbins [Frederick Ribbans] being a very smart man and a real seaman, he well new who he would wish to have. When we ware call'd up on the quarter deck, they ware so thick round the cabin that my cumrad and myself sat at a distance and concluded that if they had their compliment we would take what they allow'd us for the time we had been at work on board. But in a short time Mr. Ribbins came out of the dore and made a signal to me to come in and made room for us. The capt[ain] wished to [k]now weather we would go the voige. We both said yes. Then they offered me the advance, but this landlord that sent us down in the boat demanded the crimpage besides the pair of stockings that I had receiv'd from him. We both denied it. As the company paid for the passage, we would not sign but go a shore. When they found we ware determined to go on shore, they agree'd to satisfy the landlord and give us our full advance and crimpage. Therefore we took the money and remained on b[oar]d.

In a few days after we sailed for Spithead, where we found 17 sail of Indiamen ready for see and the chief of them for Canton in China. We received between three and four hundred soldiers on board, some for the Cape of Good Hope and the rest for the Prince of Wales'es Island, or otherwise call'd Pulleponang.[1] At length we sailed, but when those Indiamen have troops on board, all hands are upon three pints of water pr. day. We had forty men shiped for seamen, and runing down Chanel with a fresh breese, they ware turned away one after the other till they ware reduced to five in number beside the quarter masters, and we had no more during the voige. We had a verry fine passage till we arived in Sadena Bay, Cape of Good Hope, and there landed the number of troops that was apointed. We receiv'd sum sheep for refreshment.

In a few days we put to see about four P.M. We had no sooner cleared the land, and before we had time to get the cables below from between decks, being a two deck'd ship, a severe gale came on from the N.W. [17 August 1806]. We kept hur before the wind during the night, our sails being all furled excepting the fore topmast staysail, to keep hur from broaching two, and the mainsail clewed up. We had about forty men on the main yard, endeavouring to furl it, but it was in vain, therefore they ware call'd down. They ware scarcely down before the main yard gave way in the slings and the yard arms in the water on each side. The main topsail yard was blown away, though furled, with out any man seeing when it went. I was then at the wheel and was releaved by a quartermaster. I had not been away above ten or fifteen minutes before she took a yaw, stearing very bad, and was nearly broaching two, and away went the three topmasts and jib boom. We had two six oard cutters secured on the quarters by davids [davits] and well lashed on each side. A most tremendious see following us struck us in the stern and took both boats away as though they had been lashed with straw.

Though hur poop was a great highth from the water, and the largest and loftiest ship in the fleet, being a ship of eighteen hundred tons [sic, 1,200 tons], it being dark in the night I was standing on the quarter deck on the starbourd side when the capt[ain] asked me, "Who is this?"

I answered, "Nagel."

He answered, "Stay here, I shall want you presently." In the mean time he said to Mr. Ribbins, who was standing by him, "Take care of me." I then saw Capt[ain] Buckhannon was frightened. Mr. Ribbins made answer that he would endeavour to do it if he could.

Then the main topmas staysail broke loose, the stay being gon. Mr. Ribbins call'd me to go with him to pass a gasket round it, but when we got into the fore riging the sheet brocks [blocks] flew from one side to the other, that we dare not go up. We remained in this situation, roling before a tremendious wind and see, and the cables below rowling from side to side, breaking chest, tables, and all our crockery ware and every thing excepting the guns, that it was dangerous to go on the lower gun deck.

All seamen and soldiers remained on deck during the night, expecting to meet our doom every minute, and I must say, though I had been round the Cape backwards and forwards five times, I never saw so trimendious a see in a gale before, though I never did pass it without a gale but once, but about day light the wind begin to lull and the see fell, and by the 8 A.M. it fell start calm, but not one sail of the fleet in sight. The fore topmast was still hanging down along side. We cut the eyes of the riging and let the broken mast go overbourd. We now begin to rig hur at see. The carpenters begin to make caps for the lower masts heads, as they ware gon, likewise the black-smith at the forge, the sailors cuting up cabels, drawing yarns, and making rope and fitting the riging, til we got topmast up and bent sails and stood on our course. Then I was put into the sailmakers crew to repair and make sails.

Storm off the Cape of Good Hope

The morning after the gale, a small American ship spoke us, supposing we might be in distress for provisions or spars, but the capt[ain] thanked him and inform'd him we had sufficiency, but he pased a joke on us saying we had a smart breeze last night, which made them laugh. He then made sail and parted.[2] We worked on near six weeks before we ware complete, but we joined the fleet the day before we arived in Pulleponang, when we entered the harbour [14 October 1806] and come to an anchor, the *Blenom* [*Blenheim*], 84 gun ship, and two frigates. The *Blenom* pressed 25 men out of our vessel and sent 8 or 10 invaledes on board to go to England.[3] We ware loaded with Kings stores for the dock yard, as it was intended for a Kings port for men of war. We discharged and took in seven brig loads of beatle nut to take to China, which they use for scarlot die, but it is a dangerous cargo. We had to keep a vintelator going constant day and night to pump the foul air out and then it would be so hot we could not stand in it.

This island is but small, lays close to the main [mainland] and deep water, for which the British have made it a randevos for men of war. The tigers swim over from the main as I was informed and often do a great deal of mischief before they are destroyed, and allegators are very numerous. Coming off from the shore in the evening in a four oard boat, one atempted to get into the boat till we made him let go, beating him with our oars. Pullo Pinang is in Long'd 100°19'E., Lat'd 5°25'N., off the Malay Peninsula.

Chinese Tomb near Canton

When ready for see the fleet sailed for China [15 November 1806]. Having fine and pleasent weather, we run through the Straits of Sincompo on the north end of the Straits. Falling dead calm, and the current setting in was drifting us on the rocks, by signals the fleet sent their boats and towed us off. We had fine and moderate w[eathe]r. We passed an island which had a vulcany on the top of a mountain, and I was inform'd that it was dangerous to land there as the men ware jiants [giants].

We arived and went through the Bogus [Boca Tigris] and came to an anchor in Ansons Bay. The next day we got under way with a light wind and got up to the second bar. Then we had 20 or more China boats that towed us up to Deans Island and came to an anchor [14 January 1807] and there striped the ship for repair and discharged the cargo.

We got Chinamen on board to help to discharge. They are notorious theaves. One of them was ketched going over the side with a pig of tooth and egg which is call'd next to or the dross of silver. They make fals dollars of it. This Chinaman was taken aft and tied up and got a severe floging, then cast loose, the capt[ain] ordered the boatswain and his two mates to thrash him round the decks in a shocking manner till he got on the gangway and jumped overboard and swam to one of the boats.

Duck Boat at Canton

At this time I was taken out of the sailmakers crew and put into the boatswains crew to refit the ship. On Sundays we could go on shore to take our recroation. I walked over a rising hill, which went with a decent. Coming on the opposite side of the hill, I observed a great number of doors in the side of the hill and all locked with large padlocks. This I understood was their grave yard. The bodies ware imbalm'd and put into these valst [vaults], standing up an end, each family in their own vault, so that they can see their familys from one jeneration to the other.

There was a small village about a half mile from it, what they call the Chinee Tarters. All live in their own boats, every family by themselves, with their poltry, pigs, or whatever property they may have. While we lay here I saw a wedding pass the ship, about 40 boats with their colours flying and musick playing. The boat the groom and bride was in was in the center, which is given by the parents as a house to live in. These boats are all covered over in the center of the boat to shelter them from all sorts of weather. Abreast of Deans Island there is a large mash [marsh] and a great number of these boats raises ducks. The owner of the boat will land in the mash and put a gangboard out and purhaps too or three hundred ducks will walk out into the mash to feed and intermix themselves amongst thousands during the day. In the evening every boat will land, and having his board out, each one blows his whissel and every duck flies for their own boat and walks regularly into hur. The boats both large and small are so numerous going up to Canton that it is often dificult to get along and pass them.

The fleet being filled out we droped down to the second barr [23 February 1807] to take in cargos of tee, about seventeen sail. The *Lion* 50 gun ship, man of war, lay'd at Ansons Bay as our convay. The boats came down with tees. One of them will carry from 14 to 18 hundred boxes of tee. They have fine rooms in them for their families and traffick for sale. Their masts and sales are made of bamboo. They use but two ores over the stern. The men, wimen, boys, and girls scull these ores. In the small boats the wimen will come along side for clothes to wash everyday and mend them and at dinner time they will come and receive what you can give them after you have your own dinner, let it be ever so trifeling, or if none to spare that day they are content, but by washing for two or three messes they are sure of rice, soop, or meat every day and when we sail it lays to our option to give them what you please.

When we had receiv'd about half our cargoes, a circumstance hapened which detained the whole fleet about two months or better. One half of our ships crew went up to Canton to by what they thought fit, as it was a rule in every Indiaman. Some of them got into a quarrel with the Chinees [24 February 1807], and the Chinees being numerous, drove them into the Companys lazarittes or buildings with sticks and stones. The English sailors not being satisfied, split up fier wood for clubs and sallied out upon them, and other sailors joining them, both Americans and Bengalles, they drove a great number of them into the water, and in the fight a Manderien was passing which was as a majestrate and got kill'd. Immediately the tea was stoped and no supply was to be got until they received blood for blood. The comedore and all the capt[ains] and a company of mariens came up and the *Neptunes* crew was confined for trial. The time was set. The petty King and his officers, the commedore and all the capt[ains] and three or four hundred Manderins. The Chinees had there racks and gallos and other machiens brought before the buildings. They ware tried one by one and could not find out the man. They tried them three times over but all in vain. What was to be don? At length it was agreed one man was to be left behind till such times that it could be setled by the India Company. It was advertised on b[oar]d every Indiaman any one man that would remain behind should receive 20,000 dollars. At length a landsman that was in the *Bussel* agreed to stop.[4]

We then rec[eive]d tea till we ware all loaded and droped down to the Bogus and put to sea [9 May 1807]. (An English man of war brig came into the Bogas and inform'd us they had a severe action off the Ladrons Ilands, being attacted by them, and was nearly taken by them, but they beat them off with the loos of a good many men and they got two men out of our ship, volentered.) For a few days we had a head wind. We then had a leading wind. As we neared the entrance of Sinkampo, we fell in with a squadron of men a war from India. As they heard of the disturbance at China the govenors ware sending both troops and men of war, one 74, three 64, and 4 frigates and a number of smaller armed vessels. The admiral was informed that it was all settled, but he continued on to China and we stood on for Pulleponang. When ariving [30 June 1807] there we had plenty of fresh buffolou, but it is tough meat. In a few days, the fleet being ready for sea, we weighed anchor with a fine pleasent and moderate breeze for Europe.

In a few days, getting clear of the islands, we fell in with a French 74 gun ship. She came down upon us, but the *Lyon* [*Lion*] man of war standing out of the fleet for hur, she hall'd off and doged round us, the *Lyon* being only a 50 gun ship, but the smallest of the Indiaman mounted 32 guns in the whole

Chinese Version of the Rack

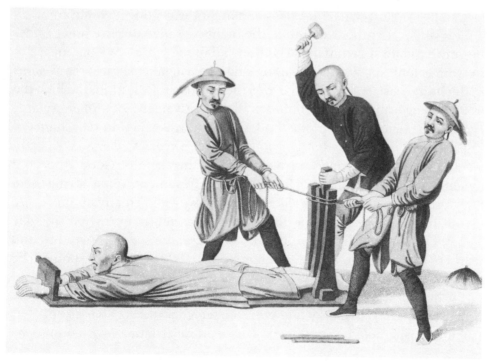

Cape of Good Hope

fleet, but she followed us three days and nights, expecting it would come on to blow and scatter the fleet, but in the night we sailed in close order under the com[modore's] command. The fourth day she left us. We had heard of this ship before. She was a fast sailing ship and had taken a great many ships on the India coast. Hur randavoos was the Morushes [Mauritius], which the French owned, and was a harbour for all their privateers. This 74 afterwards was coming home full of money to France and was taken in the Chanel of England by the Brittish after their toil for several years.[5]

We kept on our voige till we arived at the Cape of Good Hope [19 September 1807]. There we rec[eive]d good refreshment. While laying there a N. wester came on which had like to have drove a good many on shore. We lost all our anchors excepting the one we was riding by, when the gale ceased, but if a ship strikes on the sunken rocks, the see rolls over hur and nearly two miles to the beach, that it is scarcely [k]nown for any body to be saved if cast away in that bay.

A man of war brig [*Greyhound*] came in that had been in search of the *Blenom* [*Blenheim*], an eighty four gun ship which pressed 25 hands out of us in Pulleponang before mentioned. The capt[ain's] father was admiral on b[oar]d of hur. They ware coming home to England with a great number of passangers from different parts of India with all their riches and one capt[ain] of man a war that had made an independent fortune in taking so many rich vessels was in hur, likewise Govener Gray, governer of Pulleponang, and his lady and all there wealth, Gov[ernor] Gray that I sail'd with in the *Rose* Indiaman to Bengall. He was one of the oldest capt[ains] belonging to India Company before he was governor. They fell in with a gale coming round the Cape in company with one frigate [*Java*], and this brig being with them, the *Blenam* hove out a signal of distress [1 February 1807] in the highth of the gale. The brig [*Harrier*] laying two to leeward could do nothing, but the frigate which was to windward bore up and came down and run so close that it was supposed by the ad'l sun [admiral's son] and crew that the *Blenom* in foundering took the frigate with them, as well as they could see from the brig. For that reason he had been runing along the coast in hopes some might of saved themselves in boats, but had no intillegence.[6]

The fleet sailed for England. We run well to the westward to make Ierland, for fear of falling in with the French fleet. Making Cape Clear, it then wanting a few day of Chrismas, the most of our hand being sick with the white flux and 45 men died out of 96 during the voige, we got pilots on b[oar]d and put into Crook Haven, a rockey mountanious place but an excelent harbour. We could get a goose for a shilling and a hamper of potatoes for a shilling sterling. The officers smugled in great quantities of tea while laying there.[7]

(One of our officers being on shore, he fell in with two fine looking girls in a geen [genteel] looking house and agree with one to remain all night. While sitting engoying himself, thought he was snug as a bug in a rug, in came two men and told him if he was not off very quick they would skin his hid[e] for him. He soon started on board and lost his mony and Dulsana [Dulcinea] both.)

The day after Chrismas we put to see for London, but no sooner than we ware out, a gale came on from the N.W. We had to furl all our sails and lay two. It came on so suddent that the custom house officers had to remain on board, but the gale continuing, the next day we found our selves on the Welch [Welsh] coast. We made sail and beat to windward. The second day we found we ware embayed in Milford Bay, but no man on b[oar]d had ever been in there. We could not of made more than one tack more without being on the roks and no hopes of being saved, but as God would have it we discovered a small ship coming down before the wind. She being a coatser

Milford, Wales

[coaster], new the harbour. We made sig[na]l of distress and she run as close as she dare. We atempted to speak each other but could not, it blew so hard. The capt[ain] saw what we wanted, rought on his quarter board "follow me." We up hellom and squared our yards after him. He [k]nowing the chanel well, kept in the deepest water. A short distance before we came to the point, we touched, but went over and followed him round the point and then we ware safe, though abreast of the town. We let go our anchor. The cable parted. Let go another. It parted. Blowing amost tremendious by this time, a pilot got on board. We ware going to let go another anchor. The pilot told the capt[ain] not to mind it, "When in the mud, every nail's an anchor. No rocks but mud." We ware then safe without an anchor.

The press gang came on board to press us, but finding all hands sick and the chief of us in our hammocks, the pilot ordered the yards and topgallant masts to be struck. The press master had to order his gang to go aloft and strike them, and it was a bitter cold day. They cursed and swore at a bitter rate but they ware compel'd to do it. The capt[ain] that brought us in had all his hands pressed by the revenew cutter.

We lay hear a considerable time [31 December 1807–16 February

1808], all hands being sick. Letters was sent to London to inform the India House of our sittuation. The *Neptune* being the richest ship in the fleet and being the largest in tonage, she had 24 thousand chest of tea on b[oar]d, besides silks and sattins. There was a sloop of war sent round to convoy us to the Downs. Our ship being the largest ship that ever was in Milford Haven, it was rumord through the country. We had visiters of the first rank daily and hoisting the ladies in and out in chairs though it was winter, they thought it was the greatest sight they had ever seen. The young squires would give us any price for our pictures and snuff boxes that we would ask, that we brought from China, they being generally of the smutty kind.

The capt[ain] had to ship men to help to bring the ship round to London, which cost 10 guineas each man, which was one third as much as we, the full seaman, received in all our hardships for 22 months, for 10 days work. We got round to the Downs under convoy of the sloop of war and then went up to Long Reach and mored the ship [22 February 1808].

I got into a boat with a number more for London with our baggage, but I soon found my landlord was a crimp, but I could not leave him till we receiv'd our wages. In a few days after we rec[eive]d our money, but I found the landlord at the White Swan near the India House had rec[eive]d part of my wages and my cumrods. We amediately went to his house. I asked him how he dare draw part of our wages. He said we had impower'd him. We denied it. He produced the will to us. "Now, Sr., we can both prove that neither of us new anything of your defraud, and if you do not give us what you have drawn for each of us, we will amediately bring it before a Court of Justice." He delivered the money amediately, but he said if we had died he might as well have it as any other person.

To make short, in about ten days we ship'd in the *Helender* [*Highlander*] of Grinnock [Greenock] in Schotland, bound for Meremashee [Miramichi, New Brunswick]. We joined hur at Longreach, receiv'd our advance, and sailed for Spithead and lay for a convoy. We came to an anchor. At Gilkicker, the convoy being ready, the frigate gave the signal, we up anchor and droped down to Lower Cows [Cowes] and came to an anchor. By the time the fleet was all under way it was dark and the wind from the eastward. They coming before the wind, a large merchant ship run a cross our bows and caried away our bowsprit. They went on with the convoy for Newfoundland, but we had to return to Gilkicker and come to an anchor [6 May 1808].[8] The capt. [Cooper] being sick, the mate went to the dock yard for a spar with four men and a boy, and four men beside myself rem[aine]d on board. We hove up two spare topmasts by the windless and riged the shears [sheers] and got the remainder of the bowsprit out by the time the boat returned. We towed the spar on shore and the carpenter went to work. In a few days we had it fitted, riged, and put to see without a convoy. We did not fall in with the convoy on the passage.

The ships crew all lived in the steerage next to the cabin, and the capt[ain] being unwell, we asked him if it would disturb him if we had a little mirth in the evening. Being fine weather and a pleasent fair wind, the capt[ain] agreed that we might enjoy our selves, and no disturbance to him. Of course we had a pleasent evening with songs and grog, etc., till some laid on the chest and fell a sleep, but two of them, one a Dean [Dane], the other a German, went on deck. They ware both the stoutest and strongest men in the ship, and they walked the deck, one on each side, and begin to curse and swear that they could kill the whole ships company. The capt[ain] was alarmed and the chief mate likewise. They both came to the top of the companion and lisned to them. They still going on, the capt[ain] told the mate to load his pistols.

By this time I wakoned, and hearing such a noise on deck, I run up the stearage lather and stood in the scuttle, the hatch being laid over, and hollow'd out, "What is the matter?" The Dean, coming aft at the same time, made me answer, "Dot, dam you, I will let you [k]now," and up with his fist and nock'd me backwards, but the scuttle prevented me from falling. I recover'd myself and jumped on the quarter deck where he was standing and took him under the jaw and laid him sprawling and cried out not to kill him. By this time the other came and swore he would let me know. He came past the companion to make a blow, and I ketched him under the jaw and he fell senceless. He laid there.

The capt[ain] said, "You have kild him."

"I hope not, Sir," said I, and got on my nees to bring him two. In the meantime the Dean had got up and came behind me and hit me in the back of the neck. I got up. "Now, you raskal," said I, "there is no quarters," and I nocked him down and then jump'd upon him and he crying out for quarters, but I gave him what he deserved. By this time the other came to himself but said nothing. The capt[ain] and mate took me in the cabin and we had some grog, but ever after that they both respect'd me, or at least pretended so.

The first land we made was Cape Britton [Cape Breton], and standing so close in with the land, and falling nearly calm, the current had nearly set us on the rocks, but a breeze springing up, we stood to the nothord and arived at the bar and got a pilot on board and got in safe. The capt[ain] had lost one ship there some time before. We run up to the island, came to an anchor, and discharged what cargo we had on board and droped halfway down to the bar, where the timber lay in rafts that we was to take in.

Being at work one four noon, a brig apeared off and sent hur boat in, which [we] supposed to be a man of war and was coming to press. We took to the boat and went on shore, but it proved otherwise. They came with a letter to the capt[ain] that when ready for see we ware to go to Grinnock [Greenock] where she belonged to.

We sailed, and getting over the bar, we got a ground near the same place the other ship was lost before mentioned. The pilot ordered a kedge to be caried out, which we did after the anchor was let go, and by a strong current fouled the harser and cable. The chief mate and myself went over the bows, striveng to clear them, as we could not get any others to venture, the see flying over the bows to a great highth so that we ware under water the chief of the time. At lenghth the chief mate gave it up, being very cold. I finding it could be cleared by continuing and endeavouring, I hung on till I did clear it, but could not get any other man that would come to my assistance. We then hove the hawser well taught and lifted the anchor to the bows and hove upon the harser. By the swell of the see, we hove hur off. I then shifting myself, and the capt[ain] took me into the cabin to warm myself and gave me a good dose of raw liquor to prevent me from ketching cold, but it avail'd not. The next day I was very ill and remain'd so for a considerable time. We had fine weather, excepting one gale, but being a fair wind from the N.W., we receiv'd no damage and arived safe in Grinnock.

The very next morning the capt[ain] rec[eive]d orders from Sq'r Steward, which was owner of the vessel, to proceed to Liverpool. The capt[ain] came on board and ordered the boats to be hoisted in, which was done. While we ware below at breekfast, the chief mate and the carpentor had a falling out, and the mate beat the carpenter. He came down to the ships crew, crying, and told them if they went to Liverpool they would all be pressed and their voige was out according to the Articles, which we new ourselves. There was another American beside myself on b[oar]d by the name of Waterman, belonging to Rode Island. The press gang had been on b[oar]d and press'd Waterman, but having a protection, they brought him back. Nevertheless, our voige being out, we had no right to go to Liverpool without extra pay, therefore we would not lift an anchor.

The capt[ain] asked us if we would hoist the small boat out to go on shore and inform the owner [Roger Stewart, Esq.]. Imediately we got the boat and 4 hands went on shore with the capt[ain]. He inform'd the Squire. He amediately sent his son on board to read the Articles to us. When arived on b[oar]d we ware all call'd aft. The crew wished me to be spokesman, as they ware of different languages and not able to speak for themselves. I went foremast. I went a breast the Squiers son and laid my arm over the netting of the quarter deck, and all standing round, he begin reading the Articles. He pronounced that we shiped from London to Meremesha and from thence els where.

"Stop, Sir," said I, "show that to me," but he would not, as I had read the Articles and new it was to any part of Europe and we was then in Europe. He told the capt[ain] it was of no youse to read the Articles to me. Therefore he went on shore and inform'd his father. Squire Steward came on board in a six oard boat and six stout men and ordered us all aft. I, of course, was foremast, and laying my elbow on the netting, with my hand to my head, the Squire turned round to the capt[ain] and said, "Which is this dam'd rebelious raskel?" The capt[ain] pointed to me. The Squire, having a large silver mounted kain in his hand, said to me, "Ile nock you down."

"I wish I could ketch you at it," I replied.

Then, said he, "I will put you on b[oar]d the tender," he replyed.

I answered, "You may do as you please, and if you dont I will make you," which made all hands burst out a laughing.

He was very angry. "Go in the boat."

"Yes, Sir," I replyed, "when I get my papers." I went forward and got what I wanted. By the time I came up they ware all in the boat. I went down in the boat and went forward to the bows. As we ware pulling for the tender, which was not more than a quarter of a mile, the capt[ain] was informing the Squire that if it had not been for me and the matc, the ship would of been lost on the reef at Meremeshee and he thought it would be a pitty to put me on b[oar]d the tender, which cooled the Old Squire. He then asked me if I would go to Liverpool if he took me back again.

I answered, "No, Sir, I will see you dam'd first." I mus allow it was a vulger exprission to a man of his dignity, but the treatment I receiv'd from him hurt my feelings as much as he was hurt by my answer, which set him in a rage.

We came along side the tender. He enquired for the capt[ain]. The lewtenant inform'd him that he was on shore. "I have a man for you," said Sq'r Steward, and as soon as the boat tutched the gangway, I was up the side. The Squire said he would see the capt[ain] on shore. As soon as the boat was gone, the leutenant call'd me aft and asked me how the Mare [Mayor] and me came to fall out that he should take the trouble to bring me there himself. I inform'd him the whole sircumstance. He asked me weather I had any protection. I inform'd him I had and showed him my protection. He laughed and told me I need not be under any concern in respect of the Squier putting me there. I inform'd him I was sencible of that, and though I was the saving of his ship and cargo, which could be proved by the capt[ain]. He put me on b[oar]d the tender.

This hapened to be on Regulating Day. The leutenant did not confine me below as the prest men ware, which I beleive ware about 40 men. The boatswain piped to dinner and gave me my rashings [rations] in a mess below amongst the prest men. I went below and had my dinner, but when I come to look up, the lather was hall'd up. I asked the sentry to speak to the comanding officer to [k]now weather I was not purmitted to come on deck. He ordered me on deck, and shortly after the capt[ain] and regulating officers came on board, and being prepared in the cabin, I was the first man that was call'd for. I came down in the cabin. The capt[ain] asked me why

Sq'r Steward put me on b[oar]d the tender. I inform'd him of the whole afair. He then asked me if I had a protection. I showed it and they all overhall'd it. He told me they could not keep me and I was at my liberty. Then I inform'd the capt[ain] that I had been a good many years on board of men of war and showed him some of Capt[ain] Bonds surtificates when I was prize master on board the *Netley* Schooner. He was surprised and told me that he was a very particular aquaintance of his and told me Capt[ain] Bond was then in Exmouth, and if I required a passage free to Plymouth, I should have it and found I thank'd him and went on deck.

Remain'd there till all the prest men ware overhall'd, but not one got clear exept myself. They came on deck and was going on shore, when I steped up to the capt[ain] and asked him weather I was to remain on b[oar]d. He said he had forgot and gave the leuten[an]t orders as soon as the boat return'd to let me have the boat to go on board to get my clothes and then to land me where I pleased. When the boat return'd I went on board, but the rest of the crew was all sent on shore, and they had taken my clothes with them.

I never had landed in Grinnock. I landed at the old fort and walk'd up into the street and enquired of an elderly woman if she could inform me where the sailers landed from the *Hilander*. She said no but if I would wait till hur son came in, he new all the boarding houses in town and he would show me. I having a little money, I sent out for a little refreshment for myself and the old woman till hur sun arived. He took me to the main street where he had intelligence and was directed to the Widow Browns, who lived in the second storie. When I came in, Waterman, before mentioned, was coming out with a hanckerchief full of provisions to take on board of the tender, but when they saw me they ware all rejoiced. Siting round the table, I sit down with them. The ship sailed the next morning for Liverpool, but the Squire had to pay five guinias each man for the trip.[9]

In a few days we all went to the Squiers office to know weather he would pay us for our voige. He drove us away and swore the nex time we came he would shoot us. I then made application to Mr. More who was Kings atorney. He did not wish to have anything to say to it, as he said no one in Grinnock wished to have anything to say to the Old Squire.

I then went to Mr. Pots, and he told me to right down the purticulars of our voige and what we could swear to and he would give us a letter to Glasco, a friend of his, who would soon settle the business for us. Accordingly I rought it and gave it to Mr. Pots. He asked who rought it. Waterman told him I had rought it. He said that was sufficient without a loyer if we could swear to it, but I told him we required a loyer to plead for us. He then gave us a letter, and Waterman went to Glassco and delivered the letter. After reading the paper he gave him half a guinea and told him to go and refresh himself and in half an hour he would have a letter for him, which he received a cording to the time appointed, but the Squire would not answer it. He sent the second, and [the Squire] would not answer it. He sent the third, and to apear at Court on the Monday following in Glassco, but on Saturday he sent for us all to his office and paid them one by one, the remainder being out side, and sending them in, and remaining till the last, he enquired for me and desired I would come in. Accordingly I came in.

"Well, Mr. American, how do you do?" I told him as well as my friends would purmit me. He said he was sorry that we should fall out, as the capt[ain] had inform'd him that I was the principel hand that saved his vessel. I then informed him the particulars of the disturbance which sprung from the carpenter that fell out with mate and "was the fore runer of the crew not going in your vessel, and when you, Sir, enquired of the ships crew all round singly who would go, the carpenter that was the instregation of it was the man that said he would go, and I being spokesman was blamed for the whole."

Greenock Street Scene

The Squier was much pleased when he understood the rights of the whole truth and told me at anytime he would give me a recommendation if I required it and would right to the capt[ain] to discharge the carpenter from his vessel, and Sq'r Steward and me parted in a friendly manner. To make short, I got to be tolerable well aquainted in Grinnock.

CHAPTER 12

The Atlantic Trade

INTRODUCTION

*I*N THE period 1808 to 1810, Nagle recounts what must have been normal routine for a merchant sailor engaged in the Atlantic trade in the age of sail. Shipping out of Greenock and Liverpool, one voyage took him to Honduras for logwood, another to British Guiana, a third to Amelia Island in what was then Spanish Florida, a center for illicit trade of Georgia cotton at the time of the Jeffersonian embargo and the War of 1812. He then shipped aboard the *Triton* from Liverpool to New York, where he jumped ship and signed on an American vessel to Tenerife that carried staves on the outward passage and wine on the return. On this trip he again was severely chilled and frost-bitten, coming into New York in a winter storm.

The object in all such voyages, and there were literally hundreds of ships like the *Brilliant,* the *Caledonia,* and the *Triton,* was to make a profit on both ends of the trip, usually taking manufactured goods of some sort to America and bringing raw products back to Britain. Thanks to Lloyd's of London, which published an annual survey of ships afloat, it is possible to know the size, the construction, and the names of captains and owners of most of them. Lloyd's also maintained a tracking system, published regularly for company officials and the Admiralty, to know where ships had last been sighted. Both merchant and naval captains would forward information on what vessels they had sighted and where, and those reports, in combination with newspaper notices of ships in and out of port, provide a surprisingly fully documented record of the appearance and activity of what were essentially floating boxcars. Most of these oceangoing ships had a capacity of 300 or 400 tons and crews of a dozen or two dozen men. They were all armed. In spite of the hazards of the sea and the vulnerable nature of wooden hulls in sea water, the average merchant vessel in this period was about ten years old, and some, usually Dutch-built vessels, were thirty or more years in service. Nagle seems to have preferred ships of very recent construction.

Sources such as Lloyd's and existing pictorial records tell us much about the ships themselves, but Nagle gives us a feel for what life was like for the typical sailor. Since crews were small, often barely adequate to sail the ship, and voyages were of several months' duration, a sailor got to know his shipmates intimately and had to live with a strange mixture of nationalities and personality quirks. It was a rough life, but for most of these men it was the only type of employment they had ever known.

I THEN ship'd as gunner on board the *Brilliant* of 20 guns, a Letter of Mark, Capt. Morris [Morrison] com'd, bound for Jameca and from thence to the Bay of Hundoras for mahoganey and logwood.[1] The sailors was surprised when they heard that I had ship'd with Capt[ain] Morison, his caracter being such a tarter, that it was difficult for him to complete his ships crew, though he had 14 prentices of his own and the merchants. Our crew was about 60 in number. The ship drop'd down to the bar to get the seamen on board.

The evening before, the capt[ain] came to my boarding house and enquired weather I was not going on board. I inform'd him I was in the morning. He made answer, "Mind you do, or els I shall have to trouble you, and you will find the launch at the watering place," and we parted that night. I had got my chest and bedding all on board and had nothing to do but go on board as soon as I pleased. Therefore I went on board in the launch the nex morning. I got the guns properly secured and filled as many catriges as the capt[ain] thought sufficient, and the ship being fitted for sec, we sailed down the River Clide, passed the hilands, and run down the west end of Ierland, with a fine and pleasent breese.

Being out about 10 day, a sail hove in sight. She was to windward of us. Sum times she would edge away for us, and then luff up again, which made us suspicious of hur. We held our wind till we got abrest of hur. The capt[ain] [k]nowing I was an old man of warsman call'd me and asked my advice.

"Sir," said I, "we sail better than she does, therefore we will stand on till we find by tacking that we can get into hur wake and then tack again. We then can fetch to windward, and if we find she is a privateer, we have hur under our command by luffing up and giving hur our lee broad side, and then keeping away under hur lee quarter, if she continues hur course and if she bears up we can rake hur, and if she tacks we can then keep a stern of hur by manuvering our sails."

"Well done, Guner," the capt[ain] reply'd, but when in hur wake we gave hur a gun, she hoisted American colours and had but 14 guns on boa[r]d. But the reason they ware afraid to come down to us was they had a number of French passangers on board and they ware afraid of being taken out as they ware then at war. We board'd her and then made sail.

Nothing accured pirticularly till we made the island of Santa Mingo [Santo Domingo]. Runing down along shore, though a considerable distance out, came three small schooner. They stood for us, and we standing our course till they got nearly within gun shot, we ware prepared for them and by the glasses we could see they ware full of men. They then hove two. Purceiving our force, they ware doubtful. We then lufed up for them. They made sail for the shore as fast as they could, but we new we could not come up with them before they would reach the shore. We bore up and arived in Kingston, Jamaca.

We had a number of men stowed away from the press. No sooner than we came to an anchor, but the flagship's boats was on board. The second mate was stowed away in the magezene, and I having a protection was put on the books as second mate and guner, but they searching so strict, they found the second mate. Then the leutenant got foul of me, but my protection being good, he could do nothing with me, as he said Adm[ira]l Cockron

[Cochrane] would not keep an American if he had a protection. We had then 16 men hid that they did not find.

We run up to Jamaca along side the wharf and got a derick up for discharging what we had in of different kinds, etc. During the time we lay here, several of our men runaway and some was ketch'd and remain'd in prison till we sail'd and then taken out. We sail'd for the Bay of Hendorus under the convoy off a small man a war brig for that station. When we got to see the sloop of war boarded us and took three men, Germans, out and kept them several days and told them if they would inform they would let them go. One was the boatswain, one a seaman, and the other a cook. To get clear they said there was several on board English men beside the guner that passed for American but they beleived he was an Englisman. They sent them on board but did not let on at this time.

We having pleasent w[eathe]r, we passed Swan Island and entered the Triangles and came to an anchor where the rest of the shiping laid, at the Belees [Belize]. The reef is so shallow at times that a lanch [launch] load'd with water will ground even in the Chanal. When the ship was mored we cleared away to take in mahogany and logwood. We had to tow off the blocks with iron dogs, 16 or 17 in a line, with two boats and kedges. While halling up to one kedge, the other run out the other kedge ahead till we reached the ship. I suppose the distance was nearly two miles. In that manner they have to bring the blocks along side, then sling them one by one with a chain and heave them in by the capstain.

One dark night, all hands at work, I had charge of the deck, hoisting in the blocks from along side, and the capt[ain] and chief mate in the hold giving directions in placing and stowing the blocke acording to the sise and mea[s]urment which must be done and then the vacancies fill'd up with logwood. All of a sudent a long side came two men of wars boats and board'd us, all armed beside a brass 4 pounder in the largest boat. The pilot of the manawar was dressed in the capt[ain's] uniforms and the master in his own.

They ordered the capt[ain] to bring his ships books up and enquired for the guner. Imediately I answered.

"Then go in the boat, Sir."

"I am protected, Sir."

"Go in the boat, Sir," says the pilot, acting as capt[ain] of the sloop of war. I, of course, was compeled to go. I went down. The coxswain was in the stern sheets. It being very dark, I sliped up again and the capt[ain] sitting on the companion, I asked for the key of the arms chest. The rest of the men being ready for me, he told me the mate had it. The raskal of a pilot being close behind me heard what I had said to the capt[ain]: "Give me the key, we will make every raskel jump overboard."

The pilot hollowed out, "Stand to your arms," and seized me. "How dare you come out of the boat."

I repli'd, "The capt[ain] ordered me a glass of grog, and I hope you will let me have it."

"Yes," said Capt[ain] Morison, "let him have his grog." The steward brought it and I drink'd it.

"Now, go in the boat, you cant get the key of the arm chest to night. You are a brave fellow for a man of war." However, they found three more besides me. This brig run into the Triangles before mentioned, a groop of small islands about 6 or 7 miles from where we lay at the Belees, and was clearing ship and getting every thing on shore to smoke hur. When we got on board it was towards morning. I hove myself on one of the guns and there I laid till the hands was turned up and they set us to work in washing the decks till breckfast. They put me in the boatswains mates mess. In less than six hours I was informed that the boatswain of our ship informed upon me to get clear himself. However we got everything out of the brig and smoked hur. I was put into the guners crew.

After getting hur well cleaned, we got all into hur again, guns, stores, and provisions, and bent sails when ready for see, which was about thre weeks. We got under way with a fine stif breeze, going down to the Beleeze where the shiping lay, but she was so crank with all sail set that if we had not taken in sail as quick as possible, one minute more she would of been past hur bearinge and upset, but taking in sail so quick, she rightened again, got down, and came to an anchor.

It was not long before Capt[ain] Morison came on board and plead hard for me and a nephew of his. The capt[ain] was loth to let me go, but being inform'd the second mate was pressed, and not having a guner, he was entierly in distress, beside they new when there four month station was out and returned to Jamaca that my protection would clear me. Therefore he let me and his nefew return on b[oar]d again.

We continuing to take in mahogany till we ware loaded, but every day I had to go up the river about eight miles in the lanch [launch] for fresh water, (and being there so often, I got aquainted with a man and his wife, Germons, and understanding that I was born in Reading, Pensylvania, enquired if I new a man by the name of Anthony Fricker. I told them I went to school with him, and new all the family, and the last time that I saw him was in Philadelphia on board the *Sarratoga* State ship. Anthony and myself and several more young men belonging to Reading was going out in hur, but after being on b[oar]d of hur a considerable time, I left them and went out in the *Fair American*. They then told me the *Saratoga* was cast away in the Bay of Hundorus, and Anthony got on shore and opposite to where they then lived was a rigment of Brittish soldiers and Anthony Fricker listed with the cornel of the rigment and the cornel made him his clark, and he was very much liked in the whole rigment, but being over at this very place where the man and wife was in forming me, opposite to where the barroks and the cornels house was, he getting intokecated, he mad[e] an attempt to swim acroos, though he was purswaded not to attempt it, being so many allegaters, but he would not lissen to them and away he went. By the time he was half way over a large allegater laid holt of him, and they saw no more of him except the blod of him. I saw his parents since but I dare not mention it, but they being dead, I make a remand of a mans ordenation).

While laying here we lived well, fresh beef one day and turkle the nex. Amongst those islands fish and turkle is plentiful. The Brittish have a rigment of Blacks there, and all very large stout men, besides the white soldiers in the fort. We had three pasengers on b[oar]d, a man and his wife and one more. When we ware ready for see, we sailed, keeping to the N.W. to get into the gulf.

One night, being a fine pleasent breeze, I having the captn's watch, a little before 12 o'clock I thought I saw land ahead. I run forward and found us close aboard the rocke. I cried out, "Helloms a lee, down with the hellom, jump up my boys or we are on shore." The ship was hove in stays in a moment. I run down to the capt[ain]. The men coming up, we got the yards brased about and under snug sail. Standing off, the capt[ain] said he did not expect to be within 50 miles of the shore at that time, but falling in with a strong current, draged us in shore unexpected, but by a good look out we escaped. We had seventy five large turkel on board, but none lived to reach Scotland, the weather being two cold. Therefore we lived well on the passage.

This lady and the capt[ain] was very formilliar. Having a heavy squall coming on in the night, and I having the watch, I run down to the capt[ain], laying on his couch. When shaking him he took me for another and was draging me along side of him til I made him sensible of the squall and then run on deck and he followed me, taking in sail, and had snug sail set. He went below. The next day I was repairing some of the small sails on the quar[ter] deck. She came to me and asked me to take a glass of grog. I thank'd hur and she told the capt[ain], "The guner is always at work, you should allow him extra grog." The capt[ain] told hur he did whenever I wanted it. Though the capt[ain] bore the name of a tarter, I never wished to sail with a better capt[ain].

We had a good voige homward bound. Coming off the Western Islands we saw a large frigate to leeward of us and crowded all sail after us. She sail'd very fast. When in gun shot we gave hur several shot but with out effect. She never fired till we hove two. She then boarded us and overhall'd all our men but took none. She was bound to the nothord to meet the Greenland ships. We stood our course again. During our homeward bound passag the boatswain got many hard rubs for his tretchary both from the capt[ain] and myself and men and he was glad when we arived in Grinnock. The capt[ain] offered my wages to go on while fitting out in Grinnock, which I agreed to, but the *Calledonia* being a larger and finer ship, I took a notion to go in hur, as she wanted a guner and Capt[ain] Morison recommended me to Capt[ain] Tompson. She was a ship pierce'd for 22 guns, 12 and 18 pounders.[2]

Before she went over the bar I got my chest and bedding on b[oar]d. There was orders for every man to be on b[oar]d next morning. The longboat being on shore for the last load of water, I was crusing about and the capt[ain] and owner was looking for me. Coming down from the square they se me go into Mrs. Browns. They give sheet after me, and I new it. I sliped into a small cabin in the passage that no person could purceive that there was any dore unless they new of it. They came in and seeing no one, they ware surprised and searched every room and place that they could suppose I was stowed. I could hear all they said. They were certain they see me go in and was surprised that I vanished out of their sight in the course of a minute, as they ware close upon me, but I lay on a small bed till they went out.

I did not mean to stay on shore longer than when the boat was ready. I came out and see them going up street towards the boat. I followed and got close behind them and heard the owner say to the capt[ain], "It is surprising where the guner can be."

"Not a tall, Sir," said I, "for I am here."

They turned round and looked at me, "Where was you?"

"Along with Mrs. Brown." They burst out a laughing. They ware pleased to find that I came of my own accord.

The boat by this time was ready and I went on b[oar]d. When on b[oar]d, Mr. Johnston, third mate, had been in the *Brilliant* afore the mast, pretended great friendship for me, and his wife and some more wimen ware in the cabin. I mus come down and have a glass of grog. I went down and took a glass and came up again. The chief mate, a verry stout man, Mr. Cameron by name, asked me what business I had in the cabin. I told him I would not of been there if I had not been asked. He asked me who it was. Inform'd him Mr. Jonson.

"Mr. Jonson has no business to ask any body, nor you have no business there unless you are going to the magezeene." I told him I had been in a better cabin than that ever was.

He flew into a great passion and ordered me off the quarter deck. I steped off and told him to come and order me from there. "Verry well, Mr. Guner, I shall mark you on the voige."

"I disregard your marks," and went below.

The next day we sail'd and put to see. I hapened to be in Mr. Cammerens watch. One fine moon light night the prentices had to look out and one of them was sitting on the gangway. The mate call'd me, "Guner, you walk the waste [waist] and see that this fellow dont fall asleep, and if he does, I will swet you for it."

"Verry well, I will do my duty, but take kare." He walked aft and I forward two or three times. I look'd at him every time I came aft, but he being very sleepy, the mate came and found him in a doze while I was coming aft.

He call'd me, "Now, you see this fellows asleep? You [k]now what I said."

"I do, Sir, and I [k]now the old grudge, but I now swear to you if ever you lift a hand to me, we will both go overboard together. That is one word for all. Are you that man? You may try as soon as you pleas." He walked aft and said no more, and I walked forward. From that time we never had any words.

About the middle of our voige, being two ships in company from Grinnock, but the other ships name I do not recollect, but she was nearly of the same weight of mettal as we ware, it was blowing a strong breeze from the N.W., and we having a fair wind, we run down on a Spanich three decker with hur topsails on the cap. Reefing topsails, we both run under hur stern and hailed hur. They answered us but we could not make out any more than they ware from South America, but they ware in the greatest confusion

The Mouth of Demerara River at Georgetown, Guyana

I ever heard on board of a three decker. It being dark and our ships looming large we supposed was the ocasion, but the English not being at war with the Spaniards at that time, we up hellom before the wind and ware soon out of sight. Two days after we espied two large sail to leeward, making all the sail they could crowd after us, but they ware two far to leeward to come up with us and that night wee lost sight of them.

At length we made the flats of Demerara, and getting a pilot on b[oar]d, we got in safe, though the other ship got a ground and had to get boats out and lighten hur before they got hur off. It is a shoal, muddy flat as far as you can see from the land. It formerly belong'd to the Dutch, but the English took it. The produce is rum, sugar, coffee, cotton, and indigo. When inside of the fort it is a good harbour but very often sickley and a strong current in the river. We got our moring anchor down, which we brought with us.

We sent sixteen of our men on shore in the country for fear of the press, as a man of war brig was stationed there and a schooner that pressed all they could ketch. We lay at our morings abreast the merchants warf and store that

Liverpool

the ship was consign'd to. The men of warsmen came on board to press but found none that was pressable. In landing the cargo, the master of the man a war brig was very desirous to have me. He asked me a number of questions and weather I was blind of my left eye. I told him no, it was only a cast. He told me I would make a good guner on b[oar]d their ship. I inform'd him that I was guner already of a supperiour ship to theirs. He apeared a little angry at my answer and told me he had a mind to take me on board, though he new I had a protection, but my capt[ain] coming up ended the dispute and told him it would be of no use, as I was well protected, and sent me on duty on b[oar]d the boat.

Here I understood I had an unkle living within eighteen miles at a place call'd Moco. He was a twin brother of my mother, who listed for a soldier when America was under the Crown of England, and when discharged, settel'd in Moco and owned two cotton farms. His name was Linkhorn

[Lincoln] Rogers. I was informed he died twelve month before I arived in Demerara, but he left two sons living on his farms. I rought them a letter, but before I receiv'd an answer we sailed for England. I saw a letter that he rought to my mother before he died. The reason I mention this in my book is, having a great number of relations through the States, that it might give them some satisfaction in hearing what became of him and where his family remains.[3]

While in Demerara it was very sickley. A great many English and American seamen died while I remain'd there. We took in rum, sugar, coffee, indigo, and cotton. While laying here the runaway Negroes would come down out of the mountains and plunder the farms. The Govenor employed the Indians to hunt them and gave them arms and amunition and was to pay them certain sum for every man.

Capt. Tompson treated his ships crew extremely well. Likewise the chief mate was always my friend. On the fourth of July I was very purticular in loading the guns myself, and the Royal Salute was fired by the capt[ain's] watch and never a gun hung fire. We rec[eive]d the praise of the whole town before all the men of war, or merchantmen.

I must here mention of Mr. Johnson, pretending to be so great a friend to me. Finding I was in favour with the capt[ain] and chief mate and I beleive with the whole crew, excepting Mr. Jonston, he endeavour'd to set the chief mate against me, the boatswain, and carpenter. Every evening at supper Mr. Johnson would have a good long storie to relate to the mate concerning us three. Mr. Cammeron sucked all in and lisened but he new it was false, as he had a beter oppertunity of [k]nowing what our conduct was on boa[r]d than he had, till one evening he had a fine story made up and relating it to the mate, "Now, Mr. Jonson, I will see about this," and desired the cabin boy to call us all down in the cabin.

We not [k]nowing what we ware call'd for, therefor came down and they sitting at supper, Mr. Cammeron spoke, "Guner, Mr. Johnson has this long time been laying complaints against you, the boatswain, and carpenter. Now I bring you all face to face. I new it was all false. Now, Mr. Johnson, speake for your self." He turned as pail as death and could not utter a word.

"Come, Mr. Johnston," said I, "let us hear some of these fine tales that you have been relating to Mr. Cammeron." No, not a word. Then the mate related sum of it. I turned to the boats[wai]n and carpent[e]r, "Did you hear or [k]now of any such thing as what has been related?" They said no, and asked Mr. Jonson how he could inven[t] such stuff, but not an answer could we get out of Johnson.

"Mr. Cameron," said I, "you ar the gentleman on board this vessel that has the best right to [k]now our proceedinge and behaviour in general and you command this vessel when the cap[tain's] on shore on his own duty. Therefore I think you have the best right to [k]now weather we do our duty or not." He laughed and said he new it and thougt it was best that we should [k]now the deception of Mr. Johnson. We thank'd the mate for his kindness and the next day Mr. Johnson wished to come and mess in the stearage with us, but we would not receive him.

We sailed for England and arived safe in Liverpool. The chief mate call'd me in the cabin and gave me five gallons of rum and sugar and coffee for a see stock the next voige. While laying in the river I put it all in my chest, and the custom house officers coming on board, they begin to search the seamins chest[s]. I new what I had for a see stock would be taken from me, beside a quantity of tobacco that I had in my chest. Being a great many chest, as they overhall'd, they numberered the chest with a piece of chalk. They overhall'd the next chest to mine and numbered it 23. I being aware of them, had got a piece of chalk from the mate, and as they ware securing the smugled afairs, I marked my chest 24. When they begin to enquire for my key, "You have overhall'd it," and seeing it numbered, went to the next chest and so on. I went on deck and told Mr. Cammeron. He was much pleased.

We then was purmitted to get our chest on shore, and the ship hall'd into the warf for discharging. The boatwain and myself told the capt[ain] we would work to discharge hur. He was glad of it. We turned to work with the lumpers, but they said we belong'd to the ship and they did not want us. They wanted there own gang. They ware afraid to smuggel while we ware there.[4] The mate inform'd the capt[ain]. The capt[ain] call'd us aft and told me if I would come on b[oar]d once a week and wipe the small arms down and take kare of them, he would pay me every Saturday the same as the lumpers had, which was a dollar a day. I thought it a great privilage. When this was settled, up steps a stout fellow, one of the lumpers, on the quarter deck while I was talking with the chief mate, and asked me if I new him. I told him I did not recollect him. He said he had a right to [k]now me and if he was able he would give me a good thrashing.

"Well," said I, "it is good that you [k]now you cant do it yourself," and the mate laughed. "Well," said I, "where did you know me?"

"In the *Gorgeon*," he replied. "You gave me a thrashing I never shall forget."

"What was it for?"

"I stole some clothes from my shipmates and was ketched and you flog'd me on the quarter deck."

"Yes, now I recollect you, and by the capt[ain's] orders."

"Yes," he replied.

"You mus be out of your sences to come and expose your self befor a hundred men. If you had said nothing about it, I should of not have [k]nown you. Now I recollect you well. At Jiberalter you was claim'd as a deserter and taken a shore, and when I came a shore with the boatswain and guner and carpenter I treat'd you. Then you went and got some more soldiers and came to the public house to flog me. I went out to you and gave you another thrashing. Is that trew?"

He said, "Yes." Every man round laughed and I thought he mus be lunetick. At the same time it was a fact.

After this I came on board and took care of the small arms for that week. As the capt[ain] allowed they ware in better order than they ware when they came from the armerar. But the boatwain purswaded me to leave hur, where I think I done rong, to go in a brig b[oun]d to the Amelia Islands. Being on board of a Sunday morning, one of the prentices came to me and asked why I did not come for my weeks wages, which was 27 shillings sterling. I told him, as I was leaving the vessel, I would not take the money.

We went on b[oar]d. The capt[ain's] name was Johnes. We sailed again and had a good passage to the Amelia Islands. The Amelia Island then belong'd to the Spaniard, but at this time was the Embargo in America, therefore the English came to this place for cotton, smugled over in schooner from the main [mainland], where the English ships lay'd and loaded.[5] Cape St. Mares [St. Marys] lays opposite, where a Merican gun boat was stationed and laid as a guard ship. It is very shoal water coming into this harbour. It is but a small village and one store, but we lay about a quarter of a mile hier up where a Spanierd had a store where we could get what we wanted. There was several ships waiting for cargoes besides ourselves. In about three weeks we receiv'd cotton as fast as we could stow it away and a stevedore with men to help us.

Our capt[ain] was represented as a tarter in Liverpool, but he behaved very well on the passage till we got into the harbour, and while waiting for the cargo we had been up the river to the watering place, and getting water on board, the mate struck one of the men, which created a quarrel, and that night the man took the small boat and got on shore. The capt[ain] begin to make a search but he could do nothing with him. There the man walked where he pleased in defiance of him. The capt[ain] now begin to show some of his pranks. The boatswan and myself, being warm weather, slung our hammocks on deck to sleep at night, and three of us sitting on the forecastle discoursing on different subject, the capt[ain] came up and ordered us below and said we intended to run away. We told him it was not our intention, but if we wanted we could run when we pleased. He flew into a rage, went down into his cabin and loaded his pistols, and brought them up on deck and told us the first man that said a word he would blow his brains out.

I said to the boatswain, ''Stick to it, he cannot kill but one at a time.'' Therefore the three of us ketched up a handspike from the windless and hove them over our heads. He retreated to the quarter deck, where the mate was standing. I went to the brake of the quarter deck and the rest followed me. I told him we ware well inform'd of his caracter in Liverpool, but that he had got some now that would not runaway from him but would see him out till we got to Liverpool with all his pistols. He then plead that he was afraid we ware going to leave him and then he would be in distress. I told him to treat us as he had done heretofore and there was no danger of loosing a man of us. Therefore it was all settled for that night.

Everything went on as yousual till we got the vessel loaded. When there was no cargo to take in we could go a fishing or fetch oisters, which was verry plentiful and the drum fish is plentiful in this harbour. They will smash an oister as quick as you would with a sledge hammer, though I do not like them upon one acount, they are generally full of worms in the tail part, which is the most fleshey.

At length, having our cargo in and water, etc., we got over the barr and came to an anchor about four in the after noon. I then went to the capt[ain].

"Sir, we want some see stores and we must have it." I spoke for the boatswain and myself. "Eiether let him or me go in the boat with you to get it and I am satisfied, and if not we will not lift an anchor."

"Will you be satisfied if I take the boatswain with me and get what you require? I will trust to the boatswain returning," the capt[ain] being more doubtful of loosing me than the boatswain, though neither of us had the leas[t] intention to leave the vessel, as we ware determined to see him to Liverpool if God spared us. Therefore the capt[ain] went on shore with the boats[wai]n, and about nine a'clock they came on board with all we required, and the capt[ain] seemed very much pleased.

During this time there was a small man of war, a schooner, came off the bar from Jamaco [Jamaica] and their boat came on board. Being an English vessel, the officers went into the cabin and of course the sailors always wishes to treat each other when coming on b[oar]d. As stranger, we gave them grog likewise, but before they went away they stole several articles of clothing that was on deck and the three pint pot that we mixed the grog in for them. In the morning we missed those articles and we informed the capt[ain]. We maned the boat and went on board and informed the commanding officers. Amediately the boats crew was searched and the property found. We received the property and the thief was punished, which is a just rule on b[oar]d a man of war or elswhere.

The nex morning we sailed for Liverpool. We run into the gulf that sets us to the nothord till we get to the Banks. Then we are very apt to ketch the N.W. breezes and made a pleasent passage to Liverpool.

When we came to the merchants counting house to be paid our wages, the merchant asked the boatswain and myself particularly how we liked the capt[ain]. We told him we liked the capt[ain] verry well, and Capt[ain] Johne was standing by.

"It is surprising," says the merchant, "this three voiges that he has been in my vessel, what did not runaway complained greatly against him."

I answered, "That might be, but where good seamen is, they will force him to be good and have there rights," which the capt[ain] confessed he would wish to have us all again, which they did except myself, who was desirous to come to America. I boarded at Mr. Roules[?], the Signe of the Royal Oak, abrest the Old Dock.

In about six weeks I shiped in a large ship call'd the *Triton*, belonging to Pool. Being two large to sale out of that port, she sail'd out of Liverpool. The capt[ain] was very consated [conceited] in his opinion and a North Contreman. We took in salt for ballas [ballast] and grates [crates] of crockery ware on top. We hall'd out of the Queens Dock and sailed for New York. Making the banks off New found Land, our chief mate died. He was a Merican. We had moderate weather, but thick and foggy, with drisling rain, as it is chiefly on the Banks. While on the Banks we could ketch as many codfish as we could use while fresh, having no salt excepting what was under the cargo.

We arived in New York and hall'd along side of Peck Slip and made fast.[6] I thought it now time to be off, as I was once more in my own country. In the night one of my shipmates and myself got our chests and bedding out and carreing them to a boarding house, Mr. McKinsey [Alexander McKenzie] in Cherry Street, this was on Saturday.[7] The next morning when they found we ware gone, the chief of them left hur the next night and we saw them the next day.

In a few days a capt[ain] came in while we ware sitting at breckfast and enquired if any of us would go to see, but we must go amediately as the ship was all ready to hall off and go to see amediately. There was about ten boarders, but none would go at so short a notice. The capt[ain] then offered thre dollars extra beside the advance if two of us would go. I asked my comrad if he would go. He said yes, if I would go.

As we had no money and being upon expence, we started. I left my cumrod to get our chest and bedding on board while I went with the capt[ain] to receive the advance. We baught what necessaries we wanted and went on b[oar]d. We made sail from the warf, and by the time we got down to Never Sink, I mised my beding, but it was too late, and I sent word back by the pilot to take kare of my bedding, but when I return'd I could get

New York

no account of my bedding, new mattrass, sheets, blankets, and quilt, but one day I observed his wife iering [ironing] some clothes on one of my blankets, but I thought it no use to make a squable then.

We sail'd and arived at Tenereef [Tenerife] loaded with staves, discharged, and took in a cargo of wine. At this time the plauge was in St. a Cruse, on the other side of the island, and the peaple of the island would not purmit them to come out of the town for fear of it spreading over the island.

Having our cargo in, we sail'd for New York. Ariving off of Never Sink, we lay two all night with our main sail blowed a way, and the weather was so severe that the most of us was frost bitten, it being my hellem at eight a'clock at night, and there I remained till day light in the morning. Being all stowed away below out of the cold, not even first, or second mate to be found, and the capt[ain] asleep in his cabin and I could not leave the helm, I was frost bitten both hands and feat. In the morning a pilot came on b[oar]d and when he found us in such distress he was sorry he did not run up to town for men, but as God would have it, there was a fine easterly wind sprung up and run us up to New York and made fast along side a warf. The capt[ain] himself went up and cut the mainsail away from the main yard. No one else was able. When made fast, the capt[ain] came forward and encouraged us. For my part, I was past eating anything. The capt[ain] sent on shore for sume nice provisions to nourish us, but I could not touch it.

Capt[ain] Dugan was very friendly to me for several reasons. On the passage our fore topmast stay was caried away about 7 or 8 feet from the bees, and bitter cold weather, having two mates on board and could not find a man to clap a shroud not on the stay and send it down except myself, beside other afairs such as grafting and flemish eyes, etc.[8]

Capt. Dugin was a fine young man and likewise a seaman. He met me on one of warfs taking a walk on day, and falling into discourse, there was two fine ships laying in the stream. "Now, you may understand that I am well aquainted with both capt[ains] of those two ships, b[oun]d to St. a Mingo, and my vessel is repairing, and if you wish to go, I will go to either of these ships that you will chuse and get you a berth suitable, as I know you are capeble of any station on b[oar]d a ship." I thank'd him, but informed him my hands or feet was not sufficiently cured to go to see at present, but they ware getting well fast, as I chanced to fall in with a capt[ain]s lady that was then a widow, about twenty eight years of age, and was aquainted with Botanist, and I was purty well assured she woul[d] cure me very shortly, and likewise paid great attention to do so, far preferable to any docter I could aply to. The capt[ain] smiled. We shook hands and parted. My doctress cured me in a short time after.

CHAPTER 13

South America

INTRODUCTION

REPERCUSSIONS of the European wars with France were felt around the world, dramatically in South America. Nagle, while serving on the *Blanche* and the *Netley* in the Mediterranean in the 1790s, had already played a minor role in the conflict between French-dominated Spain and British-backed Portugal. This national alignment of enemies persisted when the second Anglo-French war broke out in 1803. In 1807 the French gave King Dom João of Portugal an ultimatum: break diplomatic relations with Britain and close Portuguese ports to British trade or France would invade the country. When a French army crossed the border in November, the Portuguese royal family embarked for Brazil, convoyed by British naval vessels under the command of Admiral Sir Sydney Smith. The king would remain in Brazil until 1821.

The British capitalized on Dom João's removal to the New World. They were now free to land an army on Portuguese soil without the diplomatic niceties and frustrations of previous years, and the Peninsular War of 1808–14 would prove to be particularly hard fought. Oporto was briefly taken by the French, but Lisbon never fell, and the British, led brilliantly by the future duke of Wellington and less so by other commanders, succeeded in maintaining the integrity of Portugal.

Dom João landed on Brazilian soil at Bahia on 23 January 1808, and eight days later proclaimed the ports of the country open to international commerce. The British soon achieved a most-favored-nation status, and for both British and American ships, ports that had never previously been accessible to them were now potential sourccs of trade. For British manufacturers, who had lost access to European markets through Napoleon's Continental System, and for American ship-owners, whose government had attempted an unwieldy embargo and then nonimportation agreements against both France and England, Brazilian ports offered exciting possibilities as both markets and sources of new materials. Between 1808 and 1812, South America was portrayed in the mercantile world as the new Eldorado, and shippers rushed to these new destinations.

Nagle had spent several weeks in Rio de Janeiro with the First Fleet in 1788, and his experiences in Portugal ten years before would have made the manners and customs of the region less foreign to him than to the typical American. He shipped aboard a Baltimore sloop, the *Griffin*, from New York, calling first at Bahia, then Rio. The fast-sailing ship then returned to the United States, but Nagle, because of his recurring health problems, was left behind in the hospital set up by the British for its growing community of merchants and visiting seamen. It would prove to be the beginning of a ten-year stay in Brazil.

We know less about Jacob Nagle between 1811 and 1821 than in any other period of his life. His ailment may have been either arthritis or some type of circulatory problem, and it would recur until his death. When he got out of the hospital, he worked at odd jobs in Rio de Janeiro, as bartender and bookkeeper in a tavern, as captain of a private yacht, and as a longshoreman. He then shipped on board a British merchantman that had not only a mutinous crew but also a rotting hull.

It was an interesting time to be traveling in the area. Montevideo was under siege by the Portuguese when they passed by it, and the authorities in Buenos Aires, where they landed, were publicly hanging right-wing revolutionaries: both of these events were side effects of the arrival of the king of Portugal and Napoleon's successes in Spain. Nagle's ship then started out for a homeward voyage to Britain, but it began leaking dangerously and had to put into Rio de Janeiro again, where it was eventually sold.

Once again Nagle was stranded, and because war had broken out between the United States and Britain there was almost no international shipping in the harbor. American ships feared capture by British warships, and British vessels risked capture by American privateers.

Nagle and several other stranded American seamen took a coastal vessel to Puerto Seguro, a small Brazilian fishing port up the coast. The group took turns going out with local fishermen, and while Nagle was away, the majority of his shipmates took passage inland, bringing along Nagle's belongings and his protection papers with them.

At this point the story becomes a little murky. Nagle was penniless. The war had cut off the shipping that normally could have provided sailors with a route of escape, and Puerto Seguro was infrequently visited by foreign ships even during peacetime. Nagle says that he periodically visited the American consul in Bahia, Henry Hill, but without protection papers, Hill would do nothing for him. For the years 1812 to early 1816, the explanation is credible. After 1816, when peace between the United States and Britain was an established fact, there is no obvious reason why Nagle needed a protection or could not have gotten passage on an American ship at much-visited Bahia. One suspects that in fact he was relatively happy with his situation. Perhaps Nagle developed a relationship with a woman whose existence he discreetly omitted to mention in consideration of whatever audience he later envisioned for his journal.

In 1819 he left Puerto Seguro and began working for Henry Hill. Hill was a New England merchant, drafted as a consular official because he was on the scene, who would fire off letters as long as a hundred pages to John Quincy Adams, analyzing South American politics and character. He had established what he hoped would be a colony of United States citizens near Caravelas, and Nagle was employed for about two years to sail a small vessel back and forth between Hill's plantation and Bahia. "The wages being low," Nagle left and then shipped on coastal vessels until he made Rio early in 1821. He appealed to the American consul and was given permission to sail as a passenger on board the USS *Congress*, returning from what was the first visit of an American warship to China. Nagle landed in Norfolk.

Over the next three years he resumed his career as a merchant seaman, taking one voyage to Cork, another to Liverpool, and several shorter trips to the West Indies and along the coast. But his health was again causing him problems. Arriving in New York on the *Fanny* with a cargo of molasses from Antigua in May 1824, he had to be hospitalized for a month. He was now sixty-two, and one more voyage, from New York to Baltimore, apparently convinced him that his forty-five-year career at sea was over.

I REMAIN'D in New York about siks weeks, when I shiped on board of a Baltimore cliper call'd the *Griffin,* a schooner, Capt[ain] Weldon com[mander], laying in North River. After receiving our advance, we went on board, 1810, sail'd for the Brazeels [Brazil]. We had a pleasent passage a cross the Line. Our vessel being low built for a smugler, the dolphin and beneta would be in chase of the flying fish at night, and they rising out of the water by schools, would fly on board and would strike against the sails and drop down. Though we did not get the quarter of them, we pick'd up a nuf to serve all hands the next day. As our lee scupers was full of water, the most of them would get away out of the scupers.

About five or six day before we made the land we had a heavy gale, but it being from the N.W. and fair, as it could blow right before the wind, we done very well. Our supercargo being a bulky fat man and coming up the cabin ladder, at that moment a most tremendious see came rowling after us, and the vessel being so low that a great quantity of the spray roll'd over our stern, I being at the helem at this time, I got a complete ducking, but there was something else took my attention. This same sea nocked the supercargo backwards down into the cabin and filled the cabin half full of water and the supercargo pufing and blowing like a porpose up to his middel in water, crying out for help, which we could not do till the water run off into the hold, we ware all hands ready to die a laughing at him, for he being supercargo, took more upon himself than what belong'd to him. He was overbearing to both capt[ain] and men. For that reason he was not liked, and he relating his danger made us laugh the more, which provoked him the more.

One morning after washing the decks, I was washing my face and feet in one of the ships buckets that we used for that purpose. The supercargo came to me and asked me how I could wash my feet in them buckets, as he said purhaps the cook would be washing the salt meat in the same bucket. I said nothing, but a few nights after, it blowing a fresh breeze, he did not like to put his bum over the stern, but he got holt of a buckct under the lee of the mainmast, and easing himself, I came along by acsident and purcived it. I told him that was a good deal worse than washing my feet in the bucket, that the cook was liable to take that bucket as well as any other. He said nothing, but I informed the capt[ain] and mate of it, and it cool'd his pride a little.

A few days after, we passed an island about a leven degrees from the line, but the name I do not recollect. Shortly after we made St. Salvedore, or as some call it Biea [Bahia] among the Portegees.[1] We sold part of the cargo, the flower [flour] in particular, at 25 dollars, which was then call'd a low price.

In a few days we sail'd for Riogenera [Rio de Janeiro] in company with a nother American vessel. The two capt[ains] bet a wager who should arive first in Riodegenaro. We soon parted, on the passage having a good fresh breeze and a rough sea, and our vessel being so sharp that she would go right through and take in the see over the bows and send it chock aft, that we had to lower our sails down and nock out the ports to let the water out or she would of foundered twice on the passage. On our passage to Rio, at day light, in the morning, being under easy sail and a moderate breeze, we spied a large frigate within half gun shot of us. Presently she gave us a gun. The shot flew over and over us. The mate informed the capt[ain] we ware not at war with any nation at this time, but the capt[ain] was determined to see if they could ketch us. In a few minutes the frigate was in a cloud of sale and everything she could set, with a leading wind. We then made sail, and she gave us another gun, and shortly after another, but hur shot barely reach'd us and the next fell short. They then found it in vain to fire any more. We caried on and by four o'clock in the after noon we arived in Riodegenaro and came to an anchor at the back of the island at the uper end of the town where their dock yard and large ships lays.

The next day in the afternoon the frigate came in. She was from Lisbon with a number of noblemen and lords of the highest quality. They inform'd the King [Dom João] of o[u]r sailing so amazing fast. He came in his barge and vewed hur all round. He offered the supercargo thirteen thousand dollars, and he would not take it, but asked eighteen, when she was not worth more than six thousand, though she was copper bolted. In seven days after the American capt[ain] arived that we sail'd with from St. Salvedore and came to an anchor a long side of us. We went on board and wen the capt[ain] understood that we had arived a week before him he could scarcely beleive it. We sold all our cargo and got in a new main mast, the old one being sprung.

Before we ware fit for see, I was taken sick and applyed to the American

Marquesa d'Yrujo

Counsel and I was sent to the English Hospittle. It was a severe cold I had got in my loines. The medesine they gave me was of no effect. At length I informed the do[cto]r mate that I thought a drawing blister would cure me. He said I should have it, "But do you no," said he, "that you will be in great misery during the night?" I told him it was better to be in pain one night than to continue the way I was. He put it on, but I got no sleep till about four in the morning. When the blister broke then I was easy and had a good nap. The docter came to me in the morning and when he saw it, he said he never saw a finer blister in his life. He dressed it and in two or three day I was fit to go out of the hospittle, but the very day that I had the blisters on the vessel sailed. The capt[ain] sent the mate, Mr. White, and a boats crew to fetch me on board, as the capt[ain] was desirous to take me with them, but when the mate saw me, he thought it would be dangerous to take me with them as I then was. The capt[ain] then went to the Counsel and left my wages and sailed for New York.

I remained there twenty one days at a dollar pr. day, which was stoped out of my wages, when I rec[eive]d the remainder from the Counsel. I boarded at Mr. Greens and kept his books and barr. During the time I was there two ships arived from Botney Bay and had several men and four or five wimen that there time was out but was compel'd to be landed here as the two ships was going to China, where wimen is not purmitted to go. I remained a few month with Mr. Green and then engaged with the Spanish Embassdore [Marqués de Casa Yrujo] which was at that time and was maried to Govener Kains daughter [Sally, daughter of Thomas McKean], to

Marques d'Yrujo

take charge of a six oard pleasure boat for them and their son and daughter to go a pleasureing whenever they thought proper with myself and a body servent that atended him. I liked the Marquis and the Marquest and the son and daughter, but the servants, which ware Portegees, we could not agree, therefore I left them.[2]

Shortly after I went on board an English ship to work and take in a cargo. When being ready for see, Capt. Smith wished me to go the voige to Bonefiras [Buenos Aires] and from thence to England. I promised I would. Went on shore to a wine house whare I had left a large bag of clothes till I call for it. I received my bag that contain'd all I had excepting what I stood in, to the value of about 40 dollars, and was about going home when in comes a tall stout sailor and exclaimed, "O, what shal I do. Here I am without money or anything to eat, and coming on to rain as hard as it can pore, and so dark you can scarcely sea to walk the streets."

He made such a lamentable story that I took pitty on him. "Sit down," said I, "and you shall have as much bread and cheese as you can eat, and I will give you something to drink to wash it doun." I call'd for it till he was satisfied.

"God Almighty, bless you, my brave tar," said he. The rain lasting, I was for shourdering my bag, when he said he did not [k]now where he should sleep. I told him to come with me and I would give him a lodging for the night. He seemed so rejoiced that he insisted on carrying my bag, which I gave him leave, but no sooner than we ware out, a heavy dark cloud came overhead with heavy rain. We had not reached twenty yards before it was so dark that I could not see him. I call'd out to him but no answer. I travised backwards and forwards but he gave me the slip. I went to the sentry at the corner of the street and inform'd him I would pay him well if he stop'd my property, but the next day I could receive no account, as I thought they ware both tared with one brush.

I then went on board the *Levant*, Capt[ain] Smith, and inform'd him of my loss. In the morning I went on shore with the cap[tain]. He gave me money to by sum clothes and went on board with him. We had not got all our hands on board, but that night they all came on board and I feeling about in the dark, in the forecastle clap'd my hand on my bag. I felt it and new it, but found there was but little in it. I was in hopes the fellow was on board. In the morning I enquired whose bag that was. A little Bengally claim'd it. I asked where he had got it. He discribed the man verry plainly as he could talk English and said he gave him one dollar for the bag, and I had often been offered two dollars for the same bag. The capt[ain] told me I had a right to take the bag, but not having much cloathing, I purmitted him to keep it.

Not sailing the next day, I found the chief of our seamen were Portegees and Spaniards. The carpenter was a Dean [Dane], the mate American and myself, the capt[ain] and cabin boy English, and the part owner. The carpenter and myself being at supper in the forecastle, these Portegees and Spaniards call'd me over to their birth and told me I must not go in that ship and if I did they would heave me overboard as soon as we got to see. One of them told me that he new some of my shipmates and they told him I was no seamen, but I new that to be false, as my vessel had long since sailed for America and no other new me.

That evening I informed the capt[ain]. He concluded that they ware upon some bad design and wanted me out of the ship that the capt. might be compel'd to ship another Portegee or Spaniard, then they would all be of one gang. The capt[ain] told me not to be under any apprihencion, as the part owner was going in the vessel and they ware well provided with arms, and likewise he said he would soon see their great seamanship. I had told the carpenter at supper and he was a stouter built man than myself, but he always kept his broad ax handy and said if they did begin he would make a slaughter amongst them.

The next day we put to see with a pleasent breese, bound for Bonea Seyras [Buenos Aires]. We had not been out but a few days when the capt[ain] and owner call'd me aft and told me I was to do the duty of second mate for the futer. Cap[tain] Smith was not behind hand in purforming his promise with the Spaniards and Portegees. He soon cowed them all intierly. When we entered the bay leading to the River of Plate there is a small island constantly full of seals, and the Spaniards keep men there a sealing. Entering the river, the capt[ain] call'd out for a leadsman. None of them would answer. I was at the hellom. The mate and capt[ain] call'd again for a ledsman. "Where is the fine sailors that threatened to heave the American overboard for not being a sailor? Come aft here, you raskels." They came aft and one spoke and said there sailors [k]nowed nothing about the leadline. The chief mate had to go in the chains, and being two hours there, the capt[ain] said he supposed that he would have to releive him, as them raskels new nothing about it. The mate said he new who would releave him. [K]nowing I hailed from Philadelphia, ane he being from there himself, the capt[ain] not thinking of me at the wheel, looked round and asked me if I could heave the lead. I told him I could. "Come aft here, one of you, and take the hellem while this man does your duty, you scoundrels." I releived the mate in the chanes [chains].

In passing Mount a Vedo [Montevideo], the forts and Portegees was canonading very heavily, and we got up to the bar and the next morning we got a pilot on b[oar]d and got over the bar and came to an anchor [at Buenos Aires] where the rest of the shiping lay.[3] Being shoalwater, we could not lay

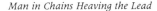
Man in Chains Heaving the Lead

Montevideo

nearer than a half a mile. An English frigate lay out side of the bar, but I do not recollect hur name. In a few days the most of these fellows run away. We discharged the cargo. The owner hired a storehouse and sold off wholesail and retail while the ship lay empty. We smoaked ship. The chiefmate took sick and went to sick quarters.

While laying here, blowing a heavy gale and striving to get into the lanch [launch] astern, one man was drownded by having a girdel of silver dollars round his body which was two heavy for him, though he was a good swimer, and the same Bengalle I before mentioned that had bought my clothes bag. At this time there was great disturbance on shore. The old Spaniards were combined and had laid a plot to murder the whole citty with there Negroes, but being discovered, they ware shooting them every day. The Leutenant Govenor [Martin de Alzaga] being the chief, he was first shot [5 July 1812] and then hung up to the gallos with about thirteen more that day, and every day, more or less, being a great number in the plot.[4]

We ware employ'd on riging our mainmast to get up new trusseltrees [trestletrees], cross trees, and new top. When we completed riging the mainmast, we begin to take in hides and tallow. In a few day after the capt[ain] sent another chief mate on board, but the first day he broached the pipe of liquor and got intoxecated and begin to fall out with the capt[ain] as soon as he came on board, and the next morning the capt[ain] sent him on shore. We then remained without a chief mate till we ware chiefly loaded. We then got a genteel young man as chief mate by the name Wherrey of London and sum men in lew of those that run away.

The money the owner received for his cargo had to be smugled, though it all came through the custom house. The silver was all in the form of sugar loves and taken on board the frigate that lay out side of the barr. This was about October 1811 [*sic,* July 1812].

Buenos Aires

The Spaniards of the country and the Old Spaniards was now at war against each other and by a carter that drove through the town to make a living it was discovered and by his information it was discovered and the list of all their names sign'd that was combined in the dreadful massacree that was to happen in a few nights after. The Old Spaniards was rich and possesed large farms in the country with for or five hundred Negroes on each farm, and by coming in for their masters, at the night apointed, they ware to murder all before them. Foreign merchants that lived in the citty to carry on trade, and the Spaniards that was born in the country, all that was not combined in the plot, was to suffer death, and the Negroes ware to have their freedom for the undertaking of this masecree. One of the priest was at the head of this plot, with the Leutenant Govenor. A few days after the Leu't Govenor was shot I saw his wife and three daughters in their own house, all dressed in mourning, and lovely young wimen they ware, but they could not help their fathers folly. They shot and then hung them up in the square till sun down, as an example. The Leut'n Governors house was searched and seven cart load of dollars was carried away. The Portegee King [Dom João], that was maried to the King of Spains daughter [Dona Carlota], was then in Riodejenara, and one of his son [Dom Pedro], which I saw both myself. They marched Portegee troop by land to Mounte Vedo, both foot and light horse, but the Spanish light horse in that country cut them all to pieces and could not face thim.[5]

Our ship being ready for see, we sailed for England, but the part owner did not go with us. After being at see a few days the ship sprung a leak and made a deal of water. We cleared away in the bows of the vessel. We found she was rotten. The carpenter and myself overhall'd the bolts in the breast piece and found we could of nearly hall'd them loos if we dare. We informed the capt[ain], and being nearly certain that she could not reach England, we

King Dom João and Retinue in Brazil

put into Riodejenaro [30 September 1812], where the owner shortly after arived. We discharged the cargo, and the carpenters were employ'd in putting new bows into hur and we ware all paid off.[6]

I then remained in Rio till the 2d of January 1812 [*sic,* 1813]. We then heard of the war between America and England.[7] The Brittis[h] had taken a Merican ship and sent hur into Rio, and they wanting hands to discharge hur, they employed eight or ten Americans, being a good many there, and those at work on b[oar]d coming down to the ballast found she had a good deal of money stowed in the ballace, all in bags. The Americans stole one bag, all in half joes, and devided them out, that they could convey them on shore the better, and before it was found out the sailors had got it on shore. One bag was missing but they could not recover what was gon, as they smugled all the rest. The American sailors "swayed away upon all topropes" while that lasted.

On the date last mentioned 14 of us, all Americans, engaged to go to Port Sagura [Puerto Seguro], which is, in English, Port Secure, and on that date we went on b[oar]d a smack and sailed, but having contrary winds, we put into a small port call'd Gulleperce [Guaripari] and remained there a week and then put to see again. Remaining at sea three days, beating against the wind and current, the pilot pretending to take the son [sun] with a kind of a hog yoke which I had heard of before, but he told the capt[ain] we had mad[e] nearly two degrees.[8] The capt[ain] new nothing about the quadron [quadrant] but new the coast well when he saw the land. One of our men having a quadron, I took the son [sun] and found by his declination we had not gain'd above 5 or 6 miles from whence we came. We inform'd the capt[ain]. He then stood in for the land to see which was right. When we got in with the land, Gulleperce [Guaripari] was close under our lee. He then bore up and run into the harbour and turned the pilot on shore.

In six days after we put to see again. In a few days after we run on a sand bank, keeping two close in shore. We carried two anchors out and at high water hove hur off without any damage, but still a head wind, we arived in Cravals [Caravelas] in two month where the Govener resided and the vessel belong'd there. We remain'd there afortnight, supplyed by the Governor, when we embarked on b[oar]d another vessel bound to Port Sagura. We arived there in a couple of day.

Port Sagura is a sucure and convenient harbour for small vessels, but vessels above 150 tons cant enter unless they are lighened. There is a hill nearly abrest the entrance of the harbour where the channel is stearing nearly west. As soon as you pass the reef of rock which the surf of the see roles over at high water, hall up south, huging the reef aboard till you come to the end of the reef where the body of the land joins the reef, then keep away west for a hundred yards or fathoms where the largest vessels comes to an anchor. There is buildings all along the beach which is call'd The Point as they have a full vew of the see or any vessel coming in, but the Lower Town lays about N.E. of the point, where the fishing boats chifly lay, on the north side of the river. It runs from the westward and forms an elbow to south till it joins the river again, the Lower Town on the side, and the island on the west. Vissels of 40 or 50 tons lay there in safety. The Upper Town is on the hill before mentioned at the entrence of the harbour. There is roads leads every way to the three towns and about half way up to the Uper Town has been a fort fronting the cannel that enters the harbour. The chief of the trade here is fishing and when loaded with salt fish they run to Biea [Bahia] or St. Salvadore, which is call'd about 80 leagues north from Port Sagura, and return with salt or what other necessaries they may want, as there is a great many groceries kept there.

In a few days after we arived, there was a vacancy for one man to go out a fishing. From the time we left Rio we ware found and supported by the King till we got into employment. We had a linkister [interpreter] with us that could talk Portegees extremely well and had been some years a mongst them and they realy thought hc was a Portegee, but he was a Bostonion. But at the first going off, by what our linkister inform us, they ware shy in taking many of us in one boat, for fear we should take hur away. When we told them we ware Americans, they did not [k]now anything about such a country, but call'd us all English men, though our linister told them otherwise, but they behaved very sivel to us, but I found they ware very ignorant in respect of any knolege of the world, but they [k]now how to ketch fish, which is there trade, as I before mentioned. Being a vacancy, we drew lots amongst us 14 and it fell to my lot, and I being the oldest and not understanding the lingo, the rest ware not willing I should go by myself, but I insisted I would go and left my scest [chest] and clothes and my Protection with Robert Star till my return. We being out about thirty day, the vessel was nearly full of fish. The capt[ain] sailed for St. Salvadore, landing us all two leagues north of the town excepting what was necessary to work the vessel.

Four days before we landed I was taken sick, but the master of the vessel and the fishermen ware very kind to me as I could not scarcely express a word of their lingo and not one on b[oar]d could under[stand] me unless it was by signs, but when we ware landed they all made the best of their way for the town and left me with my bundel to shift as well as I could. There is what they call tame Indians that settles amongst the Portegees and maries amongst each other. One of those Indians, seeing they had all left me, returned back again and remain'd with me till we came to the Upper Town where he lived.

I then went to the Lower Town, expecting to meet my comrades, but to my astonishment they ware all gon and nothing in the house where we all lived except a few logs that lay together. I was now in a distressed sittuation; I was sick and felt cold, could not speak to any of them or them to me if I went to enquire, and nothing to nourish me. I wished to find out what becam of the rest, but whenever I met any of them they would endeavour to inform me but all in vain, we could not understand each other. I return'd to the house and sat down on the logs. I then begin to reflect, in my ilness, though I had traveled a good many years through the four quarters of the globe, been a prisoner twice, cast a way three times, and the ship foundering under me, two days and a night in an open boat on the wide ocion without

Porto Seguro, Brazil

anything to eat or water to norish us, and numbers of times in want of water or victuals, at other times in action, men slain along side of me, and with all, at this minute it apeared to me that I was in greater distress and missery than I ever had been in any country during my life. I fell on my nees, and never did I pray with a sincerer hart than I did at that presentime.

I then set myself down on one of the logs for a few minutes and semed to be more composed within my brest, when the dore opened, and in came a black woman with a bason of soop and part of a fowl and farinia, which serves in the lew of bread, and presented the dish to me to eat, and then left me to reflect upon what the Lord had done for me and his merciful goodness to a sinner. When I finished my meal, I laid down on the logs and fell a sleep. When I waked in the evening the woman came again and supplied me in the same manner. This woman was a wife to one of the masters of a fishing boat, seeing my distress, gave me hur assistance as I hereafter found out, and sail'd in the same boat with hur husband and was well aquanted with them afterwards. I rested there that night.

In the morning I took a walk out, and falling in with some Portegees and an Atalion [Italian] sailor that had arived there, they inform'd him of my circumstances and where the rest was, which they could not tel me. He came up to me and spoke to me in very good Inglish. I was rejoice'd to find a man that could speak my lingo. He inform'd me, as they had told him, shortly after I went out to see the Govenor arived from Cravels and took all our men with him that was on shore. Three of us being out a fishing, he went to the nothord up a large river about 40 miles that leads to the mines and Robert Star expected I would be sent after them and took my chest with him, but he inform'd me our linkister was left behind, being sick, and his quarters was now within 5 or 6 doers of the church in the square in the Uper Town. I immediately started, after thanking him for his information, and found him, which gave us both great comfort. He got me some breekfas and then we took a walk down to the Lower Town. We then remain'd together, and shortly after the other two came in from sea.

I then made myself comfortable, having companions to talk with and linkister that understood their lingo. We done very well. By this time the lanch [launch] that I had been in returned and the owner had the account of what fish I had ketched, and I not [k]nowing that I was to receive anything, the owner sent for me by the linkester and paid me to the amount of 6 or 7 shillings sterlin, which was a good support till we went to see again.

In a short time after I went to Biea [Bahia], and when ariving, I made application to the American Counsel, Mr. [Henry] Hill, for asistance to get home, but having no Protection, he would do nothing for me, though I told him who had got my protection and chest of clothes that he had sent home in the brig call'd the *Blody Yankee* which had been a privateer and made a carteel of to send home the Americans that was there.[9] Therefore I was compelled to return again and continued a fishing, though every few months one or the other would make a trip to Biea in hopes of getting a ship for home and then return again. Shortly after John Hammon, that had been with us from Rio, returned to Biea and got command of a small schooner belonging to Mr. Hill, Counsel'r, that was employ'd runing to his plantation, which was about 90 od leagues south of Biea.

In 1819, about the 9 of November, being out in one of the fishing boats, which are vessels about 35 to 50 tons, a most tremendious gale came on with heavy rain and a thick fog. The wind from the N.E., our sails spliting, we lowered the sail down and while repairing the sail we ware drove in shore and drifted in side of the reef, the fog so thick we could not see ten yards from the vessel. We let go three anchors but we found it was not posseble to ride it out without foundering. The see runing so high, we had to cut our cables. By this time we had repair'd our sails as well as we could and maid sail, though we could not see ten yards a head, but through providence we run in between two rocks, a small channel that the oldest fisherman new nothing of, which saved us all. It coming on dark, and when we found ourselves clear, we kept away to the sotherd for our port, we being to the notherd of a small town call'd St. acruse [Santa Cruz Cabralia]. We arived next morning safe into Port Saguro, but the other two vessels that was out ware drove over the reef and their bottoms beat out and not one man saved out of about thirty od. One vessel was hall'd up and repair'd again, but the other went to pieces.

Portuguese Coast, Rio to Bahia

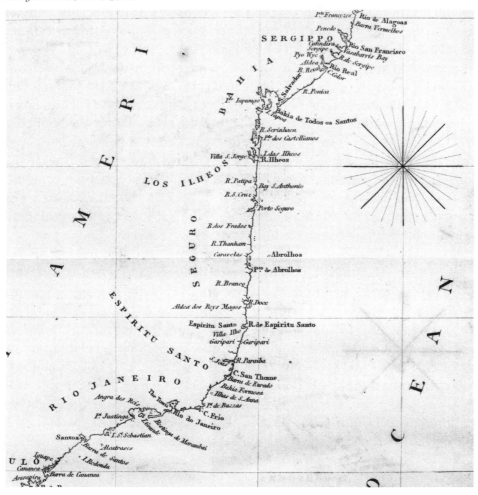

Some times when we ware out a fishing we would run in amongst for [four] small rockey islands call'd the Abrolias [Abrolhos], which means "open your eyes." There is sunken rocks all round it but in betwen them was good anchorage and lay a long side the rocks and go ashore and get turkels egs, and see fow[l] breads [brecd] on those rocks, and a gale from the norwest, you lay safe. It lays abrest of the town cal'd Cravals [Caravelas], I should suppose about three leagues.

Shortly after, John Hammon came in to Port Sagura in the schooner and wish'd me to go with him, which I did. We arived at the plantation and refited the schooner and took in a load of farenia and sailed for Biea, and ariving, we discharged our cargo. Being prepared for see, the Counsel sent two milk cows on board for the plantation. We sailed, and having fine weather till we got half way on our passage, we fell in with a gale from the south in the night. The thunder and lightening was so quick and heavy that it seemed to be one continuel flash of lightening with heavy rain. The next morning it cleared off, but the wind continued from the sotherd and we continued to beat to the sotherd but could gain no ground. During that time our provisions was out and nothing for the cattle. We got a small quantity at different times from small vessels passing to the nothord, but the poor cows we had no remidy for them. We had a few potatoes in willow baskets. We gave them the potatoes and then cut the willow baskets into one or two inches. They eat that. It being a dangerous and rockey coast we could not land without endangering the vessel and our lives, and about middle passage the capt[ain] was loth to return. At length the two cows were nothing but skin and bone. One of them got holt of a stocking jacket that laid in hur reach and swallowed it and would of choked if the capt[ain] had not put his arm down hur throat and hall'd it out. It hurt my feelings to see the distress the poor beasts was in, but they died, and we ourselves being starving, we skined them and cut them into small junks [chunks] and put it into salt pickel in the harness cack [cask]. Though like caron [carrion], we ware glad to eat it. As near as I can recollect we ware about four weeks reaching the plantation. We then refited, wanting some repairs, and took in farenia for St. Salvador and sail'd and arived there safe, we continuing going backwards and forwards.

Capt[ain] John Hammon was made overseer of the plantation and I was required by the Counsel to take his place, which I did for several month, runing backwards and forwards. When wanting melasses for the American ships we run up the rivers where it was so narrow and crooked that we would have to pole hur, the sails being of no use. At one time we went thirty leagues up from St. Salvedore but returned without any, requiring more than what the Counsel would give. There is a great number of small towns and villiges up these rivers where they manefactor Brazeel rum, sugar, cotton, and coffee, etc.

I cannot particularly say how long I remain'd in this schooner, but the wages being low, I left hur and return'd to Port Sagura and remain'd till the year 1821. I went on board a large lanch [launch] bound to St. Mathews, a town that is about ten leagues up a river [São Mateus River] on the coast, south of Port Sagura and north of Riodegenaro. When we got up to the town we had to go five leagues farther up to a plantation where we lay till the cargo was ready, and when it was ready they expected the crew to fetch it down on their backs about a quarter of a mile, though they had a great number of Negroes, therefore my comrad, which was a German sailor, and myself left hur and went down to the town. We ware well treated there by the capt[ains] and mates of vessels as they ware fitting out for see.

At length we engaged to go about three leagues below the town to fit out a smack that was bound to Riodegenaro. When we came down the carpenters was heaving hur down to repair hur bottom. The owner understanding that we understood repairing of sails, he employed us at the sails till the vessel was ready for riging. We had "good living" as is call'd in that country, jerk beef and farenia, which is made out of a tree that is call'd manyoke [manioc, or cassava]. When planted, it grows about 10 feet high and is not fit for use under sixteen or eighteen month. Then the roots grows much like a yam or a potatoe but much larger; they then [are] scraped clean and grated as we do horse redish, but they have mils for that purpose, as they make a great quantity. Then it is pressed to take the juice out of it and then sifted through two or three sives, then hove into large earthen pans made for that purpose with fiers under them and parch it. It is then fit for use, but the tree itself is useless. Oranges, limes, and lemons are plentiful but very little of any other kind of fruit at that time of year.

We fitted the smack out and took in hur cargo of farenia, having plenty of Negros to load hur, and droped down to the bar where a number of other vessels was laying ready to put to see for different ports on the Brazeele coast. In 1821 [sic, 1820], Decemb'r 17th, we got under way and got over the barr, about eight sail, but it is a shoal and dangerous bar. Our vessel a lone was bound to Rio and the rest to the norther. The weather was fine but a long passage. At length we arived and came to an anchor in Rio degenaro.

Before I was discharged I was pressed by the Portegees to help to carry stores on board of a 74 gun ship [*Dom João VI*] that the King of Portangal [Portugal] was to return in to Lisbon, but they did not keep me.[10] I return'd on board and was paid off and found the *Congress* Frigate laying there, and by applying to the Counsel who new me he gave me a letter to Capt[ain] Hanly [John D. Henley]. I went on board the 10 of April and we sailed on the 15th with a number of sick on b[oar]d with the colemagus [cholera morbus]. Nothing materiel hapened on the passage, having generally fine weather. We arived in Norfolk some time in June, but they had a great many men died on the passage from Manela [Manila].[11] The ships company being paid off [9 June 1821], I ingaged in a new light boat and went down to Smiths Point.

In about six months I returned to Norfolk and shiped on board a large ship from Baltimore bound to Cork the 1st of January 1822, but loosing some of hur men, the capt[ain] came up to Norfolk to ship more in there stead, and we sailed the 29 of Fabruary 1822. We had very severe weather, and blowing hard from the S. west on the Banks, the ship sprung a leak. We got both pumps going and hove 2,000 staves overboard and hove the ship on the starboard tacks, which was contrary to our course, till we could keep hur free with one pump. Our bull works ware all nock away with the sea, the thunder and lighening was quick and heavy. One man was nocked down along side of me by the power of a thunderbolt passing him along the deck and went through the galley and out of the harse hole. It being dark, the man washed against my legs, the deck being full of water. We got him up and he recoverd. The capt[ain's] lady being on board, she miscaried with the fright. On the 5th of April [1822], in the evening, we got into the Cove of Cork in time as a nother heavy gale came on from the N.W. There was several vessels lost off of Cork that night and one American ship full of passengers totally lost. One boat crew that atemped to go off to save some ware likewise lost. On the 15th [April 1822] we ware discharged.

The 10 of May [1822] I shiped in the Brig *Henry*, bound to Liverpool, but being seazed for debt, was taken up to the custom house and discharged and the crew paid off, but I rema[i]nd on board with the capt[ain] and mate, and shortly after the mate left hur. She was taken down to Mr. McNights dock yard and I remained in hur till the fifth of August [1822].

I left hur and shiped on board the *Eliza* Sloop, Capt. Pendergrass, bound to Giberalter.[12] We sail'd on the 14th [August 1822] from Cove, having pleasent w[eathe]r, but we had acasion to put into a small harbour call'd Portsmouth. In a few days we sailed and arived at Giberalter on the 26th [August 1822]. The crew was paid off excepting the capt[ain] and myself.

The sloop was to be sold. We lay up abreast the old mold in the bay near the newtral ground. (29 March 1823) Still remain'd on board the *Aliza*. About this time a gale came on and drove sixteen English and American ships on shore and some of them totally racked [wrecked].

(3 July 1823) Capt[ain] Pendergrass [Pendergast] left the sloop and sail'd in the *Margaret* for Dublin, and I had charge of the vessel and was supply'd by the merchant in what was necessary till the sloop was sold.

(13 Augt 1823) An action commenced between the Spanish Revolutioners and Kings troops of Spain and a French 74 and a frigate laid against the fort at Old Jib, a small iland with a few guns, as I was looking at them from the sloops mast head. The Revolutioners had to retreat to the newteral ground where the Rock of Giberalter protected them. The French men of war engaging, this small fort on the island, as I understood, had but four guns, and the 74 coming to an anchor with springs on hur cables beside the frigate, fired hur guns in platoons, which I never saw on b[oar]d of a ship before, but the 74 lost near 80 men that day beside what the frigate lost, but I never had the purticular account of the number, but they had to hall off and leave the fort, but a short time after they had to surrender for the want of water and provisions and the general was taken.

(1 Sept'r 1823) The *Eliza* being sold, I was discharged. The 4th I went on b[oar]d, Capt. Jones, til I got a ship.

(12 Sept. 1823) Shiped on board the *Leuesa,* Capt[ain] Falkner, bound to the West Indies. (4 Oct. 1823) Sailed, the wind at east. (29 Oct. 1823) At 4 P.M. made the island of Burbadoes, distance 4 or 5 leagues, bearing N.W. $\frac{1}{2}$ W., hall'd our wind S.W. The 30th, at noon, made Tobago, bearing S.S.W. November 2d (1823), passed through the Bogus and arived in the island of Trenedad. (Island is on the N.E. coast of Columbia, separated from Paria on the south by a strait about 10 miles over and from Cumana on the west by the Gulf of Paria. It is 62 miles long and 45 broad, produses sugar, cotton, indian corn, tobacco, and fruit. The air unhealthy. The capitel is Port de Espagne in the Gulf of Paria near the Bocqu. Long'd 61°30′ West, Latt'd 10°0′ North.) Employed discharging the cargo. At this time the Negroes was revolting. The plot was laid to attack the town in the night, but being discovered, 12 of the chief ringleaders ware hung. On the 12 Novr (1823) left Trenedat [Trinidad] and run down to the Bogus and took in ballast. The 15 (Nov. 1823) sailed for Antego [Antigua]. Having a pleasent passage, we arived in a few day. From thence we sailed for St. Thomases and took in a cargo of plank and lumber and returned for Antego [Antigua]. We caried

away our main topmast and sprung a leake, but we arived safe and discharged. (28 Dec. 1823) On Sunday, left the *Leuesa*, belonging to Mr.
Merson, and boarded at Mrs. Bisshops.

March 13th (1824), on Saturday night, about half past 10, we felt three
shocks of an earthquake, but one was much heavier than the other two.
March 20, (1824) ship'd on board the *Gleaner* Schooner, Capt[ain] John
Osburn. The 28th (March 1824), through the ill treatment of the capt. the
men left hur and I remain'd at Mrs. Bishups.

April 1d (1824) Shiped on board the *Fanny* Brig bound to New York,
Capt. Leubeck. 16th (April, 1824) We sailed with a cargo of melasses. (May
7, 1824) Arived in New York.[13] The 11th (May 1824), I went to the hospittle
and the 4th of June (1824) I left the hospittle.

July 11, (1824) I shiped in the Poke *Hunter* and sailed for Baltimore.[14]

CHAPTER 14

The Final Voyage

INTRODUCTION

THE fifteen years between Jacob Nagle's retirement from the sea and his death had little of the excitement of his sailing days, but they tell us a great deal about him. He was not idle. For several years in the 1830s he worked in the offices of the clerk of the court and recorder of deeds in Canton and Perrysburg, Ohio, presumably copying deeds and keeping ledgers. His handwriting, retaining the neatness more characteristic of the eighteenth than the nineteenth century, was good, and midwestern Americans of the period were not overly scrupulous about spelling.

Intermittently, he made efforts to secure bounty lands and pension money for his and his father's Revolutionary War services. Nagle was penniless for much of the period, except for the little he could earn from odd jobs and what he was given by relatives, but one senses that the primary motivation of his persistently going after the veteran's benefits was pride. Money and possessions never had been important to him: for Nagle, "a good living" was food, clothing, shelter, and companionship, not much more.

Nagle had spent his entire life moving from place to place. To be alive was to be on the move, and in these last years he seems to be trying to sail out of range of the Grim Reaper, always hoping that he would find his youthful good health, or perhaps a Captain Bond beckoning him to a comfortable berth on a new *Netley*. Nagle met the challenge of faltering health with his head up and his feet constantly in motion.

Nagle's relatives helped him in every way they could. He lived with his sister in Maryland; his sister in Canton, Ohio; a cousin in Harrisburg; and a nephew in Perrysburg, Ohio, for periods as long as three years. In each case, the drive to keep moving got the better of him. At the end of his life he seems to have been living in the last of a succession of boardinghouses.

In comparison with his neighbors and acquaintances in these last years, Nagle was very much a man of the world. The irony was that while he was out seeing the world, he had missed most of his own country's history. When Jacob Nagle left Philadelphia in 1781, the United States had not even achieved permanent existence. Ohio, where he would later reside, was then Indian territory. He missed entirely the period when the Constitution was written and ratified; he missed George Washington's presidency and the War of 1812.

If he had struck up a conversation with a store owner or a farmer in Canton in the 1830s, the probable topics would have been farming, politics, or religion. Nagle had never farmed in his life. He believed in the existence of God, but when he filed his application for a pension, he admitted that he was acquainted with no minister of the Gospel who could vouch for his character. His sister had obviously not gotten him to attend her Methodist church. As for politics, the issues and their contexts must have been incomprehensible to him, the candidates merely names. The American Revolution was the only common ground he shared with anyone, and it is not surprising that he took particular pleasure in running across an "old Revolutioner," who would understand at least some of his life's experiences.

In one particularly evocative sentence in this last section of the journal, describing the kindnesses of the Beisel family near Philadelphia, he let slip that "I felt happy while I was with them," suggesting that most of the time he was a very lonely man. It was out of this loneliness and sense of isolation from the world around him that he increasingly turned to the past. He loved to tell stories to anyone who would listen, and fortunately, he also put them on paper.

The last journey that Jacob Nagle recorded in his journal was in July 1839. He became sick on a canal boat. The bugle player on the boat took pity on him and put him up at a hotel until he was well enough to move and then paid his way to Zanesville, Ohio. He started to walk the ninety miles to Canton. He had to lie down along the road at one point, and it took him two days to go ten miles, "so weak I had to sit down every five or six hundred yards." It took him ten days to reach his destination.

His life was drawing to a close, and he seems to have known it. Although there was more room on the page, on 22 July 1840 he made an entry in his journal that he obviously considered to be the last. He died seven months later, without money and without a will, but leaving behind friends who appreciated this extraordinary man and the journal, which by remarkable good fortune has survived to the present day.

ON THE 17 (June 1824) I left Baltimore for Reading. 18 (June 1824) came to Abbington, but very sick. 19 (June 1824) came to Haverdegrass. 20th (June 1824) traveled six miles above Haverdegrass and crossed the bridge. That night stop'd within 25 miles of Lancaster. 21d (June 1824), went only 15 miles. The 22d went through Lankaster. At 9 o'clock A.M. on the 23d arived in Reading and remain'd amongst my relations till the 17th August (1824), at 10 o'clock A.M., I left Reading. Stop'd at Womelsdurf, 14 miles, went through Stouts Town, Moyers Town, Lebanon, stoped 19 Miles, from Harrisburg. (20 Aug. 1824) Came to HarrisBurg and stop'd with my cozen, Geo. Nagle, and had the pleasure of seeing Mr. J. Bealer, which ware both first cozins of my fathers side. I remained a couple of days, and started (23 Aug. 1824) for Hagorstown and arived in Hagers Town on the 27th, from thence to Salsbury Springs, 4 miles from Hagers Town, [met] Thos. McCartel, that was maried to my sister Ann and remain'd there till the 4th of May, 1826 [*sic,* 1827].

About 10 A.M. (4 May 1827), I left my sister Ann at the turnpike road with hur son Wilford McKardel.[1] Came through Clear Springs. At 4 P.M. came to Mr. Sniders, 19 miles from Hagers Town. The 5th I left Mr. Sniders, being aquainted with his family, went through Hankock (7 May 1827), went through Comberland.

Being then with a wagoner, loaded for Pitsburg, we came to Mount Pleasant the 10 (May 1827). Being on the road, the wagon broke down about two miles from where he could get any assistence. He asked me if I would remain till he returned, having six horses. I said I would. Where we had stop'd that morning there was a stout fellow was travcling to the eastward, and when he met us he turned back again and kept us company. The wagoner gave me a hint to be aware of that fellow, as he new he travel'd that road backwards and forwards for chanses. While the wagoner was gon, he wanted me to leave the wagon and go on, and he would carry my napsack. "A, ya," said I, "my good fellow, I paid dear for that trick once in my time by such a fellow as you, and I think it would be best for you to go about your business." Accordingly he did walk off.

The wagoner return'd with a carpenter and blacksmith and repair'd the wagon. We got only eight miles that day (11 May 1827). We went through Monrow and Union Town, where we saw the fellow again, but he did not come near us. Went through Redstone Old Fort, Brownswell [Brownsville], Monogohele River, through St. Evil, 18 miles from Washington, through Belvil, then through Pankake Town. That evening arived in Washington, Pennsylv[ania] (13 May 1827).

(14 May 1827) I left Washington, came to Cross Kreek Villige. Stop'd 18 miles from Washington with Mr. Wm. Hall, being a Revolutioner.[2] The 16th (May 1827), crossed the Ohio at St[e]ubenvil[le], went through Richmon[d] and Springfield. In leaving Stubenvil, I came up with Joseph Wortwell and Charles Smith with about 11 or 12 hundred sheep, and they said if I would stay with them to follow the sheep they woul[d] pay my way to Canton. Therefore I remain'd with them, and arived in Canton on the 19 May (1827), where my sister lived, and Geo. Web[b] hur sun was the first I saw at the entrance of the town of Canton.[3]

(Thurs., 7 June 1827) John Webb coming from Perrysburg for his mother and two sisters, I left Canton with them at 4 in the afternoon.[4] Went through Kendel and Maslin [Massillon]. Went through Dover and put up at Wooster and left the bagage at James Hemperleys and went [to] see Mr. Pankost, 5 miles from thence, being related. We stoped several days and then returned (13 June 1827) to Wooster and went on, came through Union Town, Ollivesburg. This day got into a mud hole and broke our gear. Had to stop til we repair'd it. Went through Parris and stop'd at New Haven (16 June 1827). Went on. Stop'd to feed at Monrow. Went on, came to Oringe Ville. Went on to Lower St. Dusky [Sandusky] hotel, brekfasted. That night remain'd [at] Mr. Howards. Went on and arived in Perrysburg that after noon with a good shower of rain. It is call'd 30 miles across the swamp.

We remaind in Perrysburg till August 16, 1827. My sister Sarah Webb left Perrysburg with hur two youngest daughters in the *Gerere* Schooner for Cleaveland and took stage for Canton, 60 miles. On the day of hur departure I was verry ill with the fever, but I shortly after recovered. The 10 of Dec'r (1827) I left Perrysburg for Canton. The 14th (Dec. 1827), about 6 miles past N[ew] Haven, I missed my road. About 6 miles I stoped at Mr. Thews, an Englishman who treated me very genteeley. Dec'r 15 (1827) I had to return another road, and being so much rain and snow and the kreeks raised that the bridges ware brok down, and striving to cross on the logs, I fell in with my napsack on my sholders, and my hat falling off, I had to swim after my hat and lost my gloves, but I swom over dripping wet and raining, snowing, and hail at different times, and walking about two miles, I came to the cross roads to Mr. Sniders and stop'd for the night and dried my clothes. I went on (Sunday, 16 Dec. 1827), but it was cruel weather. Some places I got a cross upon old trees, other places I had to waid. I had been castaway on the ocion but never was cast away in mud and dry land before this trip. I laboured on till I came within one mile of Canton (Fri., 21 Dec. 1827) but could go no farther. I was feeble and a heavy ague on me and stop'd at Mr. Smiths all night and I got to Canton the next day (22 Dec. 1827) and remained in Canton till the year 1828.

March 1, (1828), I left Canton at 10 o'clock with Mr. Cragehead. Stop'd all night at Allexander. Fed the horses at Lisbon. 2d, stop'd at Little Beaver. The 3d, stop'd Big Beaver, passed Oconnomy [Economy] on the Ohio. On the 4 we arived in Pitsburg about one o'clock, put up at the Pitsburg hotel. Mr. Cragehead sold his horses. (5 March 1828) I left Pitsburg with a wagon. The 6th I was sick and the wagon left me. I pushed on slowly, went through Greenswell [Greensburg] and through Loghlings [Laughlin] Town, stop'd on Lorrel Hill. Unwell, 11 (March 1828), I went on, though it rained. Came to Stoystown, then Shelburg. Got in company with a wagon, but the jolting of the wagon made me sick and I had to remain behind. Went through McConnels Town, came over the N. Mountain (17 March 1828). Met Mr. Cragehead. He gave me a dinner and some spirits to refresh me at the foot of it at a paper mill. On the 18th I arived in Hagers Town. Rem[aine]d at Mrs. Meltons at night, an aquaintance of my sisters.

19th (March 1828) went to Mr. McCardels and remained till the 25th and started for Harrisburg. The 27 took coach for Harrisburg. At night arived

Reading, Pennsylvania

there and remained till the 31st and left Harisburg in the coach and arived in Reading the 1st of April (1828) by kandle light and received a certificate from my unkel.

The 3d (April 1828) left Reading for Washington. Went through Lancaster. 5th, crossed Collumbus [Columbia] bridge. I stop'd about an hour in Little York and went on through Threwsbury. The 7th arived in Baltimore. The 8 left Baltimore. Went through Bledingsburg [Bladensburg] the 9 (April 1828) within five miles of Washington, but unwell. Arived in the citty (10 April 1828), went to Mr. Moyers and found Mr. Adams [William Addams], member of Congress.[5] Went to Mr. Adams [Addams] (11 April 1828), member for Pennsslvania. Was put off till Saturday the 12th and sent Mr. Mitchal, his secatary, with me and received the land for my father or at least the certificate which was 500 acres for me and my sisters.

The same day I started, but rain'd all day. I fell in with Mr. G. W. Pool, who wished me to stop till morning at his house, the roads being so bad, and stop'd to breckfast. 16th (April 1828), went through Leesburg and through

Hilsburrough and came to Keys ferry, from thence to Shepperds Town. Went on for Cravel Town and crossed the fields one mile to Morgans Mills (18 April 1828), now call'd Henrys Mills on the Potomack. Here I crossed from Virginia to Maryland, 7 miles from Williams Port, but what secmed curious, when I got on the main road, not [k]nowing at that time what distance it might be, but asking different peapel on the road, I got forther off from Williamsport than from the place I crossed, though they said I was in the right road, till I came nearly within sight, and meeting a gentle[ma]n a horse back, I asked him.

"You are close too it now, when you go over this little hillock."

I told him I only had crossed from Virgina at the mill seven miles off and by the time I traveled about two miles inquired and they told me 8 or 9 miles. He laughed and I went on, and as he said, it was so. I entered and was aquainted in the town and dined at Mr. Hiram Stecks and then parted and arived at Mr. McKardels farm and found them all well. Remain'd there till the 18th of Nov'r (1828) and then started and arived in Harrisburg on Sunday 23d, but had bad roads with rain and snow.

I remain'd all winter with my cosin, Geo. Nagle, till the eighth of April (1829), but had no success in applying for my father, as my mother was dead.

I then returned again to my sister or Mr. McKardel, 4 miles from Hagers Town, till Easter Monday (April the 20), when I left them, bound for Canton. After breckfast, came on rain. Arived that night at Mr. Sniders. The 21 fell in with a wagon and travel'd on. I do not put down every place we stoped or every day of the month as it is chiefly before mentioned. Stop'd (Fri., 24 April 1829) 83 miles from Hagers Town. The 25 went on. Mr. McKardel came up with us. He was then going up to Kain Tuckey [Kentucky]. I went on. Came to Monegehaley [Monongahela] (Apr. 28), and went on to Wash-ing[ton], Penns[ylvania]. The wagon took another cours and left me. In the morning (Apr. 29) I started but got wet. Stoped to dry myslf. I went though Middle Town, stop'd at Robert Shaw (1 May 1829), 7 miles from Ohio. Was directed a rong road and had to waid over Cross Creek and went down the branch 5 miles below. Getting information, I had to return five miles to St[e]ubenvil[le] and remain'd there all night. Traveling on, fell in with a boy that directed me a road that would be a short cut. I followed his road, was benighted, and laid in the woods all night on the 3 (May 1829). I came to a town (May 4), fell in with a wagon, and on the 5th arived in Canton.

Remained in Canton till Sept. 22. Left Canton on a visit to Mr. Pancost and arived on the 30th (Sept. 1829). Went to Wooster and return'd. Started for Canton (2 Oct. 1829) and arived in the evening. I now emp[loye]d myself in sawing wood and continued at that labour during the winter for a small support till when I left Canton for Masslin [Massillon] (4 May 1830) and went on b[oar]d a kanel [canal] boat for Cleaveland. In the morning of the 5 (May 1830) she started, call'd the *Union of Dover*. On the 6 arived at Claveland. Remained all night at Mr. Spanglers, waiting for a boat.

A steame boat came off the harbour at 8 o'clock A.M. and was sending hur boat in for pasengers. I was coming down the hill with my napsack to go on board and met a young gentelman, as I took him to be, and told me not to go in that boat as they would charge me double price. Therefore I return'd back to Mr. Spanglers, and informing him, he told me it was false and that man was in opposition to that boat, but he said there would be another in before night. At 7 P.M. the *Enterprise* (8 May 1830) steam boat came in to take in pasengers. I went on board. About 8 P.M. we sailed for Portland. It blew a fresh breeze all night. About 6 A.M. in the morning (May 9) we ware off Portland, but blowing fresh and a rough see, the capt[ain] would not venture in and passed on for Detroite. We arived about 4 o'clock P.M., the pasengers landed that was bound there, and others came on b[oar]d. 10 (May 1830), at 9 A.M., we sail'd for Portland.[6] About dusk we arived in Portland and went on shore.

I remain'd all night at Mr. Cogsdills, a boarding house. In the morning (Tues., May 11) I found Mr. Pennewells, who rec'd me kindly. I looked round for employment, went on b[oar]d (May 12) several vessels, but found nothing to my advantage. The 15 I got employment to finish a gardin. Sund[a]y, 16, strong gales from the eastward. Mon[da]y, 17 emp[loye]d planting potatoes, cloudy w[eathe]r and fresh gales from the east[war]d. The 19 finish'd my undertaking; empl[oye]d myself choping wood and making a mat for Mrs. Penewell. I skip over the wind and weather, but it has been chiefly rain and blustry w[eathe]r. On the 29 (May 1830) was Quarterly Meating [probably Methodist Quarterly Meeting] in Portland. From this date chiefly blustry and windy weather, with rain till June 11th (1830). I engaged with Mr. Townsen, went up to his plantation three mile, and loaded a wood flat with about 14 kord of wood and brought hur down to his warf. He settel'd with me, but I had to take half in store goods. The 16 (June 1830) I went to Mathew Hurin, 10 miles, where there was a steam boat and launched. Saw the capt[ain] of the boat, but having all his hands, I return'd and arived in the evening. In the morning (Tues., June 17) I started for

Canton. About two miles I met two brothers on the road and they asked me home with them and staid all night with them (June 18), Thos. Galloway on Pike Creek.

At ½ past 4 A.M. I started along the farera [parara, or prairie] and lost myself.[7] Came to a house and was directed, but being boggy and many paths, I was lost again. Came to another house, and by their directions I got into the main road at a stone house five miles from Portland. I went through Miland [Milan] and Newark [sic, Norwalk], came to a cross road, and was directed and short road through the big farara, but with the cattle making many pathes, I lost myself again, and being cloudy weather, I could see no sun and drislin rain and thunder and sumtiems half way up to my nees in mud and water. I observed by a mark that I came to one tree three times in the after noon. I thought of the Indian track [trick], stearing my course by the moss of the trees, which is north. I steared about S.E., which brought me to a new road I could see by the wagon wheels, but over flowed with water. I then follow'd the road N.E. and came to a house which was on the main road, but asking a man at the house, he directed me a cross the crick, which I had to wade, and went on about a mile and came to the house he directed me to, two miles from St. Clarks fields as I understood afterwards.[8] I was in a wet and dirty condition, my shoes I caried in my hand or loose them. This is in Huron County.

It rained, thundered, and lightening during the whole night (Sat., 19 June 1830). When I came to the dore the woman invited me in. I asked for a place to shift myself. She showed me a small room. My clothes was dry, having a painted napsack. I shifted myself and came out, and by this time hur husband came, Mr. Daniel Dills, (Sun., 20 June 1830), and acted as a genteel man would to a st[r]anger. I inform'd him the road I had come. He told me that man had directed me away from the road, as I was then in the road, and would have to go back to that road again, but he said he was a mean [man] at the best, but he advised me when I got on that road to take the Wooster road, as the new road was unpasseble and difficult to find the right road. This Vermillion River leads into Lake Erie below Black River. The wind S.W., with heavy showers of rain. Mr. Dills advised me to remain there till next morning.

A.M., clear w[eather] (June 21), started after breckfast, back the same road, and got over the creek upon some old trees, the creek being over-flowed, and got into the road as I was directed by Mr. Dills le[a]ding to New London, about four miles, otherwise call'd the Center Cross Roads. I was directed the road south, as the other roads and rivers were not pasibles. I now steared for Haney Villige, five miles. Went on three miles to N[ew] London, or Center Cross, which I supposed to be a town or a villige, but I found a log house upon each corner of the cross road but no one lived in either of them.

I went on for Haney Villige. Before I got there, I had to cross a creek that was two deep to cross without danger. I was at a stand when a young man came riding up to me on horse back. I informed him I wanted to get a cross if I could without getting me napsack wet. He said he would take me a cross. I thank'd him. He took the bundel and wish'd me to get on. I told him if I fell in I could swim across. I went on a large tree and scrambled a cross without falling in and he rode over and gave me my bundel and wish'd me good by. I went on through mud and mier till I came within two miles of Haneys Villige, and it being dark, I asked the man of the house to remain there till morning, but they refused me. It raining and dark, I went on through a dark wood, up to my nees in mud and water, however I arived in Haneys Village and the first house I applyed to was Mr. John Custard, kept open house and treated me kindly and charged me nothing for the night.

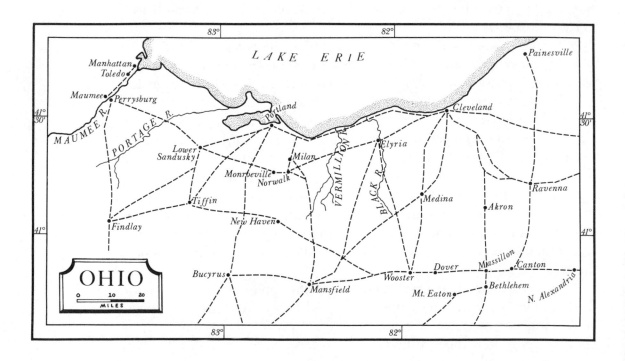

Canton, Ohio

(Tues., 22 June 1830) A.M. started on with showers of rain for Wooster, all day riding logs across the creeks, the bridges being broke down with the flods. I arived in Wooster about nine a'clock at night and got a lodging. The next day (Wed., June 23) I set out for Canton. Going four miles, fell in with a light wagon, caried my bundel as far as Dover, and I being lame and very much fateged and rain likely to continue, I stop'd for a while at the Sign of the Beehive, Mr. J. Lierd, then rested a while a[nd] went on within 12 miles of Canton and rested all night. (Thurs., 24 June 1830) A.M., started early with two waggons bound to Maslin [Massillon]. On the road one upset, loaded with flower [flour]. I stop'd till we got the flower in again and then went on again and arived in Canton in the evening.

Remaining in Canton, by the instrogation of Mr. Georg Cane [Cake], being aquainted with Mr. John Mires [Myers], Esqr., I got into his office and remain'd with him and the latter part with Mr. Brice [William Bryce] when Recorder till the year 1833, righting in their offices.[9]

Left Canton bound for Washington at 8 o'clock A.M. (1 July 1833), weather warm. I received a litter from Mr. Shorb in Canton to Major [James A.] Hook in Washington as a recomendation. Ariving in Lisbon (2 July 1833), I went to Mr. Tompson [John Thomson], Member of Congress. He backed my papers. I went on.[10] I wish to make short, and nothing particular, I only mention the chief of the villiges I went through from Lisbon: Fulks Town [Foulkstown] or West Union, Little Beaver, came to Ohio [River], crossed to Geore Town [Georgetown], came to Hooks Town, Frankford, Cross Town, Burgets Town, Washington, Pen[nsylvan]ia, went over Ginger Hill, Williams Port. Being in the rong road, went to Brownsvill[e] and crossed, then Bridgeport, Monegehele, Union Town, Munrow, went over Lorrel Hill [Laurel Hill], past Braddocks Run, Smithfield, Cumberland, Pleasent Mills Tavern, Pleasent Valley, Flintstone, Will[ia]m[s] Port, Mariland, Boonsbury [Boonsboro], Middle Town, Fredericks [Frederick] Town, George Town, Cockvile [prob. Rockville], Kenly Town.

Arived in Washington City on the (24 July 1833). I went to Mr. Laskeys, where I had been before.[11] The next day (July 25) I went to Major Hook and delivered the letter from Mr. Shorb and my papers. He sent his secatary with me and my papers was aproved and I was examined by the B[oar]d of War, or J. L. Edwards, Commissioner of Pensions, in Washington City, but by the neglect of my loyer, Mr. Brice, not sending my dockement with me, it could

Stage Stop between Washington and Baltimore

not be settled. Therefore I was in a bad sittuation and without money. Having no way to remain there while I sent to Canton, and not informing Majer Hook where I was gon, I started for Baltimore (26 July 1833) in hopes I could get work till I sent to Canton. It came on to rain heavy, which wet me to the skin, and having no money for a bed, I laid down in the porch, but the landlord taking a fancy to my staff and purhaps seeing I was in distress, I gave it to him. He gave me a good brandy sling going to bed and my bitters with a good warm breekfast and a half dollar in cash. His name was Mr. Gibbs, capt[ain] the stage house.

I started on the road, and being tierd, I steped into a porch at Mr. Rummons, an open house. While sitting the[re], a Catholic Priest came out, and having a little conversation, asked me if there was any Catholiks about Canton. I tild here [told him there] was, and as he step'd into his coach, he clap'd a half dollar into my hand and started for Baltimore.

I then travel'd on and laid all night in the woods. This day I was verry unwell. I travel'd on for Baltimore (27 July 1833). Came to a stage house. Though I had part of the money I received, I had to be careful, and being unwell, I did not wish to lay out all night. Seeing the hosler in the stable, I spoke to him. He gave me a good hayloft to lay down. I remain'd till morning. He came early and let me out. I traviled on.

I must say this of the country, they have no respet or humanity for a person in poverty. At 8 o'clock A.M. (Sunday, 28 July 1833), coming a long on the turnpike, passing a few houses, a stout able man came out of a house, runing at me with a white shirt in his hand, tearing it all to peaces and runing at me. I took him to be lunateck. I having a good stick in my hand, I put myself on a gard and told him to stand off or I would nock him down. He stepeded back and picked up three or four stones of about one lb. weight and made offers to heave them at me, but I still remained on my gard and closed in with him till I observed some men and wimen behind a corner of a house laughing. I then slaped him on the sholder. He then laughed, otherwise I should of laid him lower than he then was. I told them I was an Old Revolutioner and was not [to] be skared in so simpel amaner. They all laughed hartily at him and told him he had met his match, thoug I was an old man. They gave me a treat. I bid them good by and went on and arived in Baltimore and went to Smiths Point.

Having one shilling left, I fell in (Mon., 29 July 1833) with a gentleman ship carpenter lived next dore to the Foul Anchor, Mr. Peacock. Though I was in distress, he and his wife treated me in the most genteelest manner that

USS Pennsylvania *at Philadelphia Dockyard*

a stranger could wish, and remain'd there till Wednesd[ay] (31 July 1833). Having no prospect of getting work, I started for Philadelphia. After receiving one dollar from Mr. Pearson, an aquaintance in our family, and settled, I had 37½ cents left.

I went on for Haverdegrass and for the want of money I laid in the woods. Went through Abington Village (Thurs., 1 Aug. 1833) and crossed Benemuns Run and arived in Haver [Havre de Grace] in morning (Fri., Aug. 2). Having but seven cents, the landlord gave me a passage over the Suscahanna. I went through Charlestown on the Bay of Elk, went through another on the head of Elk, then throug Elk Town, wh[ich] is a very hansome town.

I traveled on at night. I came to a house, but they would not give me any shelter. I walked on till I came to a barn, but it was locked. I gathered the straw and laid on that, close to the dore, but I observed something under the barn flore hissing at me. I supposed it might be a snake, but having my stick, I laid till morning. Then I looked and what should it be but a goose sitting on some eggs. Went on through Christian town [Christiana] (Sat., 3 Aug. 1833)

Philadelphia Waterworks

and through Wilmington. A gentelman gave me some cakes and crakers. I went on and remain'd out all night.

At 2 o'clock P.M. (Sunday, 4 Aug. 1833) arived in the city. I made enquirey for some relations and old aquaintances but could get no intilligence. Supposing them to be dead, therefore I started (Mon., Aug. 5) to walk to Reading. On the g[o]ing out through Second Street, came into Cohockson [Cohocksink], joining Philadelphia.[12] Coming on a heavy shower of rain, I crossed the street towards a grocery. The gentalman standing in the dore desired me to come in. His name was Simon Bisel [Beisel].[13] He brought me a chair out side the bar. I sat down, and he enquiring where I came from, I inform'd him and related my case. He gave me some cracker and made me a stiff tumbler of brandy tody, he then considering on my situation and said it was two far for me to go to Reading and desired me to stop till I could settle my business, and gave me a good supper and lodging. His wife gave me a clean shirt and neck hankerchief and washed some shirts for me (6 Aug. 1833). I took a walk and walk along the Nothern Liberties and down the wharfs to the State Dock Yard, where the *Pennsylvania* then lay with a shed over hur. I never saw less shipping in the harbour than was at that time and but little work for labourers.

I rought a letter to Mr. Brice for my dockament and remain'd with Mr. Bisel for an answer from Canton. Mr. Athony Bilad and his father and mother then lived together in one house. I found out in a few day that both father and son were gunsmiths and a shop was within one dore of his own house. Therefore I assited him in grinding down turn screws and filing down worms, before they ware turned. If I see his wife and mother wanted water or wood, I woul[d] go and provide for them without askin. His sister lost hur husband while I remained there and came and lived with them. She had a fine girl about 8 years and his daughter was about 7 years, ware fond of me, but I am well ashured I had the affection of the whole three families that lived in one house.

Every Sunday Mr. Bisel would give me a quarter or half dollar and generally take a walk with me over to the water works, which is a great piece of work and a curosity. Mr. Bisel gave me a room and bed to myself and fared as they did. I felt happy while I was with them.

On the 19th (Sept. 1833) I received an answer from Mr. Brice that my dockament was gon to Washington. Mister Bisel then lent me seven dollars and I started on in the steam boat at 6 A.M. (23 Sept. 1833) for Washington and arived at New Castel and started in the steam cars [New Castle & Frenchtown R.R.] and went sixteen miles and a half in one hour.[14] Another boat being all ready at French Town, started for Baltimore and arived there at 3 o'clock (Sept. 24). I started for Washington, arived there on the 25 of Septem[be]r.

Mager Hook informd me, not [k]nowing what was become of me, he rought to Mr. Shorb and he got the dockament from Mr. Brice and sent it to him and he had got the pention ticket and sent it to Canton. I was then in a hobbel again. Being about noon, Mager Hook desired his secatary to take me home. I went with him and by the time we ware there, Major Hook was there on his poney, being wounded the last war. Dinner being ready, he introduced me to several officers that came to dine with him and we all sat down. After dinner the Major disered me to make his house my home as long as I thought fit to stay.

The Majer wish'd to send me in the stage, and every day the stage was so full that there was no room. At length I told him I woul[d] walk to Baltimore (5 Oct. 1833). He gave me a letter to the capt[ain] of the steam boat and another to Capt. Hook, his father, in Baltimore.[15] Arived in Baltimore (8

Baltimore

Oct. 1833) and went to Capt. Hook. He recev'd me very kindly and delivered the letter and wished me to remain all night, he being a Revolutioner as well as myself. After taking a glass with him, I told him I would go where the steam boat started from and see the capt[ain], as I had a letter for him, and if he did not start directly I would return. I went down and the boat was about starting. I gave the letter to the capt[ain]. When he read it over, he gave me a ticket, and w[h]en under way, I was standing on the forecastel, he came to me and we had a good deal of conversation till we ware broke off by some of the passengers.

I arived in Philadelphia (9 Oct. 1833), went to Mr. Bisels and inform'd him of my sircumstanc. I rougt to Mr. Brice and sent me ten dollars. Then I was in want of money to travel with, but Mr. Bisel said when I arived in Canton I could send it in a letter and that note was good but not very passible in Philadelphia, therefore he gave me other money in lew of it.

I left Mr. Bisel and famelies (5 Nov. 1833) for Reading. Coming to the kanel [canal], I went in a boat to Potsgrove and from thence to Reading, 10th. Left Reading, 15th, and arived in Harisburg 20th (Nov., 1833). Left

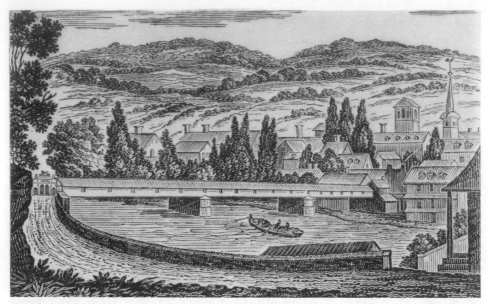

Reading, Pennsylvania

Harisburg December 17. Arived in Pitsburg the 28th. Went in the steamboat to Bever, arived at Beaver by a leven o'clock, and arived in Canton December 23 (1833) at Mr. Blacks, where I then boarded. Rec'd my money and rought a letter to Mr. Bisel with the money inclosed in the letter that I owed to him and rec'd an answer that he had receiv'd it and sent me word by righting he thougt I coul[d] do as well in Philadel[phi]a as any ware els and wished me to return, but circumstances does not purmit.

Left Canton (13 Oct. 1834) and arived in Perrysburg, October the 25. Remained there righting in the clarks office with my nephew, John Webb, Esqr., when I went to see my sister, Sally Webb. Left Perrysburg (27 Oct. 1837) and arived in Cleaveland that night, 30th. Arived in Canton on November 5 at 10 A.M. Departed from Geo. Webb, Esqr., and his family for Shanesvill[e]. Went through Bethleham, stop'd at Narr [?], Mr. John Yank, on the kanel. November the 6 (1837), went on to Sugar Creek, from thence to Shanesvill[e] and found my sister was gone to W. Dover.

Nov'r 7, went Vensburg, from thence to Mount Eton. Novemb'r 8 went on for Dover. Arived there and found my sister, Mr. Geor[g]e Cake, and Mr. Crofford that is maried to one of hur daughters. Rem[aine]d about a week and started 15 of Nov'r. 17th, arived at Cleaveland. Went on b[oar]d a schooner for Maumee, Nov'r 24. Went on shore at Manhattan, walk'd to

Perrysburg, Ohio

Toledo, and from thence to Perrysburg in the *Sun,* steam boat, and remained there in the office with Mr. John Webb till left Perrysburg (5 June 1839) in the *Newberry* for Cleaveland. On the 6 of June went on shore. The 7th, at 8 A.M., went through the locks at Cleaveland. The same day went through 21 locks at Acron [Akron].[16] Arived in Maslin [Massillon] Sunday, 9th, came to Canton 10, remain'd the 11, rem[aine]d, then went to Maslin and Dover Thursd[a]y, 12. In Dover, Monday, 17, went with my sister to Mr. Pancost. Thursday, 20, return'd to Dover with Mr. Pancost.

The 22 I started for Maslin. Stoped at Brookfield (23 June 1839), from thence to Maslin and to Canton. Remained till Saturday 29th. Came with George Webb to Maslin, from thence to Bollevor [Bolivar], then in the *Ruby,* 2d July, about 80 miles to Bradford, County Muskingum, where I was taken very sick. Went on shore at the Ohio Inn. The 4th they came for me from Dreston [Dresden]. 5, I return'd for my clothes. Sat'y, 6th the musiconer sent me to the steam boat for Sensvill [Zanesville] and paid my charges at Mr. Sellers hotel.[17] Sund'y, 7, went to Sensville [Zanesville]. Put up at the Sign of the Perry. Mon'y, July 8, left Sensvill, had to lay on the road. At day light reach'd the three mile tavern. Went on but so weak I had to sit down every five or six hundred yards. I got to Adams Ville (10 July 1839) and remained at Mr. Brothers, Salam Township, Ohio, Muskingum. Remained five days

Canton, Ohio

sick. Went on (July 16) and crossed Tuscarawa[s] River to Evensburge on the kenel. I stop'd at Docter George Day and Sampson K. White, Sign of the Washington. Being sick, there wives were very kind to me and charged very little. The kenel being broke, had to remain three day. This village is in Coshockson [Coshocton] County. The line lays near Adams Mills. At length the boat came and arived at Bethlehem (19 July 1839).

In the evening I started for Canton. Coming on dark and I raped [wrapped] myself in my cloke till morning. In the evening (July 20) I came to Mr. Stigers, Esq'r. He sent me in his light waggon to town to Mr. Jacob Hantzell. On the 27 (July, 1839) agraed to board with Mr. Hantzells, where my abode is at this present time, July 22d, 1840.

I wish to Let the publick no that this is only a Sketch of my life, as I Cannot go through with the whole Particulars of my Life in all Circumstances, but my Travels has been for Sixty four Years and I was born in the Year One thousand Seven hundred and Sixty one, which Makes me now Seventy Nine Years Old.

1837

Aug 6 went through Bethlehem Stop'd at Near Mr John Gants on the Kanul November
we went on to Sugar Creek from thence to Shanesville & found my Sister was gone to
to Dover Nov'r 7 went Oensburg from thence to Mount Eton, Novemb 8 went on for Town
Arived there and found my Sister Mr Geore Cake & Mr Crofford that is maried to one of his
Daughters Rem'd about a week & Sarted 13 of Nov 17th Arived at Cleaveland went on B'a

24 Schoner for Maumee Nov'd 24 went on Shore at Manhattan walk'd to Toledo & from thence
to Perrysburg in the Sun Steam Boat & Remained there in the Office with Mr John Webb

1839
June the Left Perrysburg on the Newberry for Cleaveland on the L of June went on Shore the
7 7th at 8 A.M. went through the Locks at Cleaveland the Same day went through 21 Locks
at Acron Arived in Maslin Sunday 9th Came to Canton to Remain this 11 Rem'd then
went to Maslin & Dover Thursd 12 in Dover Monday 17 went with my Sister to Mr Pancost Thursday 20 Returnd to Dover with Mr Pancost the 22 I Started for Maslin Stopd

23 at Brookfield from thence to Maslin & to Canton Remained till Saturday 29 Came with
July George webb to Maslin from thence to Bellevor then in the Riely 2d July about 80 miles to
1 Bradford County Muskingum where I was taken Very Sick went on Shore at the Ohio
4 Inn, the 4 the Came for my from Driston & I Returnd for my Clothes Sat'd the Musiconer
Sent me to the Steam Boat for Sensville ~~in the it~~ & paid my Charges at Mr Sellers
7 hotel Sund'y went to Sensville put up at the Sign of the Perry Mon July & Left Sensville
8 had to Say on the Road at Day Light Reach'd the three mile Tavern went on but So weak
July I had to Sit down Every five or six hundred Yards I got to Adams Ville & Remained at
10 Mr Brothers Salam Township Ohio Muskingum Remained five Days Sick
16 went in and Crofsed Tuscarawa River to Coinsburg on the Kanul I Stop at Docter George
Cay & Sampson It white Sign of the Washington being Sick there wives were very kind to me
& Charged Very Little the Kanul being Broke had to Remain three Day this Village is in
Coshocton County the Line lays near Adams Mills at length the Boat Came & arived

19 at Bethlehem in the Evening I Started for Canton Coming on Dark & I Raped myself in
20 my Cloke till Morning in the Evening I Came to Mr Stigers Esqr he Sent me in his Light
27 Waggon to Town So Mr Jacob Hantzele on the 27 agraed to Board with Mr Hantzele
where my abode is at this Present Time July 22 - 1840 -

      I wish to Let the Publick no that this is only a Sketch of my life as I cannot
go through with the whole Particulars of my Life in all Circumstances but my travels
has been for Sixty four Years & I was born in the Year one thousand Seven hundred &
Sixty one which Makes me now Seventy Nine Years old

Appendices

Three other biographical sources about Jacob Nagle exist: his 1833 application for a Revolutionary War pension, and two obituary notices, the first of which appeared in the *Stark County Democrat* (Canton, Ohio) on 20 February 1841, and the second in the Cincinnati *Advertiser and Journal* for 25 February 1841.

Jacob Nagle dictated and signed his pension application on 22 April 1833 while he resided in Canton. As we know from his journal, he would have to wait for months before the bureaucratic red tape was unwound and he finally received his annual payment of $32.46, but it is possible that the process of providing this short sketch of his military career inspired him to commit the longer record of his life to paper. The information in the pension narrative is essentially in agreement with the journal in both fact and error. In both he greatly exaggerates the duration of his imprisonment at Basseterre, St. Christopher, and slightly exaggerates the length of his service on HMS *Prudent* before being assigned to the *St. Lucia*. He also shaded the truth and glossed over the facts in describing how he had gotten into the British service.

The two obituary notices are brief but valuable insights into his personality and the only record we have of his last months, death, and funeral. The Cincinnati writer gives us a wonderfully personal picture of Nagle in his last years, sitting by the fire until late in the evening, captivating his audience with the tales of his adventuresome life. The Canton obituary notice provides reassuring confirmation that his passing was not unnoticed.

On a cold Saturday morning, 13 February 1841, Jacob Nagle attended the funeral of his sister, Sarah Webb. In the emotion of the moment, he expressed a wish that he soon join her. He took sick that evening and died four days later, on 17 February 1841. The town turned out in force for the funeral on the eighteenth, and with full honors provided by Captain Weber's company of German Guards and the music of the German Brass Band, Nagle's earthly remains were consigned to the grave. He would have greatly approved of the whole proceeding. There is little doubt but that his body now rests at the Plumb Street Cemetery, in the Webb Family Plot, in Canton, Ohio.

APPENDIX 1

The State of Ohio
 Stark County

       Court of Common Pleas April Term 1833. On the twenty second day of April: personally appeared in open Court before the Judges of the common Pleas of Stark County Ohio, now sitting: Jacob Nagle a resident of said County of Stark, aged seventy-one years, the fifteenth day of September last who being duly Sworn according to Law, doth depose, and on his oath make the following declaration, in order to obtain the benefit of the provisions made by the act of Congress, passed June Seventh Eighteen hundred and thirty-two.

  That he this deponent entered the service of the United States, at the same time the British landed at the head of Elk, to march to Philadelphia, in the year seventeen hundred and seventy-seven, as a volunteer, but for no specified time; he this deponent served by land Eight months, in the grand Park Pennsylvania line, under the Command of Col' Thomas Procter: The four first months service under Adjutant Hofner; the last four months this deponent was in service on land was under Capt' Jones: the other Officers with whom this deponent Messed, while in service on land, were Capt' Frank Procter, Capt' Samuel Procter, Capt' Courtney, and Capt' Patterson. The first Battle this deponent was in on land was the Battle of Brandywine at Shads Ford under the Command of Adjutant Hofner: An other Battle was commenced at Schuilkil But was not Continued in consequence of what was called the three day's rain. Two days before the Battle of German-Town, this deponent had leave to go home to Reading: in consequence of which he this deponent was not in that

Battle; this deponent remained two weeks in Reading and then returned to the Army, which were then lying back of chesnut-Hill: this deponent was in several Skirmishes under Capt' Jones, how many this deponent does not recollect: one of the Skirmishes, was at White-Marsh.

And when the army went to winter quarters, this deponent went to Reading; and in the winter he, this deponent returned to Valley Forge where the army, then lay to see his father who commanded the tenth Pennsylvania Regiment, and soon after, the British left Philidelphia for New-York, he, this deponent went to sea, part of the time with the Navy, and part of the time as a privateer, in all two years eight months one week and four days to wit: the first six weeks was in the Saratoga, a Naval ship of twenty Guns. Commanded by Capt' Young, the Second cruise was in the Fair-American, a Privateer of sixteen Guns, four months cruise, two actual engagements, one with the Kings Packet, of eighteen Guns, fourteen Sixes, and four Eighteens: the second Engagement, was with a Scotch Ship of twenty-six Guns—two engagements; while on board the Rising Sun, this was the third cruise, one of the engagement was with a privateer of sixteen Guns, the other a Kings Store-Ship of twenty six Guns: the fair-American, was Commanded by Capt' Decatur the Rising Sun was commanded by Capt' Young: this Deponent had two cruises in the Rising Sun one six weeks cruise, the second was a four months cruise, each cruise was commanded by Capt' Youngs, the fifth Cruise was in the Trojan, a Privateer & Copper bottom Ship of Sixteen Guns, Commanded by Capt' Fanning; he, this deponent says, after eleven days cruise in the Trogan, Commanded by Capt' Fanning they were taken prisoners of war, by the Royal Oak Seventy four gun Ship, & the Lenymph frigate rated a thirty two Gun Ship. This deponent says he was taken to the west Indies imprisoned in Bastar on the Island of St' Christopher, and remained a prisoner of war twenty month (20 Month). The French then took the Island, and this deponent was set at liberty, he this deponent says as he was going from the Island on which he was imprisoned to Martinico in a Schooner, he was taken on board the prudent, a British Sixty four Gun Ship, and in three weeks was drafted on board the St' Lucia, brig of war, remained one year aboard of her, she being sent to Antigua, an English harbour, he this deponent was drafted on board the Ardent, a Sixty four Gun Ship, and taken to England, and there discharged: tho it was then peace, having no protection, was pressed at several different times; and sailed twenty four years, in different parts of the globe: This deponent then arrived at Norfolk, from thence to Philadelphia: this deponents parents being dead, he went to Sea again; sailed twenty years, returned to Baltimore on the sixteenth day of July 1824, which was the last of this deponents seafaring: from thence this deponent went to Maryland, Washington County, and remained two years, and from thence, to Canton, Stark County, Ohio, where this deponent now resides.

This deponent further says he is not acquainted with any Clergyman who can certify as to his belief respecting his age and the general belief in his neighborhood relative to his revolutionary services; this deponent further says he knows of no persons now living who can testify as to his entering the service, nor of his service in the army—this Deponent further says he has no certificate of discharge, or any Record of discharge, he, this deponent being taken a prisoner of war, he had no regular discharge.

I do hereby relinquish every claim whatever to a pension or annuity except the present, and declare that my name is not on the pension roll of the agency of any State.

Sworn to and subscribed the day and year aforesaid,

Jacob Nagle

1ˢᵗ Where and in what year were you born?

I was born in Reading, Pennsylvania in the year seventeen hundred and Sixty One, on the fifteen day of september

2ᵈ Have you any Record of your age, and if so where is it?

I know of no record of my age, except the record of the church in which I was Christened, in Berks County, in Pennsylvania, in a place called the swamp eighteen Miles from Reading in the Presbyterian church; I have not, with me any Copy of it. My name was also recorded in my fathers Bible, But I know not what has become of it.

3ᵈ Where were you living when called into Service, where have you lived since the Revolutionary war, and where do you now live?

I was living in Berks County a place called Reading, Pennsylvania, when I entered the service, I have been forty eight years at Sea, two years near Hagers-Town, Maryland: from thence to Stark County, Ohio where I have Resided ever since.

4ᵗʰ How were you Called into service: were you drafted, did you volunteer, or were you a substitute, and if a substitute, for whome?

I volunteered as above stated, by my father's request but was a substitute for no person.

5ᵗʰ State the name of some of the regular officers who were with the Troops or aboard of the Navy, when you served: such continental and militia Regiments as you can reculect, and the general circumstances of your Service.

I reculect Col' Thomas Procter, Capt' Frank Procter, Capt' Samuel Procter, Capt' Courtney, Capt Patterson, Capt Jones and Adjutant Hofner, these were the officers in the Regiment in which I served on land. Capt' Decature father of Stephen Decature, Capt Young, and Capt' Fanning, were the officers of the Navy under which I served. I cannot reculect any other regiments except the one in which I se[r]ved.

6ᵗʰ Did you ever receive a discharge from the service, and if so by whom was it given and what has become of it?

I never received a discharge, being taken prisoner before the war ended.

7ᵗʰ State the names of some of the persons to whom you are acquainted or known in your present neighborhood, and who can testify as to your character for veracity, and their belief of your services as a soldier in the revolution.

George Dunbar Esqr. George N. Cake, George N. Webb, and Thomas L. Webb, are persons who can testify as to my Character and veracity, and their belief of my services as a soldier in the revolution

Jacob Nagle

Mr. George Dunbar, George N. Cake, George N. Webb, and Thomas L. Webb, all of Canton, Stark County, Ohio, do hereby certify that we are well acquainted with Jacob Nagle who has Subscribed and Sworn to the above declaration; that we believe him to be a man of veracity: that he is reputed and believed, in the neighborhood where he resides, to have been a soldier of the revolution; and that we concur in that opinion.

Sworn and Subscribed, the day and year aforesaid   Geo. Dunbar
                                                         G.H. Cake
                                                         Geo. N. Webb

And the said Court do hereby declare their opinion, after the investigation of the matter and after putting the interogatories prescribed by the war department that the above named applicant was a revolutionary soldier, and served as he States: and the Court further certifies, that it appears to them, that George Dunbar, George H. Cake, George N. Webb, and Thomas L. Webb, who have signed the preceding certificate, are residents of the county, Town and State aforesaid, and are credible persons, and that their Statements are entitled to credit.

State of Ohio Stark County SS

I John Myers Clerk of the Court of Common Pleas of said County of Stark do hereby certify that the papers here attached are the original papers of the examination of the said Jacob Nagle as sworn to by the said Nagle in said Court of Common Pleas on the 22 day of April AD 1833

In testimony whereof I hereunto set my hand and affix the seal of said Court at Canton the 9th day of September 1833

Jn.º Myers Clerk

APPENDIX 2

Stark County Democrat, Canton, Ohio. Saturday, 20 February 1841

ANOTHER REVOLUTIONARY SOLDIER GONE.

DIED—On Wednesday morning last, the 17th inst. Mr. Jacob Nagle, in the eightieth year of his age. Mr. Nagle was a soldier of the Revolution, and did his first service at the celebrated battle of the Brandywine, in that war, when he was not yet seventeen years of age. He afterwards entered the naval service, and was a sailor fifty years of his life, during a great portion of which time he was in foreign countries. He died, like most of that band of brave and unconquerable heroes who perilled all for the liberty we enjoy, POOR, AND DESTITUTE OF THE COMFORTS OF LIFE,—the only reward his country ever bestowed upon him was a miscalled pension of THIRTY DOLLARS a year. He was ill but four days, and retained his senses to the last.—On Saturday he attended the funeral of his sister Mrs. Webb at which time he expressed a wish that his might be the next.

His remains were interred in Canton, on the 18th with military honors by Captain Weber's company of German Guards, accompanied by the German Brass Band, and a numerous concourse of Citizens, who respected the honesty, and patriotism of the old sea beaten veteran. We are requested to offer the thanks of the surviving relatives of the deceased, to the military and to the public, for the sympathy which was manifested, for them, in their affliction.

Advertiser and Journal. Cincinnati, Ohio. Thursday, 25 February 1841

ANOTHER REVOLUTIONARY SOLDIER GONE!

Died, on Wednesday morning, the 17th inst. at Canton, Stark county, Ohio, Mr. JACOB NAGLE, in the 80th year of his age. Mr. Nagle was a Penn[s]ylvanian by birth, and entered the army before he was seventeen, and was in the battle of Brandywine. He served for some time in the army with great credit to himself, and afterwards entered the American navy. He was subsequently pressed into the British sea service, where he remained upwards of forty years. During the continuance of the memorable contests between England and the combined fleets of France and Spain, Mr. Nagle was in active service, and distinguished himself for his resolute bravery, in several of the great naval battles between those powers. He was in the expedition which made the early settlements in New South Wales, and was an active participator in the capture of the celebrated chief Bennelong. Of the utmost simplicity in his manners, he was nevertheless of undaunted courage. The writer of this article knew him well. Many an hour have we listened to him, recounting the privations he underwent in the continental army, and the perils he encountered upon the waves. Peace be to his ashes! Never did the earth cover the remains of a more honest man than Jacob Nagle. "He died like most of that band of brave and unconquerable heroes, who periled all for the liberty we enjoy:—POOR, AND DESTITUTE OF THE COMFORTS OF LIFE, the only reward his country ever bestowed upon him, was a miscalled pension of *thirty dollars* a year." The soldiers' "farewell shot" echoed over the last resting place of the old sea-beaten veteran, and he reposes from all his toils and privations with the love of all who knew him.

Notes

In preparing the Jacob Nagle journal for publication, the editor devoted much of five years comparing the manuscript with contemporary source material documenting the events the author witnessed or in which he participated. All of the tendencies of academic training tempt the scholar to employ footnotes to document the thoroughness of his work, to show how much he knows about the subject, and to expose to the unappreciative public eye every other source, contemporary or scholarly, touching upon the persons, places, and events recorded.

Hearkening to the same restraining impulse that convinced the editor to avoid the use of footnotes at the bottom of the page, he has attempted to provide notes in the following section only where additional information might be of interest to some readers, and where it serves to explain or identify something Nagle did not fully describe or did not himself know, or where he is wrong.

CHAPTER 1

1. Nagle's story of the pretended loss of dispatches from Washington is a little confusing. Presumably Mrs. Nagle sent a messenger who caught up with Jack Biddle and the other officers, asking that he take Jacob to the front. Biddle then made up an excuse to go back and get him.

   Jack, or John, Biddle (b. 1736) was a son of William and Mary Scull Biddle and brother of Edward Biddle (1739–1799), member of Continental Congress and

Reading lawyer who had greatly furthered Nagle's father's career. Another brother, Nicholas Biddle (1750–1799), had been a midshipman and lieutenant in the Royal Navy before the war and a messmate of young Horatio Nelson on the Phipps Arctic expedition. Nicholas left the British Navy when the war began and was one of the most successful and promising officers in the Continental navy until he was killed in action.

John Biddle had apparently served with the British forces during the French and Indian War. When the Revolution began, he was appointed commissary for Colonel William Thompson's battalion of riflemen, in which Nagle's father served as captain of the company from Reading. With the reorganization of forces in 1776, he was appointed assistant commissary general in the Continental army.

As the primary theater of conflict shifted to the Philadelphia area, Pennsylvania became increasingly polarized. The legislature instituted a loyalty oath, began confiscating Tory property, and deported a number of nonbelligerent Quakers from the state. In both civilian life and within the ranks of the army, men began questioning the loyalty of others, and shortly after John Biddle conducted Jacob Nagle to the army, he, Richard Peters, and Colonel Robert L. Hooper were accused of favoring Tories rather than Whigs when commandeering wagons for transporting supplies. Biddle may or may not have been guilty, but he undoubtedly resented the charges.

In February 1778 Biddle deserted to the British, taking with him a detailed map of the American encampment at Valley Forge, which he presented to the British. Biddle was rewarded with commissions as lieutenant in the West Jersey Volunteers, later the Guides and Pioneers, and at the end of the war, in 1783, he petitioned General Carleton to appoint him as a surveyor in Nova Scotia. *Pennsylvania Magazine of History and Biography,* Vol. 5 (1881), 93–94; Vol. 36 (1912), 71–72; John C. Fitzpatrick, ed., *The Writings of George Washington,* Vol. 10 (Washington, 1931–44), 497–98; John Blair Linn and William H. Egle, eds., *Pennsylvania in the War of the Revolution,* Vol. 1 (Harrisburg, Pa., 1880), 14; Henry Young Index of Loyalist Officers, Clements Library; "Nicholas Biddle," in *Appleton's Cyclopaedia of American Biography,* Vol. 1, eds. James Grant Wilson and John Fiske (New York, 1888), 256–57.

2. Proctor's artillery was placed on a hill on the east side of present Route 100, about a half mile north of Route 1, slightly beyond the Chad House.

3. Fortunately for the eighteenth-century soldiers who consumed this original form of "gunpowder tea" in order to strengthen their courage before battle, the ingredients of black powder are not particularly toxic.

4. Washington's army retreated from the Brandywine battlefield on the evening of 11 September 1777, eastward to Chester, Pennsylvania, roughly following present-day Routes 1 and 322.

5. Yellow Springs, twenty-five miles northwest of Philadelphia, had become a health resort before the Revolution and served after the Battle of the Brandywine until the end of the war as a hospital. J. Smith Futhey and Gilbert Cope, *History of Chester County, Pennsylvania* (Philadelphia, 1881), 202.

6. On 17 October 1777, Washington sent Anthony Wayne with a body of Pennsylvania and Virginia troops to annoy and confuse the British. They built large fires near Whitemarsh and returned to camp. John F. Reed, *Campaign to Valley Forge* (Philadelphia, 1965), 262.

7. The American army in the vicinity of Philadelphia celebrated the surrender of Burgoyne on October 20. Edward H. Tatum, Jr., ed., *The American Journal of Ambrose Serle* (San Marino, Cal., 1940), 260.

8. George Nagle wrote General Washington from Chestnut Hill on 3 March 1778, describing his nightly patrols. He indicated that he had cut the lines of communica-

tion on the Germantown and Ridge roads and expected to patrol the York and Frankfort roads that evening and "interrupt a few Butchers that I am told is to drive in Cattle this Evening or to Morrow Morning." Washington Papers Microfilm, Reel 47.

9. The British army, under its new commander, Sir Henry Clinton, evacuated Philadelphia on 18 June 1778. They encountered the American army at the Battle of Monmouth on June 28, then marched on to Sandy Point, where they embarked on British ships for New York City.

CHAPTER 2

1. USS *Saratoga,* a 16-gun sloop with a complement of 86 men, was built by Wharton & Humphreys of Philadelphia. Construction began in December 1779, and the ship was launched on 10 April 1780. Under the command of Captain John Young, she sailed on 13 August 1780, and in her short career made a number of captures. In March 1781, sailing in a convoy of American and French vessels out of Cap François, the ship was caught in a gale and vanished without a trace, with the loss of its entire crew. Naval History Division, Department of the Navy, *Dictionary of American Naval Fighting Ships,* Vol. 6 (Washington, D.C., 1976), 334–36.

2. Stephen Decatur (1751–1808), son of a Protestant French émigré to Rhode Island, was a merchant captain in Philadelphia before the Revolution and a privateering captain during the undeclared war with France in 1798–1801.

    His son, Stephen Decatur (1779–1820), achieved a heroic reputation for his actions against the Barbary pirates in the first two decades of the nineteenth century. He was killed in a duel with Captain James Barron in 1820. His Washington home, "Decatur House," remains a landmark. *Appleton's Cyclopaedia of American Biography,* Vol. 2 (New York, 1888), 120–22.

3. Cape May, New Jersey, is at the head of Delaware Bay, on the north, opposite Cape Henlopen on the south. The lighthouses on both points served as important landmarks for mariners. Because of its proximity to Philadelphia, Cape May, in the colonial period, became, along with Newport, Rhode Island, one of the first popular seaside resorts in the United States.

4. According to the newspaper notice of the arrival of the *Mercury* packet as a prize to the *Fair American, Holker,* and *Enterprize,* the passengers included: Capt. Campbell of the 44th Regt.; Capt. Mure, 82nd Regt.; Capt. Lyman, Prince of Wales Regt.; Capt. Murray, Wentworth's Dragoons; Capt. Wallop, Knyphausen's Regt.; Mrs. Griffiths, Mrs. Anderson, and three servants. *Pennsylvania Packet, Or, The General Advertiser,* 15 August 1780. To this list, *The Pennsylvania Gazette and Weekly Advertiser,* 16 August 1780, added Capt. Landen of a letter of marque.

5. The *Richmond,* Capt. Jameson, from Glasgow, according to the newspaper, mounted 2 nine-pounders, 8 six-pounders, and shipped a crew of thirty-four. Captain Jameson's account of the engagement between the *Fair American, Holker,* and *Richmond* was published in the *New York Gazette* for 4 December 1780: "A smart Engagement ensued, and the Richmond beat them off with the Loss of one Man killed and three wounded. They attacked her again the next Morning, and after a close Action of an Hour and twenty Minutes, were obliged to sheer off, after having received very material Damage. The same Day, at half past 11 o'Clock, the Rebels made the third Attack, and after a severe Engagement of Three Quarters of an Hour, obliged the Richmond to strike." William Bell Clark, "That Mischievous Holker,
The Story of a Privateer," *Pennsylvania Magazine of History and Biography,* Vol. 79 (1955), 47.

6. USS *Confederacy,* a 36-gun frigate with a crew complement of 260 men, was launched at Norwich, Connecticut, and fitted out at New London in early 1779. It

then cruised to Philadelphia with USS *Deane*, where both ships and USS *Trumbull* lay for considerable periods in 1780 and early 1781, all of them pressing men and making it difficult for privateers to bring prizes into port without losing their crews. The *Confederacy* was captured in 1781 while returning from the West Indies by HMS *Roebuck* and HMS *Orpheus*. *Dictionary of American Naval Fighting Ships*, Vol. 2 (1963), 161; Clark, "That Mischievous Holker," 44.

7. The two crewmen who had turned the *Richmond* over to the British in Charleston were tried by the vice admiralty court in Philadelphia on 23 April 1781. Nicholas Coleman was acquitted. Thomas Wilkinson was convicted and sentenced to death. *The Freeman's Journal* (Philadelphia), 11 November 1780; Clark, "That Mischievous Holker," 47–48.

8. The *Jay*, 12 guns and a complement of 70 men, William Havens, master, was bonded on 1 February 1781, and undoubtedly sailed from Philadelphia shortly thereafter. Continental Congress Papers Microfilm, Reel 203.

9. The brigantine *Tristram Shandy*, 100 tons burden, Captain Brice, had been taken at sea on a voyage from Tenerife to Philadelphia by HMS *Orpheus* and retaken by the *Rising Sun*, Captain Samuel Cassin. The notice of sale enumerated the cargo as Tenerife wine, salt, seven casks of raisins, and a cask of almonds. *Pennsylvania Packet* (Philadelphia), 21 July 1781 and 28 July 1781.

10. Nagle provides interesting commentary and documentation on the very real and dangerous presence of Loyalist "pirates" in Delaware Bay, even after the British had evacuated Philadelphia. The inhabitants of southern Delaware and the coastal areas of Maryland and southern New Jersey included a sizable percentage of Loyalist Episcopalians, Quakers, and Methodists. The many tidal creeks provided safe hiding places for small armed vessels, known to local inhabitants, but impenetrable for large ships and strangers who were not familiar with the waters. The area remained dangerous for small vessels and undermanned prizes until the war ended and the presence of the Royal Navy was eliminated.

11. John Goodrich had been a wealthy merchant in Portsmouth, Virginia, before the war. Captured while on a British expedition to take supplies off the Carolina coast and imprisoned for two years, he escaped to New York, where he and a son fitted out privateers that were responsible for taking several hundred American merchant vessels. When the British evacuated New York, he removed to London, where he was granted a pension and where he died in 1784. Peter Wilson Coldham, *American Loyalist Claims*, Vol. 1 (Washington, D.C.: National Genealogical Society, 1980), 189–90.

12. The sort of "off-the-record" sale of smuggled cargo recorded here by Nagle was obviously so widespread that one comes to suspect that existing records of captured ships and their cargoes to be found in vice admiralty court proceedings and newspapers represent but a modest percentage of the totals. The magnitude of illicit profits could never be documented, but it was very considerable.

13. It is probable that Nagle's memory as to the number of prizes taken by the *Rising Sun* was faulty. It would seem to be an unlikely coincidence that it had taken twenty-one ships, exactly the same number as he records for the *Fair American*.

14. Wallops Island, consisting of approximately 1,500 acres, is on the eastern coast of Accomack County, on the Eastern Shore of Virginia. There were never more than two or three houses on the island in the eighteenth century. In the late nineteenth century, it became a fishing and hunting club, and during World War II it was taken over by the Federal government as a naval ordnance station and later a launching site for satellites.

15. Nagle's geographical location of the "Old Torie," somewhere between Snow Hill, Maryland, and Lewes, Delaware, is too broad to identify him, although it was an area where British sympathizers were numerous. The plantation he describes, with

a collection of outbuildings, a large home with a porch and a central hall running from front to back of the building, was typical of the larger homes of the area, with the one exception that there are no stone houses of eighteenth-century date in the area—it was probably red brick or wood, painted to look like stone.

16. John Paul Jones, his reputation already fully earned in action in European waters and the court of France, returned to America and was in Philadelphia between February and August 1781. He was treated as a hero, and with some of his crewmen from the *Ariel* staying at Nagle's father's tavern, Jacob undoubtedly became caught up in the excitement of his exploits. It is possible that some of his fellow crewmen on the *Trojan* were former sailors who had served under Jones. Samuel Eliot Morison, *John Paul Jones* (Boston, 1959), 309–18.

17. While the exact design of the American flag was in a constant state of change during the American Revolution, thirteen stripes had begun appearing on flags even before the war, representing the unity of thirteen separate colonies, and had emerged as the device most commonly used by 1781, when Nagle reports that the *Trojan*, on November 23, "hoisted our thirteen stripes and hall'd them down again." For the authoritative study of the evolution of the flag, see Harold D. Langley, *So Proudly We Hail: The History of the United States Flag* (Washington D.C.: Smithsonian Institution Press, 1981).

CHAPTER 3

1. Isaac Coffin (1759–1839) entered HMS *Royal Oak* as sixth lieutenant on 20 February 1781 and was reassigned to HMS *London* on 17 August 1781. He therefore was officially a supernumerary at the time Nagle and his fellow crewmen were captured. HMS *Royal Oak*, Pay Register, ADM/34/559, Public Record Office (hereafter PRO). For biographical information on Coffin, see Robert P. Tristram Coffin, *Sir Isaac Coffin, Bart. (1759–1839), Admiral and Prophet*, The Newcomen Society in North America (New York, 1951); "Biographical Memoir of Sir Isaac Coffin, Bart.," *The Naval Chronicle*, Vol. 12 (1804), 1–12; Allen Johnson and Dumas Malone, eds., *Dictionary of American Biography* (New York, 1943), 1–12.

2. The names of the crew of the *Trojan* as entered in the muster book of HMS *Royal Oak*, in addition to "Jacob Noggle," were Edward Donnelly, David Simson, John Carr, John Alexander, Timothy Osgood, James Richison, Moses Beard, William Thomas, Thomas Brown, William Rigeons, John Quigg, William Gibson, Stephen Suel [probably Sewall], Michael Shehan, John Fanon [*sic*, Fanning, Captain], William Hebron, William Berryman. Because a number of these men were former British sailors, some of them probably were using false names. HMS *Royal Oak*, Muster Book, ADM/36/9524, PRO.

3. HMS *La Nymphe*, on 24 November 1781 boarded a "brig from Guadaloupe to Salem, James Bare, Master," and exchanged prisoners with them. HMS *La Nymphe*, Master's Log, ADM/52/2427, PRO.

4. The French recaptured St. Eustatius from the British on November 25, little more than a week before the *Royal Oak* and *La Nymphe* arrived. In such a situation, it would be several months before incoming ships from the North American mainland or Europe would be aware of the change, making it potentially profitable to lure ships into port by flying the enemy flag.

5. Presumably HMS *Russell*, which was stationed in the West Indies during the period Nagle was there.

6. The objective of the French fleet was actually Barbados, not Jamaica. William Laird Clowes, *The Royal Navy*, Vol. 3 (London, 1898), 510.

7. William Rigeons, fellow sailor with Nagle on the *Trojan* and the French vessel owned by de Boullé, fellow prisoner of both the British at St. Kitts and the French at Martinique, was not among the men drafted on the *Prudent* and the *St. Lucia*.

8. The Battle of Frigate Bay of 25–26 January 1782, which Nagle witnessed from shore, was a brilliant tactical victory for Admiral Hood over de Grasse, but it had no effect in raising the siege of Brimstone Hill. The British were forced to surrender the outpost on 13 February 1782. Clowes, *The Royal Navy,* Vol. 3, 510–18.

9. The *Holker,* the privateer with which the *Fair American* had so profitably cruised in 1781, embarked on a six month cruise in November 1781 to the West Indies and took 14 prizes. St. Pierre, Martinique, and Guadeloupe were the vessel's normal bases of supply. Clark, "That Mischievous Holker," 54–59.

10. "Jack" is presumably short for "Jack Tar."

11. Alice B. Gomme in *The Traditional Games of England, Scotland, and Ireland,* Vol. 1 (New York, 1964), 84–85, describes a game called "cudgel," somewhat like cricket and "cat and dog." Players used sticks and guarded holes at which a piece of wood was pitched.

12. According to the logs, muster books, and pay registers of HMS *Prudent* and HMS *St. Lucia,* cartels of exchanged prisoners from Martinique arrived at Gros Islet Bay, St. Lucia, on 14, 20, and 21 May 1782. Nagle was apparently in the second group, as he was entered on the muster roll of the *St. Lucia* as of May 20, although he actually reported for duty on May 26. It appears that rather than three weeks, as he remembered it, he spent only five or six days on HMS *Prudent.* HMS *Prudent,* Lieutenant's Log, ADM/L/P/449, National Maritime Museum, Greenwich (hereafter NMM); HMS *Prudent,* Pay Register, ADM/34/608, PRO; HMS *St. Lucia,* Muster Book, ADM/36/8890, PRO.

13. In addition to Captain Samuel Brooking, the primary officers on the *St. Lucia* with whom Nagle had frequent contacts were George Douglass, boatswain, and James Parry, purser. HMS *St. Lucia,* Pay Register, ADM/34/472, PRO.

14. Luke Avre volunteered on 26 June 1782 and was appointed quartermaster. He "ran" on 25 August 1782 at St. Lucia. HMS *St. Lucia,* Pay Register, ADM/34/472, PRO.

15. Nagle's memory here is faulty. Captain Barkley's log on HMS *Prudent* notes that he got word of Rodney's victory at the Battle of the Saints on 24 April 1782, almost a month before Nagle came on board. Rodney participated in no engagements with the French after that battle and was relieved of command in July 1782, at the fall of Lord North's ministry. HMS *Prudent,* Captain's Log, ADM/51/748, PRO; Clowes, *The Royal Navy,* Vol. 3, 536–37.

16. The "Kenash" of Nagle's journal, spelled in a variety of ways in contemporary sources, was the Carenage, an inlet with a harbor that had presumably been used at some point in the past to carene ships (laying them on their side largely out of water to clean and repair their hulls).

17. James Nuttall had been impressed on board the *St. Lucia* on 1 June 1782. He deserted on July 8 but was brought back to the ship at the end of August and returned to duty on 4 September 1782. Nagle's account of the captain's leniency would seem to be accurate, as Nuttall was not entered on the list of men who had "run" in the captain's muster reports. As with Nagle, Nuttall was later drafted on HMS *Ardent* for the trip back to England after the war. HMS *St. Lucia,* Pay Register, ADM/34/472, and Muster Book, ADM/36/8890, PRO.

18. Territorial and personnel changes occurred so rapidly in the West Indies in 1782 that documentation in the Admiralty records of minor incidents is uneven. The log of the *St. Lucia* gives no clear indication that the action described by Nagle, where a number of French merchant vessels were captured, actually took place, but a letter of Admiral Pigot to the secretary of the Admiralty of 13 December 1782, enclosing an enumeration of prizes taken between July 20 and December 11, lists four vessels (*La Fortune, Les Deux Frères, L'Hereux, St. Jacques*) taken in August from a convoy sailing to Martinique. The capturing vessels are listed as the *Leander, St. Lucia, Gros*

Islet, and *Regulator* privateer. Admiral Hugh Pigot to Philip Stevens, ALS., 13 December 1782, in Admirals' Correspondence, ADM/1/313, PRO.

19. James Dundass succeeded Samuel Brooking as commander of HMS *St. Lucia* on 22 October 1782 and served until the ship was decommissioned on 23 April 1783. HMS *St. Lucia,* Captain's Log, ADM/51/964, and Pay Book, ADM/34/472, PRO.

20. HMS *Ardent,* 64 guns, was launched at Hull in 1764. She served at New York in 1778 and was captured off the English coast on 17 August 1779 and recaptured by the British in the Battle of the Saints, 12 April 1782. The ship was in very poor condition and was sent to English Harbor, Antigua, for extensive repairs. The *Ville de Paris,* d'Estaing's flagship, was also captured, repaired, and assigned to send British troops back to England at the end of the war. The latter vessel foundered in a gale with the loss of all but one man. HMS *Ardent,* Captain's and Lieutenants' Logs, ADM/L/A/162, NMM; *Authentic Narrative of the Loss of the Ville de Paris* (London, 1809), 7–16.

21. Writing from Gros Islet Bay on 3 March 1783, Admiral Pigot informed the secretary of the Admiralty that the *Ardent* was leaking badly and had been sent into Antigua for repairs. Nagle and forty-nine other crewmen from the *St. Lucia* joined the crew on May 14, and on June 4, in company with HMS *Invincible* and HMS *Prudent,* sailed for home. The logs document that the ship was taking on water rapidly throughout the voyage, but it made an expeditious crossing, anchoring at Plymouth Sound on 7 July 1783. The crew was paid off on 11 August 1783. Hugh Pigot to Philip Stevens, ALS., 13 December 1783, Admirals' Correspondence, ADM/1/313, PRO; HMS *Ardent,* Captain's and Lieutenants' Logs, ADM/L/A/162, NMM.

22. Partly because of the confusion of wartime, partly because of the fact that such a large percentage of crewmen on British vessels in American waters were impressed Americans, muster books and pay registers for this period do not, as usual, always list place of birth. There is no way to identify the Canadian sailor who passed as Nagle's "brother" on his first visit to London.

23. The "long rooms" of the eighteenth century were precursors of the nineteenth-century dance halls, where a sailor could dance, drink, and meet women for more intimate pleasures in the after-hours at their rooming houses.

24. HMS *Scipio* was launched at Deptford in 1782 and remained on the list of active ships until 1798. Between July and early September 1783, the ship was moored at Black Stakes, taking on volunteers for the ship itself and for the *Ganges, Goliath, Pegasses,* and *Ardent.* The ship sailed on September 19 and arrived at Spithead nine days later. Nagle, who had volunteered for the *Ganges* on August 25, came on board with the rest of the crew on 28 September 1783. "Rupert Jones List," (5-vol. typed list recording cumulative histories of ships of the Royal Navy as listed in annual *Navy Lists*), National Maritime Museum, Greenwich; HMS *Scipio,* Master's Log, ADM/52/2520, PRO, and Lieutenant's Log, ADM/L/S/140, NMM.

25. The *Ganges,* in company with the *Goliath, Diadem,* and *Ardent,* sailed from Spithead on October 15 and arrived at Gibraltar on October 29. They sailed on November 14 and arrived back at Portsmouth on 13 December 1783. The ship remained in port for the next three and a half years Nagle was on board. HMS *Ganges,* Captains' Logs, ADM/51/381 and 382, PRO, and Lieutenants' Logs, ADM/L/G/171, NMM.

26. Captain Luttrell's log mentions heavy frost and snow on 22 January and 13 February 1784. HMS *Ganges,* Captain's Log, ADM/51/381, PRO.

27. Edward Riou (1762–1801) left the *Ganges* on 16 June 1784. Captain Luttrell was succeeded by Sir Roger Curtis on 16 May 1784. HMS *Ganges,* Captains' Logs, ADM/51/381 and 382, PRO.

The best documentation of Riou's career is to be found in his papers at the National Maritime Museum, Greenwich, and in "Biographical Memoir of Captain

Edward Riou," *The Naval Chronicle*, Vol. 3 (London, 1805), 482–93; Ludovic Kennedy, "The Log of the *Guardian*," in *The Naval Miscellany*, Vol. 4, The Naval Records Society (London, 1952), 295–358.

28. Although normally meaning the entryway of a man-of-war, the sally port in Portsmouth harbor was a specific landing place reserved for boats from men-of-war. Peter Kemp, ed., *The Oxford Companion to Ships & the Sea* (London, 1976), 746.

29. On 23 March 1787, seven men from the *Ganges* were discharged into the *Sirius* and three to the *Supply*. The seven from the *Ganges* were Jacob Nagle (Philadelphia, age 26), Richard Thomas (Carmarthen, age 22), John Middleton (Aberdeen, age 30), David Davis (Carmarthen, age 29), James Wilson (Philadelphia, age 22), Henry Fitzgerald (Halifax, age 32), Owen Cavenaugh (Gosport, age 25). Terence Burne (Dublin, age 25) joined the *Sirius* from the *Goliath* on 25 March 1787. HMS *Ganges*, Captain's Log, ADM/51/382, PRO; HMS *Sirius*, Pay Register, ADM/35/1563, PRO.

CHAPTER 4

1. The crew of a man-of-war in the Royal Navy was normally divided into two watches. In dividing it into three, Phillip was understandably seen by hardened naval officers such as Maxwell as pampering the men and endangering shipboard discipline. The sailors were not above taking advantage of the governor's leniency, as Nagle's account documents, but Phillip knew what he was doing. These early theatrics on his part in the interests of the sailors cemented a bond of loyalty on the part of the seamen that survived the very difficult years of early Australian settlement.

2. As "crossing the Line," or the equator, became an increasingly common occurrence for naval and merchant ships in the seventeenth and eighteenth centuries, the event was marked by ceremony and was unfailingly noted in the log books. In a sense, the "Line" represented symbolically the division between the land of the known and the land of the unknown. Above the equator a ship remained within the orbit of European civilization. Below it, the ship had nothing but its own fabric and crew to depend on.

3. One of the standard morning routines on a man-of-war was the stowing of hammocks. Seamen were required to take their hammocks down from the hooks on the deck beams, lash them securely with their blankets rolled up inside, and take them on deck and stow them on the hammock nettings on the inner sides of the upper deck and along the break of the poop deck. In their daytime positions, the hammocks provided added protection against musket fire in an engagement, and they could be easily cut free to serve as life preservers in case of disaster. Kemp, *Oxford Companion*, 372.

4. Arthur Phillip had been given permission, in 1774, to serve in the Portuguese navy. International exchanges of military and naval officers between the European powers in the eighteenth century, as unusual as it may seem today, were not uncommon, and for Phillip, stalled in terms of career advancement at lieutenant's rank in the British service, it provided him the opportunity of command with the rank of captain. Phillip had the linguistic and diplomatic skills necessary to take full advantage of the opportunity, and from the Admiralty's perspective, it would provide the British with firsthand intelligence concerning a little-known area of the world.

   Phillip served four years with distinction in the Portuguese–Spanish war over the disputed frontier territories of present-day southern Brazil and Uruguay before returning to British service. In addition to providing a wealth of experience upon which he would later draw in establishing the Australian colony, he earned a high reputation in Brazil, resulting in the unusually warm reception the First Fleet received in Rio de Janeiro in 1787. For the best accounts of Phillip's Portuguese service, see Kenneth Gordon McIntyre, *The Rebello Transcripts, Governor Phillip's*

Portuguese Prelude (London and Adelaide: Souvenir Press, 1984), and Alan Frost, *Arthur Phillip, 1738–1814, His Voyaging* (Melbourne: Oxford University Press, 1987), 59–91.

5. Nagle's journal would seem to suggest that the devilfish was caught between Rio and the Cape of Good Hope. Actually, it had been brought on board on 30 June 1787 just beyond Tenerife. Lieutenant Bradley's journal provides a detailed description of the fourteen-foot, eleven-inch monster of the deep. He noted that "some of the people eat of this Fish but it was not thought good." William Bradley, *A Voyage to New South Wales*, facsimile ed., The William Dixon Foundation (Sydney, 1969), 28–29.

6. A "grain" is a harpoon with five prongs, attached to a line and used in the era of sail for spearing fish or dolphins from the jib-boom at the bow of the ship. Kemp, *Oxford Companion*, 349.

7. Nagle is confusing with regard to Phillip's transfer from the *Sirius* to the *Supply*. On 25 November 1787 Governor Phillip, Lieutenant King, and Lieutenant Dawes of the marines went on board the *Supply*. Their intention was to proceed ahead so as to reconnoiter Botany Bay and the surrounding area ahead of the arrival of the fleet and select a location for the permanent settlement. Major Ross went on board the *Scarborough*, and the remainder of the fleet was then divided into two divisions— the *Scarborough*, *Friendship*, and *Alexander* transports under Lieutenant Shortland in one group and the three "heavy sailing" transports and the three storeships convoyed by the *Sirius* under Captain Hunter in the second contingent. The divisions created some ill will among officers, but in fact all of the ships would arrive at Botany Bay within two days of each other, so that Phillip's exploration of Port Jackson did not take place until after the initial landing of the colonists had been made. Bradley, *Voyage*, 18–19.

8. The *Supply* arrived first at Botany Bay on the afternoon of 18 January 1788, followed the next morning (January 19) by the *Scarborough*, *Alexander*, and *Friendship*, and on the morning of January 20 by the *Sirius* and the rest of the fleet. John Cobley, *Sydney Cove, 1788* (London, 1962), 19–21.

9. Dr. John White describes firing a pistol through a native's shield while at Botany Bay, which has a similarity to Nagle's story. See John White, *Journal of a Voyage to New South Wales*, ed. Alec H. Chisholm (Sydney, 1962), 110–11.

10. Nagle is slightly inaccurate concerning the personnel involved in the first two explorations of Port Jackson. On the first expedition of January 21–23, Governor Phillip and Captain Hunter were in the party, but not Lieutenant Bradley. On the expedition of January 28, when Hunter and Bradley began making careful charts of the harbor, Governor Phillip was not present, remaining behind at Sydney Cove to oversee the work of establishing the permanent settlement. Cobley, *Sydney Cove, 1788*, 24, 40–41.

11. The agricultural settlement at Rose Hill, at the head of navigation of Port Jackson, was established in October 1788. Bradley, *Voyage*, 143, 163–64.

12. Governor Phillip embarked on his first survey of Broken Bay in early March 1788 and on a second expedition in June. Nagle was probably present on both, and his brief account would appear to include elements of each. The first, accomplished by water, concentrated on surveying the lower region of the bay and was hampered by rainy weather. On the second expedition, the officers traveled from Port Jackson by land and were met in Broken Bay by the boats, and particular efforts were made to explore Hawkesbury River in its various branches. Nagle was probably also present on expeditions under Captain Hunter and Lieutenant Bradley in August– September 1789 to chart Broken and Botany Bays. Bradley, *Voyage*, 87–94, 172– 177; John Hunter, *An Historical Journal of Events at Sydney and at Sea, 1787–1792* (Sydney, 1968), 95–109.

13. Because Nagle's memory obviously combined incidents on the several explora-

tions of Broken Bay, it is difficult to exactly identify geographical locations of sites noted, such as this waterfall.

14. Captain Hunter noted the same evidence of severe flood danger on the Hawkesbury River in his entry for 6 July 1788. Hunter, *Historical Journal*, 105–6, 409.

15. This battle between two parties of natives on 24 August 1788 in Manly Cove was witnessed and described by Lieutenant Bradley and Daniel Southwell. It was suspected that it may have been staged for the benefit of the colonists, in order to demonstrate military prowess or possibly to lure them into a trap. In this early period of settlement, the natives of the North Branch had demonstrated more belligerence than those found elsewhere in Port Jackson. Bradley, *Voyage*, 121–22; White, *Journal*, 161; "Journal and Letters of Daniel Southwell," in *Historical Records of New South Wales*, ed. F. M. Bladen (Sydney, 1893), 700–704.

16. In 1788 and 1789, the native population near Port Jackson was stricken by smallpox, and the exploring parties began encountering not only the sick but the remains of men and women who had died from the disease. Dr. White brought in four natives, two of whom died and two, an eight-year-old boy named Nanbaree and a thirteen-year-old girl named Abaroo, who lived. White, himself, actually adopted the boy, and the girl was taken in by the Reverend Richard Johnson and his wife. White, *Journal*, 18–19.

17. James Daly, who invented the gold discovery hoax, was given 100 lashes for his offense. On 2 December 1788, he was again brought before a court for stealing clothes and was executed the following day. Hunter, *Historical Journal*, 57–59, 401; Watkin Tench, *A Complete Account of the Settlement at Port Jackson*, in *Sydney's First Four Years*, ed. L. F. Fitzhardinge (Sydney, 1961), 137, 303.

18. In the first year of settlement at Port Jackson, the cattle disappeared in the night, and their location or fate was one of the mysteries that was often speculated upon. Finally, in 1795 they were found grazing in a distant meadow, considerably increased in numbers, but this was well after Nagle had left the colony. He probably learned of the discovery from Jedediah Morse's *The American Universal Geography*, Vol. 2 (1812 ed.), 676, which had picked up the story from the published journal of David Collins.

19. Lieutenant Bradley, who commanded the party that captured Bennelong and Colbey on 25 November 1789, says, contrary to Nagle, that they were secured without firing a shot. This raises some question as to whether Nagle was actually present, although his duties as a crewman on the governor's boat would have made his presence likely under normal conditions. Both natives were later to escape, but Bennelong returned to Sydney, where he resided in a small house on Bennelong Point. Colbey never returned permanently to the settlement and did not, as Nagle suggests, either travel to England or die on the passage. Bennelong did accompany Phillip on his return to England in 1792 and made quite an impression as the first native Australian to visit London. He returned to the colony in 1795, no longer able to fit into either native or Western culture, and he died an alcoholic in 1813. In terms of actual chronology, Nagle misplaces this event in his journal by about a year. Bradley, *Voyage*, 181–84, 185, 225, 230–31; Robert Hughes, *The Fatal Shore* (London: Collins Harvill; New York: Knopf and Vantage Books, 1987), 11.

20. Governor Phillip was wounded on 7 September 1790, after Nagle and the crew of the *Sirius* had gone to and returned from Norfolk Island. Nagle's brief narrative agrees with the primary account of the incident by Lieutenant Waterhouse, as transcribed by Lieutenant Bradley and reported by Captain Hunter. Phillip had received word that Bennelong and Colbey, the escaped captives, wished to see him in Collins Bay. The governor met the natives and conversed with them, but one of them apparently became frightened and threw a spear, which struck Phillip. The

small party did not include a doctor, but Lieutenant Waterhouse did break the spear off, and it was probably Waterhouse who wrote down Phillip's will as the boat crew pulled back to Sydney Cove, a two-hour trip. There is no reason to doubt Nagle's presence on the expedition, but he apparently misdated the occurrence in his mind by almost a year, just as he had done with Bennelong's and Colbey's capture. Bradley, *Voyage,* 225–31; Hunter, *Historical Journal,* 140–43.

21. The journals of neither Captain Hunter nor Lieutenant Bradley mention either the sighting of Cape Flyaway or Lieutenant George Maxwell's endangerment of the *Sirius* on the voyage of late 1788 to the Cape of Good Hope for supplies, but there are probable explanations for the omissions. Disappearing capes are a constantly recurring feature of maritime literature, optical illusions caused by combinations of clouds, mist, the angle of the sun, and in this case possibly icebergs. By the late eighteenth century, when navigation was supposedly a science, an officer in the Royal Navy would have been likely to have suppressed official notice of having been fooled. Likewise, naval officers, as with fellow workers in most situations, tend to cover for their peers. Lieutenant Maxwell was declared insane by Governor Phillip after the *Sirius* returned to Port Jackson and relieved of his duties. He probably had ordered the sails set, as Nagle noticed, but recording that fact in either a log or a publication would have reflected poorly on Captain Hunter as much as on Maxwell himself. There may have been humane considerations as well.

22. The other four sailors who deserted the *Sirius* with Nagle at the Cape of Good Hope were James Lewis (Worcestershire, age 25), John William Kerr (London, age 22), John Punton (Plymouth, age 28), and James Wilson (Philadelphia, age 22). They were reported as deserters on 12 and 14 February 1789. HMS *Sirius,* Pay Register, ADM/35/1563, PRO.

23. Captain Hunter describes the storm of 21–22 March 1790, mentioned by Nagle, in considerable detail. In his career, Hunter put two ships on the rocks, and there has always been some question about his navigational skill and judgment. In this case, in passing Tasmania, incorrect calculations of position had put the *Sirius* farther north and too close to shore. The ship was very fortunate to survive the storm. See journal and editor's notes in Hunter, *Historical Journal,* 81–85, 404–7.

24. The discovery of the theft from the storehouse, at a time when supplies were dangerously low and the *Sirius* had not yet returned from the Cape of Good Hope, provided the most dramatic execution in Sydney's early history. Joseph Hunt provided evidence on 20 March 1789. The seven marines confessed to stealing 100 gallons of rum and wine, 500 pounds of flour, and 8 pounds of tobacco. Luke Haynes, James Baker, James Brown, Richard Asky, Richard Dukes, and Thomas Jones were tried on March 26 while the gallows was being erected. They were executed the following day. Jacob Nagle would not have learned of the crime until the *Sirius* returned in May, but his account is accurate and, in fact, adds details, which may have been fact or merely part of community gossip, not recorded elsewhere. John Cobley, *Sydney Cove, 1789–1790* (Sydney, 1963), 21–24.

25. Ann Davis, alias Judith Jones, was arrested on 14 November 1789 for being drunk and having in her possession clothing belonging to convict Robert Sidaway. At her trial on November 21, she attempted to implicate another female convict, Elisabeth Fowles, and also claimed that she was pregnant, both of which claims she recanted at her execution on March 23. Cobley, *Sydney Cove, 1789–1790,* 111, 114–15.

26. Francis Hill, master's mate of the *Sirius,* disappeared on 5 or 6 November 1789 while walking between the cove where the ship was being repaired and Sydney Cove. Search parties were sent out by boat and by land and the guns of the *Sirius* were fired every two hours for several days, but he was never found and was thought to have been taken by the natives. Cobley, *Sydney Cove, 1789–1790,* 106–10.

27. Peter White, sailmaker from the *Sirius*, was lost on July 11 from Sydney Cove but was found on July 14 by Governor Phillip and a party that was exploring the North Arm. Bradley, *Voyage*, 168–69; Cobley, *Sydney Cove, 1789–1790*, 68–71.

28. On 17 December 1789, Captain Hunter wrote to Governor Phillip, sending on a letter of Surgeon Worgan concerning Lieutenant Maxwell's health. Hunter noted that Maxwell had experienced a severe illness on the voyage to Australia and that from that time there had been a gradual decline in his mental faculties. Hunter said, "Since that time I have had very frequent cause when upon duty to suspect his mental incapacity." Maxwell was formally examined and relieved of his duties on 27 December 1789. Cobley, *Sydney Cove, 1789–1790*, 122–25.

29. John Caesar, the black convict, had been sentenced for theft on 29 April 1789 but escaped in early May with arms and ammunition. On May 26 he stole provisions from the brickmakers and was retaken on June 6. Captain David Collins noted in his journal that Caesar was considered to be the hardest worker in the colony but mentally little above a "brute." All of his thefts had been for the purpose of securing enough food. "He was such a wretch, and so indifferent about meeting death, that he declared while in confinement, that if he should be hanged, he would create a laugh before he was turned off, by playing off some trick upon the executioner. Holding up such a mere animal as an example was not expected to have the proper or intended effect." Governor Phillip sentenced him to be confined to Garden Island.

On 23 December 1789 Caesar escaped from the island, and two days later he stole a musket. He gave himself up on 30 January 1790 at Rose Hill. Governor Phillip pardoned him and in March 1790 sent him to Norfolk Island. He returned to Port Jackson in 1793, and after further escapes, a price was put on his head of five gallons of spirits, and he was shot by an aborigine in 1796. Cobley, *Sydney Cove, 1789–1790*, 32, 37, 39, 49–50, 124, 133–34, 158; Don Chapman, *1788: The People of the First Fleet* (Sydney: Cassell, 1981), 64.

CHAPTER 5

1. Lieutenant Philip Gidley King's journal, published in conjunction with Captain Hunter's and Lieutenant Henry Lidgbird Ball's accounts in 1793, provides a full history of the initial colonization effort on Norfolk Island, previous to the wreck of the *Sirius* and the arrival of Captain Hunter and Nagle. The first settlement of the island was made by Lieutenant King and party in early March 1788. The *Supply* then went back to Sydney Cove. The landing had been difficult, but there had been no loss of life. In July 1788 the *Supply* was sent back to Norfolk Island, and while attempting to land supplies on August 6, the colony's boat overturned with the loss of four of the colonists, among them James Cunningham, formerly master's mate, and William Westbrook, formerly a sailor on the *Sirius*. Nagle's claim that the accident was the result of poor judgment on the part of Cunningham must have been part of the gossip that later circulated in the colony, and it was published by Stockdale in London. The charge infuriated Lieutenant Bradley (who, like Nagle, was not present), and in his journal he goes out of his way to exonerate Cunningham and place the blame on the ill-advised orders of Lieutenant King. Hunter, *Historical Journal*, 201–19; Bradley, *Voyage*, 214–15.

2. While neither Hunter nor Bradley, who had their own reputations to protect, recorded the near-miss for the *Sirius* in going out of Port Jackson on 6 March 1790, Lieutenant Ralph Clark of the marines noted that "Just as we came abreast of the outer South Head it fell calm and the swell was setting us fast to leward on the North Head which, had not a puff of wind filled the Sails, we should have been drove on shore on the North Head, and every body on board thought of no other but that we should." Cobley, *Sydney Cove, 1789–1790*, 160.

3. Lord Howe's Island and Ball's Pyramid were discovered by the *Supply* on its first trip to Norfolk Island in February 1788. On the ship's return voyage in March, Lieutenant Ball had landed a party on Lord Howe's Island. They had found an abundance of green turtle but no fresh water. Hunter, *Voyage*, 50.

4. When the *Sirius* arrived at Norfolk Island on 13 March 1790, the wind prohibited landing at Sydney Bay. The ship sailed around to the northeast side of the island and on the 13th and the 15th managed to land the marines and convicts. Hunter, *Historical Journal*, 119.

5. After the arrival of the convicts and the crewmen from the *Sirius* in March 1790, the population of the island, according to Captain Hunter, was 506 persons. Hunter, *Historical Journal*, 121.

6. The desperate condition of the colonies at Sydney Cove and Norfolk Island after the wreck of the *Sirius* caused Governor Phillip to order their only oceangoing vessel, the *Supply*, to sail to Batavia to secure provisions and to rent another ship. The *Supply*, under the command of Lieutenant Ball, sailed from Port Jackson on 17 April 1790, and reached Batavia on July 6. The Dutch officials were only moderately cooperative, but Ball managed to purchase flour and rice and rent the *Waaksamheyd*. The *Supply* returned to Sydney Bay on 19 October 1790. Cobley, *Sydney Cove, 1789–1790*, 191–92, 291–93.

7. While Governor Phillip went to considerable lengths, both on the voyage out to Australia and in the early settlement of the colony, to separate the female convicts from would-be sexual partners, his heightened sense of morality was not shared by most of his fellow colonists, including the officers. Lieutenant Ball, commander of the *Supply*, who was often operating beyond Phillip's immediate supervision, fathered a child by a convict. Lieutenant King, the first commander on Norfolk Island, was devoted to a convict mistress and had children by her, and he generally permitted cohabitation on the island, which to some degree must have softened the blow of the wreck of the *Sirius* for Nagle's fellow sailors, possibly Nagle himself, although he never mentions any liaisons during his Australian career. Likewise, on at least some of the ships in the Second Fleet, Phillip's strenuous efforts to separate convict women from the ships' crews were not repeated. John Nicol, who was a seaman on the transport *Lady Julian*, which sailed in 1789, described how when "fairly out at sea, every man on board took a wife from among the convicts," and a good percentage of the women arrived in the colony pregnant or with babies in their arms. See John Nicol, *Life and Adventures* (New York, 1936), 121; Margaret Hazzard, *Punishment Short of Death* (Melbourne: Hyland House, 1984), 14, 21; Chapman, *1788*, 37.

8. Nagle's distinction between the "mount pitters" and the "mutton birds" does not seem to be supported by other contemporary sources. The terms seem to have been used interchangeably, both referring to the brown-headed petrel.

9. Captain Cook's description of abundant "New Zealand flax" had been one of the primary incentives for establishing the Norfolk Island colony in the first place, but the agricultural industry, pursued in various ways for more than a century, never was a real success. Lieutenant King had difficulty identifying the plant and eventually decided that Cook had meant a wild iris, which did have long fibres. Experiments failed to show the early colonists how this plant could be properly dressed, and two imported flax dressers brought to the colony later had no greater luck. By the mid-1790s, it was determined that the native plant was inferior, and future efforts were made with imported seed. Merval Hoare, *Norfolk Island* (Brisbane, 1978), 9.

10. According to Captain Hunter, the seven people who lost their lives when the boat bringing convicts in from the *Justinian* and the *Surprise* was upset on the reef at Sydney Bay, Norfolk Island, included only two sailors, three female convicts, one

child of a convict, and one male convict who had come out from shore to help save the women. The two seamen from the *Sirius* who were lost were David Bayne and James Coventry. Hunter, *Historical Journal*, 129; HMS *Sirius*, Pay Register, ADM/35/1563, PRO.

11. One of Nagle's fellow American sailors, James Procter of Boston, was discharged on 7 March 1791, to remain as "a settler on Norfolk Island." HMS *Sirius*, Pay Register, ADM/35/1563, PRO.

12. *Brookes'* or *Darby's Universal Gazetteer* would appear to be the one printed book that Nagle used to any extent in compiling his journal, primarily to get longitudes and latitudes and brief descriptions of ports of call. In *Darby's Edition of Brookes' Universal Gazetteer* (Philadelphia, 1823), on page 732, the entry for Norfolk Island includes the claims that "The island is supplied with many streams of good water, which abound with very fine eels," and that "anchorage is safe all round the island." Nagle objected to both statements.

13. Nagle copied most of his longitude and latitude locations from the gazetteer noted in note 12, many of which are wrong both in the book and in his manuscript. They are printed in the text as he recorded them.

14. It is fascinating to compare the various accounts that have survived of the encounter between the *Waaksamheyd* and the natives of Duke of York Island. In varying degrees, the other witnesses place some of the blame on the impetuous Dutch captain, Smith. See Hunter, *Historical Journal*, 155–62, 417; Bradley, *Voyage*, 256–63; Daniel Southwell to Mrs. Southwell, Batavia Roads, 12 October 1791, in Bladen, ed., *Historical Records of New South Wales*, 728.

15. Nagle confused the Solomon Islands and the Admiralty Islands. The *Waaksamheyd*, after making a fruitless attempt to reach Norfolk Island, essentially sailed from east to west, first reaching Lord Howe's Group (which was part of the Solomons), then sailing eastward through the straits between New Britain and New Guinea, stopping at Duke of York Island, and then encountering the Admiralty Islands as it made its way toward Mindinao in the Philippines.

16. The journal of Hunter confirms Nagle's assertion that changing winds caused the officers to revise their intended destination, but he confused the order. China was chosen as the target to aim for first, Manila second. Hunter, *Historical Journal*, 165–67.

17. A "compasant," also known as St. Elmo's Fire, was an electrical phenomenon that, under certain atmospheric conditions, would appear on the masts and spars of ships and was quite naturally seen as an omen. The old seamen Nagle had encountered apparently viewed it as foretelling a storm, but to others it meant the end of a storm and return of favorable weather. Nagle was not, apparently, superstitious, and he attempts to explain the phenomenon as some sort of blubber that rose out of the sea. A variety of natural substances do often produce an electrical glow in the water at night, but it is unlikely that there would be any connection between this and what was presumably a ball of lightning.

18. For the differing interpretations of the engagement, see Hunter, *Historical Journal*, 169–74, 274–79, and Daniel Southwell to Mrs. Southwell, Batavia Roads, 12 October 1791, in Bladen, ed., *Historical Records of New South Wales*, 729–30.

19. Lieutenant George Maxwell had died at sea on 13 April 1791. Bradley, *Voyage*, 415.

20. The Dutch captain, Detmer Smith, was discharged at Batavia, "for insolent and other improper behaviour" according to Bradley. The Dutch crew was also discharged and the British flag hoisted over the *Waaksamheyd*. Captain Hunter took command at this point, and the ship, eventually purchased by the Admiralty, would remain in British service after its return from Australia in 1792. Bradley, *Voyage*, 292.

21. While at the Cape of Good Hope, a gale caused the *Waaksamheyd* to drag her anchors. Nagle's memory was that it was the *Swan* that came to their rescue, but in fact it was Captain Bligh in the *Providence*, then on the outward passage of the second breadfruit voyage. The first lieutenant on Bligh's ship, Francis Godolphin Bond, would later become Nagle's favorite captain on HMS *Netley*. The *Swan* did not arrive at the Cape until December 23, three days after the incident, although it would have been, as Nagle says, a boat from this vessel that visited the *Waaksamheyd* at the time of the "frolick." Bradley, *Voyage,* 297–98; Hunter, *Historical Journal,* 190–91.

22. Nagle's comments on Napoleon and his tenure at St. Helena were copied verbatim from his standard reference book, *Darby's Edition of Brookes' Universal Gazetteer* (Philadelphia, 1823), 403–4.

23. There is conflicting evidence as to the price Captain Smith asked for the *Waaksamheyd,* but he did offer either to sell the ship or rent it, and Governor Phillip did choose the latter arrangement at approximately the 300 Pounds sterling per month figure mentioned by Nagle. Hunter, *Historical Journal,* 335–36, 435.

24. Although their ship had been lost in March 1790, Nagle and his fellow seamen would remain on the books as crewmen of the *Sirius* until they were discharged and paid off on 4 May 1792. When the *Waaksamheyd* reached Portsmouth, the crew was assigned to HMS *Duke* until they were discharged, but they were never formally made part of the ship's crew and were permitted shore leave. HMS *Duke,* Captain's Log, ADM/51/265, PRO, and Master's Log, ADM/52/2985, PRO.

CHAPTER 6

1. Henry Hacking (1750 or 1753–1831), from Blackburn, Lancashire, and quartermaster on the *Sirius,* was one of a number of ship's officers who would later return to Australia. Hacking went back in 1792 in the *Royal Admiral* and had a colorful career. He made an early attempt to cross the Blue Mountains, was the person who discovered the missing herd of cattle in 1795 and again in 1798, was a pilot in Port Jackson, and in 1805 helped to capture six escaped convicts. He was overly fond of spirits and occasionally got into trouble, once for shooting and wounding a woman, another time for stealing ship's stores, but he escaped the death penalty twice through the kind intervention of Governor King, fellow First Fleeter. He died at Hobart. Chapman, *1788,* 109; HMS *Sirius,* Pay Register, ADM/35/1563, PRO.

2. Unlike the crewmen of the *Sirius,* who were expeditiously paid off at Portsmouth, those of the *Supply,* which arrived in English waters just before the *Waaksamheyd,* had to take the ship around to the Thames. They were not discharged for several weeks.

3. Millicent Rose's *The East End of London* (London, 1951) is a particularly good local history of the area east of the Tower that Nagle knew so well. At the time the book was written, there were still remnants of the eighteenth-century environment, most of which have disappeared in the course of the vast docklands redevelopment projects over the past thirty years.

4. Nagle's close friend, William Beard, was twenty-five and listed as coming from Edinburgh when he enlisted in 1786 on the *Sirius.* He had been an "ablebodied seaman" on the voyage out, but was appointed quartermaster's mate on 1 March 1790. HMS *Sirius,* Pay Register, ADM/35/1563, PRO.

CHAPTER 7

1. Although Nagle covers his tour of duty on HMS *Hector* in little more than a page, he actually served on the 74-gun vessel for almost seven months. From early August until early December, the ship was moored at Portsmouth. During this period, the captain's cabin was temporarily converted into cells to house the ten crewmen

from HMS *Bounty* who were tried for the mutiny. Six were sentenced to death on September 12, two of them later pardoned (Haywood and Morrison), and four (Musprat, Milward, Ellison, and Burket) executed on October 29 from the flagship in view of the entire fleet.

On 8 December 1792, the ship moved out of the harbor to Spithead, and on 17 February 1793 she sailed in company with HMS *Hannibul*. They encountered HMS *Atalanta* and the *Ganges*, East Indiaman, on February 21. Sixty-one men were impressed out of the *Ganges* on the 22nd, and a lieutenant, a master's mate, a midshipman, and forty seamen, Nagle among them, were placed on board the *Ganges* to take her to the Thames. The *Hector* returned to Spithead on March 3, drafted men from the *Brunswick* and *Royal William*, and cleared port for Barbados on March 24–25, before Nagle and his fellow crewmen had made it back to the ship. HMS *Hector*, Captain's Log, ADM/51/448, PRO.

2. Although Nagle and the other sailors from the *Hector* were transferred from the *Ganges*, East Indiaman, to *La Nymphe* to *L'Aigle* and then to the *Brunswick* between 22 February and 3 April 1793, they were officially crewmen of the *Hector* until assigned to the *Brunswick* on March 23. They actually reported for duty on the *Brunswick* on 3 April 1793. HMS *Hector*, Pay Register, ADM/35/760, PRO; HMS *Brunswick*, Pay Register, ADM/35/266, PRO.

3. Of all the sights of the eighteenth century that have been lost because of technological change, there are very few that must have been as spectacular as a fleet of as many as a thousand merchant ships, protected by several dozen warships, sailing from Spithead, heading for the four corners of the globe. The protection of commercial shipping was a primary responsibility, however irksome, of the British navy in Nagle's era, but it is part of the job that tends to get lost in naval histories. Occasionally, naval vessels and fleets would move from one part of the globe to another for purely military reasons, but in most cases, during wartime and in dangerous waters, these moves would be timed to protect the tobacco fleet, or the wine or codfish trades, or some other segment of Britain's lucrative international trade.

4. The account of the Glorious First of June that Nagle provides was obviously based on, or largely copied from, a general history of British naval exploits during the French Wars. There are many similarities to the 1818 edition of John Campbell's *The Naval History of Great Britain* (London, 1818), 411–16. In addition to relying on a work of this sort, Nagle probably had picked up some firsthand details from fellow sailors on the *Brunswick* with whom he would have later come into contact.

5. Discipline on board an East Indiaman or any merchant vessel was not as systematic as it was in the Royal Navy. The log of Captain Gray records that on 10 September 1794, "At 6 P.M. 4 of the Seamen run away with the Jolly Boat." The second officer and petty officers were sent after them and brought them back at 11:00 P.M. The four were not named, but five days later, William Osborn, Thomas Barret, Thomas Lewis, and John Robinson were punished with "1 dozen for desertion." Such infractions were apparently to be entered in the Crew List/Receipt Books, and it is so recorded for Thomas Barry or Barret, but a similar entry is obviously erased for William Osborn. Jacob Nagle, alias Lincoln, receives no mention for the infraction in either the log book or pay book, and yet there is no reason to think that he was not guilty or that he was not punished. Either the officers entered his name wrong, or as in the case with Osborn, later good behaviour caused them to erase or change the record.

The difference was that in the Royal Navy, disciplinary offenses were crimes against the state. In the East India Company and on merchant vessels, while tradition and statute did support the use of corporal punishment, it did not have the same weight of law behind it. Particularly during the French Wars, when the East

India Company and merchant ships in general were woefully short of able-bodied seamen, discipline was not so much to effect justice as merely to correct an immediate problem. After the fact, the record could be easily changed so as to encourage reenlistment. One senses that East India Company log books must be used with considerable caution as complete and true historical records. There were too many incentives encouraging omission and falsification for all concerned, including the company itself. *Rose,* "Ledger, 4th Voyage, Arrived 1795," "Receipt Book," and Log of Alexander Gray, L/MAR/B/59V, L/MAR/59 V-2, and L/MAR/59D, India Office Library, London.

6. It would be interesting to know the identity of these two "ladies" of the First Fleet who had escaped to Calcutta by 1795 and established themselves as high-class courtesans. They probably had coaxed sailors or officers of one of the transports or storeships to stow them away in return for keeping their hammocks warm on the long voyage home. Nagle would have been one of very few First Fleeters to have gotten to Calcutta by this time and one of very few who would have recognized the women. It is entirely likely that had he spoken up, he could have caused them considerable trouble and perhaps even got them sent back to Australia.

7. The ships that bore down on the *Rose* on July 17 included the "*Poliphemus* 64, *Apollo, Cerberus & Margretta* frigates & *Hazard* under Capt. Manly." Log of Alexander Gray, *Rose,* L/MAR/59D, India Office Library, London.

8. A general history of the Quiberon Bay invasion fiasco, and the political and diplomatic background, can be found in John Ehrman, *The Younger Pitt: The Reluctant Transition* (London, 1983), 567–79. The troops that had assembled in the area were not raised to repel a French invasion but to be part of the French invasion themselves. Nagle's group avoided the main roads until they got to Poplar. Although he notes that there were reportedly four press gangs in the village, it was essentially an East India Company town at this period, and the men felt relatively safe beyond this point.

9. The White Swan tavern was apparently very near the East India Company headquarters on Leadenhall Street, and from Nagle's comments concerning arrangements for his voyages of 1795 and 1805–7, it appears that the company had an official or unofficial arrangement with the tavern for recruiting men. While the company had to be careful about the methods it used, the tavern and its landlord could and apparently did resort to whatever practices would raise men for the company and make money for themselves.

10. Although the eastern, riverside gate to the Tower of London was eliminated in the late eighteenth century, Irongate Stairs, giving access to the Thames, remained in Nagle's day. The name was apparently used by a nearby tavern, where Captain Edward Tyrrell established the "rendezvous" for his press gang. Tyrrell was an interesting, resourceful man, and his correspondence to the Admiralty concerning the problems associated with impressment is interesting to read. Captain's Correspondence "T," ADM/1/2596 (1795) and ADM/1/2597 (1796–97), PRO; John Charlton, *The Tower of London* (London, 1978), 112–13.

11. There may have been an unusual infestation of rats on shipping at this time. The log of George Chatterton, Master on the *Gorgon,* to which Nagle was assigned, contemporaneously noted that the crew was "pointing the Foresail and repairing the Damaged Mainsail which had been eat by the Rats in several Places." HMS *Gorgon,* Master's Log, ADM/52/3057, PRO.

12. According to George Rude in *Hanoverian London, 1714–1808* (Berkeley, Cal., 1971), 228–29, shipbuilding was the most depressed of the major industries of Britain in the 1790s, particularly along the Thames. Nagle's in-laws, the Pitmans, were a family of boat and shipbuilders who apparently had migrated from their home on the Isle of Wight in the 1780s or at the beginning of the French Wars. As

of 1795, they were thinking of going back, and by 1796, it would seem that the Pitmans were at Portsmouth.

13. Presumably John Greatrise Smyth, who had been first mate on the *Rose* under Captain Gray on the previous voyage. *Rose,* "Ledger" and "Receipt Book," L/MAR/B/59V, L/MAR/59 V-2, India Office Library, London.

CHAPTER 8

1. Nagle's geographical description of Corsica is taken, almost verbatim, from *Darby's Edition of Brookes' Universal Gazetteer* (Philadelphia, 1823), 232–33.

2. Nagle's old friend from the *Sirius* and London, William Beard, was a sailor on the *Blanche,* and his presence may have influenced Nagle's decision to make the transfer. Nagle left the ship on 27 July 1798 to join the crew of the *Netley,* and Beard left the next month to serve on the *Royal William.* HMS *Blanche,* Pay Register, ADM/35/239, PRO.

3. Jacob Nagle's incidental remarks provide a wonderfully complete portrait of life at sea in his era. His description of the exchange of cannon fire between the *Blanche* and fortifications on shore emphasize two of the realities of naval warfare in the age of black powder and solid shot: (1) the extent to which a ship firing round after round became quickly enveloped in smoke, making it not only hard to see any target but to know what was going on on your own vessel, and (2) the amount of damage a cannonball could do on deck after it had initially landed. There were undoubtedly more casualties due to splintering wood from the ship than from direct hits by the balls themselves.

4. Nelson got himself into some diplomatic difficulties for keeping these Austrians. According to the Genoese, they were hired by the Spanish to join a Swiss regiment at Barcelona. Nelson considered the Genoese nothing more than puppets of the French, and he claimed that the Austrians themselves were delighted to enter British service. Horatio Nelson to John Jervis, 5 June 1796, in Nicholas Harris Nicolas, ed., *The Dispatches and Letters of Vice Admiral Lord Viscount Nelson,* Vol. 2 (London, 1845), 182–83.

5. French victories and diplomatic alliances in Italy not only put military pressure on the British navy but created serious supply problems for the Mediterranean fleet. The fall of Leghorn cut off the supply of hemp used to manufacture cordage at Ajaccio. The supply of beef became critically low in early 1796, requiring the assignment of vessels such as the *Blanche* to special missions to purchase cattle wherever they could be obtained. When the Mediterranean fleet pulled back to Lisbon, closer to supplies from Britain and to fresh beef from North Africa, the situation improved.

6. Captain D'Arcy Preston's log on the *Blanche* for 1 December 1796 notes that "the *Victory* ran foul of us & carried away the Barracading on the Starboard side the Quarter Deck, two Main Shrouds & split the Main Top sail." HMS *Blanche,* Captain's Log, ADM/L/B/97, NMM.

7. Captain George Cockburn of *La Minerve* recorded in his log for 19 December 1796 that at Cape de Gatte, at 7:30, the *Blanche* in company, they "Spoke a Genoese Polaere from Carthegena bound for Malaga, Took 8 Bales & One Trunk of Silk out of her being Spanish Property," and allowed the ship to go on. *La Minerve,* Captain's Log, ADM/51/1204, PRO.

8. In addition to the accounts found in the logbooks of *La Minerve* and the *Blanche* of the engagement between these two vessels and the *Santa Sabina* and the *Ceres* on 19–20 December 1796 see also Nelson to Jervis, 20 December 1796; D'Arcy Preston to Nelson, enclosed in Nelson to Jervis, 29 December 1796; "Bulletin" of Mr. Bromley, a merchant of Lisbon, 20 and 24 December 1796, enclosed in Jervis to Nepean, 12 January 1797, in Admirals' Correspondence, ADM/1/395 and 396,

PRO. For the Captains' Logs, see ADM/51/1204, PRO, and ADM/L/B/97, NMM.

9. The editor has found no contemporary documentation confirming Nagle's story that the British had managed to capture Napoleon's baggage.

10. The logs of HMS *Dido* while Hotham was in command provide no convincing evidence that he was unusually strict, but it is very difficult to evaluate a captain's leadership abilities from the sort of evidence that survives. Hotham was meticulous, and he was dealing with a crew that had a lofty sense of their own rights and had recently lived through the emotional divisions associated with Captain Sawyer's court-martial. The *Blanche* was Captain Hotham's third and last command.

11. Nagle was fortunate that the *Blanche* was not chosen to be part of the expedition to Santa Cruz, the harbor he had visited nine years earlier with the outgoing First Fleet. Nelson's Tenerife expedition was foiled by unfortunate weather conditions, and Nelson was severely wounded in the right elbow, requiring the amputation of his arm. Carola Oman, *Nelson* (New York, 1946), 236–43.

CHAPTER 9

1. HMS *Netley*, a 16-gun schooner with a sliding keel, was designed by General Samuel Bentham and launched in 1798. The ship was 82.6 feet in length, and had a tonnage of 177 and a mean draft of 9.3. The ship surrendered to the French in the West Indies in 1806. "Rupert Jones List," NMM.

2. In a letter of 12 September 1798, from Haslar Hospital, Portsmouth, Captain Bond wrote to Evan Nepean, secretary of the Admiralty, that he not only suffered from the wound in the thigh, but also from having received "a violent contusion in my breast, the effect of which is not a little alarming, though the pain, by blistering etc. is something palliated." Health may have been a factor in limiting his active career. Captain's Correspondence, ADM/1/2756, PRO.

3. In a letter of 4 July 1797, Samuel Hood wrote to Admiral Jervis describing his ill-fated effort to take Vigo. He attributed the failure to "extraordinary" poor intelligence provided by Vice-Consul Allen. Allen's kindness to Nagle may have been, in part, an effort to improve his reputation with the Royal Navy.

4. Nagle is confusing with regard to his acquaintances at Vigo. The editor's reading of the journal is that the consul, Mr. Allen, arranged for Nagle to board with neighbors. Although Nagle is not clear about how close the relationship became, he suggests that the wife of Allen's friend exceeded the bounds of propriety in her show of affection for him. Nagle may be teasing his reader a bit, or he may be salving a guilty conscience.

CHAPTER 10

1. *The London Gazette* regularly published public notices of the distribution of prize money from the sale of vessels captured by the *Netley*. Those of the spring of 1802 are signed by Joseph Lyne and Co., presumably the London half of the firm Nagle identifies as "Loyns & Gill & Co." See *London Gazette*, 6–9 March 1802; 30 March– 3 April 1802; 8–12 June 1802.

2. William Jarvis arrived in Lisbon on 1 August 1802, President Jefferson's newly appointed American consul. His correspondence during his first year in office is primarily concerned with the terrible yellow fever epidemic that killed Nagle's wife and children. The main goal of the consul's correspondence was to try to convince Portuguese authorities to permit American vessels to unload cargoes and clear the port without going through a lengthy quarantine. U.S. Consular Dispatches, T-180, roll T1, National Archives, Washington, D.C.

3. Nagle does not provide enough detail in his journal for us to be certain exactly which ship he took passage on from Lisbon to Norfolk. He had been discharged

from the *Gorgon* on 19 April 1802 and shortly thereafter shipped with his family to Lisbon. The fever was at its height at that period, and the family had probably died by the middle of summer. *The Commercial Register* of Norfolk, Virginia, notes the arrival of the *Victory,* Captain Halton, from Lisbon on August 15 after a passage of sixty-two days. Fifteen days later the brig *Mary,* Captain Wakefield, arrived in Norfolk from Lisbon after a passage of sixty-six days. *The Commercial Register* (Norfolk, Va.), Nos. 1, 8, 24, 25.

4. The *Success,* Captain Tice, entered the port of Norfolk on 1 September 1802, and it cleared Portsmouth, presumably for Philadelphia, on October 8. *The Commercial Register* (Norfolk, Va.), Nos. 8, 24.

5. White's *Philadelphia Directory* for 1785 lists a Benjamin Carr on 3rd, between South and Lombard, and the 1791 *Philadelphia Directory* includes Joseph Carr, a joiner, at 220 3rd Street.

6. This entry in Jacob Nagle's journal is the only record that has come to light of his "youngest sister Polly." She would have been an infant, or perhaps not yet born, when he left Philadelphia in 1781. The reference would suggest that she was unmarried in 1802 and lived in Reading or the Philadelphia area. Nagle cared about family, and the fact that Polly is never mentioned on later visits to the United States might indicate that she had died before he returned permanently in the 1820s.

7. The schooner *Sally,* Captain Tice, cleared the port of Philadelphia for Norfolk in early October 1803, which was either the voyage, or a similar trip, that Nagle made to Richmond for coal. Until the discovery and exploitation of the massive coal deposits of Pennsylvania in the 1820s, the area northwest of Richmond, Virginia, was the most productive coal field in the United States. *Gazette of the United States* (Philadelphia), 6 October 1803.

8. The Trap was a small village twenty-six miles northwest of Philadelphia, and Potts Grove a larger settlement eleven miles farther on the road to Reading. Reading was fifty-four miles from the city. Thomas F. Gordon, *A Gazetteer of the State of Pennsylvania* (Philadelphia, 1832), 386, 392, 452.

9. In his will, Jacob Nagle's grandfather Joachim Nagel left "the sum of ten Pounds unto my Grandson," adding the provision that "Should my Grandson (who is now absent) not return to the State of Pennsylvania and make demand of the aforementioned Legacy within seven years after my decease," it was to be divided between Jacob Nagle's uncles, Peter Nagel and John Nagel. Joachim Nagel died on 26 July 1795, at the age of ninety, and his grave is marked by a stone of that date in the Fritz Burial Ground, Douglass Township, where it was rediscovered by Mrs. Marion Rhoads in recent years. The seven years since the grandfather's death had actually elapsed before Jacob Nagle returned to Reading, but the bequest was paid by Nagle's uncle Peter. Nagel Family Record, provided the editor by Mrs. Marion Rhoads, Reading, Pennsylvania.

10. Anna Margaretha Nagel (b. ca. 1740), who married Valentine Geiger, Jr. (ca. 1720–1778), was a half sister of Jacob Nagle's father, George Nagel. She married in 1766 and moved the following decade to Sunbury, Pennsylvania. Geiger had four children by a previous marriage and two by his union with Anna. Nagel Family Record, from Mrs. Marion Rhoads, Reading, Pennsylvania.

11. Elias Youngman (1738–1817), of Youngmantown, now Mifflinburg, Pennsylvania, was the husband of Caterina Nagel Youngman (1743–1822), half sister of Jacob Nagle's father. The Youngmans had two sons and a daughter. Nagel Family Record, from Mrs. Marion Rhoads, Reading, Pennsylvania.

12. Metheglin was a beverage made from fermented honey.

13. Sarah Nagle Webb (1774–1841), the second of Jacob Nagle's three younger sisters, married John Webb, a hatter, of Reading, Pennsylvania, in 1794. They moved to New York City, where Webb had a shop on Maiden Lane, then moved to Young-

mantown or Mifflinburg, Lancaster County, Pennsylvania, and to Canton, Ohio, in 1814. His children included George N. Webb of Canton and John Webb and Thomas L. Webb, who moved to Perrysburg, Ohio, in 1822. John Webb, Sr., died in Canton about 1825. *Commemorative Historical and Biographical Record of Wood County, Ohio* (Chicago, 1897), 366, 826–27.

14. Ann or Anna Nagle McCardell (b. ca. 1762) was the oldest of Jacob Nagle's three sisters. She married Thomas McCardell. They lived on a farm in the vicinity of Hagerstown, Maryland. Nagel Family Record, from Mrs. Marion Rhoads, Reading, Pennsylvania.

15. On his brief visit to Philadelphia, Nagle presumably stayed with his youngest sister, Polly, and their first cousin Betsy Lincoln.

16. The *James,* on its return from St. Thomas, entered the port of Philadelphia on 4 April 1804. *New-York Price-Current* (New York), 7 April 1804.

17. The acquisition of Louisiana by the United States in 1803, at a period when war in Europe increased the risks of transatlantic trade, offered great promise for American shipowners. Captain Richard Tice, whose permanent address in the early years of this decade was Spruce Street, Philadelphia, had purchased a new schooner, the *Eliza,* in 1803. It was built at Gloucester, New Jersey, was 99-tons burden, 62 feet long, had one deck, two masts, a square stern, and a woman figurehead. Beginning in 1803, the ship made regular voyages between Philadelphia and New Orleans and Natchez. Robinson's *Philadelphia Directories,* 1803–7; WPA, *Ship Registers and Enrollments of New Orleans,* Vol. 1, for 1804–20 (Baton Rouge, La., 1941), 39; *New-York Price-Current* and *Gazette of the United States,* 1803–5.

18. The *Gazette of the United States* for 11 May 1805 reported that the *Eliza,* Captain Tice, was spoken to on April 21 "in Rock passage" on its way to Jaquemel, Santa Domingo.

19. *New-York Price-Current* for 28 December 1805 notes the arrival on December 23 of the *Patriot,* Captain Hudson, a coastal vessel coming from Virginia. Nagle had probably shipped to New York on the previous voyage.

   The Minutes of the Common Council of the City of New York, Vol. 3, for 22 June 1801–13 May 1805 (New York, 1917) show that John McCombs was one of the primary contractors for paving the streets of New York in this period.

   The 1806 New York directory lists John M'Comb, "paver," at 12 Duane Street, and John M'Comb, "paver & grocer," at Crosby, corner of Spring Street. John Moneypenny, grocer, resided at 272 Greenwich Street. *Longworth's American Almanac, New-York Register and City Directory, 1806* (New York, 1806).

   Hay Scale slip, where Nagle landed, was between Duane and Jay streets. *Elliot's Improved New-York Double Directory* (New York, 1812), 17.

20. The *Mercantile Advertiser* (New York) for 11 December 1805 contained an advertisement for the ship *Science,* Thomas Howard, master, then lying at Pine Street wharf, "having two thirds of her cargo engaged. For the remainder or passage, having elegant accommodations, apply to the master on board or to Thomas Harvey & Son." Thomas Harvey and Son were located at 73 South Street. *Longworth's Directory* (New York, 1806).

   Lloyd's Register indicates that the *Science* had a short career. Its first year was 1806, and the *Register* of 1809 notes that she had been "captured."

CHAPTER 11

1. The fleet assembled at Mother Bank as of 14 May 1806, convoyed by HMS *Lion,* included the following East India Company ships: *Neptune, Marchioness of Exeter, Marquis of Wellesley, Thames, Glatton, Royal Charlotte, Cirencester, Marquis of Ely, Monarch,* and *Experiment,* along with transports. *Neptune,* Log Book, L/MAR/B/98 O, India Office Library, London.

2. According to the log of the *Neptune,* the American ship that they spoke to the day

after the storm, on 18 August 1806, was returning to Boston from Bengal. L/MAR/B/98 O, India Office Library, London.

3. The *Neptune's* log for 14 October 1806 reported that sixteen men had been pressed by HMS *Blenheim*. L/MAR/B/98 O, India Office Library, London.

4. The details of the *Neptune* incident are to be found in the "Canton Consultations" and "Canton Diary," 1807–8, G/12/156–162, India Office Library, London. The $20,000 offer to any man who would remain behind, mentioned by Nagle, is not part of the official record.

5. The two most famous French captains of the era who terrorized British shipping were Rear Admiral Linois and privateer Captain Robert Surcouf, although neither would have been following the fleet Nagle was part of in 1807. Linois, who commanded the 74-gun *Marengo*, had been captured by the British in 1806 and brought into Portsmouth at the time Nagle's fleet was about to sail. Surcouf, in the fast sailing *Clarisse*, but mounting only 14 guns, was operating on the trade route between Madras and Bengal. C. Northcote Parkinson, *War in the Eastern Seas, 1793–1815* (London, 1954), 275, 311.

6. HMS *Blenheim*, with Admiral Thomas Troubridge aboard, and HMS *Java* foundered off the southeast end of Madagascar in a gale. HMS *Harrier* had sighted them in distress and had then lost contact. Admiral Pellew sent the admiral's son, Captain E. Troubridge, under a flag of truce to the Isle de France and Madagascar in search of the vessels. There were persistent rumors that the crews had survived, but Captain Troubridge concluded, as the hard evidence indicated, that the ships had been lost. Parkinson, *War in the Eastern Seas*, 298–99; Admirals' Correspondence, Cape of Good Hope, 1807, ADM/1/59, PRO.

   Alexander Gray, Nagle's former captain on the *Rose*, had gone out to Prince of Wales Island in 1806, as the British navy decided to establish a repair station there. He was not, as Nagle remembered it, governor, but had been appointed "Third in Council, Superintendent and Paymaster of Marine, and Naval and Military Store-keeper." The official records of the colony indicate that Gray became sick, and he may have left the island on the *Blenheim*. Correspondence from Prince of Wales Island, 1805–9, G/34/179; Dispatches from Co. to Straits Settlement, G/34/196, India Office Library, London.

7. The *Neptune* was at Crook Haven, 18–31 December 1807. The official company records do not make it clear whether Ireland was an original, or unwritten, objective of the voyage, but such a stop certainly made possible private profits for officers and crewmen, if not the company itself. *Neptune* Logbook, L/MAR/B/98 O, India Office Library, London.

8. *Lloyd's List*, No. 4250 (6 May 1808) reported that the *Highlander*, Captain Cooper, bound for Quebec, had put back to Portsmouth because of the loss of its bowsprit.

9. The *Highlander* arrived at Liverpool after the dispute described by Nagle on 13 October 1808. *Lloyd's List*, No. 4293 (18 October 1808).

CHAPTER 12

1. The *Brilliant*, Captain D. Morrison, was a vessel of 367 tons and 14 guns. It was built in 1806 and was engaged in 1808 and 1809 in trade between Greenock and Liverpool and Honduras. *Lloyd's Register* (1808–9).

2. The *Caledonia*, Captain S. Thomson, was a vessel of 445 tons and 20 guns. She was built in 1807, was copper sheathed, and in the period 1808–10 shipped between Greenock and Liverpool and Demerara. *Lloyd's Register* (1808–10).

3. Lincoln Rogers, a former British soldier who settled at Demerara and died there in about 1808 or 1809, was a twin brother of Nagle's mother. Nagle's mother was Rebecca Rogers, daughter of Roger Rogers and Mary Robeson Lincoln Rogers. Mary Robeson, Jacob's grandmother, had first married Mordecai Lincoln (1686–1736), a widower, among whose previous six children was John Lincoln, Abraham Lincoln's

great-grandfather. Mordecai and Mary Robeson Lincoln had three children. After Mordecai Lincoln's death, she married Roger Rogers (d. 1758), and they were the parents of Jacob Nagle's mother and her twin brother, Lincoln Rogers. J. Henry Lea and J. R. Hutchinson, *The Ancestry of Abraham Lincoln* (Boston, 1909).

4. Corruption among the lumpers, or in American terminology, longshoremen, made possible smuggling in a regular British port. Obviously, if anyone else was allowed to be present when a ship was loaded or unloaded, the smugglers' freedom of action would have been severely limited.

5. Frustrated by the unwillingness of Britain or France to respect the "rights" of neutral American ships during the Napoleonic Wars, from 1807 to 1809 President Jefferson imposed an embargo on American trade to Europe in the hope that it would create sufficient hardship in London and Paris to change their policies. The embargo was repealed in 1809, but it was replaced by the Nonintercourse Act, prohibiting trade to Britain and France. These measures failed in part because of genuine difference in opinion between the British and the Americans over the nature of the war with France, but to a considerable degree because it was not supported by shipping interests in the United States. Most of the illicit trade that developed was in New England, but on the southern border with Florida, Amelia Island became a lucrative shipping point for Georgia and South Carolina cotton. For American sailors, the embargo was a disaster, forcing them, as was the case with Nagle, to ship largely on European ships, or to restrict themselves to coastal voyages.

6. There were several ships bearing the name *Triton* plying the Atlantic in 1809. Beginning in April 1809, ads appear in *The Public Advertiser* (New York) of the availability of the "new, fast sailing, and handsome brig Triton, captain Porter, 202 tons" lying at Peck Slip wharf. Nagle may have sailed into New York on this ship.

7. Alexander McKenzie kept a tavern at 76 Cherry Street. *Longworth's New York Directory . . . 1808* (New York, 1808).

8. Edward Dugan, "shipmaster," lived at 15 Lombard Street in 1809 and at 8 George Street in 1810–11. *Longworth's Directories . . . New York* (New York, 1809–11).

CHAPTER 13

1. Bahia, or St. Salvador, not to be confused with the island in the Bahamas of the same name, was the old capital of Brazil, slightly over 800 miles north of Rio de Janeiro.

2. Nagle's employer as master of a pleasure boat at Rio de Janeiro in 1811 was Carlos María Martínes, marqués de Casa Irujo, or Yrujo (1763–1824), then Spanish ambassador to the Portuguese court at Rio de Janeiro, and minister to the United States during the administrations of Washington, Adams, and Jefferson. On 10 April 1798 he had married one of the beauties of Philadelphia, Sally McKean (pronounced by the family McKane), daughter of Thomas McKean (1734–1817), signer of the Declaration of Independence, congressman, chief justice of Pennsylvania, and governor of Delaware, 1799–1808. The boy whom Nagle helped to take care of, later the duke of Sotomayer, became prime minister of Spain. William S. Baker, "Washington after the Revolution, 1784–99," *Pennsylvania Magazine of History and Biography,* Vol. 21 (1897), 43; John Howard Brown, ed., *Lamb's Biographical Dictionary of the United States,* Vol. 5 (Boston, 1903), 259–60; John Street, *Artigas and the Emancipation of Uruguay* (Cambridge, 1959), 139–40.

3. Buenos Aires declared itself independent in 1810. Montevideo, governed by Francisco Xavier de Elio, tended to be Spanish in its leanings and was ever distrustful of Buenos Aires. Elio saw himself as defender of the Spanish empire in America, and on his return from Spain in 1811 declared open hostilities with the forces of independence in Buenos Aires and the Banda Oriental, who retaliated by besieging Montevideo. The city was being bombarded at the time Nagle's vessel passed by early in 1812. John Street, *Artigas,* 78–161.

4. Captain Pitt Burnaby Greene wrote to Admiral Sir Manley Dixon from Buenos Aires

describing the discovery of "a most diabolical plot . . . amongst the Old Spaniards resident here, having in mediation the massacre of the creoles." The leader, Martin de Alzaga, was executed on 5 July 1812. There were at least twenty-six further executions. Contained in letter of Dixon to John Wilson Croker, *Montagu*, Rio de Janeiro, 30 August 1812, in Gerald S. Graham and R. A. Humphreys, eds., *The Navy and South America, 1807–1823*, Navy Records Society (London, 1962), 76–77.

5. The Portuguese and Rio de Janeiro had always felt that Uruguay was rightfully theirs, and the independence movement in the Banda Oriental and Buenos Aires provided the necessary excuse for an invasion. Claiming that they were trying to rescue the Spanish viceroy, Elio, who was being besieged at Montevideo and who had urged Portuguese intervention in his behalf, troops entered Uruguay under the command of General de Souza in June 1811 and began slowly to gain control of territory. The British were supportive of the Portuguese regime in Rio de Janeiro, but they were not enthusiastic about a Portuguese conquest of Uruguay. In the summer of 1812 they succeeded in bringing about a truce and the retreat of Portuguese troops. Nagle witnessed the Portuguese advance in Uruguay before the treaty went into effect. Street, *Artigas*, 140–61.

6. *Lloyd's List* (No. 4732) for 29 December 1812 reported intelligence from Rio de Janeiro that the *Levant*, Captain Smith, had arrived there from Buenos Aires, intending for Liverpool, "in distress." On March 2, it reported that "The Levant, Smith, from the River Plate to Liverpool . . . has been condemned and sold." *Lloyd's List*, No. 4751, 2 March 1813.

7. The United States declared war against Great Britain on 18 June 1812, and news of the conflict reached Rio de Janeiro in the middle of September. Graham and Humphreys, *Navy and South America*, 79.

8. The "hog yoke" that the Brazilian pilot attempted to use to ascertain the altitude of the sun was presumably a rudimentary form of cross-staff or forestaff. In the vicinity of the equator, because the Polar Star and the Guards (two bright stars in the Lesser Bear) were close to or below the horizon and because of haze, noonday solar sightings were often necessary. The cross-staff was devised in the fifteenth century by Portuguese explorers, and although far less accurate than the quadrant or astrolabe for determining latitude, it remained in use as late as the early nineteenth century. E. G. R. Taylor and M. W. Richey, *The Geometrical Seaman, A Book of Early Nautical Instruments* (London, 1962), 37–40.

9. Henry Hill (1794–1892), born in New York, was a merchant in Bahia, Brazil, and American consul there from 1808 until 1817, then consul at Rio de Janeiro and Valparaiso, Chile. He owned an extensive plantation near Caravelas, between Rio and Bahia, on which Jacob Nagle worked. Hill returned to the United States in 1821 and in 1822 accepted the position of treasurer of the American Board of Commissioners of Foreign Missions, from which he retired in 1854. *Missionary Herald*, Vol. 88 (March 1892), 89.

10. Dom João and the royal family of Portugal embarked on the *Dom João IV* on 25 April 1821, accompanied by twelve vessels and 4,000 governmental officials and dependents, to resurrect the monarchy in Portugal. Dom Pedro, the king's son, assumed the throne of Brazil, which shortly thereafter declared its independence. Neill Macaulay, *Dom Pedro: The Struggle for Liberty in Brazil and Portugal, 1798–1834* (Durham, N.C.: Duke University Press, 1986), 86.

11. USS *Congress* was one of six frigates authorized by Congress in 1794. It was nearing the end of its career when sent under Captain John D. Henley on a two-year cruise to the Pacific. The voyage was a success in extending the presence of the American navy to China and the Philippines, but it had been a particularly unhealthy cruise. Seventy-three men died of cholera or dysentery. The ship arrived at Rio de Janeiro on 8 March 1821, and the log of Captain Henley records that on April 1, at 6:30

P.M., "Jacob Nigle" came aboard. The ship sailed on April 15 and arrived at Norfolk on the evening of 29 May 1821. *Dictionary of American Naval Fighting Ships,* Vol. 2, 163; USS *Congress,* Captain's Log, RG24, National Archives, Washington, D.C.

12. The *Eliza,* according to *Lloyd's Register for 1822,* was an American brig of only 125 tons. It was then eleven years old.

13. The *New-York American* for 8 May 1824 reported the arrival the night before of the brig *Fanny,* Captain Lubeck, fourteen days from Antigua, with a cargo of sugar, hides, and lead.

14. During the months of June and early July, Boorman & Johnston, 57 South Street, advertised for sale the brig *Hunter,* 152 tons, then lying at Gouverneur's Wharf. The last ad appeared on July 10. This may be the ship on which Nagle made his last voyage. *New-York American,* June–July, 1824.

CHAPTER 14

1. Wilford D. McCardell (1814–1861), Nagle's nephew, served as a Whig member of the Maryland House of Delegates for Washington County. He drowned accidentally at Williamsport. Nagel Family Record, from Mrs. Marion Rhoads, Reading, Pennsylvania.

2. William Hall (b. 1756), who put Nagle up for the night at Cross Creek, Washington County, Pennsylvania, was a fellow veteran of the Battle of the Brandywine. He was born in Ireland and came to Pennsylvania with his father in 1760. He lived in Lancaster County until 1779–80, Westmoreland County until 1800, and Washington County thereafter. He saw three full years of service as a drummer, beginning with service around Boston in Captain Slough's Company in 1775, and including participation in the battles of Long Island, White Plains, Trenton, Princeton, the Brandywine, and Monmouth, the Paoli Massacre, and the Crawford Expedition. He was granted a pension in 1836. Revolutionary War Pension Files, National Archives, Washington, D.C. (Microfilm, Reel 390).

3. George N. Webb (b. 1802), nephew of Jacob Nagle, was a hatter by trade. He was first sergeant of the Canton Blues, the local militia company. He was a Democrat in politics; in 1828 he was elected coroner of Stark County, and in 1833 he successfully ran for sheriff of Stark County. Nagel Family Record, from Mrs. Marion Rhoads, Reading, Pennsylvania; *The Ohio Repository,* Canton, Ohio, 4 January 1827–27 December 1833.

4. John Webb (1795–1885), like his father, John Webb, and his brother George N. Webb, was a hatter by trade. He was born in New York City and moved with his parents to Mifflinburg, Pennsylvania, where he married Elizabeth Charles (1794–1833). He moved to Canton, Ohio, in 1820 and was one of the first settlers in Perrysburg, Ohio. He practiced his trade there from 1824 to 1828 and served many years as the sheriff of Wood County and as county clerk between 1826 and 1860. He had three wives and fourteen children. *Commemorative Historical and Biographical Record of Wood County, Ohio* (Chicago, 1897), 366, 826–27; Charles W. Evers, *The Pioneer Scrap Book of Wood County and the Maumee Valley* (n.p., n.d.), 239–41.

5. William Addams (1776–1858), of Reading, Pennsylvania, served as Democratic representative in Congress from 1825 to 1829. *A Biographical Congressional Directory* (Washington, D.C., 1913), 430.

6. Portland was the former name of Sandusky, Ohio.

7. "Farara" is Nagle's word for prairie. W. Bruce Finnie's *Topographical Terms in the Ohio Valley, 1748–1800,* Pub. of the American Dialect Society No. 53 (University of Alabama, 1970), 86–87, 118, records use of "parara" by a Virginia clergyman traveling in Ohio in 1795.

8. The reference to "St. Clarks fields" would seem to be an incorrect reference to St. Clair's battlefield, which is actually in northwestern Ohio, near the Indiana border,

a part of the state that Nagle never visited. General St. Clair was defeated there by the Indians in October 1791.

9. George Cake must have been either the father-in-law or brother-in-law of Jacob Nagle's nephew, George N. Webb, and he, George N. Webb, and Thomas L. Webb, another nephew, were character witnesses for Nagle's pension application. John Myers and John Bryce successively served as recorders of deeds for Stark County. Nagle worked in their office in the early 1830s, and the original land plats for the towns of Minerva (1833) and Liverpool (1834), used as illustrations in Edward T. Heald's *The Stark County Story, Volume 1* (Canton, Ohio, 1949), 225, 273, are in Nagle's unmistakable handwriting. This is one of the two probable times when he might have written his journal. *The Ohio Repository,* Canton, Ohio, 25 August and 14 October 1831.

10. Major James A. Hook of Washington was apparently a private agent who assisted veterans to get pensions—he was not a War Department employee. John Thomson (1780–1852), a physician in New Lisbon, Ohio, was a Democratic member of the House of Representatives in Washington, D.C., 1825–27, 1829–37. *Biographical Congressional Directory,* 1055.

11. Richard Laskey, who came to Washington in 1812 from England, was a tavern keeper. John C. Proctor, *Washington, Past and Present,* Vol. 4 (New York, 1930), 457; Gaither & Addison, *The Washington Directory . . . for 1846* (Washington, 1846).

12. The Cohocksink section in the Northern Liberties was named for the creek that emptied into the Delaware. The stream and the name disappeared within a few years after Nagle's residence there. Joseph Jackson, *Encyclopedia of Philadelphia,* Vol. 2 (Harrisburg, 1931), 492.

13. It was probably the family of Simon Beisel who befriended Nagle. Beisel first appears in a Philadelphia directory in 1840 as a gunsmith, on Germantown Road, near 5th Street. The following year, at the same address, his trade is listed as "brick press maker," and in 1845 as "black and whitesmith." He must have died in the late 1840s, and in the directory for 1850 Wilhelmina, at the same location and presumably his widow, supplies "trimmings." *McElroy's Philadelphia Directory (1840, 1841, 1845, 1850).*

14. The New Castle and Frenchtown Railroad, connecting the Delaware River and Chesapeake Bay, was completed in 1831. It employed horse-drawn cars at first, but on 10 September 1831 a locomotive of English construction was used, providing the first regular steam passenger service in the United States. WPA, *Delaware, A Guide to the First State* (New York, 1938), 75–76.

15. Joseph Hook, Sr., Revolutionary War veteran and father of Major James A. Hook of Washington, received a pension in 1832 for three years of service in the Maryland Line. He lived in Baltimore at 65 N. Green Street. Revolutionary War Pension Files, National Archives, Washington, D.C. (Microfilm, Reel 440); *Matchett's Baltimore Director . . . 1831* (Baltimore, 1831).

16. Akron is situated on the crest of Portage Summit. The Ohio Canal, beginning near Cleveland, ascended almost 400 feet in twenty-five miles by means of a series of two dozen locks.

17. Many of the early steamboats included a bugle player as a member of the crew, partly to add excitement for the passengers, partly for musical entertainment, but primarily to provide advance warning of the boat's approach to the persons responsible for operating locks and bridges and for providing changes of horses or mules.

Glossary

Nagle's journal is a wonderfully rich document of seamen's terms. While his spellings are often unorthodox, the meanings of the words he uses are true to the objects and actions being described and to the times.

The following glossary is a modest attempt to define those terms used in the journal that might not be obvious to the nonexpert. No attempt has been made to create a complete or authoritative dictionary or provide every definition of any term listed. In creating this list, Peter Kemp's *The Oxford Companion to Ships & the Sea* (London: Oxford University Press, 1976) and William Falconer's *A New Universal Dictionary of the Marine* (London, 1815) have been particularly useful.

abaft. Toward the stern, from whatever object is referred to.

accommodation ladder. A light ladder of rope or chain hung over the side of a vessel for entering or leaving small boats.

aft. To the rear, toward, or at the stern of a vessel.

athwart. Running across, from side to side.

backstays. Long ropes extending from the topmast heads to the chains on either side of the ship. There were two pairs of backstays on each mast, breast-backstays and after-backstays, and their purpose was to reinforce the shrouds in supporting the mast while under sail.

ballast. Weight, either in the form of iron pigs, loose sand, gravel, or cargo, used to stabilize a ship and maximize its sailing qualities.

beam ends. A ship "on her beam ends" has heeled over on her side to the point that her beams approach to a vertical position. If the ship did not right itself, this might be accomplished by putting out an anchor and shifting the cargo. In extreme cases, the masts would be cut away.

bees. A piece of wood fastened to the outer end of the bowsprit, to which were attached the fore-topmast stays.

before the mast. In the age of sail, the seamen, as opposed to the officers, were quartered in the forecastle, in the bow of the ship. A man who "shipped before the mast" had therefore signed on as a seaman, not an officer.

before the wind. With the wind propelling the vessel from behind, a ship sailing "before the wind" was sailing in the same direction as the wind.

bend. A knot or hitch used to join two ropes or a rope with an object. To bend a sail is to tie it to a yard or boom; to bend an anchor is to attach it to a cable.

bilge of the cask. The point of largest circumference, where the bung hole is situated.

binnacle. The pedestal, just before the helm, supporting the ship's compass. The housing was also sometimes used to store charts, log-line, and the twenty-eight-second glass used to measure the ship's speed.

bits, or *bitts.* A frame made up of two vertical posts, attached firmly to the deck in the bow, used to secure the fall of cables from the rigging. Bitts were to be found elsewhere on some ships as well.

boatswain's call. The silver pipe or whistle used by the boatswain to produce a variety of calls, ordering the seamen to and from duties on deck.

bore. A particularly strong tidal flow, accompanied by waves or a noticeable rise in the water level, caused by the juncture of two currents or the concentration of water by the narrowing of a channel.

bow. The forepart of the ship. In Nagle's era, often referred to in the plural, "the bows," because shipbuilders and crewmen thought of a ship as having two distinct halves, larboard and starboard.

bowline knot. A knot tied at the end of a rope so as to produce a loop that will not slip.

brace of pistols. A pair of pistols.

break. The line of sudden rise or fall in deck level, such as "the break of the quarterdeck."

breast piece. Part of the copper sheathing, presumably at the bow. Copper-bottomed ships, with plates attached by copper bolts, came into common usage in the late eighteenth century to deter weed growth, improve sailing speed, and protect the hulls from worms, particularly in warm waters.

broach to. When, because of too great a press of sail, the ship flies up into the wind, making the vessel vulnerable to losing its masts or even foundering if there is a sudden change of wind direction.

broadside. The simultaneous firing of all guns that can be brought to bear on an enemy vessel. The primary objective of much of eighteenth-century battle tactics was to make possible the firing of broadsides at enemy ships while they were not in a position to return the fire.

bulkhead. A vertical partition between the decks of a ship. In the eighteenth century they served largely to create cabins or compartments, although the powder magazine and arms room had strong oak siding for security. Later, in the age of steel ships, bulkheads became important as firewalls and compartments to contain water.

bulwark, or *bullwork.* Planking along the sides of a ship, above the level of the deck, to prevent water from washing over the deck and to keep objects or men from going overboard in rough seas.

bumboat. A small boat used to supply vessels with provisions from shore and usually manned by local merchants.

buttocks. The breadth of the convex afterpart of a ship, where the hull rounds down to meet the stern.

canister. Musket-sized shot encased for easy handling. The case breaks apart, releasing the balls individually, when fired. Used for relatively close artillery fire.

cap. The wooden block separating and attaching the lower and upper mast. It is secured to the lower mast by a square hole and the upper mast is fitted through a round hole and held there by a fid, lashings, and rigging.

capstan. A barrel mounted vertically on a spindle, around which anchor and rigging cables were wound, both for the mechanical advantage provided and in order to minimize the clutter of the fall of cable on deck. The capstan was normally in the center of the main deck, and it was operated by men pushing capstan bars that fitted into pigeonholes at the top. They could be removed when not in use. A capstan was most likely to be found on large vessels. Its function was accomplished by a windlass, mounted horizontally, on smaller vessels.

cartel. The agreement between belligerent nations to exchange prisoners; the prisoners themselves; or the ship on which they were transported.

cat (noun). The "purchase" or mechanical device, made up of ropes and pullies, used to hoist an anchor. Also the colloquial name given to the cat-o'-nine-tails with which men in the Royal Navy were flogged.

cat (verb). The process of hoisting an anchor to the cat head.

cat head. A piece of heavy timber, securely fastened to the bulwark on the outside of each bow, to which the top of the anchor is slung, attached to the cat. It permitted the anchor to swing free of the hull of the ship when being lowered or weighed.

catharpins. Short ropes under the "top" (the horizontal platform between the lower and upper masts) connecting and keeping taut the "futtock shrouds" (which were cables below the platform to secure it in place).

chain pumps. The most efficient and common type of pump used on eighteenth-century vessels for clearing bilge water.

chains. The small platform mounted on either side of the ship, supported by chain plates and to which the shrouds were attached. The chains was the common place used by the leadsman when taking a sounding.

chefortus. A term, apparently original to Nagle and possibly a corrupted non-English word, indicating a flammable liquid, possibly alcohol.

clewed up. The clews of a square sail are the two lowermost corners. If "clewed up," they were tightly secured, making the sail taut, risking sail and mast damage in exceptionally strong winds.

clinch. A knot or method of fastening a large cable to an object by bending it around the object and back on itself, these being bound or "seized" with a small rope. An anchor would be clinched at both ends—to the ring of the anchor and to the mast when all cable was extended.

coble. A flat-bottomed fishing boat, fitted with a sail and oars and notable in design for a rudder and forefoot extending below the keel. A coble is launched and landed bow seaward.

colors. The flag indicating a ship's nationality.

companion. The framed skylight on the quarterdeck that permitted natural light to enter the cabin below.

compasant. St. Elmo's Fire, or a ball of lightning occasionally seen on the decks and masts during atmospheric change, which gave rise to much superstition among sailors.

coppers. The cooking vessels in which all meat, vegetables, and puddings on shipboard were boiled.

counter. The portion of the deck overhanging the rear of the vessel, behind the rudder.

crab. A capstan without a drumhead. The crab was turned by bars inserted through holes in the barrel itself at different heights and angles. It was used for any heavy lifting of cables.

crank. A ship is crank when its ballast is not sufficient or well enough balanced to permit it to carry a normal amount of sail without being in danger of upsetting.

crimpage. The portion of a merchant seaman's wages paid to the crimp who had enticed him to sign on a vessel.

cross trees. Timber braces attached at right angles to the trestletrees at the top of the lower mast and near the top of the topmast. Their purpose was to support the platform at the top of the lower mast and to spread the shrouds.

crowd sail. To carry the maximum, or more than the maximum, sail for prevailing weather conditions.

cut the mast. Under severe weather conditions, or when a ship heeled over on its beam ends, it was sometimes necessary to "cut" the upper masts and let them go over the side. The process did not normally involve cutting the mast itself, but cutting or disengaging the shrouds and stays that held the upper masts in place.

cutter. A small decked ship with one mast and a bowsprit, which was light in the water and fast. Used for coastal duty and messenger service between ships in a large fleet.

davits. Wooden or metal arms used to hoist and secure the small boats of a ship. On small vessels, lacking cat heads, davits were used to secure anchors.

dipsey lead; dipsey line. A line, with lead weight attached, used to "sound" or measure depth.

downhaul. A rope used to lower a sail.

ensign. A flag indicating the nationality of a ship, hoisted usually on an ensign staff erected over the stern of a ship.

eye. The circular loop in a rigging cable where it passes over a mast.

fall. The end of a rope that is pulled to secure the system of pulley and ropes making up the ship's tackle. In the process of raising a sail, the fall of a cable could clutter the deck unless a windlass, capstan, or crab was available to take up the slack.

false keel. An additional keel, secured outside the main one, intended to protect it in case of grounding. In the late eighteenth century, additional keels were added to experimental vessels to improve sailing qualities.

fathom. The distance of six feet, approximately a man's reach. This was the standard unit of measurement for water depth and for cables.

fid. A square block of wood that is passed through the lower end of a topmast or topgallant mast and serves much like a cotter pin to support the upper mast on the trestletrees.

fish (verb). On a ship in Nagle's day, one would "fish" an anchor or "fish" a yard or mast. Fishing an anchor involved drawing up the flukes to the cat davit in preparation for hauling it on deck and storing it on the anchor bed on deck. To fish a mast, a "fish" (long piece of wood, rounded and concave on one side) was bound to any spot where a mast or yard had weakened and was in danger of breaking. It was a temporary repair, used in lieu of a spare mast or under rough weather conditions when it was impractical to completely replace a mast at sea.

fleet a purchase. To adjust the blocks of any tackle, placing them farther apart, so as to be able to pull the tackle more tightly.

flemish eyes. To make an eye (a firm loop at the end of a rope) by unbraiding one strand, folding the end, and using the loose strand to secure the loop. The loop is then bound or "marled" (using a small rope secured by marlin hitches and covered with spun yarns). Flemish eyes were not as strong as regular eyes and were used for temporary repairs.

flip. A favorite drink of eighteenth-century seamen, being a mixture of beer, spirits, and sugar, often heated with a hot iron.

fore course. The sail set on the lower yard of the foremast.

forecastle. Pronounced "foksil," the term referred both to the raised deck at the bow of the ship and the living quarters below it, which were inhabited by the seamen. To be a "forecastle man," as Nagle was, meant that you were a seaman, not an officer.

forefoot. The point where the stem (which is the almost vertical timber forming the bow, under the bowsprit) joins the keel.

foretop. The platform between the lower and upper foremasts. See *top.*

fusee. A flintlock gun.

galyot. A small, Dutch-style trading vessel having a distinctive rounded bow, a single mast, and fore and aft sails.

gangway. The platforms (skids) on either side of the spare masts in the waist of the ship that run between the forecastle and the quarterdeck. They were used to stow the ship's boats, and they also provided a walkway between the two decks, fore and aft, avoiding the necessity of descending to and ascending from the main deck.

gasket. A rope or strip of canvas used to secure a furled sail to the yard or boom.

gig. A light narrow boat built for speed, with oars and short masts for lug or lateen sails.

grafting. A technique for splicing two ropes together, similar to making flemish eyes, where strands of the rope are used to cover the joint in such a way that the circumference of the rope is not increased. It could be run through tackle blocks, but it did not make a particularly strong connection and would be used only in emergency.

grain. A five-pronged harpoon used to spear fish or dolphins, usually at the bow of a ship.

grape. A cluster of iron shot held together by cast-iron plates and a connecting rod. Grape was used at close range to scatter shot.

gratings. Open hatch covers with latticelike openings to permit light and air to circulate below deck. In extreme weather, they would be covered with tarpaulin.

grog. A mixture of one part rum to three parts water, the standard daily drink of seamen in Nagle's era. In the British navy, crewmen were issued a half-pint of rum per day.

guarda-costa. A Spanish coast guard vessel, found in both European and South American waters.

gun deck. On frigates or sloops, the main deck.

gunnel, or *gunwale.* Pronounced "gunnel," the gunwale was the plank balustrade forming a low wall along the sides of a vessel on either side of the waist.

gunroom. An apartment on the after-end of the ship, occupied by the gunner on a large ship and by the lieutenants as a dining room on a frigate.

hand lead. The lead or hand lead was a weight of seven to ten pounds attached to a lead line of approximately twenty fathoms' length, used for measuring depth.

hand pump. The hand pump was located in the middle of the ship, on the main deck. It was somewhat unwieldy, raising water by means of a long wooden tube that descended to the bottom of the ship. It was useful in clearing small amounts of bilge water and provided a backup for the more efficient chain pumps, common on newer and larger vessels.

handspike. Handspikes were handles that were detached from the machinery, such as the windlass, to save space on deck when not in use. Like belaying pins or pump bolts, they were easily converted into weapons when a sailor got into a fight.

hardway. The area of shoreline in a harbor above high water mark where the banks are firmed up and perhaps paved, making possible easy landing or mooring of small boats.

hatchway. The hatches or hatchways are the oblong or square openings between decks. On larger naval vessels there would be three: the fore-, main-, and after-hatchways. Ships often had smaller openings between decks, primarily for ventilation, which were called scuttles.

haul. In seamen's language, the verb "haul" was used exclusively to denote pulling something by a single rope without the mechanical benefit of any blocks.

hawse (to Nagle, *harse*). The portion of the bow of the ship where the hawse-holes (through which the anchor cables pass) are situated. It is also a general reference to the portion of the bow between the head of the ship and the anchor chain.

hawser (to Nagle, *harser*). A very heavy cable used to secure an anchor or to secure the ship to a wharf.

head. The carved figurehead of the ship; a general reference to the entire forepart of the vessel. The term also had a specific reference to the places, "the heads," on either side of the stem of the ship, for the forecastle men to relieve themselves—hence the modern use of the term for a water closet or restroom.

heart (*of the forestay*). A heart-shaped flat board with one large hole in the middle that was used as a deadeye on staysail rigging. In contrast, a normal deadeye employed on the shrouds had three holes.

heavy sea. A rough sea with high waves.

housed. A gun on deck was housed by pulling it back from the porthole and removing the quoin under the breech, thus allowing it to point upward and the muzzle to rest on the side above the port. It was then lashed in place and the muzzle "stoppered," or plugged. In the cabins below, a housed gun might be stored fore and aft to save space.

hoy. A small vessel, rigged as a sloop, used for coastal traffic and for ferrying stores from shore to vessels in port.

jack. A small flag denoting a vessel's nationality, generally displayed from a staff on the outer end of the bowsprit.

jib. A triangular sail or one of several, set on a stay between the top of the foremast and the outer end of the jib boom at the bow of a ship.

jolly boat.   The smallest of the open boats kept on a man-of-war, used primarily for going to and from shore.

kedge.   The smallest of the anchors, used as an auxiliary to keep a ship clear of its bower anchor with a change of tide or wind or used to pull a ship out of a harbor or up a river. The kedge is transported by the long boat in the proper direction and the ship then pulled up to it.

kites.   A general term for all the sails above the topsails. They were used to maximize the advantage of light and moderate afterwinds.

klinch (see *clinch*).

knots.   The nautical measure of speed. One knot is equal to going one nautical mile in an hour. The term was derived from the equipment used to determine this rate. The log was thrown out, and as the line ran out, knots, 42 to 50 feet apart were counted over a period of 24 to 28 seconds (measured by a sand glass).

krank (see *crank*).

lanyards.   Short pieces of rope used for a variety of purposes on shipboard, including securing machinery in place and stretching the shrouds and stays of the masts in conjunction with deadeyes and hearts. When used with deadeyes, they were greased with lard or tallow.

larboard.   The left side of the ship when looking forward from the stern.

lazaretto.   A storage compartment in the fore part of the lower deck on some merchant vessels.

lead (see *hand lead*).

leadsman.   The man who operates the lead and the leadline to ascertain depth.

league.   Three nautical miles, which is one-twentieth part of a degree of a great circle.

lee.   The side of a ship away from that upon which the wind is blowing. A ship is on the lee shore when she is near the coast toward which the wind is blowing.

lighter.   A large, open, flat-bottomed boat, propelled by oars, used to carry goods and supplies to and from a ship.

log.   A piece of wood, one-quarter of an inch thick and shaped like a quarter-wedge of a pie. It is attached to a log line at the two rounded corners so that in the water it will maintain its position while the ship moves beyond it. The log-line is marked by knots. The number of these knots passed in 24 to 28 seconds determined the speed the vessel was going.

luff.   To luff a ship, the bow was brought round closer to the direction of the wind.

lugger.   A small vessel, primarily found in the Mediterranean, having two or three masts and a bowsprit, set with distinctive squared lug sails and two or three jibs set on the bowsprit.

mainsail.   The largest single sail on the ship, usually the lowest sail on the main mast.

minute gun.   The firing of a gun at regular intervals, either as a mark of honor, or in order to establish position for another party that is out of sight but not out of hearing range.

muffled oars.   Placing cloth or some other substance around the locks of the oars and the gunnels so as to enable a boat to move silently through the water.

northwesters.   The predominant, cold winter wind of the northern Atlantic coast of America, blowing from the northwest.

oakum.   The fibres of old ropes which have been untwisted and drawn apart. Oakum was used for caulking seams and repairing leaks in the hull.

painter.   A rope used to attach a boat to a ship or wharf.

part a cable.   To have an anchor cable break in rough weather.

pennant.   The pennant or pendant is a long, narrow flag, flown at the mast head, which indicated that the vessel was in commission. The ''broad pendant'' was flown by the commodore of a squadron or convoy.

phlip (see *flip*).

pinnace.   The pinnace of the Royal Navy of Nagle's era was a long, narrow, and light boat pulling eight oars. While the larger barge was used by admirals and captains, the pinnace was used by the lieutenants. In the sixteenth century, the term was used to describe small sailing vessels of about 20 tons, having two masts and either lug sails or schooner rigging.

poop.   The highest and aftmost deck of a ship.

ports.   The square holes cut in the sides of ships through which the guns were fired. When not in use, they could be closed by port lids. During wartime and in the age of pirates and privateers, much attention was paid to ascertaining the number of ports in any strange sail that was spotted, to determine whether the potential opponent had superior firepower.

preferment.   Advancement or promotion in rank: an officer would ''be preferred,'' or ''go on preferment.''

press.   Synonymous with ''to impress.''

protection.   An officially issued document attesting to a man's nationality, occupation, age, etc., aimed at protecting him from impressment. British naval captains tended to pay little attention to American protections until after the end of the Napoleonic Wars.

pump bolt.   One or two pieces of iron with a handle at one end, used to operate the hand pump of a ship.

quadrant.   A mathematical instrument used to ascertain the position of a fixed star, the sun, or planets to determine latitude (the north/south position) of a ship relative to the equator.

quarter board.   Planking above the bulwarks, along the quarterdeck of a ship.

quarterdeck.   The portion of the upper deck of the ship behind the mainmast, usually raised above the level of the main deck but below the level of the poop deck. The quarterdeck was largely the preserve of the captain and the commissioned officers, and it was from there that warrant officers received orders and the captain commanded the ship. Sailors only went on the quarterdeck to fulfill a specific duty, and it was standard procedure for all on board to salute when ascending the ladder to this level of the ship.

quarters. When seamen were summoned by the call "All hands to quarters," each crewman took a preassigned position on deck, ready for action. Lieutenants were assigned to command the guns, the master to oversee the movements of the ship and the sails. The boatswain and a party of men were stationed to repair damaged rigging. The seamen were divided into gun stations, with crews under first and second gun captains for each gun, with additional men assigned as firemen, winch men to work the pumps, powder men to fetch powder, etc.

rake. To fire at a ship, head-on or stern-on with canister or grape shot, scouring the deck "fore and aft."

rattan. A short whip cane carried by boatswains in the Royal Navy until prohibited shortly after Nagle left the service. Used to prod seamen to more quickly complete their duties, the rattan became something of a symbol of naval brutality to seamen.

riders. Auxiliary timbers, bolted to existing timbers in the hold and running between the keelson and the beams of the lower deck, used to support the frame of the ship. Because they would take up valuable space in the hold, they were used only when it was feared that the existing frame could not withstand heavy seas.

ringtail sail. A small sail extended on a mast from the bow of the ship, used only in light and favorable winds.

roadstead. An area of a harbor, river, or bay where ships could safely moor.

royal sciscraper. A small triangular sail set on the mainmast at the very top in favorable weather.

sally port. The place at Portsmouth that was restricted exclusively for the landing of boats from naval vessels.

scuppers. Lead-lined channels cut through the bulwarks of a ship to permit water to run off the deck.

scuttle. A small hatchway or hole cut through the deck or sides of a vessel, or even through the hatchways. It could be closed with a lid.

scuttlebutt. A cask with a square piece cut out at the point of largest circumference, which is lashed on deck and contains the fresh water for the daily use of the crew.

sea cunnies. Helmsmen.

sheers. A temporary structure of two or three spars raised and secured on deck to lift and set a replacement mast.

sheet anchor. One of two spare anchors carried in case the bower anchors failed.

sheet home. To fix the placement of a sail by securing the sheets and tacks (which are ropes fastened to the lower corners).

shiver. A sail will shiver, fluttering in the breeze, when positioned neither behind nor before the wind. At times, a sail would be temporarily set in that position on purpose so as to cut down the amount of working sail the ship was carrying.

shoulder of mutton sail. A triangular sail, similar to a lateen sail, but attached to the mast rather than to the yards.

shrouds. Heavy ropes extending from the tops of the masts to the sides of the ships, which by spreaders and tackle are pulled taut. They support the masts, giving them the necessary strength to carry sails.

skiff. A small boat, pulled by oars, used in relatively calm water.

slack water. The interval between the flux and reflux of the tide.

slings of a yard. Ropes fixed around the middle of a yard to suspend it for work or secure it in case of damage during an engagement.

slip her cable. To slip an anchor cable, as opposed to cutting it, is to let it run all the way out. If possible, a buoy would be attached to the cable to make it easier to find the anchor later.

smack. A small-rigged vessel used as a tender or fishing boat.

snatch block. One of many variant blocks used to secure ropes in the rigging of a ship. A snatch block was iron bound and attached by a hinge to a fixed support.

snow. An exclusively European design of ship, having two masts with square sails and a third small mast behind the mainmast for a triangular sail. Snows were the largest of the two-masted vessels and weighed up to 1,000 tons.

snug sail. A vessel under snug sail was well prepared in its rigging and sails to weather a storm.

sound the well. To measure the depth of the water in the hold by means of a sounding rod lowered in the pump well.

spar deck. Either a temporary deck laid in any part of the ship on skid beams or the quarterdeck or forecastle when used to store spare spars. HMS *Sirius* had a spar deck laid over the main deck the entire length between the forecastle and the quarterdeck.

spring a mast. A mast is sprung when it has developed a horizontal or oblique crack that makes it dangerous to carry any sail.

spring on the cable. A rope attached from a different part of the ship to the anchor cable so as to hold the vessel, when under the pressure of wind or current, at a steady angle rather than have it swing back and forth.

spritsail yard. A yard attached to and at right angles to the bowsprit.

squaresail boom. A boom on a single-masted vessel lashed across the deck and used to spread the foot of the squaresail.

starboard. The right side of the ship when looking forward from the stern.

staysail. A triangular sail, running fore and aft, that is attached to a stay (rigging running before and after a mast to give it support).

steerage. The open area below the quarterdeck and in front of the great cabin. It was only an entryway to the cabin on a man-of-war but on merchant ships was used to house crewmen and "steerage passengers."

stem. The heavy, circular wooden timber at the bow of a ship, which runs from the keel to the bowsprit, into which the planking of both sides of the ship are rabbeted.

stern sheets.   The aft section of a boat between the last of the seats for rowers and the stern, where the helmsman and commanding officer are usually stationed.

stopper the cable.   A stopper is a short piece of knotted rope that can be attached to a stopper bolt in the deck and to the anchor cable by a lanyard so as to hold the ship at a particular length from the anchor, keeping its cable from running entirely out.

stow hole.   A space under the cargo in the hold of a ship used by seamen to escape impressment. Sailors were often surprisingly successful in creating unnoticeable hiding places, of course, with the full cooperation of the officers of the ship, who did not want to lose hands.

strip a vessel.   Stripping a vessel involved removing guns, rigging, and masts. In the Royal dockyards, guns, masts, and rigging were transferred back and forth between the ship and the hulks (floating warehouses of naval stores made out of older vessels). It took several months to thoroughly refit a ship.

supercargo.   The merchant's representative on a cargo vessel responsible for the cargo and the ship's accounts. Younger sons of merchants frequently learned the business in this capacity. There was often a degree of friction between the ship's captain and the supercargo, each of whom had separate interests and thought of themselves as the primary officer.

sweeps.   Large oars used on a man-of-war to turn a vessel, to increase its speed in a chase, or to propel the ship in a calm.

swivel.   A small piece of artillery fixed in an iron crotch that was mounted in sockets attached to the ship's stern, bow, tops, or elsewhere. It could be pointed in any direction and it was balanced so that it could easily be aimed by hand.

tackle.   The combination of ropes and blocks making up pulleys, used to rig a ship.

top.   The platform near the lower masthead that served both to spread the shrouds supporting the masts and as a useful resting place, lookout post, and fighting station during close engagements with an enemy vessel.

topsails.   The large sails on the topmasts.

trestletrees.   Two strong oak timbers fixed horizontally on the sides of the lower masthead, which support the frame of the top and the weight of the topmast.

van.   The lead position or squadron in a fleet or battle formation.

ventilator.   Beginning in the middle of the eighteenth century, ships were equipped with hand-operated ventilators so that the foul air in the hold, storerooms, and living quarters could be replaced by clean air. The process involved a certain amount of scheduled work for the crew, opening and closing various passageways and doors and hand pumping the fan. The foul air was expelled through the ventilator and passageways to the deck, drawing in fresh air by the open doors and hatchways. Continuously operating ventilators were not introduced until the nineteenth century.

waist. The midsection of a ship, between the forecastle and the quarterdeck.

ware. To ware or wear a ship is to cause it to change its course by turning its stern to the wind.

warp. To warp a ship is to change her position in a harbor, often when the sails are unbent, by pulling it with warps (ropes) attached to fixed objects, such as buoys, stakes on shore, or other ships.

water sail. A small sail spread under the studding sail, at the sides and below the mainsails. They would be employed only when there was very little wind.

weather beam. An object beyond the ship is "on the beam" when it is on a line with the ship's beams, or at right angles to the keel. "On the weather beam" refers to something on the weather side of the ship.

weather gauge. To have the "weather gauge" is to be on the weather side, or upwind from another ship.

weather side. That side of the ship from which the wind is blowing. The opposite is the "lee side."

wherry. A light vessel, powered with one or two sets of oars, used in rivers or harbors to carry passengers from place to place. In a sense, they were small water taxies, and in places like London their fares were strictly regulated by law.

windlass. The machinery used, like a capstan, to heave up anchors. Unlike the capstan, the shaft on which it turns is mounted horizontally to the deck.

windward. Toward the wind.

worm. An instrument on a pole with a large screw on the end. The primary purpose of worming a gun during action was to remove an unexploded cartridge or the smoldering remains of the previous charge, which could ignite the new cartridge while it was being rammed home. A gun was sponged between firing and reloading.

yarns. A yarn is a single thread of a rope. To "draw yarns" is to pull apart old rope, creating "junk" or "rope yarns," which had many uses on shipboard.

yaw. A movement of a ship deviating from the set course, equivalent to a shimmy in an automobile. A ship would "take a yaw" when poorly designed, when the ballast was insufficient or poorly distributed in the hold, or when the wind rapidly shifted in intensity or direction.

yawl. A small vessel, in form like a small cutter, fitted with sails and oars and used for transporting goods to and from ships and shore.

Illustrations

The illustrations used in this volume were selected from printed books and the picture collections of sixteen libraries, historical societies, and museums. Permission to publish has been requested and gratefully received from each. In the following list of credits, the illustrations are identified by the number of the page on which each illustration appears in the text. Color illustrations are identified by plate number.

Berks County Historical Society. Reading, Pennsylvania.

Page 6. Woodcut by Preiss Bros., Reading, Pennsylvania.
Page 326. "A View of Reading." Separately published lithograph by F. A. Holzwart.

British Library, Book Division. London.

Page 152. Samuel Ireland, *Picturesque Views on the River Thames* (London, 1791), vol. 2, opposite p. 232.
Page 180. Thomas and William Daniell, *Oriental Scenery,* Part 2 (London, 1797), Plate 7.
Page 235. James Murphy, *Travels in Portugal* (London, 1795), Plate I.
Page 279. J. Stuart, del., Joseph Swan, sc., "White Hart Inn, etc.," in Daniel Weir, *History of the Town of Greenock* (Greenock, 1829), opposite p. 45.
Page 310. James Henderson, *History . . . Brazil* (London, 1821), frontispiece.

British Library, Map Division. London.

Plate 2. Pages ii, 48. Augustus Brunias, del., I. F. Miller, sc., two-part large folio, colored engraving of Basseterre, St. Christopher, ca. 1780–85. K. Top. 124, 80.

Plate 3. Anonymous watercolor, Brimstone Hill, St. Christopher, n.d. K. Top. 123, 80d.

Plate 5. Anonymous watercolor, Plymouth Harbor, n.d. K. Top. 11, 84k.

Plate 13. William Duvall, "London from Greenwich Park," Colored engraving, n.d. K. Top. 21, 57.5.

Pages 54–55. Chevalier d'Epernay, "Vue du Fort de la Martinique," n.d. K. Top. 123, 103c.

Page 64. Lieutenant Charles Forrest, del., F. Chesman, eng., "A View of Pigeon Island and Gros-Is-Let Bay, in the Island of St. Lucia" (London, 1786). K. Top. 106m.

Page 254. P. M. Vieilot, del., I. C. Stadler, sc., "View of St. Thomas, Taken from Havensicht" (London, 1810). K. Top. 123, 70.

Jacket illustration. Anonymous watercolor, Gibraltar, n.d. K. Top. 72, 48k.

British Museum, Print Department. London.

Page 62. Lieutenant Charles Forrest, del., Archibald Robertson, sc., "St. Lucia—View toward Martinique" (London, 1783).

Page 244. "A View of the Splendid Illumination at M. Otto's House in Portman Square on the Evening of the Proclamation of Peace, April 29, 1802" (London, 1802).

William L. Clements Library. Ann Arbor, Michigan.

(Photographs by Paul Jaronski, University of Michigan Photographic Services.)

Page xiv. Nagle Journal Ms., p. 1.

Page 9. George Washington. Unascribed nineteenth-century engraving.

Page 22. "A View of the Lighthouse on Cape Henlopen; taken at Sea, August 1780," *The Columbian Magazine* (February 1788), opposite p. 108.

Page 49. Mathew M. Richmond, *A Map of the Caribee, Granadilles and Virgin Isles* (London, 1779).

Page 51. M. F. Dien, sc., "Marquis de Bouillé." Engraving from a bound collection of portraits of French participants in the American War for Independence.

Page 59. J. N. Bellin, *Carte Reduite des Isles Antilles* (Paris, 1758).

Page 67. *Authentic Narrative of the Loss of the Ville de Paris* (London, 1809), frontispiece.

Page 101. "Fasciated Mullet," in John White, *Journal of a Voyage to New South Wales* (London, 1790), opposite p. 268.

Page 102. John White, *Journal of a Voyage,* opposite p. 129.

Page 102. *The Voyage of Governor Phillip to Botany Bay* (London, 1789), opposite p. 106.

Hubert Stacy Smith personal library.

Page 189. Rowlandson, del., "Sheerness Boat," in Alfred Burton, *The Adventures of Johnny Newcome in the Navy* (London, 1818), opposite p. 26.

Independence National Historical Park Collection. Philadelphia.

Page 305. Pastel portrait of Don Carlos, Marques d'Yrujo, by James Sharpless or another member of his family.

Mitchell Library, State Library of New South Wales. Sydney, Australia.
(Photographs by Brian Bird, Leighton Studios.)

Plates 6, 7, 8, 9, 10. Pages 95, 100, 119, 128, 130, 135, 140–41. William Bradley Ms., "A Voyage to New South Wales."
Page 98. Philip Gidley King Ms., watercolor sketch of Australian native.
Page 105. J. Neagle, sc., portrait engraving of Bennelong in Western dress, presumably as he appeared in London, early 1790s.
Page 110. Juan Revenet, watercolor sketch of Australian convicts, 1793.

National Portrait Gallery. London.

Page 88. F. Wheatley, oil portrait of Arthur Phillip, 1786.

National Maritime Museum. Greenwich.

Plate 4. Nicholas Pocock, "The Battle of Frigate Bay, Jan. 26, 1782," oil painting.
Plate 12. Nicholas Pocock, "The Fight between the 'Brunswick' and the 'Vengeur' at the Battle of the Glorious First of June, 1794," oil painting.
Plate 14. J. H. Schmidt, pastel portrait of Horatio Nelson, 1806.
Plate 16. William Daniell, "The Mast House at Blackwall," 1803, oil painting.
Plate 19. Edmund Patton, del., W. Walton, sc., "A View of the City of Bahia, in the Brazils," 1833.
Page 27. J. Buys, del., R. Vinkels, sc., "Dutch Brig Cunningham Captures an English Packet," 2 May 1777.
Pages 34–35. "An East Prospective View of the City of Philadelphia . . . ," Carrington Bowles reissue of view by Nicholas Scull and George Heap, 1778.
Pages 68–69. Nicholas Pocock, "Plymouth Dock," oil painting.
Page 74. R. A. Jackson, "Capt. Edward Riou," watercolor portrait.
Page 158. Cartoon collection, Picture Department.
Page 203. Anonymous, "Horatio Nelson," 1795, miniature portrait.
Page 205. Gilbert Stuart, "John Jervis," ca. 1790, unfinished oil portrait.
Page 210. T. Buttersworth, "The Inside Squadron off Cadiz," oil painting.
Page 220. William Opie, "William Sidney Smith," oil portrait.
Page 221. Anonymous silhouette of Francis Godolphin Bond.
Page 223. Laurie & Whittle, pub., "A View of the City of Oporto," 1794.
Pages 272–73. Desenhado, del., F. L. Canacho, sc., "S.W. View Milford Town, Pembrokeshire," 1832.

Page 289. W. S. Hedges, del., L. Haghe, sc., "View of Georgetown, Taken from the Entrance of the River Demerara."

Pages 290–91. H. James, del., W. J. Bennett, sc., "A View of the Town and Harbour of Liverpool," 1817.

Page 307. "Man in the Main Chains Heaving the Lead," unascribed woodcut.

New York Public Library. New York.
(Photograph by Precision Chromes, Inc.)

Plate 1. Archibald Robertson, "View of Philadelphia, 28 Nov. 1777," sepia wash watercolor. Spencer Collection.

Peabody Museum. Salem, Massachusetts.

Plate 17. Anonymous, "Chinese Court of Inquiry re. Neptune Incident, 1807 [Canton]," watercolor.

Public Record Office. Kew.

Page 52. ADM 36/ 9524.
Page 97. ADM 48/ 67.
Page 208. ADM 1/ 5125.

Stark County Historical Society. Canton, Ohio.

Page 331. Adolphus Weaver, del., "View of Canton, State of Ohio, North America," lithographed by Klaupreck and Menzel, Cincinnati, Ohio.

Yale Center for British Art. New Haven, Connecticut. Paul Mellon Collection.
(Photographs by Richard Caspole.)

Plate 11. Joseph Farington, del., Joseph Constantine Stadler, sc., "The Tower," from J. & J. Boydell, *History of the River Thames* (London, 1795), vol. 2, opposite p. 236.

Plate 15. Captain James Weir, del., Francis Jukes, sc., "View of Porto Ferrajo from within the Bay," from James Daniell, *Island of Elba* (London, 1814).

Plate 18. Page 240. Joseph Constantine Stadler, sc., "View up the Tejo [Lisbon]," from Lieutenant Colonel George Thomas Landmann, *History of Portugal* (London, 1818), vol. 2, foldout plate between pp. 212–13.

Plate 20. Lieutenant Henry Chamberlain, del., T. Hunt, sc., "S.W. View of the City of Rio de Janeiro," in Chamberlain, *Views . . . of the City of Rio de Janeiro* (London, 1822), Plate 21.

Page 174. Joseph Farington, del., Joseph Constantine Stadler, sc., "View of Purfleet, Erith, and Long-Reach," from J. & J. Boydell, *History of the River Thames,* vol. 2, opposite p. 260.

Page 179. Thomas Daniell, *Views in Calcutta* (London, 1786–88), Plate 5.

Page 182. Samuel Davis, del., William Daniell, sc., "St. Helena, Viewed from the Road to Long Wood," from Alexander Beatson, *Tracts Relative to the Island of St. Helena* (London, 1816).

Page 207. Captain James Weir, del., Francis Jukes, sc., "View of the West Side of Porto Ferrajo Bay," from James Daniell, *Island of Elba*.

Pages 308–09. Thomas Sutherland, sc., "Monte Video" and "Buenos Ayres," from Emeric Essex Vidal, *Picturesque Illustrations of Buenos Ayres* (London, 1820), opposite p. 1.

Harlan Hatcher Graduate Library, University of Michigan. Ann Arbor.

Page 49. Nicholas Pocock, del., Medland, sc., "View of St. Kitts," *Naval Chronicle*, 13 (1805), 203.

Page 60. Northcote, del., Ridley, sc., "Captain Samuel Brooking," *Naval Chronicle*, 10 (1803), 177.

Page 75. Rivers, del., Ridley, sc., "Sir Roger Curtis," *Naval Chronicle*, 6 (1801), 261.

Page 122. Ridley, sc., "Captain John Hunter," *Naval Chronicle*, 6 (1801), 349.

Page 139. Captain John Hunter, del., Greig, sc., "Engagement between the Crew of the Waaksamheyd Transport & the Natives of an Island near Mindanao," *Naval Chronicle*, 6 (1801), 381.

Page 161. F. Gibson, del., Wells, sc., "View of the Town & Harbour of Ostend," *Naval Chronicle*, 11 (1804), 21.

Page 197. J. F. Lee, del., Hall, sc., "Martello Tower, St. Fiorenzo Bay, Corsica," *Naval Chronicle*, 22 (1809), 107.

Page 199. Nicholas Pocock, del., Medland, sc., "A View of Bastia," *Naval Chronicle*, 2 (1799), 68.

Page 229. Wood engraving, *Naval Chronicle*, 16 (1806), 221.

Page 234. Nicholas Pocock, del., "Lisbon Harbour," *Naval Chronicle*, 2 (1799), 209.

Page 242. Anderson, del., Wells, sc., "View of Malta," *Naval Chronicle*, 8 (1802), 121.

Page 249. G. T., del., Baily, sc., "A Virginia Pilot-Boat, with a Distant View of Cape Henry, at the Entrance of the Chesapeak," *Naval Chronicle*, 33 (1815), 304.

Page 297. G. T., del., Hall, sc., "New York," *Naval Chronicle*, 14 (1805), 296.

Page 313. *Reise nach Brasilien in den Jahren 1815 bis 1817 von Maximilian Prinz zu Wied-Neuweid* (Frankfurt, 1820–21), Plate 16.

United States Naval Academy Museum. Annapolis, Maryland.

Page 18. Saint-Mémin portrait of Captain Stephen Decatur, Sr. (1752–1808).

Page 20. Contemporary model of the *Fair American*, almost certainly the Philadelphia-based vessel on which Jacob Nagle served.

Collection of the Editor.

Page 269. Dadley, sc., "The Rack," in William Miller, *The Punishments of China* (London, 1801), Plate 9.

Index

The Lifetime Voyaging
of
JACOB NAGLE
· · · · · · · ·
traced on
Mercator's Projection

based on map of Robert de Vaugondy, 1778